BAKER'S POCKET HARMONY OF THE GOSPELS

Benjamin Davies, Editor

BAKER BOOK HOUSE
Grand Rapids, Michigan

Formerly published
under the title,
Harmony of the Four Gospels
Reprinted 1975 by
Baker Book House
ISBN: 0-8010-2843-4

SYNOPSIS OF THE HARMONY.

PART I.—Events connected with the Birth and Childhood of our Lord
Time: *About thirteen years and a half.*

SECT.	Matt.	Mark	Luke	John
1. Preface to Luke's Gospel			1. 1–4	
2. An angel appears to Zacharias.—*Jerusalem; in the Temple*			1. 5–25	
3. The same angel appears to Mary.—*Nazareth*			1. 26–38	
4. Mary visits Elisabeth.—*Jutta?*			1. 39–56	
5. Birth of John the Baptist.—*Jutta?*			1. 57–80	
6. An angel appears to Joseph.—*Nazareth*	1. 18–25			
7. The birth of Jesus.—*Bethlehem*			2. 1–7	
8. An angel appears to the shepherds.—*Near Bethlehem*			2. 8–20	
9. The circumcision of Jesus, and His presentation in the temple.—*Bethlehem. Jerusalem*			2. 21–38	
9. The Magi.—*Jerusalem. Bethlehem*	2. 1–12			
. The flight into Egypt. Herod's cruelty. Return. *Bethlehem. Nazareth*	2. 13–23		2. 39, 40	
. At twelve years of age Jesus goes to the passover. *Jerusalem*			2. 41–52	
. The Genealogies	1. 1–17		3. 23–38	

PART II.—The Announcement and Introduction of our Lord's Public Ministry.—Time: *About one Year.*

	Matt.	Mark	Luke	John
. Ministry of John the Baptist.—*Desert. Jordan*	3. 1–12	1. 1–8	3. 1–18	
. The baptism of Jesus.—*The Jordan*	3. 13–17	1. 9–11	3. 21–23	
. The temptation.—*Desert of Judea*	4. 1–11	1. 12, 13	4. 1–13	
. Preface to John's Gospel				1. 1–18
. Testimony of John the Baptist to Jesus.—*Bethabara beyond Jordan*				1. 19–34
. Jesus gains disciples.—*The Jordan. Galilee?*				1. 35–51
. The marriage at Cana of Galilee.				2. 1–12

PART III.—Our Lord's First Passover, and the Subsequent Transactions until the Second.—Time: *One year.*

	Matt.	Mark	Luke	John
At the passover Jesus drives the traders out of the temple.—*Jerusalem*				2. 13–25
Our Lord's discourse with Nicodemus.—*Jerusalem*				3. 1–21
Jesus leaves Jerusalem, but remains in Judea and baptizes. Further testimony of John the Baptist.—*Ænon*				3. 22–36
Jesus departs into Galilee after John's imprisonment	{ 4. 12; 14. 3–5 }	{ 1. 14; 6. 17–20 }	{ 4. 14; 3. 19, 20 }	} 4. 1–3
Our Lord's discourse with the Samaritan woman. Many of the Samaritans believe on Him.—*Sychar, that is, Shechem or Neapolis*				4. 4–42
Jesus teaches publicly in Galilee	4. 17			4. 43–45
Jesus again at Cana, where He heals the son of a nobleman at Capernaum.—*Cana of Galilee*		1. 14, 15	4. 14, 15	4. 46–54
Jesus at Nazareth; He is there rejected, and fixes His abode at Capernaum	4. 13–16		4. 16–31	

Sect.	Matt.	Mark	Luke	John
85. Further public teaching of our Lord. He reproves the unbelieving Jews, and escapes from their hands.—*Jerusalem*	....	....	....	8. 12–59
86. A lawyer instructed. Love to our neighbour defined. Parable of the good Samaritan.—*Near Jerusalem*	....	....	10. 25–37	
87. Jesus in the house of Martha and Mary.—*Bethany*	....	....	10. 38–42	
88. The disciples again taught how to pray.—*Near Jerusalem*	....	....	11. 1–13	
89. The Seventy return.—*Jerusalem?*	....	....	10. 17–24	
90. A man born blind is healed on the sabbath. Our Lord's subsequent discourses.—*Jerusalem*	....	....	....	{ 9. 1–41 \ 10. 1–21
91. Jesus in Jerusalem at the festival of dedication. He retires beyond Jordan.—*Jerusalem. Bethabara beyond Jordan*	....	....	....	10. 22–42
92. The raising of Lazarus.—*Bethany*	....	....	....	11. 1–46
93. The counsel of Caiaphas against Jesus. He retires from Jerusalem.—*Jerusalem. Ephraim.*	....	....	....	11. 47–54
94. Jesus beyond Jordan is followed by multitudes. The healing of the infirm woman on the sabbath.—*Valley of Jordan. Peræa*	19. 1, 2	10. 1	13. 10–21	
95. Our Lord goes teaching and journeying towards Jerusalem. Is warned against Herod.—*Peræa*	....	....	13. 22–35	
96. Our Lord dines with a chief Pharisee on the sabbath. Incidents.—*Peræa*	....	....	14. 1–24	
97. What is required of true disciples.—*Peræa*	....	....	14. 25–35	
98. Parable of the lost sheep, etc. Parable of the prodigal son.—*Peræa*	....	....	15. 1–32	
99. Parable of the unjust steward.—*Peræa*	....	....	16. 1–13	
100. The Pharisees reproved. Parable of the rich man and Lazarus.—*Peræa*	....	....	16. 14–31	
101. Jesus inculcates forbearance, faith, humility. *Peræa*	....	....	17. 1–10	
102. Christ's coming will be sudden.—*Peræa*	....	....	17. 20–37	
103. Parables: The importunate widow. The Pharisee and publican.—*Peræa*	....	....	18. 1–14	
104. Precepts respecting divorce.—*Peræa*	19. 3–12	10. 2–12		
105. Jesus receives and blesses little children.—*Peræa*	19. 13–15	10. 13–16	18. 15–17	
106. The rich young man. Parable of the labourers in the vineyard.—*Peræa*	19. 16–30 \ 20. 1–16	10. 17–31	18. 18–30	
107. Jesus a third time foretells His death and resurrection.—*Peræa*	20. 17–19	10. 32–34	18. 31–34	
108. James and John make their ambitious request. *Peræa*	20. 20–28	10. 35–45		
109. The healing of two blind men near Jericho	20. 29–34	10. 46–52	18. 35–43 \ 19. 1	
110. The visit to Zaccheus. Parable of the ten pounds. *Jericho*	....	....	19. 2–28	
111. Jesus arrives at Bethany six days before the passover.—*Bethany*	....	....	....	{ 11. 55–57 \ 12. 1, 9–11

PART VII.—Our Lord's Public Entry into Jerusalem, and the Subsequent Transactions before the Fourth Passover.—Time: *Five days.*

	Matt.	Mark	Luke	John
Introductory Note.				
112. Our Lord's Public Entry into Jerusalem.—*Bethany. Jerusalem*	21. 1–11, 14–17	11. 1–11	19. 29–44	12. 12–19
113. The barren fig-tree. The cleansing of the temple.—*Bethany. Jerusalem*	21. 12, 13, 18, 19	11. 12–19	19. 45–48 \ 21. 37, 38	
114. The barren fig-tree withers away.—*Between Bethany and Jerusalem*	21. 20–22	11. 20–26		

	Matt.	Mark	Luke	John
SECT.				
145. Jesus before Caiaphas and the Sanhedrim. He declares Himself to be the Christ; is condemned and mocked.—*Jerusalem*	26. 59-68	14. 55-65	22. 63-71	18. 19-24
146. The Sanhedrim lead Jesus away to Pilate.—*Jerusalem*	27. 1, 2, 11-14	15. 1-5	23. 1-5	18. 28-38
147. Jesus before Herod.—*Jerusalem*			23. 6-12	
148. Pilate seeks to release Jesus. The Jews demand Barabbas.—*Jerusalem*	27. 15-26	15. 6-15	23. 13-25	18. 39, 40
149. Pilate delivers up Jesus to death. He is scourged and mocked.—*Jerusalem*	27. 26-30	15. 15-19		19. 1-3
150. Pilate, after again seeking to release Jesus, delivers Him to be crucified.—*Jerusalem*				19. 4-16 ACTS
151. Judas repents and hangs himself.—*Jerusalem*	27. 3-10			1. 18, 19 JOHN
152. Jesus is led away to be crucified.—*Jerusalem*	27. 31-34	15. 20-23	23. 26-33	19. 16, 17
153. The crucifixion.—*Jerusalem*	27. 35-38	15. 24-28	23. 33, 34, 38	19. 18-24
154. The Jews mock at Jesus on the cross. He commends His mother to John.—*Jerusalem*	27. 39-44	15. 29-32	23. 35-37 39-43	19. 25-27
155. Darkness prevails. Christ expires on the cross. *Jerusalem*	27. 45-50	15. 33-37	23. 44-46	19. 28-30
156. The veil of the temple rent, and graves opened. Judgment of the centurion. The women at the cross.—*Jerusalem*	27. 51-56	15. 38-41	23. 45, 47-49	
157. Taking down from the cross. Burial.—*Jerusalem*	27. 57-61	15. 42-47	23. 50-56	19. 31-42
158. The watch at the sepulchre.—*Jerusalem*	27. 62-66			

PART IX.—OUR LORD'S RESURRECTION, HIS SUBSEQUENT APPEARANCES, AND HIS ASCENSION.—TIME: *Forty days.*

Introductory Note.				
159. Morning of the resurrection.—*Jerusalem*	28. 2-4	16. 1		
160. Visit of the women to the sepulchre. Mary Magdalene returns.—*Jerusalem*	28. 1	16. 2-4	24. 1-3	20. 1, 2
161. Vision of angels in the sepulchre.—*Jerusalem*	28. 5-7	16. 5-7	24. 4-8	
162. The women return to the city. Jesus meets them.—*Jerusalem*	28. 8-10	16. 8	24. 9-11	
163. Peter and John run to the sepulchre.—*Jerusalem*			24. 12	20. 3-10
164. Our Lord is seen by Mary Magdalene at the sepulchre.—*Jerusalem*		16. 9-11		20. 11-18
165. Report of the watch.—*Jerusalem*	28. 11-15			
166. Our Lord is seen by Peter. Then by two disciples on the way to Emmaus.—*Jerusalem. Emmaus.*	1 COR. 15. 5	16. 12, 13	24. 13-35	
167. Jesus appears in the midst of the apostles, Thomas being absent.—*Jerusalem*	1 COR. 15. 5	16. 14-18	24. 36-49	20. 19-23
168. Jesus appears in the midst of the apostles, Thomas being present.—*Jerusalem*				20. 24-29
169. The apostles go away into Galilee. Jesus shows Himself to nine of them at the sea of Tiberias. *Galilee*	MATT. 28. 16			21. 1-24
170. Jesus meets His apostles and about five hundred brethren on a mountain in Galilee.	28. 16-20 ACTS			1 COR. 15. 6
171. Our Lord is seen of James; then of all the apostles.—*Jerusalem*	1. 3-8 ACTS			1 COR. 15. 7
172. The Ascension.—*Bethany*	1. 9-12	16. 19, 20	24. 50-53	
178. Conclusion of John's Gospel				JOHN 20. 30, 31 21. 25

PART I.

EVENTS CONNECTED WITH THE BIRTH AND CHILDHOOD OF OUR LORD.

TIME: *About Thirteen Years and a Half.*

---

§ 1. PREFACE TO LUKE'S GOSPEL.

Luke 1. 1-4.

[1]FORASMUCH as many have taken in hand to set forth in order a declaration of those things which are most surely believed among us, [2]even as they delivered them unto us, which from the beginning were eyewitnesses, and ministers of the word; [3]it seemed good to me also, having had perfect understanding of all things from the very first, to write unto thee in order,[a] most excellent Theophilus,[b] [4]that thou mightest know the certainty of those things, wherein thou hast been instructed.

§ 2. AN ANGEL APPEARS TO ZACHARIAS.[c]—*Jerusalem: in the Temple.*

Luke 1. 5-25. [5]There was in the days of Herod, the king of Judea, a certain priest named Zacharias, of the course of Abia:[d] and his wife *was* of the daughters of Aaron, and her name *was* Elisabeth. [6]And they were both righteous before God, walking in all the commandments and ordinances of the Lord blameless. [7]And they had no child, because that Elisabeth was barren, and they both were *now* well stricken in years.

[8]And it came to pass, that while he executed the priest's office before God in the order of his course, [9]according to the custom of the priest's office, his lot was to

---

[a] *In order* (καθεξῆς), *i. e.,* in succession or continuously, without necessarily implying a strictly *chronological* arrangement. Though the order of time is generally followed in Luke's narrative, yet there are cases of obvious departure from it, as in ch. 3, where our Lord's baptism is related (vers. 21, 22) *after* John's imprisonment (ver. 19, 20). Even Greswell, who strenuously maintains the chronological regularity of this Gospel, allows that the order of time has not been strictly followed in the above instance, as well as in ch. 4. 5-8; ch. 21. 37, 38; ch. 22. 20; and ch. 22. 63-65.

[b] Acts 1. 1.

[c] The vision of Zacharias is assumed by some to have occurred on the great day of Atonement, the tenth of the seventh month. But on that day the high priest himself officiated, entering into the holy of holies, Lev. 16. 3, 29, 32-34. Zacharias was an ordinary priest of the class of Abia, one of the twenty-four classes instituted by David for the service of the temple, which relieved each other in succession every sabbath: see 1 Chron. 24. 3-19; 2 Chron. 8. 14; Joseph. Antiq. 7. 14. 7. Their service included the daily burning of incense on the altar of incense in the first or outer sanctuary; and this was what Zacharias was now doing: Luke 1. 9; Ex. 30. 6-8; 1 Chron. 23. 13. It follows, that no inference whatever can hence be drawn as to the year, or season of the year, when the vision took place. Nor is it said how long a time elapsed between the vision and Elisabeth's conception; the expression *after those days,* ver. 24, being quite vague.   [d] 1 Chron. 24. 10, 19.

Luke 1.

burn incense when he went into the temple [*] of the Lord. ¹⁰And the whole multitude of the people were praying without at the time of incense. ¹¹And there appeared unto him an angel of the Lord standing on the right side of the altar of incense. ¹²And when Zacharias saw *him*, he was troubled, and fear fell upon him. ¹³But the angel said unto him, Fear not, Zacharias: for thy prayer is heard; and thy wife Elisabeth shall bear thee a son, and thou shalt call his name John. ¹⁴And thou shalt have joy and gladness; and many shall rejoice at his birth. ¹⁵For he shall be great in the sight of the Lord, and shall drink neither wine nor strong drink; [f] and he shall be filled with the Holy Ghost, even from his mother's womb. ¹⁶And many of the children of Israel shall he turn to the Lord their God. ¹⁷And he shall go before him in the spirit and power of Elias, to turn the hearts of the fathers to the children, and the disobedient to the wisdom of the just; to make ready a people prepared for the Lord. [g] ¹⁸And Zacharias said unto the angel, Whereby shall I know this? for I am an old man, and my wife well stricken in years. ¹⁹And the angel answering said unto him, I am Gabriel, that stand in the presence of God; and am sent to speak unto thee, and to show thee these glad tidings. ²⁰And, behold, thou shalt be dumb, and not able to speak, until the day that these things shall be performed, because thou believest not my words, which shall be fulfilled in their season. ²¹And the people waited for Zacharias, and marvelled that he tarried so long in the temple. ²²And when he came out, he could not speak unto them: and they perceived that he had seen a vision in the temple: for he beckoned unto them, and remained speechless.

²³And it came to pass, that, as soon as the days of his ministration were accomplished, he departed to his own house. ²⁴And after those days his wife Elisabeth conceived, and hid herself five months, saying, ²⁵Thus hath the Lord dealt with me in the days wherein he looked on *me*, to take away my reproach [h] among men.

§ 3. The same Angel appears to Mary.—*Nazareth.*

Luke 1. 26-38. ²⁶And in the sixth month [i] the angel Gabriel was sent from God unto a city of Galilee, named Nazareth, ²⁷to a virgin espoused to a man whose name was Joseph, of the house of David; [j] and the virgin's name *was* Mary. ²⁸And the angel came in unto her, and said, Hail, *thou that art* highly favoured, the Lord *is* with thee: blessed *art* thou among women. ²⁹And when she saw *him*, she was troubled at his saying, and cast in her mind what manner of salutation this should be.

³⁰And the angel said unto her, Fear not, Mary: for thou hast found favour with God. ³¹And, behold, thou shalt conceive in thy womb, and bring forth a son, and shalt call his name JESUS. ³²He shall be great, and shall be called the Son of the Highest: and the Lord God shall give unto him the throne of his father David: ³³and he shall reign over the house of Jacob for ever; and of his kingdom there shall be no end. [k] ³⁴Then said Mary unto the angel, How shall this be, seeing I know not a man? ³⁵And the angel answered and said unto her, The Holy Ghost shall come upon thee, and the power of the Highest shall over-

---

[*] *Temple* (ναός), *i. e.*, the holy place or sanctuary, where the altar of incense stood (Ex. 30. 1, 6-8). When *temple* is used (as in most cases in the Gospels) for the courts or whole area about the sanctuary, it is always expressed by another word (ἱερόν).

[f] Num. 6. 2-4.

[g] Comp. Mal. 4. 5, 6.

[h] Gen. 30. 23; Isa. 4. 1.

[i] The sixth month here refers back, not to the vision, but to the conception of Elisabeth: ver. 36.

[j] The words *of the house of David* are, probably, intended here to describe, not Joseph, though he too was of the royal descent, but Mary; for in ver. 32 she is told that her Son is to have the throne of *his father David*. See also the Note to § 13 in the Appendix.

[k] Comp. Mic. 7. 4.

Luke 1.

shadow thee: therefore also that holy thing which shall be born of thee shall be called the Son of God. [36] And, behold, thy cousin Elisabeth, she hath also conceived a son in her old age: and this is the sixth month with her, who was called barren. [37] For with God nothing shall be impossible. [38] And Mary said, Behold the handmaid of the Lord; be it unto me according to thy word. And the angel departed from her.

§ 4. MARY VISITS ELISABETH.—*Jutta?*

Luke 1. 39-56. [39] And Mary arose in those days, and went into the hill country with haste, into a city of Juda; [1] [40] and entered into the house of Zacharias, and saluted Elisabeth. [41] And it came to pass, that, when Elisabeth heard the salutation of Mary, the babe leaped in her womb; and Elisabeth was filled with the Holy Ghost: [42] and she spake out with a loud voice, and said, Blessed *art* thou among women, and blessed *is* the fruit of thy womb. [43] And whence *is* this to me, that the mother of my Lord should come to me? [44] for, lo, as soon as the voice of thy salutation sounded in mine ears, the babe leaped in my womb for joy. [45] And blessed *is* she that believed: for there shall be a performance of those things which were told her from the Lord.

[46] And Mary said, My soul doth magnify the Lord, [47] and my spirit hath rejoiced in God my Saviour. [48] For he hath regarded the low estate of his handmaiden; for, behold, from henceforth all generations shall call me blessed. [49] For he that is mighty hath done to me great things; and holy *is* his name. [50] And his mercy *is* on them that fear him from generation to generation. [51] He hath showed strength with his arm; he hath scattered the proud in the imagination of their hearts. [52] He hath put down the mighty from *their* seats, and exalted them of low degree. [53] He hath filled the hungry with good things; and the rich he hath sent empty away. [54] He hath holpen his servant Israel, in remembrance of *his* mercy; [55] as he spake to our fathers, to Abraham, and to his seed for ever.[m] [56] And Mary abode with her about three months, and returned to her own house.

§ 5. BIRTH OF JOHN THE BAPTIST.—*Jutta?*

Luke 1. 57-80. [57] Now Elisabeth's full time came that she should be delivered, and she brought forth a son. [58] And her neighbours and her cousins heard how the Lord had showed great mercy upon her; and they rejoiced with her.

[59] And it came to pass, that on the eighth day [n] they came to circumcise the child; and they called him Zacharias, after the name of his father. [60] And his mother answered and said, Not *so;* but he shall be called John. [61] And they said unto her, There is none of thy kindred that is called by this name. [62] And they made signs to his father, how he would have him called. [63] And he asked for a writing table, and wrote, saying, His name is John. And they marvelled all. [64] And his mouth was opened immediately, and his tongue *loosed*, and he spake, and praised God. [65] And fear came on all that dwelt round about them; and all these sayings were noised abroad throughout all the hill country of Judea. [66] And all they that heard *them* laid *them* up in their hearts, saying, What manner of child shall this be? And the hand of the Lord was with him.

[67] And his father Zacharias was filled with the Holy Ghost, and prophesied, saying, [68] Blessed *be* the Lord God of Israel; for he hath visited and redeemed his people, [69] and hath raised up an horn of salvation for us in the house of his servant David;

---

[1] Or, *into a city*, *Juda* (εἰς πόλιν Ἰούδα). *Juda* here is probably a softened form for *Juta*, Heb. יָטָה or יֻטָּה, i. e., *Jutah* or *Juttah*, a city of the priests in the mountains of Judah, south of Hebron: Josh. 15. 55; 21. 16. The place still exists under the same name. Robinson's Bibl. Res. ii. p. 628.

[m] Comp. Isa. 41. 8, 9; Gen. 22. 16. sq.

[n] Lev. 12. 3.

Luke 1.

[70] as he spake by the mouth of his holy prophets, which have been since the world began: [71] that we should be saved from our enemies, and from the hand of all that hate us; [72] to perform the mercy *promised* to our fathers, and to remember his holy covenant; [73] the oath which he sware to our father Abraham,[c] [74] that he would grant unto us, that we being delivered out of the hand of our enemies might serve him without fear, [75] in holiness and righteousness before him, all the days of our life. [76] And thou, child, shalt be called the prophet of the Highest: for thou shalt go before the face of the Lord to prepare his ways; [77] to give knowledge of salvation unto his people by the remission of their sins, [78] through the tender mercy of our God; whereby the dayspring from on high[p] hath visited us, [79] to give light to them that sit in darkness and *in* the shadow of death, to guide our feet into the way of peace. [80] And the child grew, and waxed strong in spirit, and was in the deserts till the day of his showing unto Israel.

§ 6. An Angel appears to Joseph.—*Nazareth.*

Matt. 1. 18-25. [18] Now the birth of Jesus Christ was on this wise: When as his mother Mary was espoused to Joseph, before they came together, she was found with child of the Holy Ghost. [19] Then Joseph her husband, being a just *man*, and not willing to make her a public example, was minded to put her away privily. [20] But while he thought on these things, behold, the angel of the Lord appeared unto him in a dream, saying, Joseph, thou son of David, fear not to take unto thee Mary thy wife: for that which is conceived in her is of the Holy Ghost. [21] And she shall bring forth a son, and thou shalt call his name JESUS: for he shall save his people from their sins. [22] Now all this was done, that it might be fulfilled which was spoken of the Lord by the prophet, saying,[q] [23] Behold, a virgin shall be with child, and shall bring forth a son, and they shall call his name Emmanuel, which being interpreted is, God with us.

[24] Then Joseph being raised from sleep did as the angel of the Lord had bidden him, and took unto him his wife: [25] and knew her not till she had brought forth her firstborn son; and he called his name JESUS.

§ 7. The Birth of Jesus.[r]—*Bethlehem.*

Luke 2. 1-7. [1] And it came to pass in those days, that there went out a decree from Cæsar Augustus, that all the world should be taxed. [2] (*And* this taxing was first made when Cyrenius was governor of Syria.[s]) [3] And all went to be taxed, every one into his own city. [4] And Joseph also went up from Galilee, out of the city of Nazareth, into Judæa, unto the city of David, which is called Bethlehem, (because he was of the house and lineage of David:) [5] to be taxed with Mary his espoused wife, being great with child.

[6] And so it was, that, while they were there, the days were accomplished that she should be delivered. [7] And she brought forth her firstborn son, and wrapped him in swaddling clothes, and laid him in a manger; because there was no room for them in the inn.

§ 8. An Angel appears to the Shepherds.—*Near Bethlehem.*

Luke 2. 8-20. [8] And there were in the same country shepherds abiding in the

---

[c] Gen. 22. 15–18.
[p] Mal. 4. 2; Isa. 9. 2.
[q] Isa. 7. 4.
[r] On the time of the Nativity, see Note on this section in the Appendix.
[s] The rendering of this verse, according to Greswell (Dissert. XII. vol. i. p. 523) ought rather to be—*This enrolment took place be-*fore Cyrenius was governor of Syria.* Wieseler forcibly maintains nearly the same opinion. *Chron. Synops.*, p. 111–121 (p. 102 Eng. ed.) It has, however, been rendered highly probable by the researches of Dr. A. W. Zumpt, that Cyrenius (P. Sulpicius Quirinus) was twice governor of Syria. See Note in Appendix.

Luke 2.

field, keeping watch over their flock by night. ⁹ And, lo, the angel of the Lord came upon them, and the glory of the Lord shone round about them : and they were sore afraid. ¹⁰ And the angel said unto them, Fear not : for, behold, I bring you good tidings of great joy, which shall be to all people. ¹¹ For unto you is born this day in the city of David a Saviour, which is Christ the Lord. ¹² And this *shall be* a sign unto you ; Ye shall find the babe wrapped in swaddling clothes, lying in a manger. ¹³ And suddenly there was with the angel a multitude of the heavenly host praising God, and saying, ¹⁴ Glory to God in the highest, and on earth peace, good will toward men.

¹⁵ And it came to pass, as the angels were gone away from them into heaven, the shepherds said one to another, Let us now go even unto Bethlehem, and see this thing which is come to pass, which the Lord hath made known unto us. ¹⁶ And they came with haste, and found Mary, and Joseph, and the babe lying in a manger. ¹⁷ And when they had seen *it*, they made known abroad the saying which was told them concerning this child. ¹⁸ And all they that heard *it* wondered at those things which were told them by the shepherds. ¹⁹ But Mary kept all these things, and pondered *them* in her heart. ²⁰ And the shepherds returned, glorifying and praising God for all the things that they had heard and seen, as it was told unto them.

§ 9. The Circumcision of Jesus, and His Presentation in the Temple.
Bethlehem, Jerusalem.

Luke 2. 21-38. ²¹ And when eight days were accomplished for the circumcising of the child,ᶠ his name was called JESUS, which was so named of the angel before he was conceived in the womb. ²² And when the days of her purification according to the law of Moses were accomplished, they brought him to Jerusalem, to present *him* to the Lord ; ²³ (as it is written in the law of the Lord,ᵘ Every male that openeth the womb shall be called holy to the Lord ;) ²⁴ and to offer a sacrifice according to that which is said in the law of the Lord,ᵛ A pair of turtle-doves, or two young pigeons.

²⁵ And, behold, there was a man in Jerusalem, whose name *was* Simeon ; and the same man *was* just and devout, waiting for the consolation of Israel : and the Holy Ghost was upon him. ²⁶ And it was revealed unto him by the Holy Ghost, that he should not see death, before he had seen the Lord's Christ. ²⁷ And he came by the Spirit into the temple : and when the parents brought in the child Jesus, to do for him after the custom of the law, ²⁸ then took he him up in his arms, and blessed God, and said, ²⁹ Lord, now lettest thou thy servant depart in peace, according to thy word : ³⁰ for mine eyes have seen thy salvation, ³¹ which thou hast prepared before the face of all people ; ³² a light to lighten the Gentiles, and the glory of thy people Israel. ³³ And Joseph and his mother marvelled at those things which were spoken of him. ³⁴ And Simeon blessed them, and said unto Mary his mother, Behold, this *child* is set for the fall and rising again of many in Israel ; and for a sign which shall be spoken against ;ᵂ ³⁵ (yea, a sword shall pierce through thy own soul also,) that the thoughts of many hearts may be revealed.

³⁶ And there was one Anna, a prophetess, the daughter of Phanuel, of the tribe of Aser : she was of a great age, and had lived with an husband seven years from her virginity ; ³⁷ and she *was* a widow of about fourscore and four years, which departed not from the temple, but served *God* with fastings and prayers night and day. ³⁸ And she coming in that instant gave thanks likewise unto the Lord, and spake of him to all them that looked for redemption in Jerusalem.

ᶠ Gen. 17. 12.
ᵘ Ex. 13. 2 ; comp. Numb. 8. 16, 17.

ᵛ Lev. 12. 6, 8.
ᵂ Comp. Isa. 8. 14.

§ 10. The Magi.—*Jerusalem, Bethlehem.*

Matt. 2. 1-12. ¹ Now when Jesus was born in Bethlehem of Judea in the days of Herod the king, behold, there came wise men from the east to Jerusalem, ² saying, Where is he that is born King of the Jews? for we have seen his star in the east, and are come to worship him. ³ When Herod the king had heard *these things*, he was troubled, and all Jerusalem with him. ⁴ And when he had gathered all the chief priests and scribes of the people together, he demanded of them where Christ should be born. ⁵ And they said unto him, In Bethlehem of Judea: for thus it is written by the prophet,ʸ ⁶ And thou, Bethlehem, *in* the land of Juda, art not the least among the princes of Juda; for out of thee shall come a Governor, that shall rule my people Israel. ⁷ Then Herod, when he had privily called the wise men, inquired of them diligently what time the star appeared. ⁸ And he sent them to Bethlehem, and said, Go and search diligently for the young child; and when ye have found *him*, bring me word again, that I may come and worship him also.

⁹ When they had heard the king, they departed; and, lo, the star, which they saw in the east, went before them, till it came and stood over where the young child was. ¹⁰ When they saw the star, they rejoiced with exceeding great joy. ¹¹ And when they were come into the house, they saw the young child with Mary his mother, and fell down and worshipped him; and when they had opened their treasures, they presented unto him gifts; gold, and frankincense, and myrrh. ¹² And being warned of God in a dream that they should not return to Herod, they departed into their own country another way.

§ 11. The Flight into Egypt. Herod's Cruelty. The Return.
Bethlehem, Nazareth.

Matt. 2. 13-23. ¹³ And when they were departed, behold, the angel of the Lord appeared to Joseph in a dream, saying, Arise, and take the young child and his mother, and flee into Egypt, and be thou there until I bring thee word: for Herod will seek the young child to destroy him. ¹⁴ When he arose, he took the young child and his mother by night, and departed into Egypt: ¹⁵ and was there until the death of Herod: that it might be fulfilled which was spoken of the Lord by the prophet, saying,ᶻ Out of Egypt have I called my son.

¹⁶ Then Herod, when he saw that he was mocked of the wise men, was exceeding wroth, and sent forth, and slew all the children *a* that were in Bethlehem, and in all the coasts thereof, from two years old and under, according to the time which ne had diligently inquired of the wise men. ¹⁷ Then was fulfilled that which was spoken by Jeremy the prophet, saying,ᵇ ¹⁸ In Rama there was a voice heard, lamentation and weeping, and great mourning, Rachel weeping *for* her children, and would not be comforted, because they are not.

¹⁹ But when Herod was dead, behold, an angel of the Lord appeareth in a dream to Joseph in Egypt, ²⁰ saying, Arise, and take the young child and his mother, and go into the land of Israel: for they are dead which sought the young child's life. ²¹ And he arose, and took the young child and his mother, and came into the land of Israel. ²² But when he heard that Archelaus did reign in Judea in the room of his father Herod,

---

ᵃ The visit of the Magi at Bethlehem naturally follows the presentation in the temple; since, after the jealousy of Herod had been once roused, this public presentation could not well have taken place. Joseph and Mary return from Jerusalem to Bethlehem, distant five English miles, where they had now been detained for nearly two months.

Luke indeed does not allude to this return (2. 39); but neither does he mention the flight into Egypt.   ʸ Mic. 5. 2.
ᶻ Hos. 11. 1.
ᵃ *All the children*, rather *all the boys* (πάντας τοὺς παῖδας): there was no inducement to kill the female children.
ᵇ Jer. 31. 15; comp. Jer. 40. 1.

Matt. 2.

he was afraid to go thither: notwith-standing, being warned of God in a dream, he turned aside into the parts of Galilee: ²³ and he came and dwelt in a city called Nazareth: that it might be fulfilled which was spoken by the prophets, He shall be called a Nazarene.*c*

Luke 2. 39, 40. ³⁹ And when they had performed all things according to the law of the Lord, they returned into Galilee, to their own city Nazareth. ⁴⁰ And the child grew, and waxed strong in spirit, filled with wisdom: and the grace of God was upon him.

§ 12. AT TWELVE YEARS OF AGE JESUS GOES TO THE PASSOVER.—*Jerusalem.*

Luke 2. 41-52. ⁴¹ Now his parents went to Jerusalem every year at the feast of the passover. ⁴² And when he was twelve years old, they went up to Jerusalem after the custom *d* of the feast. ⁴³ And when they had fulfilled the days, as they returned, the child Jesus tarried behind in Jerusalem; and Joseph and his mother knew not of *it.* ⁴⁴ But they, supposing him to have been in the company, went a day's journey; and they sought him among *their* kinsfolk and acquaintance. ⁴⁵ And when they found him not, they turned back again to Jerusalem, seeking him.

⁴⁶ And it came to pass, that after three days they found him in the temple, sitting in the midst of the doctors, both hearing them, and asking them questions. ⁴⁷ And all that heard him were astonished at his understanding and answers. ⁴⁸ And when they saw him, they were amazed: and his mother said unto him, Son, why hast thou thus dealt with us? behold, thy father and I have sought thee sorrowing. ⁴⁹ And he said unto them, How is it that ye sought me? wist ye not that I must be about my Father's business? ⁵⁰ And they understood not the saying which he spake unto them.

⁵¹ And he went down with them, and came to Nazareth, and was subject unto them: but his mother kept all these sayings in her heart. ⁵² And Jesus increased in wisdom and stature, and in favour with God and man.

§ 13. THE GENEALOGIES.*e*

Matt. 1. 1-17. ¹ The book of the generation of Jesus Christ, the Son of David, the son of Abraham.*g*

Luke 3. 23-38 (*Inverted*). ³⁸ *The son* of God,*f the son* of Adam, *the son* of Seth, ³⁷ *the son* of Enos, *the son* of Cainan, *the son* of Maleleel, *the son* of Jared, *the son* of Enoch, *the son* of Mathusala, ³⁶ *the son* of Lamech, *the son* of Noe, *the son* of Sem, *the son* of Arphaxad, *the son* of Cainan, ³⁵ *the son* of Sala, *the son* of Heber, *the son* of Phalec, ³⁴ *the son* of Ragau, *the son* of Saruch, *the son* of Nachor, *the son* of Thara, *the son* of Abraham, *the son* of

---

c Isa. 11. 1, in the Hebrew. Comp. Isa. 53. 2; Zech. 6. 12; Rev. 5. 5.
d Deut. 16. 1-8.
e See Note on this section in the Appendix.
f The words *which was the son* are supplied in our version all through, and as such ought to be in *italics.* It would be better, however, to supply simply *son of,* and to understand it of Jesus, all through the list. This change is accordingly made in the text, especially because it facilitates the inversion of Luke's order.
g Matthew, as writing particularly for

Jews, traces our Lord's descent only to David and to Abraham; but Luke, as writing for Gentiles, traces it rather to Adam. The two genealogies thus prove Jesus to be—1. *The Son of David,* who should, according to promise, sit on the throne of Israel (Isa. 9. 6, 7; Luke 1. 32; Acts 2. 30). 2. *The Seed of Abraham,* in whom all nations of the earth should be blessed, according to the covenant made with the father of the faithful (Gen. 22. 18; Gal. 3. 14). 3. *The Son of man,* or "the seed of the woman," who should bruise the serpent's head (Gen. 3. 15; Heb. 2. 14).

Matt. 1.

² Abraham begat Isaac; and Isaac begat Jacob; and Jacob begat Judas and his brethren; ³ and Judas begat Phares and Zara of Thamar; and Phares begat Esrom; and Esrom begat Aram; ⁴ and Aram begat Aminadab; and Aminadab begat Naasson; and Naasson begat Salmon; ⁵ and Salmon begat Booz of Rachab; and Booz begat Obed of Ruth; and Obed begat Jesse; ⁶ and Jesse begat David the king;

And David the king begat Solomon of her *that had been the wife* of Urias; ⁷ and Solomon begat Roboam; and Roboam begat Abia; and Abia begat Asa; ⁸ and Asa begat Josaphat; and Josaphat begat Joram; and Joram begat Ozias; ⁹ and Ozias begat Joatham; and Joatham begat Achaz; and Achaz begat Ezekias; ¹⁰ and Ezekias begat Manasses; and Manasses begat Amon; and Amon begat Josias; ¹¹ and Josias begat Jechonias and his brethren, about the time they were carried away to Babylon.

¹² And after they were brought to Babylon, Jechonias begat Salathiel; and Salathiel begat Zorobabel; ¹³ and Zorobabel begat Abiud; and Abiud begat Eliakim; and Eliakim begat Azor; ¹⁴ and Azor begat Sadoc; and Sadoc begat Achim; and Achim begat Eliud; ¹⁵ and Eliud begat Eleazar; and Eleazar begat Matthan; and Matthan begat Jacob; ¹⁶ and Jacob begat Joseph the husband of Mary, of whom was born Jesus, who is called Christ.¹

¹⁷ So all the generations from Abraham to David *are* fourteen generations; and from David until the carrying away into Babylon *are* fourteen generations; and from the carrying away into Babylon unto Christ *are* fourteen generations.

Luke 3.

Isaac, *the son* of Jacob, ³³ *the son* of Juda, *the son* of Phares, *the son* of

Esrom, *the son* of Aram, *the son* of Aminadab, ³² *the son* of Naasson,

the son of Salmon, *the son* of Booz, *the son* of Obed, *the son* of Jesse, ³¹ *the son* of David, *the son* of

Nathan, *the son* of Mattatha, *the son* of Menan, ³⁰ *the son* of Melea, *the son* of Eliakim, *the son* of Jonan, *the son* of Joseph, *the son* of Juda, *the son* of Simeon, ²⁹ *the son* of Levi, *the son* of Matthat, *the son* of Jorim, *the son* of Eliezer, *the son* of Jose, ²⁸ *the son* of Er, *the son* of Elmodam, *the son* of Cosam, *the son* of Addi, *the son* of Melchi, ²⁷ *the son* of Neri, *the son* of

Salathiel, *the son* of Zorobabel, *the son* of Rhesa, *the son* of Joanna, ²⁶ *the son* of Juda, *the son* of Joseph, *the son* of Semei, *the son* of Mattathias, *the son* of Maath, ²⁵ *the son* of Nagge, *the son* of Esli, *the son* of Naum, *the son* of Amos, *the son* of Mattathias, ²⁴ *the son* of Joseph, *the son* of Janna, *the son* of Melchi, *the son* of Levi, *the son* of Matthat, *the son* of Heli, the son of Joseph,—²³ and Jesus himself . . . being (as was supposed)—

---

¹ According to the conclusions maintained in detail in the Appendix to § 13, both Mary and Joseph were descendants of David: Joseph in the kingly line through Solomon, Mary in the line of Nathan. It may be noted further in the genealogy as given by Matthew, that the names of women are introduced, Tamar, Rahab, Ruth, and Bathsheba, thus connecting the Christ with the heathen world, and with the names of two, at least, whose personal guilt had been great, as if to show that he had come as the Saviour of *all*. There is no record in the Old Testament of the marriage of Salmon to Rahab; the fact, however, must have been preserved in the genealogies. Salmon was a prince of the house of Judah (1 Chron. 2. 10, 11), and the first proprietor, or perhaps the founder, of Bethlehem (ver. 54).

PART II.

ANNOUNCEMENT AND INTRODUCTION OF OUR LORD'S PUBLIC MINISTRY.

TIME: *About One Year.*[h]

§ 14. THE MINISTRY OF JOHN THE BAPTIST.[i]—*The Desert. The Jordan.*

Luke 3. 1-18.

Now in the fifteenth year of the reign of Tiberius Cæsar, Pontius Pilate being governor of Judea, and Herod being tetrarch of Galilee, and his brother Philip tetrarch of Iturea and of the region of Trachonitis, and Lysania, the tetrarch of Abilene, [2] Annas and Caiaphas being the high priests, the word

Matt. 3. 1-12.	Mark 1. 1-8.	of God came unto John

Matt. 3. 1-12. [1] In those days came John the Baptist, preaching in the wilderness of Judea, [2] and saying, Repent ye: for the kingdom of heaven is at hand. [3] For this is he that was spoken of by the prophet Esaias, saying,[k] The voice of one crying in the wilderness, Prepare ye the way of the Lord, make his paths straight. [4] And the same John had his raiment of camel's hair, and a leathern girdle about his loins; and his meat was locusts and wild honey. [5] Then went out to him Jerusalem, and all Judea, and all the region round about Jordan, [6] and were baptized of him in Jordan, confessing their sins.

Mark 1. 1-8. [1] The beginning of the gospel of Jesus Christ, the Son of God.—[4] John did baptize in the wilderness, and preach the baptism of repentance for the remission of sins. —[2] As it is written in the prophets,[j] Behold, I send my messenger before thy face, which shall prepare thy way before thee. [3] The voice of one crying in the wilderness,[k] Prepare ye the way of the Lord, make his paths straight.—[6] And John was clothed with camel's hair,[l] and with a girdle of a skin about his loins; and he did eat locusts and wild honey.—[5] And there went out unto him all the land of Judea, and they of Jerusalem, and were all baptized of him in the river of Jordan, confessing their sins.—

of God came unto John the son of Zacharias in the wilderness. [3] And he came into all the country about Jordan, preaching the baptism of repentance for the remission of sins; [4] as it is written in the book of the words of Esaias the prophet, saying,[k] The voice of one crying in the wilderness, Prepare ye the way of the Lord, make his paths straight. [5] Every valley shall be filled, and every mountain and hill shall be brought low; and the crooked shall be made straight, and the rough ways *shall be* made smooth, [6] and all flesh shall see the salvation of God.

Matt. 3.	Luke 3.

Matt. 3.

[7] But when he saw many of the Pharisees and Sadducees come to his baptism, he said unto them, O generation of vipers, who hath warned

Luke 3.

[7] Then said he to the multitude that came forth to be baptized of him, O generation of vipers, who hath warned

---

[h] This is made out by reckoning the six months of John's ministry before he baptized the Saviour, and about six more between that event and our Lord's first passover: see § 21.

The time of John's entering on his minis-try, as specified in Luke 3. 1, is stated in the second paragraph of the Note to § 7, in the Appendix.

[j] Mal. 3. 1; Isa. 40. 3.　[k] Isa. 40. 3. sq.

[l] Comp. Isa. 20. 2; Zech. 13. 4.

Matt. 3.

tion of vipers, who hath warned you to flee from the wrath to come? ⁸ Bring forth therefore fruits meet for repentance; ⁹ and think not to say within yourselves, We have Abraham to *our* father: for I say unto you, that God is able of these stones to raise up children unto Abraham. ¹⁰ And now also the axe is laid unto the root of the trees: therefore every tree which bringeth not forth good fruit is hewn down, and cast into the fire.

Luke 3.

you to flee from the wrath to come? ⁸ Bring forth therefore fruits worthy of repentance, and begin not to say within yourselves, We have Abraham to *our* father: for I say unto you, that God is able of these stones to raise up children unto Abraham. ⁹ And now also the axe is laid unto the root of the trees: every tree therefore which bringeth not forth good fruit is hewn down, and cast into the fire. ¹⁰ And the people asked him, saying, What shall we do then? ¹¹ He answereth and saith unto them, He that hath two coats, let him impart to him that hath none; and he that hath meat, let him do likewise. ¹² Then came also publicans ᵐ to be baptized, and said unto him, Master, what shall we do? ¹³ And he said unto them, Exact no more than that which is appointed you. ¹⁴ And the soldiers likewise demanded of him, saying, And what shall we do? And he said unto them, Do violence to no man, neither accuse *any* falsely; and be content with your wages.

¹⁵ And as the people were in expectation, and all men mused in their hearts of John, whether he were the Christ or not; ¹⁶ John answered, saying unto *them* all,ⁿ I indeed baptize you with water;

Matt. 3.

¹¹ I indeed ⁿ baptize you with water unto repentance: but he that cometh after me is mightier than I, whose shoes I am not worthy to bear: he shall baptize you with the Holy Ghost,ᵒ and *with* fire: ¹² whose fan *is* in his hand, and he will throughly purge his floor, and gather his wheat into the garner; but he will burn up the chaff with unquenchable fire.

Mark 1.

⁷ And preached, saying, ⁸—I indeed have baptized you with water; ⁷—There cometh one mightier than I after me, the latchet of whose shoes I am not worthy to stoop down and unloose:—⁸ but he shall baptize you with the Holy Ghost.ᵒ

but one mightier than I cometh, the latchet of whose shoes I am not worthy to unloose: he shall baptize you with the Holy Ghostᵒ and with fire: ¹⁷ whose fan *is* in his hand, and he will throughly purge his floor, and will gather the wheat into his garner; but the chaff he will burn with fire unquenchable.

¹⁸ And many other things in his exhortation preached he unto the people.ᵒ

ᵐ The *publicans* (τελῶναι) were farmers of the taxes imposed on the Jews by the Roman government. They were particularly odious to the people, who considered them as no better than traders in the slavery of their country, often abusing their office for the purpose of extortion.

ⁿ There is a difference, here, in the words of the Baptist as quoted by the three Evangelists; so also in the utterance of the voice at Christ's baptism, Matt. 3. 17; Mark 1. 11; Luke 3. 22. A like difference is seen in the four copies of the title on the cross, Matt. 27. 37; Mark 15. 26; Luke 23. 38; John 19. 19. And still more, in the solemn words of our Lord at the institution of the cup, Matt. 26.

28; Mark 14. 24; Luke 22. 20; 1 Cor. 11. 25. Similar varieties of expression in the different reports of the same language are found in the following passages, as well as very many others: Matt. 3. 11; Mark 1. 7; Luke 3. 16; John 1. 27.—Matt. 9. 11; Mark 5. 16; Luke 5. 30.—Matt. 15. 27; Mark 7. 28.—Matt. 16. 6-9; Mark 8. 17-19.—Matt. 20. 33; Mark 10. 51; Luke 18. 41.—Matt. 21. 9; Mark 11. 9; Luke 19. 38.—Matt. 25. 39; Mark 14. 36; Luke 22. 42.—Matt. 28. 5, 6; Mark 16. 6; Luke 24. 5, 6. These examples go to show that the evangelists record the expressions used by our Lord and others according to the *sense*, and not according to the *letter*.

ᵒ Acts 1. 5; 2. 2-4. ᵖ Ver. 19, 20 in ? 24.

§ 15. The Baptism of Jesus.[*]—*The Jordan.*

Matt. 3. 13-17. [13]Then cometh Jesus from Galilee to Jordan unto John, to be baptized of him. [14]But John forbade him, saying, I have need to be baptized of thee, and comest thou to me? [15]And Jesus answering said unto him, Suffer *it to be so* now: for thus it becometh us to fulfil all righteousness. Then he suffered him.

[16]And Jesus, when he was baptized, went up straightway out of the water: and, lo, the heavens were opened unto him, and he saw the Spirit of God descending like a dove, and lighting upon him: [17]and lo a voice from heaven, saying, This is my beloved Son, in whom I am well pleased.

Mark 1. 9-11. [9]And it came to pass in those days, that Jesus came from Nazareth of Galilee, and was baptized of John in Jordan.

[10]And straightway coming up out of the water, he saw the heavens opened, and the Spirit like a dove descending upon him: [11]and there came a voice from heaven, *saying*, Thou art my beloved Son, in whom I am well pleased.

Luke 3. 21-23. [21]Now when all the people were baptized, it came to pass, that Jesus also being baptized,

and praying, the heaven was opened, [22]and the Holy Ghost descended in a bodily shape like a dove upon him, and a voice came from heaven, which said, Thou art my beloved Son; in thee I am well pleased.

[23]And Jesus himself began to be about thirty years of age,—

§ 16. The Temptation.^r—*Desert of Judea.*

Matt. 4. 1-11. [1]Then was Jesus led up of the Spirit into the wilderness to be tempted of the devil. [2]And when he had fasted forty days and forty nights, he was afterward an hungered. [3]And when the tempter came to him, he said, If thou be the Son of God, command that these stones be made bread. [4]But he answered and said, It is written,^s Man shall not live by bread alone, but by every word that proceedeth out of the mouth of God. [5]Then the devil taketh him up into the holy city, and setteth him on a pinnacle of the temple, and

Mark 1. 12, 13. [12]And immediately the Spirit driveth him into the wilderness. [13]And he was there in the wilderness forty days, tempted of Satan; and was with the wild beasts; and the angels ministered unto him.

Luke 4. 1-13. [1]And Jesus being full of the Holy Ghost returned from Jordan, and was led by the Spirit into the wilderness, [2]being forty days tempted of the devil. And in those days he did eat nothing: and when they were ended, he afterward hungered. [3]And the devil said unto him, If thou be the Son of God, command this stone that it be made bread. [4]And Jesus answered him, saying, It is written,^s That man shall not live by bread alone, but by every word of God. —[9]And he brought him to Jerusalem, and set him on a pinnacle of the tem-

---

^p As to the time of the baptism, as indicated in Luke 3. 23, see Note to § 7 in the Appendix.

^q Comp. Numb. 4. 3, 35, 39, 43, 47.

^r That the temptation of Jesus took place immediately after his baptism, appears from Mark 1. 12; and also from a comparison of John 1. 29, 35, 44.—According to Mark and Luke, Jesus was tempted during the forty days. Matthew and Luke specify three instances of temptation, but in a different order. One of these apparently must have occurred at the end of the forty days. The order of Matthew is perhaps the most natural of the two: it is, at least, clearly indicated by the words *then—again.* ^s Deut. 8. 3.

Matt. 4.

saith unto him, * If thou be the Son of God, cast thyself down: for it is written,[i] He shall give his angels charge concerning thee: and in *their* hands they shall bear thee up, lest at any time thou dash thy foot against a stone. [7] Jesus said unto him, It is written again,[u]

Thou shalt not tempt the Lord thy God. [8] Again, the devil taketh him up into an exceeding high mountain, and showeth him all the kingdoms of the world, and the glory of them; [9] and saith unto him, All these things will I give thee,

if thou wilt fall down and worship me. [10] Then saith Jesus unto him, Get thee hence, Satan: for it is written,[v] Thou shalt worship the Lord thy God, and him only shalt thou serve. [11] Then the devil leaveth him, and, behold, angels came and ministered unto him.

Luke 4.

ple, and said unto him, If thou be the Son of God, cast thyself down from hence: [10] for it is written,[i] He shall give his angels charge over thee, to keep thee: [11] and in *their* hands they shall bear thee up, lest at any time thou dash thy foot against a stone. [12] And Jesus answering said unto him, It is said,[u] Thou shalt not tempt the Lord thy God.—[5] And the devil, taking him up into an high mountain, showed unto him all the kingdoms of the world in a moment of time. [6] And the devil said unto him, All this power will I give thee, and the glory of them: for that is delivered unto me; and to whomsoever I will I give it. [7] If thou therefore wilt worship me, all shall be thine. [8] And Jesus answered and said unto him, Get thee behind me, Satan: for it is written,[v] Thou shalt worship the Lord thy God, and him only shalt thou serve. —[13] And when the devil had ended [w] all the temptation,[x] he departed from him for a season.[y]

§ 17. Preface to John's Gospel.

John 1. 1-18. [1] In the beginning was the Word, and the Word was with God, and the Word was God. [2] The same was in the beginning with God. [3] All things were made by him; and without him was not any thing made that was made. [4] In him was life; and the life was the light of men. [5] And the light shineth in darkness; and the darkness comprehended it not.

[6] There was a man sent from God, whose name *was* John. [7] The same came for a witness, to bear witness of the Light, that all *men* through him might believe. [8] He was not that Light, but *was sent* to bear witness of that Light. [9] *That* was the true Light, which lighteth every man that cometh into the world. [10] He was in the world, and the world was made by him, and the world knew him not. [11] He came unto his own, and his own received him not. [12] But as many as received him, to them gave he power to become the sons of God, *even* to them that believe on his name: [13] which were born, not of blood, nor of the will of the flesh, nor of the will of man, but of God. [14] And the Word was made flesh, and dwelt among us, (and we beheld his glory, the glory as of the only begotten of the Father,) full of grace and truth.

[15] John bare witness of him, and cried, saying, This was He of whom I spake, He that cometh after me is preferred before me: for he was before me. [16] And of his fulness have all we received, and grace for grace. [17] For the law was given by Moses, *but* grace and truth came by Jesus Christ. [18] No man hath seen God at any time; the only begotten Son, which is in the bosom of the Father, he hath declared *him*.

---

[i] Psa. 91. 11.   [u] Deut. 6. 16.
[v] Deut. 6. 13.
[w] *All the temptation* (πάντα πειρασμόν), rather *every temptation*, the three cases being regarded as types or samples of the three

classes into which all temptations may be divided; namely, the lust of the flesh, the lust of the eyes, and the pride of life, according to 1 John 2. 16. Comp. Gen. 3. 6.
[x] Comp. Heb. 4. 15. [y] Comp. John 14. 30.

§ 18. TESTIMONY OF JOHN THE BAPTIST TO JESUS.—*Bethabara beyond Jordan.*

John 1. 19-34. ¹⁹ And this is the record of John, when the Jews sent priests and Levites from Jerusalem to ask him, Who art thou ? ²⁰ And he confessed, and denied not, but confessed, I am not the Christ. ²¹ And they asked him, What then ? Art thou Elias ? And he saith, I am not.ᵃ Art thou that prophet ?ᵃ And he answered, No. ²² Then said they unto him, Who art thou ? that we may give an answer to them that sent us. What sayest thou of thyself ? ²³ He said, I *am* the voice of one crying in the wilderness, Make straight the way of the Lord, as said the prophet Esaias.ᵇ ²⁴ And they which were sent were of the Pharisees. ²⁵ And they asked him, and said unto him, Why baptizest thou then, if thou be not that Christ, nor Elias, neither that prophet ? ²⁶ John answered them, saying, I baptize with water : but there standeth one among you, whom ye know not ; ²⁷ he it is, who coming after me is preferred before me, whose shoe's latchet I am not worthy to unloose. ²⁸ These things were done in Bethabara ᶜ beyond Jordan, where John was baptizing.

²⁹ The next day John seeth Jesus coming unto him, and saith, Behold the Lamb of God, which taketh away the sin of the world ! ³⁰ This is he of whom I said, After me cometh a man which is preferred before me : for he was before me. ³¹ And I knew him not :ᵈ but that he should be made manifest to Israel, therefore am I come baptizing with water. ³² And John bare record, saying, I saw the Spirit descending from heaven like a dove, and it abode upon him. ³³ And I knew him not : but he that sent me to baptize with water, the same said unto me, Upon whom thou shalt see the Spirit descending, and remaining on him, the same is he which baptizeth with the Holy Ghost. ³⁴ And I saw, and bare record that this is the Son of God.

§ 19. JESUS GAINS DISCIPLES.—*The Jordan. Galilee ?*

John 1. 35-51. ³⁵ Again the next day after John stood, and two of his disciples ; ³⁶ and looking upon Jesus as he walked, he saith, Behold the Lamb of God ! ³⁷ And the two disciples heard him speak, and they followed Jesus. ³⁸ Then Jesus turned, and saw them following, and saith unto them, What seek ye ? They said unto him, Rabbi (which is to say, being interpreted, Master,) where dwellest thou ? ³⁹ He saith unto them, Come and see. They came and saw where he dwelt, and abode with him that day : for it was about the tenth hour.

⁴⁰ One of the two which heard John *speak,* and followed him, was Andrew, Simon Peter's brother. ⁴¹ He first findeth his own brother Simon, and saith unto him, We have found the Messias, which is, being interpreted, the Christ. ⁴² And he brought him to Jesus. And when Jesus beheld him, he said, Thou art Simon the son of Jona : thou shalt be called Cephas, which is by interpretation, a stone.ᵉ

⁴³ The day following Jesus would go forth into Galilee, and findeth Philip, and

---

ᵃ Here John declares that he was not Elias, meaning that he was not Elias risen from the dead : in Matt. 17. 12, Christ declares that " Elias is come already," meaning that John had come "in the spirit and power of Elias," Luke 1. 17.
ᵇ Deut. 18. 15, 18.   ᵇ Isa. 40. 3.
ᶜ *Bethabara* (or as the best texts reads, *Bethany*) was a place on the eastern bank of the Jordan, and taking its name (*place of passage*) from a ford of the river at that spot. It is probably the same as *Bethbarah* in Judges 7. 24.
ᵈ Here the Baptist says he knew not Jesus ; yet in Matt. 3. 14 (⸹ 15) he appears to have known who He was. The discrepancy is

removed by supposing that John did not know Jesus as the Messiah before He came to be baptized, when a sign was given to point Him out.
ᵉ The evangelist John in this paragraph records the first *discipleship* of three who were afterwards called to be *apostles* (see ⸹ 29). (It is most probable that the disciple with Andrew was John himself, who here, as elsewhere, suppresses his own name.) There is thus no difficulty in the comparison of this passage with the "call" as related by the other three evangelists ; but rather a beautiful harmony. The command, "Follow Me," was willingly and instantaneously obeyed by those who already knew the Lord.

John 1.

saith unto him, Follow me. ⁴⁴ Now Philip was of Bethsaida, the city of Andrew and Peter. ⁴⁵ Philip findeth Nathanael, and saith unto him, We have found him of whom Moses in the law, and the prophets, did write, Jesus of Nazareth, the son of Joseph. ⁴⁶ And Nathanael said unto him, Can there any good thing come out of Nazareth? Philip saith unto him, Come and see. ⁴⁷ Jesus saw Nathanael coming to him, and saith of him, Behold an Israelite indeed,* in whom is no guile! ⁴⁸ Nathanael saith unto him, Whence knowest thou me? Jesus answered and said unto him, Before that Philip called thee, when thou wast under the fig-tree, I saw thee. ⁴⁹ Nathanael answered and said unto him, Rabbi, thou art the Son of God; thou art the King of Israel. ⁵⁰ Jesus answered and said unto him, Because I said unto thee, I saw thee under the fig-tree, believest thou? thou shalt see greater things than these. ⁵¹ And he saith unto him, Verily, verily, I say unto you, Hereafter ye shall see heaven open, and the angels of God ascending and descending upon the Son of man.*

§ 20. THE MARRIAGE AT CANA OF GALILEE.

John 2. 1-12. ¹ And the third day* there was a marriage in Cana of Galilee; and the mother of Jesus was there: ² and both Jesus was called, and his disciples, to the marriage. ³ And when they wanted wine, the mother of Jesus saith unto him, They have no wine. ⁴ Jesus saith unto her, Woman, what have I to do with thee? mine hour is not yet come. ⁵ His mother saith unto the servants, Whatsoever he saith unto you, do *it*. ⁶ And there were set there six waterpots of stone, after the manner of the purifying of the Jews,* containing two or three firkins * apiece. ⁷ Jesus saith unto them, Fill the waterpots with water. And they filled them up to the brim. ⁸ And he saith unto them, Draw out now, and bear unto the governor of the feast. And they bare *it*. ⁹ When the ruler of the feast had tasted the water that was made wine, and knew not whence it was: (but the servants which drew the water knew;) the governor of the feast called the bridegroom, ¹⁰ and saith unto him, Every man at the beginning doth set forth good wine; and when men have well drunk, then that which is worse: *but* thou hast kept the good wine until now. ¹¹ This beginning of miracles did Jesus in Cana of Galilee, and manifested forth his glory; and his disciples believed on him.

¹² After this he went down to Capernaum, he, and his mother, and his brethren, and his disciples: and they continued there not many days.

---

* Psa. 73. 1; Rom. 2. 28.

f Comp. Gen. 28. 12; Heb. 1. 14. The Nathanael to whom these words were spoken is generally, and with reason, supposed to have been the same with Bartholomew (Bar-Tolmai, "son of Tolmai") the apostle, and associate of Philip in all the lists of the twelve. It should be observed that the prediction addressed "to him" is widened by our Lord in its application: "*Ye* shall see." It is a promise to all the spiritually-minded, to all who had "eyes to see." Our Lord now for the first time assumes the title which He was so constantly and exclusively to appropriate, "Son of Man;" the use of which in all the four Gospels is one striking feature in their harmony. His disciples never address *Him* thus; but He claims and constantly employs the name, denoting His true and deep oneness with our humanity. Those who truly knew Him would *henceforth* (not

hereafter, as our version reads, although some texts omit the particle altogether) discern in Him the true "ladder" or link between earth and heaven—"angels ascending and descending:"—type of the mystic union of the human and Divine.

g The *third day* refers back to John 1. 43. The journey in returning to Galilee did not require more than two days; the distance being, in any position of Bethabara, not beyond about fifty miles. Cana, now *Kana-el-Jelil* (!), was situated about seven miles north of Nazareth, and about three miles N. by E. of Sepphoris: see Bibl. Res. in Palest. III. p. 204. *h* Comp. Mark 7. 3.

i Firkins (μετρητὰς): one of these is generally reckoned at seven and a half gallons. The large quantity made the miracle more striking and serviceable, since the feast probably lasted seven days (Judges 14. 12), and many guests were present.

PART III.

OUR LORD'S FIRST PASSOVER AND THE SUBSEQUENT TRANS-ACTIONS UNTIL THE SECOND.

TIME: *One Year.*

---

21. AT THE PASSOVER JESUS DRIVES THE TRADERS OUT OF THE TEMPLE.—*Jerusalem.*

John 2. 13-25.

[13] AND the Jews' passover was at hand,[j] and Jesus went up to Jerusalem, [14] and found in the temple those that sold oxen and sheep and doves, and the changers of money sitting: [15] and when he had made a scourge of small cords, he drove them all out of the temple, and the sheep, and the oxen; and poured out the changers' money, and overthrew the tables; [16] and said unto them that sold doves, Take these things hence; make not my Father's house an house of merchandise. [17] And his disciples remembered that it was written,[k] The zeal of thine house hath eaten me up.

[18] Then answered the Jews and said unto him, What sign showest thou unto us, seeing that thou doest these things? [19] Jesus answered and said unto them, Destroy this temple, and in three days[l] I will raise it up. [20] Then said the Jews, Forty and six years was this temple in building, and wilt thou rear it up in three days? [21] But he spake of the temple of his body. [22] When therefore he was risen from the dead, his disciples remembered that he had said this unto them; and they believed the Scripture, and the word which Jesus had said.

[23] Now when he was in Jerusalem at the passover, in the feast *day*, many believed in his name, when they saw the miracles which he did. [24] But Jesus did not commit himself unto them, because he knew all *men*, [25] and needed not that any should testify of man: for he knew what was in man.[m]

---

j This, our Lord's first passover during his public ministry, is mentioned only by John; though the language of the other evangelists implies that he had been again in Judea: Matt. 4. 12; Mark 1. 14. John connects with this first passover the cleansing of the temple and the casting out of the traders; while the other evangelists describe a like transaction at his last passover: Matt. 21. 12, sq.; Mark 11. 15, sq.; Luke 19. 45, sq. The question is raised, whether these were different transactions. That our Lord was accustomed to repeat the substance of his discourses, or at least the more striking parts of them, at different times and before different persons, is sufficiently obvious. Compare Luke 11. 37-54, uttered in Galilee, with Matt. 23. 1-39, delivered at Jerusalem; likewise Matt. 5. 13, in the sermon on the mount, with Mark 9. 50, and Luke 14. 34, 35, spoken elsewhere; and also the different examples of the Lord's prayer, Matt. 6. 9-13; Luke 11. 2-4. Such examples indeed may be multiplied almost indefinitely, as the pages of the Harmony everywhere show. Why might he not have repeated, after an interval of two or three years, and before different persons, this public symbolical *act*, so significant in itself, and so expressive of his character and authority as the Messiah? The Jews, it seems, did not question his right to perform such an act, provided he was a true prophet. They only demanded some sign of his authority, John 2. 18. This Jesus had already given in his mighty works, wrought at the same passover, ver. 23; works which drew from Nicodemus, a Pharisee and member of the Sanhedrim, the admission, that he was "a teacher come from God," John 3. 2.

k Psa. 69. 9.

l On the *three days* here, see Note to Matt. 12. 40, in ¿ 49.

m Comp. John 4. 17-19; 16. 19; Matt. 9. 4; 12. 25; Mark 12. 15; Luke 6. 8; 9. 47.

§ 22. Our Lord's Discourse with Nicodemus.—*Jerusalem.*

John 3. 1-21. [1] There was a man of the Pharisees, named Nicodemus, a ruler of the Jews: [2] the same came to Jesus by night, and said unto him, Rabbi, we know that thou art a teacher come from God: for no man can do these miracles[n] that thou doest, except God be with him. [3] Jesus answered and said unto him, Verily, verily, I say unto thee, Except a man be born again, he cannot see the kingdom of God. [4] Nicodemus saith unto him, How can a man be born when he is old? can he enter the second time into his mother's womb, and be born? [5] Jesus answered, Verily, verily, I say unto thee, Except a man be born of water and *of* the Spirit, he cannot enter into the kingdom of God. [6] That which is born of the flesh is flesh; and that which is born of the Spirit is spirit. [7] Marvel not that I said unto thee, Ye must be born again. [8] The wind bloweth where it listeth, and thou hearest the sound thereof, but canst not tell whence it cometh, and whither it goeth: so is every one that is born of the Spirit.

[9] Nicodemus answered and said unto him, How can these things be? [10] Jesus answered and said unto him, Art thou a master of Israel, and knowest not these things? [11] Verily, verily, I say unto thee, We speak that we do know, and testify that we have seen; and ye receive not our witness. [12] If I have told you earthly things, and ye believe not, how shall ye believe, if I tell you *of* heavenly things? [13] And no man hath ascended up to heaven, but he that came down from heaven, *even* the Son of man which is in heaven. [14] And as Moses lifted up the serpent in the wilderness,[o] even so must the Son of man be lifted up: [15] that whosoever believeth in him should not perish, but have eternal life.

[16] For God so loved the world, that he gave his only begotten Son, that whosoever believeth in him should not perish, but have everlasting life. [17] For God sent not his Son into the world to condemn the world; but that the world through him might be saved. [18] He that believeth on him is not condemned: but he that believeth not is condemned already, because he hath not believed in the name of the only begotten Son of God. [19] And this is the condemnation, that light is come into the world, and men loved darkness rather than light, because their deeds were evil. [20] For every one that doeth evil hateth the light, neither cometh to the light, lest his deeds should be reproved. [21] But he that doeth truth cometh to the light, that his deeds may be made manifest, that they are wrought in God.

§ 23. Jesus leaves Jerusalem, but remains in Judea and Baptizes.[p] Further Testimony of the Baptist.—*Ænon.*

John 3. 22-36. [22] After these things came Jesus and his disciples into the land of Judea; and there he tarried with them, and baptized. [23] And John also was baptizing in Ænon near to Salim,[q] because there was much water there: and they came, and were baptized. [24] For John was not yet cast into prison.[r]

[25] Then there arose a question between *some* of John's disciples and the Jews about purifying. [26] And they came unto John, and said unto him, Rabbi, he that was with thee beyond Jordan, to whom thou barest witness, behold, the same baptizeth,

---

• John 2. 23.

• Comp. Num. 21. 8, sq.

[p] The order of this section and the following is determined by comparing John 3. 24 with Matt. 4. 12; Mark 1. 14. Jesus goes out with his disciples from Jerusalem into the country of Judea; where he remains until after John was cast into prison. See the Note on John 4. 35, in § 25.

[q] *Ænon* and *Salim* appear, according to

Eusebius and Jerome, to have been both situated on the Jordan, about eight miles to the south of Scythopolis, the ancient Beth-shean.—*Relandi Palæstina,* p. 480.

[r] This is the only mention made of the Baptist's imprisonment in this Gospel. Its brief and incidental character may be regarded as one proof that John intended his Gospel to follow the others as a supplement: see § 24.

John 3.

and all *men* come to him.   ²⁷ John answered and said, A man can receive nothing, except it be given him from heaven.   ²⁸ Ye yourselves bear me witness, that I said, I am not the Christ, but that I am sent before him.   ²⁹ He that hath the bride is the bridegroom : but the friend of the bridegroom, which standeth and heareth him, rejoiceth greatly because of the bridegroom's voice : this my joy therefore is fulfilled.   ³⁰ He must increase, but I *must* decrease.   ³¹ He that cometh from above is above all : he that is of the earth is earthy, and speaketh of the earth : he that cometh from heaven is above all.   ³² And what he hath seen and heard, that he testifieth ; and no man receiveth his testimony.   ³³ He that hath received his testimony hath set to his seal that God is true.   ³⁴ For he whom God hath sent speaketh the words of God : for God giveth not the Spirit by measure *unto him.*   ³⁵ The Father loveth the Son, and hath given all things into his hand.   ³⁶ He that believeth on the Son hath everlasting life : and he that believeth not the Son shall not see life ; but the wrath of God abideth on him.

§ 24.   Jesus departs into Galilee after John's Imprisonment.

Matt. 4. 12. Now when Jesus had heard that John was cast into prison, he departed into Galilee.

Mark 1. 14. Now after that John was put in prison, Jesus came into Galilee,—

Luke 4. 14. And Jesus returned in the power of the Spirit into Galilee :—

Matt. 14. 3-5.   ³ For Herod had laid hold on John, and bound him, and put *him* in prison for Herodias' sake, his brother Philip's wife.

Mark 6. 17-20.   ¹⁷ For Herod himself had sent forth and laid hold upon John, and bound him in prison for Herodias' sake, his brother Philip's wife : for he had married her.   ¹⁸ For John had said unto Herod, It is not lawful for thee to have thy brother's wife.   ¹⁹ Therefore Herodias had a quarrel against him, and would have killed him : but she could not :   ²⁰ for Herod feared John, knowing that he was a just man and an holy, and observed him ; and when he heard him, he did many things, and heard him gladly.

Luke 3. 19, 20.   ¹⁹ But Herod the tetrarch, being reproved by him for Herodias his brother Philip's wife, and for all the evils which Herod had done,   ²⁰ added yet this above all, that he shut up John in prison.

⁴ For John said unto him, It is not lawful for thee to have her.   ⁵ And when he would have put him to death, he feared the multitude, because they counted him as a prophet.

John 4. 1-3.   ¹ When therefore the Lord knew how the Pharisees had heard that Jesus made and baptized more disciples than John, ² (though Jesus himself baptized not, but his disciples,) ³ he left Judea, and departed again into Galilee.

§ 25.   Our Lord's Discourse with the Samaritan Woman.   Many of the Samaritans believe on Him.—*Sychar*, i.e., *Shechem or Neapolis.*

John 4. 4-42.   ⁴ And he must needs go through Samaria.   ⁵ Then cometh he to a city of Samaria, which is called Sychar,* near to the parcel of ground that Jacob gave to his son Joseph.ᶠ   ⁶ Now Jacob's well was there.   Jesus therefore, being wearied with *his* journey, sat thus on the well : *and* it was about the sixth hour.ᵘ

---

* *Sychar* is the ancient *Shechem*, either with the same name slightly changed by the Jews, in their enmity, so as to denote a *lie*, or *a drunkard*; or more probably with a distinct name, in the sense of *purchase* (from סָכַר *sachar*, to buy), not expressive of contempt, but commemorative of Jacob's purchase of the parcel of ground close by (Gen. 33. 19).   See Wieseler, pp. 256-258.

ᶠ Josh. 24. 32.

ᵘ *Sixth hour,* i.e., about *noon*, when the heat was greatest.

John 4.

[7] There cometh a woman of Samaria to draw water: Jesus saith unto her, Give me to drink. [8] (For his disciples were gone away unto the city to buy meat.) [9] Then saith the woman of Samaria unto him, How is it that thou, being a Jew, askest drink of me, which am a woman of Samaria? for the Jews have no dealings with the Samaritans. [10] Jesus answered and said unto her, If thou knewest the gift of God, and who it is that saith to thee, Give me to drink; thou wouldest have asked of him, and he would have given thee living water. [11] The woman saith unto him, Sir, thou hast nothing to draw with, and the well is deep: from whence then hast thou that living water? [12] Art thou greater than our father Jacob, which gave us the well, and drank thereof himself, and his children, and his cattle? [13] Jesus answered and said unto her, Whosoever drinketh of this water shall thirst again: [14] but whosoever drinketh of the water that I shall give him shall never thirst; but the water that I shall give him shall be in him a well of water springing up into everlasting life. [15] The woman saith unto him, Sir, give me this water, that I thirst not, neither come hither to draw. [16] Jesus saith unto her, Go, call thy husband, and come hither. [17] The woman answered and said, I have no husband. Jesus said unto her, Thou hast well said, I have no husband: [18] for thou hast had five husbands; and he whom thou now hast is not thy husband: in that saidst thou truly. [19] The woman saith unto him, Sir, I perceive that thou art a prophet. [20] Our fathers worshipped in this mountain;* and ye say that in Jerusalem is the place where men ought to worship. [21] Jesus saith unto her, Woman, believe me, the hour cometh, when ye shall neither in this mountain, nor yet at Jerusalem, worship the Father. [22] Ye worship ye know not what: we know what we worship: for salvation is of the Jews.*w* [23] But the hour cometh, and now is, when the true worshippers shall worship the Father in spirit and in truth: for the Father seeketh such to worship him. [24] God *is* a Spirit: and they that worship him must worship *him* in spirit and in truth. [25] The woman saith unto him, I know that Messias cometh, which is called Christ: when he is come, he will tell us all things. [26] Jesus saith unto her, I that speak unto thee am *he.*

[27] And upon this came his disciples, and marvelled that he talked with the woman: yet no man said, What seekest thou? or, Why talkest thou with her? [28] The woman then left her waterpot, and went her way into the city, and said to the men, [29] Come, see a man, which told me all things that ever I did: is not this the Christ? [30] Then they went out of the city, and came unto him.

[31] In the mean while his disciples prayed him, saying, Master, eat. [32] But he said unto them, I have meat to eat that ye know not of. [33] Therefore said the disciples one to another, Hath any man brought him *ought* to eat? [34] Jesus saith unto them, My meat is to do the will of him that sent me, and to finish his work. [35] Say not ye, There are yet four months,*x* and *then* cometh harvest? behold, I say unto you, Lift up your eyes, and look on the fields; for they are white already to harvest. [36] And he that reapeth receiveth wages, and gathereth fruit unto life eternal: that both he that soweth and he that reapeth may rejoice together. [37] And herein is that saying true, One soweth, and another reapeth. [38] I sent you to reap

---

* *This mountain,* i.e., *Gerizim,* between which and mount *Ebal* the town of Sychar or Shechem lay: see Deut. 11. 29, 30; Judges 9. 7.

w Isa. 2. 1–3; Zech. 8. 20–23.

x John 4. 35 contains a specification of time which is tolerably definite: "Say ye not, There are yet four months, and the harvest cometh?" According to Lev. 23. 5–7, 10, 11, 14, 15, and Jos. Antiq. 3. 10. 5, the first-fruits of the barley-harvest were presented on the second day of the paschal week; while the wheat-harvest was two or three weeks later; see Bibl. Res. in Palest. II. p. 99, sq. Hence this journey of our Lord must have been made in the latter part of November or in December, about eight months after the preceding passover. It follows (allowing one year to the events in Part II.) that the public ministry of John the Baptist had continued for at least a year and six months, before his imprisonment.

John 4.

that whereon ye bestowed no labour: other men laboured, and ye are entered into their labours.

[39] And many of the Samaritans of that city believed on him for the saying of the woman, which testified, He told me all that ever I did. [40] So when the Samaritans were come unto him, they besought him that he would tarry with them: and he abode there two days. [41] And many more believed because of his own word; [42] and said unto the woman, Now we believe, not because of thy saying: for we have heard *him* ourselves, and know that this is indeed the Christ, the Saviour of the world.

§ 26. Jesus Teaches Publicly in Galilee.

John 4. 43–45. [43] Now after two days he departed thence, and went into Galilee. [44] For Jesus himself testified, that a prophet hath no honour in his own country.[y] [45] Then when he was come into Galilee,[z] the Galileans received him, having seen all the things that he did at Jerusalem at the feast:[a] for they also went unto the feast.

| **Matt. 4. 17.** From that time Jesus began to preach, and to say, Repent: for the kingdom of heaven is at hand.[b] | **Mark 1. 14, 15.** [14] Preaching the gospel of the kingdom of God, [15] and saying, The time is fulfilled, and the kingdom of God is at hand: repent ye, and believe the gospel. | **Luke 4. 14, 15.** [14] And there went out a fame of him through all the region round about. [15] And he taught in their synagogues, being glorified of all. |

§ 27. Jesus again at Cana,[c] where He heals the Son of a Nobleman lying Ill at Capernaum.—*Cana of Galilee.*

John 4. 46–54. [46] So Jesus came again into Cana of Galilee where he made the water wine. And there was a certain nobleman, whose son was sick at Capernaum. [47] When he heard that Jesus was come out of Judea into Galilee, he went unto him, and besought him that he would come down, and heal his son: for he was at the point of death. [48] Then said Jesus unto him, Except ye see signs and wonders, ye will not believe. [49] The nobleman saith unto him, Sir, come down ere my child die. [50] Jesus saith unto him, Go thy way; thy son liveth. And the man believed the word that Jesus had spoken unto him, and he went his way. [51] And as he was now going down, his servants met him, and told *him*, saying, Thy son liveth. [52] Then inquired he of them the hour when he began to amend. And they said unto him, Yesterday at the seventh hour the fever left him. [53] So the father knew that *it was* at the same hour, in the which Jesus said unto him, Thy son liveth: and himself believed, and his whole house. [54] This *is* again the second[d] miracle *that* Jesus did, when he was come out of Judea into Galilee.

§ 28. Jesus at Nazareth; He is there Rejected; and fixes His Abode at Capernaum.

Luke 4. 16–31. [16] And he came to Nazareth,[e] where he had been brought up: and, as his custom was, he went into the synagogue on the sabbath day, and stood up for to read. [17] And there was delivered unto him the book of the prophet Esaias.

---

y *His own country:* as applied to Christ, this means here *Judea,* where he had been born: comp. ver. 47. Only in this place do we find John alluding to the fact that our Lord was born in Bethlehem; but this slight passing allusion is a striking confirmation of the statements of Matthew (ch. 2. 1) and Luke (ch. 2. 4).

z Comp. Luke 4. 24.

a John 2. 23.
b Ver. 13–16 in § 28.
c See § 20.
d John 2. 11.
e The visit to Nazareth is inserted here on the testimony of Luke 4. 16, sq., which is supported by Matt. 4. 13. The visit mentioned in Matt. 13. 54, sq.; Mark 6. 1, sq., was later, and took place after the raising of Jairus's daughter.

Luke 4.

And when he had opened the book, he found the place where it was written,[f] [18] The Spirit of the Lord *is* upon me, because he hath anointed me[g] to preach the gospel to the poor; he hath sent me to heal the brokenhearted, to preach deliverance to the captives, and recovering of sight to the blind, to set at liberty them that are bruised, [19] to preach the acceptable year of the Lord.[h] [20] And he closed the book, and he gave *it* again to the minister,[i] and sat down. And the eyes of all them that were in the synagogue were fastened on him. [21] And he began to say unto them, This day is this scripture fulfilled in your ears. [22] And all bare him witness, and wondered at the gracious words which proceeded out of his mouth. And they said, Is not this Joseph's son? [23] And he said unto them, Ye will surely say unto me this proverb, Physician, heal thyself: whatsoever we have heard done in Capernaum,[j] do also here in thy country. [24] And he said, Verily I say unto you, No prophet is accepted in his own country. [25] But I tell you of a truth, many widows were in Israel in the days of Elias, when the heaven was shut up three years and six months, when great famine was throughout all the land; [26] but unto none of them was Elias sent, save unto Sarepta, *a city* of Sidon, unto a woman *that was* a widow.[k] [27] And many lepers were in Israel in the time of Eliseus the prophet; and none of them was cleansed, saving Naaman the Syrian.[l] [28] And all they in the synagogue, when they heard these things, were filled with wrath, [29] and rose up, and thrust him out of the city, and led him unto the brow of the hill whereon their city was built, that they might cast him down headlong. [30] But he passing through the midst of them went his way, [31] and came down to Capernaum, a city of Galilee.[m]

Matt. 4. 13-16. [13] And leaving Nazareth, he came and dwelt in Capernaum, which is upon the sea coast, in the borders of Zabulon and Nephthalim: [14] that it might be fulfilled which was spoken by Esaias the prophet, saying,[n] [15] The land of Zabulon, and the land of Nephthalim, *by* the way of the sea, beyond Jordan, Galilee of the Gentiles; [16] the people which sat in darkness saw great light; and to them which sat in the region and shadow of death light is sprung up.[o]

§ 29. CALL OF SIMON PETER AND ANDREW, OF JAMES AND JOHN: THE MIRACULOUS DRAUGHT OF FISHES.[p]—*Sea of Galilee; near Capernaum.*

Luke 5. 1-11. [1] And it came to pass, that, as the people pressed upon him to hear the word of God, he stood by the lake of Gennesaret, [2] and saw two ships

---

[f] Isa. 61 1. Comp. Isa. 58. 6.

[g] *Hath anointed me:* by the application of this prophecy our Lord intimated that he was *The Christ,* or the *Messiah,* i.e., *The Anointed One.*

[h] Comp. Lev. 25. 8–10.

[i] *The minister,* rather *servant,* or *attendant,* whose business it was to take care of the sacred rolls (books) and other things in the synagogue, not very unlike the clerk of a parish church.

[j] What is here meant we gather only from John 4. 46–54: see § 27.

[k] 1 Kings 17. 1, 9.   [l] 2 Kings 5. 14.

[m] See in § 30.   [n] Isa. 9. 1, 2.

[o] Ver. 17 in § 26.

[p] That the call of the four apostles belongs here, in accordance with Mark's order, is obvious; since they were present with Jesus at the healing of the demoniac and of Peter's wife's mother, §§ 30, 31.—The three accounts all probably relate to the same transaction.

though many writers prefer to take what is narrated in Luke 5. 1–11, as a wholly distinct and later event, which preference is very ably supported by Greswell, Dissert. IX. vol. ii. Luke relates more particularly the former part, including the putting off upon the lake in Simon's boat and also the miraculous draught, and passes lightly over the latter part. Matthew and Mark, on the other hand, narrate the former part only generally, but the latter part with more detail. In the one part, Luke introduces circumstances which the others omit; in the other part, Matthew and Mark mention facts which Luke has not noted. The remark of Spanheim is just: that particulars are frequently omitted by one evangelist, which are supplied by others; *lest the sacred writers should even seem to have used collusion,* and lest we should delight to read one of them to the neglect of the rest.—*Dubia Evang.* tom. iii. Dub. 72. vii.

Luke 5.

standing by the lake; but the fishermen were gone out of them, and were washing *their* nets. ³ And he entered into one of the ships, which was Simon's, and prayed him that he would thrust out a little from the land. And he sat down, and taught the people out of the ship. ⁴ Now when he had left speaking, he said unto Simon, Launch out into the deep, and let down your nets for a draught. ⁵ And Simon answering said unto him, Master, we have toiled all the night, and have taken

| **Matt. 4.** 18-22. ¹⁸ And Jesus, walking by the sea of Galilee, saw two brethren, Simon called Peter, and Andrew his brother, casting a net into the sea: for they were fishers. | **Mark 1.** 16-20 ¹⁶ Now as he walked by the sea of Galilee, he saw Simon and Andrew his brother casting a net into the sea: for they were fishers. | nothing: nevertheless at thy word I will let down the net. ⁶ And when they had this done, they inclosed a great multitude of fishes: and their nets brake. ⁷ And they beckoned unto *their* partners, which were in the other ship, that they |

should come and help them. And they came, and filled both the ships, so that they began to sink. ⁸ When Simon Peter saw *it* he fell down at Jesus' knees, saying, Depart from me;⁹ for I am a sinful man, O Lord.ʳ ⁹ For he was astonished, and all that were with him, at the draught of the fishes which they

| **Matt. 4.** ¹⁹ And he saith unto them, Follow me, and I will make you fishers of men. ²⁰ And they straightway left *their* nets, and followed him. ²¹ And going on from thence, he saw other two brethren, James *the son of* Zebedee, and John his brother, in a ship with Zebedee their father, mending their nets; and he called them. ²² And they immediately left the ship and their father, and followed him.ˢ | **Mark 1.** ¹⁷ And Jesus said unto them, Come ye after me, and I will make you to become fishers of men. ¹⁸ And straightway they forsook their nets, and followed him. ¹⁹ And when he had gone a little farther thence, he saw James the *son of* Zebedee and John his brother, who also were in the ship mending their nets. ²⁰ And straightway he called them: and they left their father Zebedee in the ship with the hired servants, and went after him. | had taken: ¹⁰ and so *was* also James and John, the sons of Zebedee, which were partners with Simon. And Jesus said unto Simon, Fear not; from henceforth thou shalt catch men. ¹¹ And when they had brought their ships to land, they forsook all, and followed him.

¹¹ And when they had brought their ships to land, they forsook all, and followed him.ᵗ |

§ 30. The Healing of a Demoniac in the Synagogue.—*Capernaum.*

| **Mark 1.** 21-28. ²¹ And they went into Capernaum; and straightway on the sabbath day he entered into the synagogue, and taught. ²² And they were astonished at his doctrine: for he taught them as one that had authority, and not as the scribes. ²³ And there was in their synagogue a man with an unclean spirit; and he cried out, ²⁴ saying, | **Luke 4.** 31-37. ³¹ — And taught them on the sabbath days. ³² And they were astonished at his doctrine: for his word was with power. ³³ And in the synagogue there was a man, which had a spirit of an unclean devil, and cried out with a |

ˢ It may be inferred from this expression, that our Lord's Divinity was now first discerned by Peter.

ʳ Comp. Ex. 20. 19; Judg. 13. 22; Isa. 6. 5.
ˢ See in § 32.
ᵗ See in § 33.

Mark 1.

Let us alone; what have we to do with thee, thou Jesus of Nazareth? art thou come to destroy us? I know thee who thou art, the Holy One of God. ¹⁵ And Jesus rebuked him, saying, Hold thy peace, and come out of him. ²⁶ And when the unclean spirit had torn him, and cried with a loud voice, he came out of him. ²⁷ And they were all amazed, insomuch that they questioned among themselves, saying, What thing is this? what new doctrine *is* this? for with authority commandeth he even the unclean spirits, and they do obey him. ²⁸ And immediately his fame spread abroad throughout all the region round about Galilee.

Luke 4.

loud voice, ³⁴ saying, Let *us* alone; what have we to do with thee, *thou* Jesus of Nazareth? art thou come to destroy us? I know thee who thou art; the Holy One of God. ³⁵ And Jesus rebuked him, saying, Hold thy peace, and come out of him. And when the devil had thrown him in the midst, he came out of him, and hurt him not. ³⁶ And they were all amazed, and spake among themselves, saying, What a word *is* this! for with authority and power he commandeth the unclean spirits, and they come out. ³⁷ And the fame of him went out into every place of the country round about.

§ 31.   The Healing of Peter's Wife's Mother, and many others.
Capernaum.

Matt. 8. 14-17. ¹⁴ And when Jesus was come into Peter's house,

he saw his wife's ᵘ mother laid, and sick of a fever.

¹⁵ And he touched her hand, and the fever left her: and she arose, and ministered unto them.

¹⁶ When the even was come, they brought unto him many that were possessed with devils: and he cast out the spirits with *his* word, and healed all that were sick: ¹⁷ that it might be fulfilled which was spoken by Esaias the prophet, saying,ʷ Himself took our infirmities, and bare *our* sicknesses.ʸ

Mark 1. 29-34. ²⁹ And forthwith, when they were come out of the synagogue, they entered into the house of Simon and Andrew, with James and John. ³⁰ But Simon's wife's mother lay sick of a fever, and anon they tell him of her. ³¹ And he came and took her by the hand, and lifted her up; and immediately the fever left her, and she ministered unto them. ³² And at even, when the sun did set,ᵛ they brought unto him all that were diseased, and them that were possessed with devils. ³³ And all the city was gathered together at the door. ³⁴ And he healed many that were sick of divers diseases, and cast out many devils; and suffered not the devils to speak,ˣ because they knew him.

Luke 4. 38-41. ³⁸ And he arose out of the synagogue, and entered into Simon's house.

And Simon's wife's ᵘ mother was taken with a great fever; and they besought him for her. ³⁹ And he stood over her, and rebuked the fever; and it left her: and immediately she arose and ministered unto them. ⁴⁰ Now when the sun was setting,ᵛ all they that had any sick with divers diseases brought them unto him; and he laid his hands on every one of them, and healed them. ⁴¹ And devils also came out of many, crying out, and saying, Thou art Christ the Son of God. And he rebuking *them* suffered them not to speak: ˣ for they knew that he was Christ.

ᵘ Comp. 1 Cor. 9. 5.
ᵛ The sabbath was then over, and the people felt at liberty to come for healing.

ʷ Isa. 53. 4.
ˣ Comp. Acts 16. 16-18.
ʸ See § 56.

§ 32. Jesus with his Disciples goes from Capernaum throughout Galilee.

Mark 1. 35-39. [35] And in the morning, rising up a great while before day, he went out, and departed into a solitary place, and there prayed. [36] And Simon and they that were with him followed after him. [37] And when they had found him, they said unto him, All *men* seek for thee. [38] And he said unto them, Let us go into the next towns, that I may preach there also: for therefore came I forth. [39] And he preached in their synagogues throughout all Galilee, and cast out devils.

Luke 4. 42-44. [42] And when it was day, he departed and went into a desert place: and the people sought him, and came unto him, and stayed him, that he should not depart from them. [43] And he said unto them, I must preach the kingdom of God to other cities also: for therefore am I sent. [44] And he preached in the synagogues of Galilee.

Matt. 4. 23-25. [23] And Jesus went about all Galilee, teaching in their synagogues, and preaching the gospel of the kingdom, and healing all manner of sickness and all manner of disease among the people. [24] And his fame went throughout all Syria: and they brought unto him all sick people that were taken with divers diseases and torments, and those which were possessed with devils, and those which were lunatic, and those that had the palsy; and he healed them. [25] And there followed him great multitudes of people from Galilee, and *from* Decapolis,[2] and *from* Jerusalem, and *from* Judea, and *from* beyond Jordan.[a]

§ 33. The Healing of a Leper.—*Galilee.*

Matt. 8. 2-4. [2] And behold, there came a leper and worshipped him, saying,

Lord, if thou wilt, thou canst make me clean.

[3] And Jesus put forth *his* hand, and touched him,[b] saying, I will; be thou clean.

And immediately his leprosy was cleansed.

[4] And Jesus saith unto him, See thou tell no man; but go thy way, show thyself to the priest, and offer the gift

Mark 1. 40-45. [40] And there came a leper to him, beseeching him, and kneeling down to him, and saying unto him, If thou wilt, thou canst make me clean. [41] And Jesus, moved with compassion, put forth *his* hand, and touched him,[b] and saith unto him, I will; be thou clean. [42] And as soon as he had spoken, immediately the leprosy departed from him, and he was cleansed. [43] And he straitly charged him, and forthwith sent him away; [44] and saith unto him, See thou say nothing to any man: but go thy way, show thyself to the priest, and offer

Luke 5. 12-16. [12] And it came to pass, when he was in a certain city, behold a man full of leprosy: who seeing Jesus fell on *his* face, and besought him, saying, Lord, if thou wilt, thou canst make me clean. [13] And he put forth *his* hand, and touched him,[b] saying, I will: be thou clean. And immediately the leprosy departed from him.

[14] And he charged him to tell no man: but go, and show thyself to the priest, and offer for thy cleansing,

---

[2] *Decapolis :* a region embracing *ten cities,* on the east of the sea of Galilee and the Jordan.

[a] Matt. ch. 5 in ¶ 41.

[b] *Touched him :* this act, according to the law of Moses, rendered unclean (Lev. 13. 44-46; Num. 5. 2, 3); but the contact did not so affect our Lord, the touch being in his case a sure means of curing the disease, and not of contracting its defilement.

Matt. 8.	Mark 1.	Luke 5.
that Moses commanded, for a testimony unto them.[c]	for thy cleansing those things which Moses commanded, for a testimony unto them.[c] [45] But he went out, and began to publish *it* much, and to blaze abroad the matter, insomuch that Jesus could no more openly enter into the city, but was without in desert places: and they came to him from every quarter.	according as Moses com manded, for a testimony unto them.[c] [15] But so much the more went there a fame abroad of him: and great multitudes came together to hear, and to be healed by him of their infirmities. [16] And he withdrew himself into the wilderness, and prayed.

§ 31. THE HEALING OF THE PARALYTIC.—*Capernaum.*

Mark 2. 1-12. [1] And again he entered into Capernaum after *some* days; and it was noised that he was in the house. [2] And straightway many were gathered together, insomuch that there was no room to receive *them*, no, not so much as about the door: and he preached the word unto them. [3] And they come unto him, bringing one sick of the palsy, which was borne of four. [4] And when they could not come nigh unto him for the press, they uncovered the roof where he was: and when they had broken *it* up, they let down the bed wherein the sick of the palsy lay.

Matt. 9. 2-8. [2] And, behold, they brought to him a man sick of the palsy, lying on a bed:

and Jesus seeing their faith said unto the sick of the palsy; Son, be of good cheer; thy sins be forgiven thee. [3] And, behold, certain of the scribes said within themselves, This *man* blasphemeth.[d]

[4] And Jesus knowing their thoughts said,

[5] When Jesus saw their faith, he said unto the sick of the palsy, Son, thy sins be forgiven thee. [6] But there were certain of the scribes sitting there, and reasoning in their hearts. [7] Why doth this *man* thus speak blasphemies? who can forgive sins but God only?[d] [8] And immediately when Jesus perceived in his spirit that they

Luke 5. 17-26. [17] And it came to pass on a certain day, as he was teaching, that there were Pharisees and doctors of the law sitting by, which were come out of every town of Galilee, and Judea, and Jerusalem: and the power of the Lord was *present* to heal them. [18] And, behold, men brought in a bed a man which was taken with a palsy: and they sought *means* to bring him in, and to lay *him* before him. [19] And when they could not find by what *way* they might bring him in because of the multitude, they went upon the housetop, and let him down through the tiling with *his* couch into the midst before Jesus. [20] And when he saw their faith, he said unto him,

　　Man, thy sins are forgiven thee.

[21] And the scribes and the Pharisees began to reason, saying, Who is this which speaketh blasphemies? Who can forgive sins, but God alone?[d] [22] But when Jesus perceived their

---

[c] Comp. Lev. 14. 2, sq. § 42.　　　　[d] Comp. Isa. 43. 25.

Matt. 9.	Mark 2.	Luke 5.
	so reasoned within themselves, he said unto them, Why reason ye these things in your hearts?	thoughts, he answering said unto them,
Wherefore think ye evil in your hearts? For whether is easier, to say, *Thy* sins be forgiven thee; or to say, Arise, and walk?	⁹ Whether is it easier to say to the sick of the palsy, *Thy* sins be forgiven thee; or to say, Arise, and take up thy bed, and walk?	What reason ye in your hearts? ²³ Whether is easier, to say, Thy sins be forgiven thee; or to say, Rise up and walk?
⁶ But that ye may know that the Son of man hath power on earth to forgive sins, then saith he to the sick of the palsy,) Arise, take up thy bed, and go unto thine house.	¹⁰ But that ye may know that the Son of man hath power on earth to forgive sins, (he saith to the sick of the palsy,) ¹¹ I say unto thee, Arise, and take up thy bed, and go thy way into thine house. ¹² And immediately he arose, took up the bed, and went forth before them all; insomuch that they were all amazed, and glorified God, saying, We never saw it on this fashion.	²⁴ But that ye may know that the Son of man hath power upon earth to forgive sins, (he said unto the sick of the palsy,) I say unto thee, Arise, and take up thy couch, and go unto thine house. ²⁵ And immediately he rose up before them, and took up that whereon he lay, and departed to his own house, glorifying God. ²⁶ And they were all amazed, and they glorified God, and were filled with fear, saying, We have seen strange things to-day.
⁷ And he rose, and departed to his house. ⁸ But when the multitude saw *it*, they marvelled, and glorified God, which had given such power unto men.		

§ 35. The Call of Matthew.—*Capernaum.*

Matt. 9. 9.	Mark 2. 13, 14.	Luke 5. 27, 28.
⁹ And as Jesus passed forth from thence, he saw a man, named Matthew, sitting at the receipt of custom: and he saith unto him, Follow me. And he arose, and followed him.ᶠ	¹³ And he went forth again by the sea side; and all the multitude resorted unto him, and he taught them. ¹⁴ And as he passed by, he saw Levi the *son* of Alphæusᵉ sitting at the receipt of custom, and said unto him, Follow me. And he arose and followed him.ᶠ	²⁷ And after these things he went forth, and saw a publican, named Levi, sitting at the receipt of custom: and he said unto him, Follow me. ²⁸ And he left all, rose up, and followed him.ᶠ

ᵉ This Alphæus may very possibly have been the same with the father of James the less (Mark 3. 18): therefore of "Judas the brother of James" (Acts 13.; Jude 1); and perhaps of Thomas also, "the twin" brother Matthew. (*Prof. Plumptre.*) Alphæus and Mary (Mark 16. 1) would thus be the favoured parents of four apostles.

See in § 58. The instantaneousness of Matthew's obedience may be explained by the statement in Mark that our Lord had already spent some time in teaching. Matthew would thus know who He was, and would have a heart already prepared for the summons. It is observable that Mark and Luke speak of the publican as "Levi." Matthew alone gives in this connexion his own well-known apostolic name (explicitly calling himself "the publican," Matt. 10. 3): while farther on, in the same spirit of humility, he does not speak of *himself* as the giver of the feast.

PART IV.

OUR LORD'S SECOND PASSOVER AND THE SUBSEQUENT TRANSACTIONS UNTIL THE THIRD.

TIME: *One Year.*

---

§ 36. THE POOL OF BETHESDA; THE HEALING OF THE INFIRM MAN; AND OUR LORD'S SUBSEQUENT DISCOURSE.—*Jerusalem.*

John 5. 1-47.

¹ AFTER this there was a feast of the Jews;ᵍ and Jesus went up to Jerusalem ² Now there is at Jerusalem by the sheep *market* a pool, which is called in the Hebrew tongue Bethesda,ʰ having five porches. ³ In these lay a great multitude of impotent folk, of blind, halt, withered, waiting for the moving of the water. ⁴ For an angel went down at a certain season into the pool, and troubled the water: whosoever then first after the troubling of the water stepped in was made whole of whatsoever disease he had. ⁵ And a certain man was there, which had an infirmity thirty and eight years. ⁶ When Jesus saw him lie, and knew that he had been now a long time *in that case,* he saith unto him, Wilt thou be made whole? ⁷ The impotent man answered him, Sir, I have no man, when the water is troubled, to put me into the pool: but while I am coming, another steppeth down before me. ⁸ Jesus saith unto him, Rise, take up thy bed, and walk. ⁹ And immediately the man was made whole, and took up his bed, and walked: and on the same day was the sabbath.

¹⁰ The Jews therefore said unto him that was cured, It is the sabbath day: is not lawful for thee to carry *thy* bed.ⁱ ¹¹ He answered them, He that made me whole, the same said unto me, Take up thy bed, and walk. ¹² Then asked they him, What man is that which said unto thee, Take up thy bed, and walk? ¹³ And he that was healed wist not who it was: for Jesus had conveyed himself away, a multitude being in *that* place.

¹⁴ Afterward Jesus findeth him in the temple, and said unto him, Behold, thou art made whole: sin no more, lest a worse thing come unto thee. ¹⁵ The man departed, and told the Jews that it was Jesus which had made him whole. ¹⁶ And therefore did the Jews persecute Jesus, and sought to slay him, because he had done these things on the sabbath day.

¹⁷ But Jesus answered them, My Father worketh hitherto, and I work. ¹⁸ Therefore the Jews sought the more to kill him, because he not only had broken the sabbath, but said also that God was his Father, making himself equal with God.ʲ

¹⁹ Then answered Jesus and said unto them, Verily, verily, I say unto you, The Son can do nothing of himself, but what he seeth the Father do: for what things

---

ᵍ That this *feast of the Jews* was our Lord's second passover, is shown in the Note to this Section in the Appendix.

ʰ *Bethesda* (בֵּית חַסְדָּא *place of mercy*) was near the sheep *gate* (see Neh. 3. 1, 32; 12. 39) and not *market,* and hence it must have been on the north-east side of the temple. It is perhaps the same as the pool

Amygdalon of Josephus (*Wars,* 5. 11. 4) which lay on the north side of the old town, and which was possibly so named (from מִגְדַּל אֵל *God's boon,* which is in effect the same as *Bethesda*) in reference to the cure effected in it. See Wieseler, p. 259

ⁱ Comp. Jer. 17. 21, 22.

ʲ Phil. 2. 6.

John 5.

soever he doeth, these also doeth the Son likewise. [20] For the Father loveth the Son, and showeth him all things that himself doeth: and he will show him greater works than these, that ye may marvel. [21] For as the Father raiseth up the dead, and quickeneth *them;* even so the Son quickeneth whom he will. [22] For the Father judgeth no man, but hath committed all judgment unto the Son: [23] that all *men* should honour the Son, even as they honour the Father. He that honoureth not the Son honoureth not the Father which hath sent him. [24] Verily, verily, I say unto you, He that heareth my word, and believeth on him that sent me, hath everlasting life, and shall not come into condemnation; but is passed from death unto life. [25] Verily, verily, I say unto you, The hour is coming, and now is, when the dead shall hear the voice of the Son of God: and they that hear shall live. [26] For as the Father hath life in himself: so hath he given to the Son to have life in himself; [27] and hath given him authority to execute judgment also, because he is the Son of man. [28] Marvel not at this: for the hour is coming, in the which all that are in the graves shall hear his voice, [29] and shall come forth; they that have done good, unto the resurrection of life; and they that have done evil, unto the resurrection of damnation.[k] [30] I can of mine own self do nothing: as I hear, I judge: and my judgment is just; because I seek not mine own will, but the will of the Father which hath sent me.

[31] If I bear witness of myself, my witness is not true. [32] There is another that beareth witness of me; and I know that the witness which he witnesseth of me is true. [33] Ye sent unto John, and he bare witness unto the truth. [34] But I receive not testimony from man: but these things I say, that ye might be saved. [35] He was a burning and a shining light: and ye were willing for a season to rejoice in his light.[l] [36] But I have greater witness than *that* of John: for the works which the Father hath given me to finish, the same works that I do, bear witness of me, that the Father hath sent me. [37] And the Father himself which hath sent me, hath borne witness of me. Ye have neither heard his voice at any time, nor seen his shape. [38] And ye have not his word abiding in you: for whom he hath sent, him ye believe not. [39] Search [m] the Scriptures; for in them ye think ye have eternal life: and they are they which testify of me.[n] [40] And ye will not come to me, that ye might have life. [41] I receive not honour from men. [42] But I know you, that ye have not the love of God in you. [43] I am come in my Father's name, and ye receive me not: if another shall come in his own name, him ye will receive. [44] How can ye believe, which receive honour one of another, and seek not the honour that *cometh* from God only? [45] Do not think that I will accuse you to the Father: there is *one* that accuseth you, *even* Moses, in whom ye trust. [46] For had ye believed Moses, ye would have believed me: for he wrote of me.[o] [47] But if ye believe not his writings, how shall ye believe my words?

§ 37. THE DISCIPLES PLUCK EARS OF GRAIN ON THE SABBATH.—*On the way to Galilee?*

Matt. 12. 1-8.	Mark 2. 23-28.	Luke 6. 1-5.
[1] At that time Jesus went on the sabbath day through	[23] And it came to pass, that he went through the corn	[1] And it came to pass on the second[p] sabbath after the

---

[k] Comp. Dan. 12. 2.
[l] Comp. Matt. 21. 26.   = Acts 17. 11, 12.
    Comp. Luke 24. 27.
[m] Comp. Gen. 3. 15; 49. 10; Num. 24. 17; Deut. 18. 15-18.
[p] The circumstances narrated show that a Passover had just been celebrated: see Note a § 25. The sabbath here named was pro-

bably *the first sabbath after the second day of the passover,* or of unleavened bread; that is, the first of the seven sabbaths reckoned between that day and Pentecost: see the Lexicons, also Scaliger *Emendat. Temp.* VI. 557. Our Lord would seem to have hastened away from Jerusalem; for which a reason is found in John 5. 16, 18.

Matt. 12.

the corn; and his disciples were an hungred, and began to pluck the ears of corn, and to eat.ᵠ ² But when the Pharisees saw *it*, they said unto him, Behold, thy disciples do that which is not lawful to do upon the sabbath day. ³ But he said unto them, Have ye not read what David did, when he was an hungred, and they that were with him;ʳ ⁴ how he entered into the house of God, and did eat the show-bread, which was not lawful for him to eat, neither for them which were with him, but only for the priests?ᵗ ⁵ Or have ye not read in the law,ᵘ how that on the sabbath days the priests in the temple profane the sabbath, and are blameless? ⁶ But I say unto you, That in this place is *one* greater than the temple. ⁷ But if ye had known what *this* meaneth, I will have mercy, and not sacrifice,ᵛ ye would not have condemned the guiltless. ⁸ For the Son of man is Lord even of the sabbath day.

Mark 2.

fields on the sabbath day; and his disciples began, as they went, to pluck the ears of corn.ᵠ ²⁴ And the Pharisees said unto him, Behold, why do they on the sabbath day that which is not lawful?

²⁵ And he said unto them, Have ye never read what David did, when he had need, and was an hungred, he, and they that were with him;ʳ ²⁶ how he went into the house of God in the days of Abiathar ˢ the high priest, and did eat the show-bread, which is not lawful to eat but for the priests, and gave also to them which were with him?

²⁷ And he said unto them, The sabbath was made for man, and not man for the sabbath: ²⁸ therefore the Son of man is Lord also of the sabbath.

Luke 6.

first, that he went through the corn fields; and his disciples plucked the ears of corn, and did eat, rubbing *them* in *their* hands.ᵠ ² And certain of the Pharisees said unto them, Why do ye that which is not lawful to do on the sabbath days? ³ And Jesus answering them, said, Have ye not read so much as this, what David did, when himself was an hungred, and they which were with him; ⁴ how he went into the house of God, and did take and eat the show-bread, and gave also to them that were with him; which it is not lawful to eat but for the priests alone? ᵗ

⁵ And he said unto them, That the Son of man is Lord also of the sabbath.

§ 38. THE HEALING OF THE WITHERED HAND ON THE SABBATH.—*Galilee Capernaum ?*

Matt. 12. 9-14. ⁹ And when he was departed thence, he went into their synagogue ; ¹⁰ and, behold, there was a man which had *his* hand withered. And they asked him, say-

Mark 3. 1-6. ¹ And he entered again into the synagogue : and there was a man there which had a withered hand. ² And they watched him whether he would heal him on the

Luke 6. 6-11. ⁶ And it came to pass also on another sabbath, that he entered into the synagogue and taught: and there was a man whose right hand was withered

---

ᵠ Deut. 23. 25.   ʳ 1 Sam. 21. 1-7.

ˢ *Abiathar* is here named as the high priest, but in 1 Sam. 21. 1-6 we find that his father *Ahimelech* was then in the office. This discrepancy may be removed by understanding the words to mean—'in the days of Abiathar, afterwards high priest.' His name is men-

tioned rather than his father's, because he too was present on the occasion alluded to (see 1 Sam. 22. 22), and having immediately succeeded his father, became better known in the history of David.

ᵗ Lev. 24. 9.   ᵘ Num. 28. 9, 10, 18, 19.

ᵛ Hos. 6. 6.

Matt. 12.

ing, Is it lawful to heal on the sabbath days? that they might accuse him.

¹¹ And he said unto them, What man shall there be among you, that shall have one sheep, and if it fall into a pit on the sabbath day, will he not lay hold on it, and lift *it* out? ¹² How much then is a man better than a sheep? Wherefore it is lawful to do well on the sabbath days.

¹³ Then saith he to the man, Stretch forth thine hand. And he stretched *it* forth; and it was restored whole, like as the other.

¹⁴ Then the Pharisees went out, and held a council against him, how they might destroy him.

Mark 3.

sabbath day; that they might accuse him.

³ And he saith unto the man which had the withered hand, Stand forth. ⁴ And he saith unto them, Is it lawful to do good on the sabbath days, or to do evil? to save life, or to kill? But they held their peace. ⁵ And when he had looked round about on them with anger,[*] being grieved for the hardness of their hearts, he saith unto the man, Stretch forth thine hand. And he stretched *it* out: and his hand was restored whole as the other. ⁶ And the Pharisees went forth, and straightway took counsel with the Herodians [ᶻ] against him, how they might destroy him.

Luke 6.

⁷ And the scribes and Pharisees watched him, whether he would heal on the sabbath day; that they might find an accusation against him. ⁸ But he knew their thoughts, and said to the man which had the withered hand, Rise up, and stand forth in the midst. And he arose and stood forth. ⁹ Then said Jesus unto them, I will ask you one thing; Is it lawful on the sabbath days to do good, or to do evil? to save life, or to destroy *it*? ¹⁰ And looking round about upon them all,

he said unto the man, Stretch forth thy hand. And he did so: and his hand was restored whole as the other. ¹¹ And they were filled with madness; and communed one with another what they might do to Jesus.[ᵞ]

§ 39. Jesus at the Sea of Tiberias is followed by Multitudes.

Matt. 12. 15-21. ¹⁵ But when Jesus knew *it*, he withdrew himself from thence: and great multitudes followed him, and he healed them all;

Mark 3. 7-12. ⁷ But Jesus withdrew himself with his disciples to the sea: and a great multitude from Galilee followed him, ⁸ and from Judea, and from Jerusalem, and from Idumea, and *from* beyond Jordan; and they about Tyre and Sidon, a great multitude, when they had heard what great things he did, came unto him. ⁹ And he spake to his disciples, that a small ship should wait on him because of the multitude, lest they should throng him. ¹⁰ For he had healed many; insomuch that they pressed upon him for to touch him, as many as had plagues. ¹¹ And unclean spirits, when they saw him, fell down before him, and cried, saying, Thou art the Son of God. ¹² And

¹⁶ and charged them that they should not make him known: ¹⁷ that it

he straitly charged them that they should not make him known.

---

[*] *With anger :* this is a remarkable statement respecting the meek and gracious Redeemer. Comp. Eph. 4. 26, "Be ye angry, and sin not." Anger, therefore, is not necessarily sinful.

[ᶻ] *The Herodians* were Jews who were ad-

herents of Herod, and maintained, in opposition to the Pharisees, the propriety of yielding obedience and tribute to the Roman government, from which Herod derived his authority. See § 118.

[ᵞ] See in § 40.

Matt. 12.

might be fulfilled which was spoken by Esaias the prophet, saying.[*] ¹⁸ Behold **my** servant, whom I have chosen; my beloved, in whom my soul is well pleased: I **will** put my spirit upon him, and he shall show judgment to the Gentiles. ¹⁹ He shall not strive, nor cry; neither shall any man hear his voice in the streets. ²⁰ A bruised reed shall he not break, and smoking flax shall he not quench, till he send forth judgment unto victory. ²¹ And in his name shall the Gentiles trust.[a]

§ 40. JESUS WITHDRAWS TO THE MOUNTAIN, AND CHOOSES THE TWELVE;[b] THE MULTITUDES FOLLOW HIM.—*Near Capernaum.*

Mark 3. 13-19. ¹³ And he goeth up into a mountain, and calleth *unto him* whom he would: and they came unto him. ¹⁴ And he ordained twelve, that they should be with him, and that he might send them forth to preach, ¹⁵ and to have power to heal sickness, and to cast out devils: ¹⁶ and Simon he surnamed Peter;[c] ¹⁷ and James the *son* of Zebedee, and John the brother of James; and he surnamed them Boanerges, which is, The sons of thunder: ¹⁸ and Andrew, and Philip, and Bartholomew, and Matthew, and Thomas, and James the *son* of Alphæus, and Thaddæus, and Simon the Canaanite, ¹⁹ and Judas Iscariot, which also betrayed him.[d]

Matt. 10. 2-4. ² Now the names of the twelve apostles are these; The first, Simon, who is called Peter, and Andrew his brother; James *the son of* Zebedee, and John his brother: ³ Philip, and Bartholomew; Thomas, and Matthew the publican; James *the son* of Alphæus, and Lebbæus, whose surname was Thaddæus; ⁴ Simon the Canaanite, and Judas Iscariot, which also betrayed him.[d]

Luke 6. 12-19. ¹² And it came to pass in those days, that he went out into a mountain to pray, and continued all night in prayer to God. ¹³ And when it was day, he called *unto him* his disciples: and of them he chose twelve, whom also he named apostles; ¹⁴ Simon (whom he also named Peter,[e]) and Andrew his brother, James and John, Philip and Bartholomew, ¹⁵ Matthew and Thomas, James the *son* of Alphæus, and Simon called Zelotes, ¹⁶ and Judas *the brother* of James, and Judas Iscariot, which also was the traitor. ¹⁷ And he came down with them, and stood in the plain,[e] and the company of his disciples and a great multitude of people out of all Judea and Jerusalem, and from the sea coast of Tyre and Sidon, which came to hear him, and to be healed of their diseases; ¹⁸ and they that were vexed with unclean spirits: and they were healed. ¹⁹ And the whole multitude sought to touch him: for there went virtue out of him, and healed *them* all.

---

[*] Isa. 42. 1-3. Comp. Isa. 11. 10.

[a] See in § 48.

[b] The appointment of the twelve follows here according to Mark and Luke. Matt. 10. 2-4 gives their names, as having been already appointed. Lebbæus, called also Thaddæus by Matthew and Mark, is the same as Jude the brother of James in Luke. The epithet Zelotes, *Zealot*, is the Greek translation of ὁ κανανίτης (improperly given as *the Canaanite* in our version), derived from Heb. אָנָק, Aram. אָנְק.

[c] Comp. John 1. 42.   [d] See in § 22.

[e] *In the plain,* properly *on a level place,* i.e., a piece of table-land on a mountain, and not what we should call *the plain.* That this level spot lay on some high ground is indicated by the use (in preference to the dative) of the genitive case, which is not employed with ἐπί except when the noun governed denotes something that is conceived to be itself elevated; so in Luke 22. 40, we have ἐπὶ τοῦ τόπου (on the spot) used of Gethsemane, which lay on the slope of Mount Olivet; comp. also Matt. 24. 3, 30; Luke 4. 29; 22. 21; Acts 20. 9; 21. 40; and Zech. 14. 10 in the Septuagint. This peculiarity (hitherto unnoticed) in the usage of the genitive after ἐπί is submitted to the examination of Greek scholars. The result of this strict rendering of the expression is highly interesting, as it enables us at once to harmonize the statements of the evangelists, inasmuch as Luke too shows that the sermon was delivered on a mountain, or some high ground, though on a level place.

§ 41. THE SERMON ON THE MOUNT./—*Near Capernaum.*

Matt. 5. 1 to 8. 1. ¹ And seeing the multitudes, he went up into a mountain: and when he was set, his disciples came unto him: ² and he opened his mouth, and taught them, saying, ³ Blessed *are* the poor in spirit: for theirs is the kingdom of heaven.ᵍ ⁴ Blessed *are* they that mourn: for they shall be comforted.ʰ ⁵ Blessed *are* the meek: for they shall inherit the earth.ⁱ ⁶ Blessed *are* they which do hunger and thirst after righteousness: for they shall be filled.ʲ ⁸ Blessed *are* the pure in heart: for they shall obtain mercy. ⁸ Blessed *are* the pure in heart: for they shall see God.ˡ ⁹ Blessed *are* the peacemakers: for they shall be called the children of God.ᵐ ¹⁰ Blessed *are* they which are persecuted for righteousness' sake: for theirs is the kingdom of heaven. ¹¹ Blessed are ye, when *men* shall revile you, and persecute *you*, and shall say all manner of evil against you falsely, for my sake. ¹² Rejoice, and be exceeding glad: for great *is* your reward in heaven: for so persecuted they the prophets which were before you.ⁿ

Luke 6. 20-49. ²⁰ And he lifted up his eyes on his disciples, and said, Blessed *be ye* poor: for yours is the kingdom of God.ᵍ ²¹ Blessed *are ye* that hunger now: for ye shall be filled. Blessed *are ye* that weep now: for ye shall laugh.

⁷ Blessed *are* the merciful: for they shall see

²² Blessed are ye, when men shall hate you, and when they shall separate you *from their company*, and shall reproach *you*, and cast out your name as evil, for the Son of man's sake. ²³ Rejoice ye in that day, and leap for joy: for, behold, your reward *is* great in heaven, for in the like manner did their fathers unto the prophets.ⁿ ²⁴ But woe unto you that are rich! for ye have received your consolation. ²⁵ Woe unto you that are full! for ye shall hunger. Woe unto you that laugh now! for ye shall mourn and weep. ²⁶ Woe unto you, when all men shall speak well of you! for so did their fathers unto the false prophets.

¹³ Ye are the salt of the earth: but if the salt have lost his savour, wherewith shall it be salted? it is thenceforth good for nothing, but to be cast out, and to be trodden under foot of men. ¹⁴ Ye are the light of the world. A city that is set on an hill cannot be hid. ¹⁵ Neither do men light a candle, and put it under a bushel, but on a candlestick; and it giveth light unto all that are in the house. ¹⁶ Let your light so shine before men, that they may see your good works, and glorify your Father which is in heaven.

¹⁷ Think not that I am come to destroy the law, or the prophets: I am not come to destroy, but to fulfil. ¹⁸ For verily I say unto you, Till heaven and earth pass, one jot or one tittle shall in no wise pass from the law, till all be fulfilled. ¹⁹ Whosoever therefore shall break one of these least commandments, and shall teach men so, he shall be called the least in the kingdom of heaven: but whosoever shall do and teach *them*, the same shall be called great in the kingdom of heaven. ²⁰ For I say unto you, That except your righteousness shall exceed *the righteousness* of the scribes and Pharisees,ᵒ ye shall in no case enter into the kingdom of heaven.

---

f See the Note to this § in the Appendix.
g Isa. 66. 2.   *h* Isa. 61. 2, 3.
i Comp. Psa. 37. 11; 22. 29.
j Isa. 25. 6; 55. 1-3.   *k* Isa. 58. 10, 11. Heb. 12. 14.   *m* Rom. 12. 18.
n 1 Kings 19. 10; 2 Chron. 16. 10; 24. 19-21; Jer. 26. 8, 20-23.
o *The Scribes and Pharisees:* the former

were a learned profession (not a religious sect), whose business was to write copies of the law, and also to expound its meaning; hence they were called also *lawyers* (Matt. 22. 35 comp. with Mark 12. 28) and *doctors of the law* (Luke 5. 17 comp. with 21). They generally favoured the views and abetted the party of the Pharisees; hence the mention of

Matt. 5.

[21] Ye have heard that it was said by them of old time,[p] Thou shalt not kill; and whosoever shall kill shall be in danger of the judgment: [22] but I say unto you, That whosoever is angry with his brother without a cause shall be in danger of the judgment: and whosoever shall say to his brother, Raca, shall be in danger of the council: but whosoever shall say, Thou fool, shall be in danger of hell-fire.[q] [23] Therefore if thou bring thy gift to the altar, and there rememberest that thy brother hath ought against thee; [24] leave there thy gift before the altar, and go thy way; first be reconciled to thy brother, and then come and offer thy gift. [25] Agree with thine adversary quickly, whiles thou art in the way with him; lest at any time the adversary deliver thee to the judge, and the judge deliver thee to the officer, and thou be cast into prison. [26] Verily I say unto thee, Thou shalt by no means come out thence, till thou hast paid the uttermost farthing.

[27] Ye have heard that it was said by them of old time,[r] Thou shalt not commit adultery: [28] but I say unto you, That whosoever looketh on a woman to lust after her hath committed adultery with her already in his heart. [29] And if thy right eye offend thee, pluck it out, and cast *it* from thee: for it is profitable for thee that one of thy members should perish, and not that thy whole body should be cast into hell. [30] And if thy right hand offend thee, cut it off, and cast *it* from thee: for it is profitable for thee that one of thy members should perish, and not that thy whole body should be cast into hell.

[31] It hath been said,[s] Whosoever shall put away his wife, let him give her a writing of divorcement: [32] but I say unto you, That whosoever shall put away his wife, saving for the cause of fornication, causeth her to commit adultery: and whosoever shall marry her that is divorced committeth adultery.

[33] Again, ye have heard that it hath been said by them of old time,[t] Thou shalt not forswear thyself, but shalt perform unto the Lord thine oaths: [34] but I say unto you, Swear not at all; neither by heaven; for it is God's throne: [35] nor by the earth; for it is his footstool: neither by Jerusalem; for it is the city of the great King. [36] Neither shalt thou swear by thy head, because thou canst not make one hair white or black. [37] But let your communication be, Yea, yea; Nay, nay: for whatsoever is more than these cometh of evil.

[38] Ye have heard that it hath been said,[u] An eye for an eye, and a tooth for a tooth; [39] but I say unto you, That ye resist not evil; but whosoever shall smite thee on thy right cheek, turn to him the other also. [40] And if any

---

both together in this and many other places. The *Pharisees* were the most numerous sect among the Jews, professing (as the name *separatists* imports) to distinguish themselves from such religionists as the Sadducees by a peculiar devotedness and strictness in the observance of the law; to which however they added the "tradition of the elders," and so made void the commands of God (see in § 67). They believed that, by observing the law and the traditions, a man might be justified before God, and even attain to the merit of supererogation; and accordingly they were generally self-righteous, and manifested a proud aversion to the gospel doctrine of justification by faith, or salvation by grace (see Luke 18. 9–14; Rom. 10. 3).

[p] Ex. 20. 13; Lev. 24. 21.

[q] Christ here speaks of three degrees of punishment, according to what was then known among the Jews. 1. *The judgment* (κρίσις), or inferior court of seven judges, which existed in every city. 2. *The council* (συνέδριον, commonly called *Sanhedrim*), consisting of seventy men—"elders of the people and the chief priests and scribes" (Luke 22. 66), who alone could inflict the severer punishments. 3. *Hell fire* (γέεννα τοῦ πυρός), properly *gehenna of fire*, so called from the *Valley of Hinnom* (הנם גיא) on the south of Jerusalem, where once children had been burnt to Moloch, and afterwards the dead bodies of beasts and malefactors were consumed in a fire constantly kept up (2 Kings 23. 10); hence it served as a figure to denote the place "where the worm dieth not, and the fire is not quenched" (Mark 9. 44).

[r] Ex. 20. 14.
[s] Deut. 24. 1.
[t] Ex. 20. 7; Lev. 19. 12.
[u] Ex. 21. 24; Lev. 24. 20.

Matt. 5.

man will sue thee at the law, and take away thy coat, let him have *thy* cloak also. ⁴¹ And whosoever shall compel thee to go a mile, go with him twain. ⁴² Give to him that asketh thee, and from him that would borrow of thee turn not thou away.

⁴³ Ye have heard that it hath been said,*ʷ* Thou shalt love thy neighbour, and hate thine enemy. ⁴⁴ But I say unto you, Love your enemies, bless them that curse you,*ˣ* do good to them that hate you, and pray for them which despitefully use you, and persecute you; ⁴⁵ That ye may be the children of your Father which is in heaven: for he maketh his sun to rise on the evil and on the good, and sendeth rain on the just and on the unjust.*ʸ* ⁴⁶ For if ye love them which love you, what reward have ye? do not even the publicans the same? ⁴⁷ And if ye salute your brethren only, what do ye more than others? do not even the publicans so?

⁴⁸ Be ye therefore perfect, even as your Father which is in heaven is perfect.

Luke 6.

—²⁹ And unto him that smiteth thee on the one cheek offer also the other; and him that taketh away thy cloak forbid not to take thy coat also. ³⁰ Give to every man that asketh of thee; and of him that taketh away thy goods ask *them* not again.*ᵛ*

—³⁷ But I say unto you which hear, Love your enemies, do good to them which hate you, ²⁸ bless them that curse you, and pray for them which despitefully use you.—

³² For if ye love them which love you, what thank have ye? for sinners also love those that love them. ³³ And if ye do good to them which do good to you, what thank have ye? for sinners also do even the same. ³⁴ And if ye lend *to them* of whom ye hope to receive, what thank have ye? for sinners also lend to sinners, to receive as much again. ³⁵ But love ye your enemies, and do good, and lend, hoping for nothing again; and your reward shall be great, and ye shall be the children of the Highest: for he is kind unto the unthankful and *to* the evil. ³⁶ Be ye therefore merciful, as your Father also is merciful.

Matt. 6. ¹ Take heed that ye do not your alms before men, to be seen of them: otherwise ye have no reward of your Father which is in heaven. ² Therefore when thou doest *thine* alms, do not sound a trumpet before thee, as the hypocrites do in the synagogues and in the streets, that they may have glory of men. Verily I say unto you, They have their reward. ³ But when thou doest alms, let not thy left hand know what thy right hand doeth: ⁴ that thine alms may be in secret: and thy Father which seeth in secret himself shall reward thee openly.

⁵ And when thou prayest, thou shalt not be as the hypocrites *are*: for they love to pray standing in the synagogues and in the corners of the streets, that they may be seen of men. Verily I say unto you, They have their reward. ⁶ But thou, when thou prayest, enter into thy closet, and when thou hast shut thy door, pray to thy Father which is in secret; and thy Father which seeth in secret shall reward thee openly. ⁷ But when ye pray, use not vain repetitions, as the heathen *do*: for they think that they shall be heard for their much speaking. ⁸ Be not ye therefore like unto them: for your Father knoweth what things ye have need of before ye ask him. ⁹ After this manner therefore pray ye: Our Father which art in heaven, Hallowed be thy name. Thy kingdom come. ¹⁰ Thy will be done in earth, as *it is* in heaven. ¹¹ Give us this day our daily bread. ¹² And forgive us our debts, as we

---

⸰ Ver. 31 on p. 35, parallel with Matt. 7. 12.   ⸰ Comp. Prov. 25. 21.   ⸰ Acts 14. 17.
⸰ Comp. Lev. 19. 18; Deut. 23. 6.   ⸰ Luke 11. 2–4; § 88.

Matt. 6.

forgive our debtors. [13] And lead us not into temptation, but deliver us from evil: For thine is the kingdom, and the power, and the glory, for ever. Amen. [14] For if ye forgive men their trespasses, your heavenly Father will also forgive you: [15] but if ye forgive not men their trespasses, neither will your Father forgive your trespasses.

[16] Moreover when ye fast, be not, as the hypocrites, of a sad countenance:[a] for they disfigure their faces, that they may appear unto men to fast. Verily I say unto you, They have their reward. [17] But thou, when thou fastest, anoint thine head, and wash thy face; [18] that thou appear not unto men to fast, but unto thy Father which is in secret: and thy Father, which seeth in secret, shall reward thee openly.

[19] Lay not up for yourselves treasures upon earth, where moth and rust doth corrupt, and where thieves break through and steal: [20] but lay up for yourselves treasures in heaven, where neither moth nor rust doth corrupt, and where thieves do not break through nor steal: [21] for where your treasure is, there will your heart be also. [22] The light of the body is the eye: if therefore thine eye be single, thy whole body shall be full of light. [23] But if thine eye be evil, thy whole body shall be full of darkness. If therefore the light that is in thee be darkness, how great *is* that darkness! [24] No man can serve two masters: for either he will hate the one, and love the other; or else he will hold to the one, and despise the other. Ye cannot[b] serve God and mammon.[c] [25] Therefore I say unto you, Take no thought for your life, what ye shall eat, or what ye shall drink; nor yet for your body, what ye shall put on. Is not the life more than meat, and the body than raiment? [26] Behold the fowls of the air: for they sow not, neither do they reap, nor gather into barns; yet your heavenly Father feedeth them. Are ye not much better than they? [27] Which of you by taking thought can add one cubit unto his stature? [28] And why take ye thought for raiment? Consider the lilies of the field, how they grow; they toil not, neither do they spin: [29] and yet I say unto you, That even Solomon in all his glory was not arrayed like one of these. [30] Wherefore, if God so clothe the grass of the field, which to-day is, and to-morrow is cast into the oven, *shall he* not much more *clothe* you, O ye of little faith? [31] Therefore take no thought, saying, What shall we eat? or, What shall we drink? or, Wherewithal shall we be clothed? (for after all these things do the Gentiles seek:) [32] for your heavenly Father knoweth that ye have need of all these things. [33] But seek ye first the kingdom of God, and his righteousness; and all these things shall be added unto you. [34] Take therefore no thought for the morrow: for the morrow shall take thought for the things of itself. Sufficient unto the day *is* the evil thereof.

Matt. 7. [1] Judge not, that ye be not judged. [2] For with what judgment ye judge, ye shall be judged: and with what measure ye mete, it shall be measured to you again.	**Luke 6.** [37] Judge not, and ye shall not be judged: condemn not, and ye shall not be condemned: forgive, and ye shall be forgiven: [38] give, and it shall be given unto you; good measure, pressed down and shaken together, and

running over, shall men give into your bosom. For with the same measure that ye mete withal it shall be measured to you again. [39] And he spake a parable unto them, Can the blind lead the blind? shall they not both fall into the ditch?

[3] And why beholdest thou the mote that is in thy brother's eye, but considerest

[40] The disciple is not above his master: but every one that is perfect shall be as

---

a Isa. 58. 5–7.
b Comp. Luke 16. 9, 11, 13.
c An Aramean word for *riches*, probably

from the idea of *support* and *reliance*. Our Lord personifies wealth as an idol god.
d Phil. 4. 6; 1 Pet. 5. 7.

Matt. 7.

not the beam that is in thine own eye? ⁴ Or how wilt thou say to thy brother, Let me pull out the mote out of thine eye; and, behold, a beam *is* in thine own eye? ⁵ Thou hypocrite, first cast out the beam out of thine own eye; and then shalt thou see clearly to cast out the mote out of thy brother's eye. ⁶ Give not that which is holy unto the dogs, neither cast ye your pearls before swine, lest they trample them under their feet, and turn again and rend you.

⁷ Ask,*e* and it shall be given you; seek, and ye shall find; knock, and it shall be opened unto you: ⁸ for every one that asketh receiveth; and he that seeketh findeth; and to him that knocketh it shall be opened. ⁹ Or what man is there of you, whom if his son ask bread, will he give him a stone? ¹⁰ or if he ask a fish, will he give him a serpent? ¹¹ If ye then, being evil, know how to give good gifts unto your children, how much more shall your Father which is in heaven give good things to them that ask him? ¹² Therefore all things whatsoever ye would that men should do to you, do ye even so to them: for this is the law and the prophets.

¹³ Enter ye in at the strait gate: for wide *is* the gate, and broad *is* the way, that leadeth to destruction, and many there be which go in thereat: ¹⁴ because strait *is* the gate, and narrow *is* the way, which leadeth unto life, and few there be that find it. ¹⁵ Beware of false prophets, which come to you in sheep's clothing, but inwardly they are ravening wolves.*f* ¹⁶ Ye shall know them by their fruits. Do men gather grapes of thorns, or figs of thistles? ¹⁷ Even so every good tree bringeth forth good fruit; but a corrupt tree bringeth forth evil fruit. ¹⁸ A good tree cannot bring forth evil fruit, neither *can* a corrupt tree bring forth good fruit. ¹⁹ Every tree that bringeth not forth good fruit is hewn down, and cast into the fire. ²⁰ Wherefore by their fruits ye shall know them. ²¹ Not every one that saith unto me, Lord, Lord, shall enter into the kingdom of heaven: but he that doeth the will of my Father which is in heaven. ²² Many will say to me in that day, Lord, Lord, have we not prophesied in thy name? and in thy name done many wonderful works? ²³ And then will I profess unto them, I never knew you: depart from me, ye that work iniquity.

²⁴ Therefore whosoever heareth these sayings of mine, and doeth them, I will liken him unto a wise man, which built his house upon a rock: ²⁵ and the rain

Luke 6.

his master. ⁴¹ And why beholdest thou the mote that is in thy brother's eye, but perceivest not the beam that is in thine own eye? ⁴² Either how canst thou say to thy brother, Brother, let me pull out the mote that is in thine eye, when thou thyself beholdest not the beam that is in thine own eye? Thou hypocrite, cast out first the beam out of thine own eye, and then shalt thou see clearly to pull out the mote that is in thy brother's eye.—

³¹ And as ye would that men should do to you, do ye also to them likewise.—

⁴⁴ For every tree is known by his own fruit. For of thorns men do not gather figs, nor of a bramble bush gather they grapes.—⁴³ For a good tree bringeth not forth corrupt fruit; neither doth a corrupt tree bring forth good fruit.—⁴⁵ A good man out of the good treasure of his heart bringeth forth that which is good; and an evil man out of the evil treasure of his heart bringeth forth that which is evil: for of the abundance of the heart his mouth speaketh.

⁴⁶ And why call ye me, Lord, Lord, and do not the things which I say? ⁴⁷ Whosoever cometh to me, and heareth my sayings, and doeth them, I will show you to whom he is like: ⁴⁸ he is like a man which built an house, and digged deep, and laid the foundation on

e Comp. Luke 11. 9–13.   *f* Comp. Acts 20. 29, 30.

Matt. 7.	Luke 6.

descended, and the floods came, and the winds blew, and beat upon that house and it fell not: for it was founded upon a rock. **26** And every one that heareth these sayings of mine, and doeth them not, shall be likened unto a foolish man, which built his house upon the sand: **27** and the rain descended, and the floods came, and the winds blew, and beat upon that house; and it fell: and great was the fall of it.

a rock: and when the flood arose, the stream beat vehemently upon that house, and could not shake it: for it was founded upon a rock. **49** But he that heareth, and doeth not, is like a man that without a foundation built an house upon the earth; against which the stream did beat vehemently, and immediately it fell: and the ruin of that house was great.

28 And it came to pass, when Jesus had ended these sayings, the people were astonished at his doctrine: **29** for he taught them as *one* having authority, and not as the scribes.

Matt. 8. **1** When he was come down from the mountain, great multitudes followed him.*

§ 42. The Healing of the Centurion's Servant.—*Capernaum.*

Matt. 8. 5-13. **5** And when Jesus was entered into Capernaum, there came unto him a centurion,[h] beseeching him, **6** and saying, Lord, my servant lieth at home sick of the palsy, grievously tormented.

Luke 7. 1-10. **1** Now when he had ended all his sayings in the audience of the people, he entered into Capernaum. **2** And a certain centurion's servant, who was dear unto him, was sick, and ready to die. **3** And when he heard of Jesus, he sent unto him the elders of the Jews, beseeching him that he would come and heal his servant. **4** And when they came to Jesus, they besought him instantly, saying, That he was worthy for whom he should do this: **5** for he loveth our nation, and he hath built us a synagogue. **6** Then Jesus went with them. And when he was now not far from the house, the centurion sent friends to him, saying unto him, Lord, trouble not thyself: for I am not worthy that thou shouldest enter under my roof: **7** wherefore neither thought I myself worthy to come unto thee: but say in a word,[i] and my servant shall be healed. **8** For I also am a man set under authority, having under me soldiers, and I say unto one, Go, and he goeth; and to another, Come, and he cometh; and to my servant, Do this, and he doeth it. **9** When Jesus heard these things, he marvelled at him, and turned him about, and said

7 And Jesus saith unto him, I will come and heal him. **8** The centurion answered and said, Lord, I am not worthy that thou shouldest come under my roof: but speak the word only,[i] and my servant shall be healed. **9** For I am a man under authority, having soldiers under me: and I say to this *man*, Go, and he goeth: and to another, Come, and he cometh; and to my servant, Do this, and he doeth *it*. **10** When Jesus heard *it*, he marvelled, and said to them that followed, Verily

---

g Ver. 2–4 in § 33.

[h] In Matthew, the centurion seems to come in person to Jesus; in Luke, he sends the elders of the Jews. This diversity is satisfactorily explained by the old law-maxim: *Qui facit per alium, facit per se;* that is, What one does by means of another, he does himself. In like manner, in John 4. 1, Jesus is said to baptize, when He did it by His disciples. In John 19. 1, and elsewhere, Pilate is said to have scourged Jesus; certainly not with his own hands. In Mark 10. 35, James and John come to Jesus with a certain request; in Matt. 20. 20, it is their mother who prefers the request.

[i] Comp Gen. 1. 3; John 1. 1–3.

Matt. 8.

I say unto you, I have not found so great faith, no, not in Israel. ¹¹ And I say unto you, That many shall come from the east and west, and shall sit down with Abraham, and Isaac, and Jacob, in the kingdom of heaven. ¹² But the children of the kingdom shall be cast out into outer darkness: there shall be weeping and gnashing of teeth.ʲ said unto the centurion, Go thy way; and as thou hast believed, *so* be it done unto thee. And his servant was healed in the selfsame hour.ᵏ

Luke 7.

unto the people that followed him, I say unto you, I have not found so great faith, no, not in Israel. ¹⁰ And Jesus ¹⁰ And they that were sent, returning to the house, found the servant whole that had been sick.

§ 43. The Raising of the Widow's Son.—*Nain*.

Luke 7. 11-17. ¹¹ And it came to pass the day after, that he went into a city called Nain; and many of his disciples went with him, and much people. ¹² Now when he came nigh to the gate of the city, behold, there was a dead man carried out, the only son of his mother, and she was a widow: and much people of the city was with her. ¹³ And when the Lord saw her, he had compassion on her, and said unto her, Weep not. ¹⁴ And he came and touched the bier: and they that bare *him* stood still. And he said, Young man, I say unto thee, Arise. ¹⁵ And he that was dead sat up, and began to speak. And he delivered him to his mother. ¹⁶ And there came a fear on all: and they glorified God, saying, That a great prophet is risen up among us; and, That God hath visited his people. ¹⁷ And this rumour of him went forth throughout all Judea, and throughout all the region round about.

§ 44. John the Baptist in Prison sends Disciples to Jesus.—*Galilee: Capernaum?*

Matt. 11. 2-19. ² Now whenˡ John had heard in the prison ᵐ the works of Christ, he sent two of his disciples, ³ and said unto him, Art thou he that should come, or do we look for another?

⁴ Jesus answered and said unto them, Go and show John again those things which ye do hear and see: ⁵ the blind receive their sight, and the lame walk, the lepers are cleansed, and the deaf hear, the dead are raised up, and the

Luke 7. 18-35. ¹⁸ And the disciples of John showed him of all these things. ¹⁹ And John calling *unto him* two of his disciples sent *them* to Jesus, saying, Art thou he that should come? or look we for another? ²⁰ When the men were come unto him, they said, John Baptist hath sent us unto thee, saying, Art thou he that should come? or look we for another? ²¹ And in that same hour he cured many of *their* infirmities and plagues, and of evil spirits; and unto many *that were* blind he gave sight. ²² Then Jesus answering said unto them, Go your way, and tell John what things ye have seen and heard; how that the blind see, the lame walk, the lepers are cleansed, the deaf hear, the dead are raised, to the poor the gospel is

---

ʲ Comp. Luke 13. 25-28.
ᵏ See in § 31.
ˡ Matthew places this narrative after the sending out of the twelve, Matt. 11. 1: see § 62. But it was during that absence John was beheaded: see Mark 6. 30; Matt. 14. 13. The order of Luke is therefore followed. Our Lord was probably at or near Capernaum, or perhaps Nain: comp. § 45.

ᵐ *In the prison:* this was, according to Josephus (Antiq. 18. 5. 2), in Machærus, a castle or fortress situated on the southern border of Peræa, near the Dead Sea, and not very far from Livias (see Wieseler, p. 243-247), a town in which Herod had a residence, and where he probably held a grand feast, during which he ordered the beheading of the Baptist: see in § 63.

Matt. 11.

poor have the gospel preached to them.[n] [5] And blessed is *he*, whosoever shall not be offended in me.

[7] And as they departed, Jesus began to say unto the multitudes concerning John, What went ye out into the wilderness to see? A reed shaken with the wind? [8] But what went ye out for to see? A man clothed in soft raiment? Behold, they that wear soft *clothing* are in kings' houses. [9] But what went ye out for to see? A prophet? yea, I say unto you, and more than a prophet. [10] For this is *he*, of whom it is written,[o] Behold, I send my messenger before thy face, which shall prepare thy way before thee. [11] Verily I say unto you, Among them that are born of women there hath not risen a greater than John the Baptist: notwithstanding he that is least in the kingdom of heaven is greater than he. [12] And from the days of John the Baptist until now the kingdom of heaven suffereth violence, and the violent take it by force. [13] For all the prophets and the law prophesied until John. [14] And if ye will receive *it*, this is Elias, which was for to come.[q] [15] He that hath ears to hear, let him hear. [16] But whereunto shall I liken this generation? It is like unto children sitting in the markets, and calling unto their fellows, [17] and saying, We have piped unto you, and ye have not danced; we have mourned unto you, and ye have not lamented.

[18] For John came neither eating nor drinking, and they say, He hath a devil.

[19] The Son of man came eating and drinking, and they say, Behold a man gluttonous, and a winebibber, a friend of publicans and sinners. But wisdom is justified of her children.[r]

Luke 7.

preached.[n] [23] And blessed is *he*, whosoever shall not be offended in me.

[24] And when the messengers of John were departed, he began to speak unto the people concerning John, What went ye out into the wilderness for to see? A reed shaken with the wind? [25] But what went ye out for to see? A man clothed in soft raiment? Behold, they which are gorgeously apparelled, and live delicately, are in kings' courts. [26] But what went ye out for to see? A prophet? Yea, I say unto you, and much more than a prophet. [27] This is *he*, of whom it is written,[o] Behold, I send my messenger before thy face, which shall prepare thy way before thee. [28] For I say unto you, Among those that are born of women there is not a greater prophet than John the Baptist: but he that is least in the kingdom of God is greater than he. [29] And all the people that heard *him*, and the publicans, justified God, being baptized with the baptism of John. [30] But the Pharisees and lawyers rejected the counsel of God against themselves, being not baptized of him.

[31] And the Lord said, Whereunto then shall I liken the men of this generation? and to what are they like? [32] They are like unto children sitting in the marketplace, and calling one to another, and saying, We have piped unto you, and ye have not danced; we have mourned to you, and ye have not wept. [33] For John the Baptist came neither eating bread nor drinking wine; and ye say, He hath a devil. [34] The Son of man is come eating and drinking; and ye say, Behold a gluttonous man, and a winebibber, a friend of publicans and sinners! [35] But wisdom is justified of all her children.[r]

---

[a] Comp. Isa. 35. 5, sq.; 42. 6, 7; 61. 1.
[o] Mal. 3. 1.   [o] Comp. Gal. 4. 1–7.
[q] Mal. 4. 5.

[r] *But* (rather, *And*) *wisdom is justified, etc.*: this obscure sentence has been explained, in harmony with the context, thus,—The Divine wisdom, which has done all that was possible to draw her children to herself, by using diverse methods in the ministry of John, and in that of Christ (see

ver. 16–19), is in this manner absolved from the complaints of the wayward Jewish people, who are called also "the children of the kingdom" (Matt. 8. 12), and "the children of the prophets and of the covenant" (Acts 3. 25). Or, the "children of wisdom" are the *really wise*, who, unlike their captious fellow-countrymen, recognise and "justify" true wisdom, under whatever diverse forms it may appear.[r]

§ 45.   Reflections of Jesus on Appealing to His mighty Works.
Capernaum ?

Matt. 11. 20-30. [20] Then began he to upbraid the cities wherein most of his mighty works were done, because they repented not: [21] Woe unto thee,* Chorazin! woe unto thee, Bethsaida! for if the mighty works, which were done in you, had been done in Tyre and Sidon, they would have repented long ago in sackcloth and ashes. [22] But I say unto you, It shall be more tolerable for Tyre and Sidon at the day of judgment, than for you. [23] And thou, Capernaum, which art exalted unto heaven, shalt be brought down to hell: for if the mighty works, which have been done in thee, had been done in Sodom, it would have remained until this day. [24] But I say unto you, That it shall be more tolerable for the land of Sodom in the day of judgment, than for thee.

[25] At that time *t* Jesus answered and said, I thank thee, O Father, Lord of heaven and earth, because thou hast hid these things from the wise and prudent,[u] and hast revealed them unto babes. [26] Even so, Father: for so it seemed good in thy sight. [27] All things are delivered unto me of my Father: and no man knoweth the Son, but the Father; neither knoweth any man the Father, save the Son, and *he* to whomsoever the Son will reveal *him*. [28] Come unto me, all *ye* that labour and are heavy laden, and I will give you rest. [29] Take my yoke upon you, and learn of me; for I am meek and lowly in heart: and ye shall find rest unto your souls. [30] For my yoke *is* easy, and my burden is light.*v*

§ 46.   While sitting at Meat with a Pharisee, Jesus is Anointed by a Woman who had been a Sinner.—*Capernaum ?*

Luke 7. 36-50. [36] And one of the Pharisees desired him that he would eat with him. And he went into the Pharisee's house, and sat down to meat. [37] And, behold, a woman *w* in the city, which was a sinner, when she knew that *Jesus* sat at meat in the Pharisee's house, brought an alabaster box of ointment, [38] and stood at his feet behind *him* weeping, and began to wash his feet with tears, and did wipe *them* with the hairs of her head, and kissed his feet, and anointed *them* with the ointment. [39] Now when the Pharisee which had bidden him saw *it*, he spake within himself, saying, This man, if he were a prophet, would have known who and what manner of woman *this is* that toucheth him: for she is a sinner. [40] And Jesus answering said unto him, Simon, I have somewhat to say unto thee. And he saith, Master, say on. [41] There was a certain creditor which had two debtors: the one owed five hundred pence,*x* and the other fifty. [42] And when they had nothing to pay, he frankly forgave them both. Tell me, therefore, which of them will love him most? [43] Simon answered and said, I suppose that *he* to whom he forgave most. And he said unto him, Thou hast rightly judged. [44] And he turned to the woman, and said unto Simon, Seest thou this woman? I entered into thine house, thou gavest me no water for my feet:*y* but she hath washed my feet with tears, and wiped *them* with the hairs of her head. [45] Thou gavest me no kiss:*z* but this woman since the time I came in hath not ceased to kiss my feet. [46] My head with

---

* Comp. Luke 10. 13-15; see in § 81.
t Comp. Luke 10. 21.   * 1 Cor. 2. 14.
* Ch. 12. 1-21 in §§ 37-39.
w *And, behold, a woman :* the common opinion, that this was Mary Magdalene, is wholly without foundation, for she is evidently mentioned by Luke, as for the first time, in ch. 8. 2, and that not as a *sinner* (like this woman), but as afflicted formerly with *seven devils*, which is no evidence of a

depraved life.—The omission of this woman's name may be attributed to delicacy of feeling in the evangelist, who, though relating this most touching and instructive story, thought it right to withhold the name.

x *Pence:* the Roman penny (*denarius*), a silver coin, equal to seven pence halfpenny of our money, but with a much larger purchasing power.

y Gen. 18. 4.   * 2 Sam. 15. 5.

Luke 7.

oil thou didst not anoint: but this woman hath anointed my feet with ointment. [47] Wherefore I say unto thee, Her sins, which are many, are forgiven; for she loved much: but to whom little is forgiven, *the same* loveth little. [48] And he said unto her, Thy sins are forgiven. [49] And they that sat at meat with him began to say within themselves, Who is this that forgiveth sins also? [50] And he said to the woman, Thy faith hath saved thee; go in peace.

§ 47. JESUS, WITH THE TWELVE, MAKES A SECOND CIRCUIT IN GALILEE.[a]

Luke 8. 1-3. [1] And it came to pass afterward, that he went throughout every city and village, preaching and showing the glad tidings of the kingdom of God: and the twelve *were* with him, [2] and certain women, which had been healed of evil spirits and infirmities, Mary called Magdalene,[b] out of whom went seven devils, [3] and Joanna the wife of Chuza Herod's steward, and Susanna, and many others, which ministered unto him of their substance.[c]

§ 48. THE HEALING OF A DEMONIAC,[d] THE SCRIBES AND PHARISEES
BLASPHEME.—*Galilee.*

Mark 3. 19-30. [19] And they went into an house. [20] And the multitude cometh together again, so that they could not so much as eat bread. [21] And when his friends heard *of it,* they went out to lay hold on him: for they said, He is beside himself.

Matt. 12. 22-37. [22] Then was brought unto him one possessed with a devil, blind, and dumb: and he healed him, insomuch that the blind and dumb both spake and saw. [23] And all the people were amazed, and said, Is not this the Son of David? [24] But when the Pharisees heard *it,* they said, This *fellow* doth not cast out devils, but by Beelzebub,[f] the prince of the devils. [25] And Jesus knew their thoughts, and said unto them, Every kingdom divided against itself is brought to desolation; and every city or house divided against itself shall not stand: [26] and if Satan cast out Satan, he is divided against himself; how shall then his

Mark 3.

[22] And the scribes which came down from Jerusalem said, He hath Beelzebub,[f] and by the prince of the devils casteth he out devils. [23] And he called them *unto him,* and said unto them in parables, How can Satan cast out Satan? [24] And if a kingdom be divided against itself, that kingdom cannot stand. [25] And if a house be divided a-

Luke 11. 14, 15, 17-23.[e]

[14] And he was casting out a devil, and it was dumb. And it came to pass, when the devil was gone out, the dumb spake; and the people wondered. [15] But some of them said, He casteth out devils through Beelzebub,[f] the chief of the devils.— [17] But he, knowing their thoughts, said unto them, Every kingdom divided against itself is brought to desolation; and a house *divided* against a house falleth. [18] If Satan also be divided against himself, how shall his kingdom stand? because ye

---

[a] See § 32.

[b] *Magdalene:* so called from Magdala, the town she belonged to, and to distinguish her from the other Marys mentioned in the Gospels, of whom there are at least three, namely, the mother of our Lord, the wife of Alphæus or Clopas, and the sister of Lazarus.

[c] Comp. 2 Cor. 8. 9.

[d] The order of Mark is here resumed, who places these transactions next after the appointment of the twelve, omitting the sermon

on the mount and other intervening matters. The narrative of Luke is obviously parallel, although given by him in a different place. See Introductory Note to Part VI.

[e] Ver. 16 in § 49.

[f] *Beelzebub, lord of flies* (2 Kings 1. 2)—more correctly *Beelzebul, lord of dung*—a name employed by the Israelites to express their contempt for that idol, and their sense of the filthiness of idolatry. Hence a name for the devil.

Matt. 12.	Mark 3.	Luke 11.

kingdom stand? **27** And if I by Beelzebub cast out devils, by whom do your children cast *them* out?*g* therefore they shall be your judges. **28** But if I cast out devils by the Spirit of God, then the kingdom of God is come unto you.

gainst itself, that house cannot stand. **26** And if Satan rise up against himself, and be divided, he cannot stand, but hath an end.

say that I cast out **devils** through Beelzebub. **19** And if I by Beelzebub cast out devils, by whom do your sons cast *them* out?*g* therefore shall they be your judges. **20** But if I with the finger of God cast out devils, no doubt the kingdom of God is come upon you. **21** When a strong man armed keepeth his palace, his goods are in peace: **22** but when a stronger than he shall come upon him and overcome him, he taketh from him all his armour wherein he trusted, and divideth his spoils. **23** He that is not with me is against me; and he that gathereth not with me scattereth.

29 Or else how can one enter into a strong man's house, and spoil his goods, except he first bind the strong man? and then he will spoil his house.

27 No man can enter into a strong man's house, and spoil his goods, except he will first bind the strong man; and then he will spoil his house.

30 He that is not with me is against me; and he that gathereth not with me scattereth abroad.

Mark 3.

31 Wherefore I say unto you, All manner of sin and blasphemy shall be forgiven unto men: but the blasphemy *against* the *Holy* Ghost shall not be forgiven unto men.*h* **32** And whosoever speaketh a word against the Son of man, it shall be forgiven him: but whosoever speaketh against the Holy Ghost, it shall not be forgiven

28 Verily I say unto you, All sins shall be forgiven unto the sons of men, and blasphemies wherewith soever they shall blaspheme: **29** but he that shall blaspheme against the Holy Ghost hath never forgiveness,*h* but is in danger of eternal damnation: **30** because they said, He hath an unclean spirit.*i*

him, neither in this world, neither in the *world* to come. **33** Either make the tree good, and his fruit good; or else make the tree corrupt, and his fruit corrupt: for the tree is known by *his* fruit.*j* **34** O generation of vipers, how can ye, being evil, speak good things? for out of the abundance of the heart the mouth speaketh. **35** A good man out of the good treasure of the heart bringeth forth good things, and an evil man out of the evil treasure bringeth forth evil things. **36** But I say unto you, That every idle word that men shall speak, they shall give account thereof in the day of judgment. **37** For by thy words thou shalt be justified,*k* and by thy words thou shalt be condemned.

§ 49. The Scribes and Pharisees seek a Sign. Our Lord's Reflections.
Galilee.

Matt. 12. 38-45. **38** Then certain of the Scribes and of the Pharisees answered, saying, Master, we would see a sign from thee. **39** But he answered and said unto them, An evil and adulterous generation seeketh after a sign;

Luke 11. 16, 24-36. **16** And others, tempting *him*, sought of him a sign from heaven.—

29 And when the people were gathered thick together, he began to say, This

---

g Comp Acts 19. 13–16.   *h* Comp. Luke 12. 10.   *i* See in § 50.
j Comp. Matt. 7. 16–18.   *k* Rom. 10. 10.

Matt. 12.

and there shall no sign be given to it, but the sign of the prophet Jonas: [40]for as Jonas was three days and three nights in the whale's belly;[l] so shall the Son of man be three days and three nights in the heart of the earth. [41]The men of Nineveh shall rise in judgment with this generation, and shall condemn it: because they repented at the preaching of Jonas;[m] and, behold, a greater than Jonas *is* here. [42]The queen of the south shall rise up in the judgment with this generation, and shall condemn it: for she came from the uttermost parts of the earth to hear the wisdom of Solomon;[n] and, behold, a greater than Solomon *is* here.—

Luke 11.

is an evil generation: they seek a sign; and there shall no sign be given it, but the sign of Jonas the prophet. [30]For as Jonas was a sign unto the Ninevites, so shall also the Son of man be to this generation.—

[32]The men of Nineve shall rise up in the judgment with this generation, and shall condemn it: for they repented at the preaching of Jonas;[m] and, behold, a greater than Jonas *is* here.—[31]The queen of the south shall rise up in the judgment with the men of this generation, and condemn them: for she came from the utmost parts of the earth to hear the wisdom of Solomon;[n] and, behold, a greater than

[29]No man, when he hath lighted a candle, putteth *it* in a secret place, neither under a bushel, but on a candlestick, that they which come in may see the light. [34]The light of the body is the eye: therefore when thine eye is single, thy whole body also is full of light; but when *thine eye* is evil, thy body also *is* full of darkness. [35]Take heed therefore that the light which is in thee be not darkness. [36]If thy whole body therefore *be* full of light, having no part dark, the whole shall be full of light, as when the bright shining of a candle doth give thee light.—[24]When the unclean spirit is gone out of a man, he walketh through dry places, seeking rest; and finding none, he saith, I will return unto my house whence I came out. [25]And when he cometh, he findeth *it* swept and garnished. [26]Then goeth he, and taketh to *him* seven other spirits more wicked than himself; and they enter in, and dwell there: and the last *state* of that man is worse than the first.[o]

[43]When the unclean spirit is gone out of a man, he walketh through dry places, seeking rest, and findeth none. [44]Then he saith, I will return into my house from whence I came out; and when he is come, he findeth *it* empty, swept, and garnished. [45]Then goeth he, and taketh with himself seven other spirits more wicked than himself, and they enter in and dwell there: and the last *state* of that man is worse than the first.[o] Even so shall it be also unto this wicked generation.

[27]And it came to pass, as he spake these things, a certain woman of the company lifted up her voice, and said unto him, Blessed *is* the womb that bare thee, and the paps which thou hast sucked. [28]But he said, Yea rather, blessed *are* they that hear the word of God, and keep it.

§ 50. THE TRUE DISCIPLES OF CHRIST HIS NEAREST RELATIVES.—*Galilee.*

Mt. 12. 46-50. [46]While he yet talked to the people, behold, *his* mother and his brethren stood without, desiring to

Mark 3. 31-35. [31]There came then his brethren and his mother, and, standing without, sent unto him, calling him.

Luke 8. 19-21. [19]Then[r] came to him *his* mother and his brethren, and could not come at him for the press.

---

[l] Jonah 1. 17.
[m] Jonah 3. 4, 5.
[n] 1 Kings 10. 1-13.

[o] Comp. Heb. 6. 4-8; 2 Pet. 2. 20-22.
[r] *Then* is here a mistranslation of δέ, which merely connects without denoting time.

Matt. 12.

speak with him. [47] Then one said unto him, Behold, thy mother and thy brethren stand without, desiring to speak with thee. [48] But he answered and said unto him that told him, Who is my mother? and who are my brethren? [49] And he stretched forth his hand toward his disciples, and said, Behold my mother and my brethren! [50] For whosoever shall do the will of my Father which is in heaven, the same is my brother, and sister, and mother.[q]

Mark 3.

[32] And the multitude sat about him, and they said unto him, Behold, thy mother and thy brethren without seek for thee. [33] And he answered them, saying,

Who is my mother, or my brethren? [34] And he looked round about on them which sat about him, and said, Behold my mother and my brethren! [35] For whosoever shall do the will of God, the same is my brother, and my sister, and mother.[q]

Luke 8.

[20] And it was told him *by certain* which said, Thy mother and thy brethren stand without, desiring to see thee. [21] And he answered and said unto them,

My mother and my brethren are these which hear the word of God, and do it.[q]

§ 51. JESUS DENOUNCES WOES AGAINST THE PHARISEES AND OTHERS. *Galilee.*

Luke 11. 37-54. [37] And as he spake,[r] a certain Pharisee besought him to dine with him: and he went in, and sat down to meat. [38] And when the Pharisee saw *it*, he marvelled that he had not first washed before dinner.[s] [39] And the Lord said unto him, Now do ye Pharisees make clean the outside of the cup and the platter;[t] but your inward part is full of ravening and wickedness. [40] *Ye* fools, did not he that made that which is without make that which is within also? [41] But rather give alms of such things as ye have; and, behold, all things are clean unto you. [42] But woe unto you, Pharisees! for ye tithe mint and rue and all manner of herbs, and pass over judgment and the love of God: these ought ye to have done, and not to leave the other undone.[u] [43] Woe unto you, Pharisees! for ye love the uppermost seats in the synagogues, and greetings in the markets.[v] [44] Woe unto you, scribes and Pharisees, hypocrites! for ye are as graves which appear not,[w] and the men that walk over *them* are not aware *of them.*

[45] Then answered one of the lawyers, and said unto him, Master, thus saying thou reproachest us also. [46] And he said, Woe unto you also, *ye* lawyers! for ye lade men with burdens grievous to be borne, and ye yourselves touch not the burdens with one of your fingers. [47] Woe unto you![x] for ye build the sepulchres of the prophets, and your fathers killed them. [48] Truly ye bear witness that ye allow the deeds of your fathers: for they indeed killed them, and ye build their sepulchres. [49] Therefore also said the wisdom of God,[y] I will send them prophets and apostles, and *some* of them they shall slay and persecute: [50] that the blood of all the prophets, which was shed from the foundation of the world, may be required of this generation; [51] from the blood of Abel unto the blood of Zacharias, which perished between the altar and the temple:[z] verily I say unto you, It shall be required of this genera-

q See in § 54.

r The order here connects back with Luke 11. 36, in § 49. Jesus received the invitation of the Pharisee while He was speaking. See Introductory Note to Part VI.

s Mark 7. 3.

u Matt. 23. 23.

t Matt. 23. 25, 26.

v Matt. 23. 6.

w Matt. 23. 27, 28.   x Matt. 23. 29-36.

y *The wisdom of God:* by this our Saviour means Himself (1 Cor. 1. 24), as may be seen from the corresponding utterance in Matt 23. 34.

z Gen. 4. 8; 2 Chron. 24 20-22.

Luke 11.

tion. [52] Woe unto you, lawyers![a] for ye have taken away the key of knowledge: ye enter not in yourselves, and them that were entering in ye hindered. [53] And as he said these things unto them, the scribes and the Pharisees began to urge *him* vehemently, and to provoke him to speak of many things: [54] laying wait for him, and seeking to catch something out of his mouth, that they might accuse him.

§ 52. JESUS DISCOURSES TO HIS DISCIPLES AND THE MULTITUDE.—*Galilee.*

Luke 12. 1-59. [1] In the mean time,[b] when there were gathered together an innumerable multitude of people, insomuch that they trode one upon another, he began to say unto his disciples first of all, Beware ye of the leaven of the Pharisees,[c] which is hypocrisy. [2] For there is nothing covered, that shall not be revealed;[d] neither hid, that shall not be known. [3] Therefore whatsoever ye have spoken in darkness shall be heard in the light; and that which ye have spoken in the ear in closets shall be proclaimed upon the housetops. [4] And I say unto you my friends, Be not afraid of them that kill the body, and after that have no more that they can do. [5] But I will forewarn you whom ye shall fear: Fear him, which after he hath killed hath power to cast into hell; yea, I say unto you, Fear him. [6] Are not five sparrows sold for two farthings, and not one of them is forgotten before God? [7] But even the very hairs of your head are all numbered. Fear not therefore: ye are of more value than many sparrows. [8] Also I say unto you, Whosoever shall confess me before men, him shall the Son of man also confess before the angels of God: [9] but he that denieth me before men shall be denied before the angels of God. [10] And whosoever shall speak a word against the Son of man, it shall be forgiven him: but unto him that blasphemeth against the Holy Ghost it shall not be forgiven. [11] And when they bring you unto the synagogues,[e] and *unto* magistrates, and powers, take ye no thought how or what thing ye shall answer, or what ye shall say: [12] for the Holy Ghost shall teach you in the same hour what ye ought to say.

[13] And one of the company said unto him, Master, speak to my brother, that he divide the inheritance with me. [14] And he said unto him, Man, who made me a judge or a divider over you? [15] And he said unto them, Take heed, and beware of covetousness: for a man's life consisteth not in the abundance of the things which he possesseth. [16] And he spake a parable unto them, saying, The ground of a certain rich man brought forth plentifully: [17] and he thought within himself, saying, What shall I do, because I have no room where to bestow my fruits? [18] And he said, This will I do: I will pull down my barns, and build greater; and there will I bestow all my fruits and my goods. [19] And I will say to my soul, Soul, thou hast much goods laid up for many years; take thine ease, eat, drink, *and* be merry. [20] But God said unto him, *Thou* fool, this night thy soul shall be required of thee: then whose shall those things be which thou hast provided? [21] So *is* he that layeth up treasure for himself, and is not rich toward God.

[22] And he said unto his disciples, Therefore I say unto you, Take no thought[f] for your life, what ye shall eat; neither for the body, what ye shall put on. [23] The life is more than meat, and the body *is more* than raiment. [24] Consider the ravens: for they neither sow nor reap; which neither have storehouse nor barn; and God feedeth them: how much more are ye better than the fowls? [25] And which of you with taking thought can add to his stature one cubit? [26] If ye then be not able to do that thing which is least, why take ye thought for the rest? [27] Consider the

---

* Matt. 23. 13.

* Luke ch. 12 is directly connected with the preceding by the phrase, *In the mean time.*

c Comp. Matt. 16. 6.

d Matt. 10. 26-33.

* Matt. 10. 19, 20.

f Comp. Matt. 6. 25-33.

Luke 12.

lilies how they grow: they toil not, they spin not; and yet I say unto you, that Solomon in all his glory was not arrayed like one of these. ²⁸ If then God so clothe the grass, which is to-day in the field, and to-morrow is cast into the oven; how much more *will he clothe* you, O ye of little faith? ²⁹ And seek not ye what ye shall eat, or what ye shall drink, neither be ye of doubtful mind. ³⁰ For all these things do the nations of the world seek after: and your Father knoweth that ye have need of these things. ³¹ But rather seek ye the kingdom of God; and all these things shall be added unto you. ³² Fear not, little flock; for it is your Father's good pleasure to give you the kingdom. ³³ Sell that ye have, and give alms; provide yourselves bags which wax not old, a treasure in the heavens that faileth not, where no thief approacheth, neither moth corrupteth. ³⁴ For where your treasure is, there will your heart be also. ³⁵ Let your loins be girded about, and *your* lights burning; ³⁶ and ye yourselves like unto men that wait for their lord, when he will return from the wedding; that when he cometh and knocketh, they may open unto him immediately. ³⁷ Blessed *are* those servants, whom the lord when he cometh shall find watching: verily I say unto you, that he shall gird himself, and make them to sit down to meat, and will come forth and serve them. ³⁸ And if he shall come in the second watch, or come in the third watch,⁹ and find *them* so, blessed are those servants. ³⁹ And this know, that if the goodman of the house had known what hour the thief would come, he would have watched, and not have suffered his house to be broken through. ⁴⁰ Be ye therefore ready also: for the Son of man cometh at an hour when ye think not.

⁴¹ Then Peter said unto him, Lord, speakest thou this parable unto us, or even to all? ⁴² And the Lord said, Who then is that faithful and wise steward,ʰ whom *his* lord shall make ruler over his household, to give *them their* portion of meat in due season? ⁴³ Blessed *is* that servant, whom his lord when he cometh shall find so doing. ⁴⁴ Of a truth I say unto you, that he will make him ruler over all that he hath. ⁴⁵ But and if that servant say in his heart, My lord delayeth his coming; and shall begin to beat the men-servants and maidens, and to eat and drink, and to be drunken; ⁴⁶ the lord of that servant will come in a day when he looketh not for *him*, and at an hour when he is not aware, and will cut him in sunder, and will appoint him his portion with the unbelievers. ⁴⁷ And that servant, which knew his lord's will, and prepared not *himself*, neither did according to his will, shall be beaten with many *stripes*. ⁴⁸ But he that knew not,ⁱ and did commit things worthy of stripes, shall be beaten with few *stripes*. For unto whomsoever much is given, of him shall be much required: and to whom men have committed much, of him they will ask the more.

⁴⁹ I am come to send fire on the earth; and what will I, if it be already kindled? ⁵⁰ But I have a baptism to be baptized with; and how am I straitened till it be accomplished! ⁵¹ Suppose ye that I am come to give peace on earth? I tell you Nay;ʲ but rather division: ⁵² for from henceforth there shall be five in one house divided, three against two, and two against three. ⁵³ The father shall be divided against the son, and the son against the father; the mother against the daughter, and the daughter against the mother; the mother-in-law against her daughter-in-law, and the daughter-in-law against her mother-in-law.

⁵⁴ And he said also to the people, When ye see a cloud rise out of the west, straightway ye say, There cometh a shower; and so it is. ⁵⁵ And when *ye see* the south wind blow, ye say, There will be heat; and it cometh to pass. ⁵⁶ *Ye* hypocrites, ye can discern the face of the sky and of the earth; but how is it that ye do not discern this time? ⁵⁷ Yea, and why even of yourselves judge ye not what

---

⁹ The dead of night, which made the vigilance more commendable.
ʰ Matt. 24. 45–51.

ⁱ Even those who sin *in ignorance* may be guilty, the ignorance itself being sinful.
ʲ Matt. 10. 24–36.

Luke 12.

is right? ⁵⁸ When thou goest with thine adversary to the magistrate, *as thou art* in the way, give diligence that thou mayest be delivered from him; lest he hale thee to the judge, and the judge deliver thee to the officer, and the officer cast thee into prison. ⁵⁹ I tell thee, thou shalt not depart thence, till thou hast paid the very last mite.

§ 53. SLAUGHTER OF CERTAIN GALILEANS. THE BARREN FIG TREE.—*Galilee.*

Luke 13. 1-9. ¹ There were present at that season [k] some that told him of the Galileans, whose blood Pilate had mingled with their sacrifices. ² And Jesus answering said unto them, Suppose ye that these Galileans were sinners above all the Galileans, because they suffered such things? ³ I tell you, Nay: but, except ye repent, ye shall all likewise perish. ⁴ Or those eighteen, upon whom the tower in Siloam fell, and slew them, think ye that they were sinners above all men that dwelt in Jerusalem? ⁵ I tell you, Nay: but, except ye repent, ye shall all likewise perish.

⁶ He spake also this parable; A certain *man* had a fig tree planted in his vineyard; and he came and sought fruit thereon, and found none. ⁷ Then said he unto the dresser of his vineyard, Behold, these three years I come seeking fruit on this fig tree, and find none: cut it down; why cumbereth it the ground? ⁸ And he answering said unto him, Lord, let it alone this year also, till I shall dig about it, and dung *it:* ⁹ and if it bear fruit, *well:* and if not, *then* after that thou shalt cut it down.[l]

§ 54. PARABLE OF THE SOWER.[m]—*Sea of Galilee: near Capernaum?*

Matt. 13. 1-23.	Mark 4. 1-25.	Luke 8. 4-18.
¹ The same day went Jesus out of the house,[n] and sat by the sea side. ² And great multitudes were gathered together unto him, so that he went into a ship, and sat; and the whole multitude stood on the shore. ³ And he spake many things unto them in parables, saying,	¹ And he began again to teach by the sea side: and there was gathered unto him a great multitude, so that he entered into a ship, and sat in the sea; and the whole multitude was by the sea on the land. ² And he taught them many things by parables, and said unto them in his doctrine, ³ Hearken; Behold, there went out a sower to sow:	⁴ And when much people were gathered together, and were come to him out of every city, he spake by a parable·
Behold, a sower went forth to sow; ⁴ and when he sowed, some *seeds* fell by the way side, and the fowls came and devoured them up: ⁵ some fell upon stony places, where they had not much earth: and forthwith they sprung up, because they had no deepness of earth: ⁶ and when	⁴ and it came to pass, as he sowed, some fell by the way side, and the fowls of the air came and devoured it up. ⁵ And some fell on stony ground, where it had not much earth; and immediately it sprang up, because it had no depth of earth: ⁶ but when the	⁵ A sower went out to sow his seed: and as he sowed, some fell by the way side; and it was trodden down, and the fowls of the air devoured it. ⁶ And some fell upon a rock; and as soon as it was sprung up, it withered away, because it lacked moisture.

---

[k] This verse fixes the order of this chapter, as coming properly next to ch. 12.

Isa. 5. 5–7.

[m] The order here depends on Matt. 13. 1;

the intervening events in §§ 51–53 being supplied by Luke. The place was probably Capernaum.

[n] *The house:* that in which Christ usually tarried at Capernaum.

Matt. 13.	Mark 4.	Luke 8.
the sun was up, they were scorched ; and because they had no root, they withered away. [7] And some fell among thorns ; and the thorns sprung up, and choked them : [8] but other fell into good ground, and brought forth fruit, some an hundredfold,[o] some sixtyfold, some thirtyfold.	sun was up, it was scorched ; and because it had no root, it withered away. [7] And some fell among thorns, and the thorns grew up, and choked it, and it yielded no fruit. [8] And other fell on good ground, and did yield fruit that sprang up and increased ; and brought forth, some thirty, and some sixty, and some an hundred. [9] And he said unto them, he that hath ears to hear, let him hear.	[7] And some fell among thorns ; and the thorns sprang up with it, and choked it. [8] And other fell on good ground, and sprang up, and bare fruit an hundredfold.[o]
[9] Who hath ears to hear, let him hear.		And when he had said these things, he cried, He that hath ears to hear, let him hear.
[10] And the disciples came, and said unto him, Why speakest thou unto them in parables ? [11] He answered and said unto them, Because it is given unto you to know the mysteries of the kingdom of heaven,[p] but to them it is not given. [12] For whosoever hath, to him shall be given, and he shall have more abundance : but whosoever hath not, from him shall be taken away even that he hath. [13] Therefore speak I to them in parables : because they seeing see not ; and hearing they hear not, neither do they understand. [14] And in them is fulfilled the prophecy of Esaias, which saith,[q] By hearing ye shall hear, and shall not understand ; and seeing ye shall see, and	[10] And when he was alone, they that were about him with the twelve asked of him the parable. [11] And he said unto them, Unto you it is given to know the mystery of the kingdom of God :[p] but unto them that are without, all *these* things are done in parables :	[9] And his disciples asked him, saying, What might this parable be ? [10] And he said, Unto you it is given to know the mysteries of the kingdom of God :[p] but to others in parables ;
	[12] that seeing they may see, and not perceive ; and hearing they may hear and not understand ;[q] lest at any time they should be converted, and *their* sins should be forgiven them.	that seeing they might not see, and hearing they might not understand.[q]

shall not perceive : [15] for this people's heart is waxed gross, and *their* ears are dull of hearing, and their eyes they have closed ; lest at any time they should see with *their* eyes, and hear with *their* ears, and should understand with *their* heart, and should be converted, and I should heal them. [16] But blessed *are* your eyes, for they see : and your ears, for they hear.[r] [17] For verily I say unto you, that many prophets and righteous *men* have desired to see *those things* which ye see, and have not seen *them ;* and to hear *those things* which

---

o Such increase is commonly yielded in the more fertile parts of Palestine.

p 1 Cor. 2. 6–10.

r Comp. Eph. 1. 17–19.

q Isa. 6. 9, 10

Matt. 13.

ye hear, and have not heard *them.* [18] Hear ye therefore the parable of the sower. [19] When any one heareth the word of the kingdom, and understandeth *it* not, then cometh the wicked *one,* and catcheth away that which was sown in his heart. This is he which received seed by the way side. [20] But he that received the seed into stony places, the same is he that heareth the word, and anon with joy receiveth it; [21] yet hath he not root in himself, but dureth for a while: [s] for when tribulation or persecution ariseth because of the word, by and by he is offended.

[22] He also that received seed among the thorns is he that heareth the word; and the care of this world, and the deceitfulness [t] of riches, choke the word, and he becometh unfruitful. [23] But he that received seed into the good ground is he that heareth the word, and understandeth *it;* which also beareth fruit, and bringeth forth, some an hundredfold, some sixty, some thirty.

Mark 4.

[13] And he said unto them, Know ye not this parable? and how then will ye know all parables? [14] The sower soweth the word. [15] And these are they by the way side, where the word is sown; but when they have heard, Satan cometh immediately, and taketh away the word that was sown in their hearts.

[16] And these are they likewise which are sown on stony ground; who, when they have heard the word, immediately receive it with gladness; [17] and have no root in themselves, and so endure but for a time: [s] afterward, when affliction or persecution ariseth for the word's sake, immediately they are offended. [18] And these are they which are sown among thorns; such as hear the word, [19] and the cares of this world, and the deceitfulness [t] of riches, and the lusts of other things entering in, choke the word, and it becometh unfruitful. [20] And these are they which are sown on good ground; such as hear the word, and receive *it,* and bring forth fruit, some thirtyfold, some sixty, and some an hundred. [21] And he said unto them, Is a candle [u] brought to be put under a bushel, or under a bed? and not to be set on a candlestick?

Luke 8.

[11] Now the parable is this: The seed is the word of God. [12] Those by the way side are they that hear; then cometh the devil, and taketh away the word out of their hearts, lest they should believe and be saved.

[13] They on the rock *are they,* which, when they hear, receive the word with joy; and these have no root, which for a while believe, and in time of temptation fall away. [s]

[14] And that which fell among thorns are they, which, when they have heard, go forth, and are choked with cares and riches and pleasures of *this* life, and bring no fruit to perfection.

[15] But that on the good ground are they, which in an honest and good heart, having heard the word, keep *it,* and bring forth fruit with patience. [16] No man, when he hath lighted a candle, [u] covereth it with a vessel, or putteth *it* under a bed; but setteth *it* on a candlestick, that they which enter in may see the light. [17] For nothing is secret, that shall not be made manifest; neither *any thing* hid, that shall not be known and come abroad.

[22] For there is nothing hid, which shall not be manifested; neither was any thing kept secret, but that it should come abroad. [23] If any man have ears to hear, let him hear. [23] And he saith unto them, Take heed what ye hear : with what

Mark 4.

measure ye mete, it shall be measured to you: and unto you that hear shall more be given. ²⁵For he that hath,^v to him shall be given: and he that hath not, from him shall be taken even that which he hath.

Luke 8.

¹⁸Take heed therefore how ye hear: for whosoever hath,^v to him shall be given; and whosoever hath not, from him shall be taken even that which he seemeth to have.^w

§ 55. PARABLE OF THE TARES. OTHER PARABLES.—*Near Capernaum?*

Matt. 13. 24-53. ²⁴Another parable put he forth unto them, saying, The kingdom of heaven is likened unto a man which sowed good seed in his field; ²⁵but while men slept, his enemy came and sowed tares among the wheat, and went his way. ²⁶But when the blade was sprung up, and brought forth fruit, then appeared the tares also. ²⁷So the servants of the householder came and said unto him, Sir, didst not thou sow good seed in thy field? from whence then hath it tares? ²⁸He said unto them, An enemy hath done this. The servants said unto him, Wilt thou then that we go and gather them up? ²⁹But he said, Nay; lest while ye gather up the tares, ye root up also the wheat with them. ³⁰Let both grow together until the harvest: and in the time of harvest I will say to the reapers, Gather ye together first the tares, and bind them in bundles to burn them: but gather the wheat into my barn.

Mark 4. 26-34. ²⁶And he said, So is the kingdom of God, as if a man should cast seed into the ground; ²⁷and should sleep, and rise night and day, and the seed should spring and grow up, he knoweth not how. ²⁸For the earth bringeth forth fruit of herself; first the blade, then the ear, after that the full corn in the ear. ²⁹But when the fruit is brought forth, immediately he putteth in the sickle, because the harvest is come.

Matt. 13. ³¹Another parable put he forth unto them, saying, The kingdom of heaven is like to a grain of mustard seed, which a man took and sowed in his field: ³²which indeed is the least of all seeds: but when it is grown, it is the greatest among herbs, and becometh a tree, so that the birds of the air come and lodge in the branches thereof. ³³Another parable spake he unto them; The kingdom of heaven is like unto leaven, which a woman took, and hid in three measures of meal, till the whole was leavened.

³⁴All these things spake Jesus unto the multitude in parables; and without a parable spake he not unto them: ³⁵that it might be fulfilled which was spoken by the prophet, saying,^x I will open my mouth in parables; I will utter things which have been kept secret from the foundation of the world.

³⁰And he said, Whereunto shall we liken the kingdom of God? or with what comparison shall we compare it? ³¹*It is* like a grain of mustard seed, which, when it is sown in the earth, is less than all the seeds that be in the earth; ³²but when it is sown, it groweth up, and becometh greater than all herbs, and shooteth out great branches; so that the fowls of the air may lodge under the shadow of it.

³³And with many such parables spake he the word unto them, as they were able to hear *it.* ³⁴But without a parable spake he not unto them: and when they were alone, he expounded all things to his disciples.

³⁶Then Jesus sent the multitude away, and went into the house: and his disciples came unto him, saying, Declare unto us the parable of the tares of the field. ³⁷He

---

^v Comp. Matt. 13. 12. ^w See in § 50. ^x Psa. 78. 2.

Matt. 13.

answered and said unto them, He that soweth the good seed is the Son of man;[v] [20] the field is the world; the good seed are the children of the kingdom; but the tares are the children of the wicked *one;* [39] the enemy that sowed them is the devil; the harvest is the end of the world; and the reapers are the angels. [40] As therefore the tares are gathered and burned in the fire; so shall it be in the end of this world. [41] The Son of man shall send forth his angels, and they shall gather out of his kingdom all things that offend, and them which do iniquity; [42] and shall cast them into a furnace of fire: there shall be wailing and gnashing of teeth. [43] Then shall the righteous shine forth as the sun in the kingdom of their Father. Who hath ears to hear, let him hear.

[44] Again, the kingdom of heaven is like unto treasure hid in a field; the which when a man hath found, he hideth, and for joy thereof goeth and selleth all that he hath, and buyeth that field.

[45] Again, the kingdom of heaven is like unto a merchant man, seeking goodly pearls: [46] who, when he had found one pearl of great price, went and sold all that he had, and bought it.

[47] Again, the kingdom of heaven is like unto a net, that was cast into the sea, and gathered of every kind: [48] which, when it was full, they drew to shore, and sat down, and gathered the good into vessels, but cast the bad away. [49] So shall it be at the end of the world: the angels shall come forth, and sever the wicked from among the just, [50] and shall cast them into the furnace of fire: there shall be wailing and gnashing of teeth.

[51] Jesus saith unto them, Have ye understood all these things? They say unto him, Yea, Lord. [52] Then said he unto them, Therefore every scribe *which is* instructed unto the kingdom of heaven is like unto a man *that is* an householder, which bringeth forth out of his treasure *things* new and old.

[53] And it came to pass, *that* when Jesus had finished these parables, he departed thence.[s]

§ 56. JESUS DIRECTS TO CROSS THE LAKE. INCIDENTS. THE TEMPEST STILLED.—*Sea of Galilee.*

| Matt. 8. 18-27. [18] Now when Jesus saw great multitudes about him, he gave commandment to depart unto the other side. [19] And a certain scribe came, and said unto him, Master, I will follow thee whithersoever thou goest. [20] And Jesus saith unto him, The foxes have holes, and the birds of the air *have* nests; but the Son of man[b] hath not where to lay *his* head. [21] And another of his disciples said unto him, Lord, suffer me first to go and bury my father. [22] But Jesus said unto him, Follow me; and let the dead bury their dead. | Mark 4. 35-41. [35] And the same day, when the even was come,[a] he saith unto them, Let us pass over unto the other side. [36] And when they had sent away the multitude, they took him even as he | Luke 8. 22-25. [22] Now it came to pass on a certain day, that he went into a ship with his disciples: and he said unto them, Let us go over unto the other side of the lake. |

[v] Comp. Dan. 7. 13.   [s] See in § 61.

[a] Mark here fixes the order of time, "the same day at evening." Very similar to Matt. 8. 19-22 is the incident related by Luke, ch. 9. 57-62, but which is in a wholly different connexion (see § 80).

[b] *The Son of man:* a name often applied to himself by Christ (comp. Dan. 7. 13, 14; Rev. 1. 13), to indicate that he was the Messiah; to indicate also that he was *the* son of Adam who was to bruise the serpent's head (comp. 1 Cor. 15. 47).

Matt. 8.	**Mark 4.**	**Luke 8.**
23 And when he was entered into a ship, his disciples followed him. 24 And behold, there arose a great tempest in the sea, insomuch that the ship was covered with the waves: but he was asleep. 25 And his disciples came to *him*, and awoke him, saying, Lord, save us: we perish. 26 And he saith unto them, Why are ye fearful, O ye of little faith? Then he arose, and rebuked the winds and the sea; and there was a great calm.	was in the ship. And there were also with him other little ships. 37 And there arose a great storm of wind, and the waves beat into the ship, so that it was now full. 38 And he was in the hinder part of the ship, asleep on a pillow: and they awake him, and say unto him, Master, carest thou not that we perish? 39 And he arose, and rebuked the wind, and said unto the sea, Peace, be still. And the wind ceased, and there was a great calm. 40 And he said unto them, Why are ye so fearful? how is it that ye have no faith?	And they launched forth. 23 But as they sailed he fell asleep: and there came down a storm of wind on the lake; and they were filled *with water*, and were in jeopardy. 24 And they came to him, and awoke him, saying, Master, master, we perish. Then he arose, and rebuked the wind and the raging of the water: and they ceased, and there was a calm.
27 But the men marvelled, saying, What manner of man is this, that even the winds and the sea obey him!	41 And they feared exceedingly, and said one to another, What manner of man is this, that even the wind and the sea obey him?	25 And he said unto them, Where is your faith? And they being afraid wondered, saying one to another, What manner of man is this! for he commandeth even the winds and water, and they obey him.

§ 57. The Two Demoniacs of Gadara.—*S.E. coast of the Sea of Galilee.*

Matt. 8. 28–34; 9. 1.	**Mark 5. 1-21.**	**Luke 8. 26-40.**
28 And when he was come to the other side into the country of the Gergesenes, there met him two possessed with devils, coming out of the tombs,[d] exceeding fierce, so that no man might pass by that way.	1 And they came over unto the other side of the sea, into the country of the Gadarenes. 2 And when he was come out of the ship, immediately there met him out of the tombs[d] a man with an unclean spirit, 3 who had *his* dwelling among the tombs; and no man could bind him, no, not with chains: 4 be-	26 And they arrived at the country of the Gadarenes,[c] which is over against Galilee. 27 And when he went forth to land, there met him out of the city a certain man, which had devils long time, and ware no clothes, neither abode in *any* house, but in the tombs.

cause that he had been often bound with fetters and chains, and the chains had been plucked asunder by him, and the fetters broken in pieces: neither could any *man* tame him. 5 And always, night and day, he was in the moun-

---

[c] Origen says that a city *Gergesa* anciently stood on the eastern shore of the lake of Tiberias, Opp. iv. p. 140. *Gadara* was a larger city, whose district or jurisdiction apparently extended to the lake, and included Gergesa.

Mark and Luke speak of only one demoniac; Matthew of two. Something peculiar in the circumstances or character of one of the persons rendered him more prominent, and led the two former evangelists to speak of him particularly. But their language does not *exclude* another.

[d] These are, in the East, either excavations in rocky cliffs and hills, or like our vaults; hence easily serving for shelters and lurking-places.

Matt. 8.   **Mark 5.**   **Luke 8.**

²⁹ And, behold, they cried out, saying, What have we to do with thee, Jesus, thou Son of God? art thou come hither to torment us before the time?

tains, and in the tombs, crying, and cutting himself with stones. ⁶ But when he saw Jesus afar off, he ran and worshipped him, ⁷ and cried with a loud voice, and said, What have I to do with thee, Jesus, *thou* Son of the most high God? I adjure thee by God, that thou torment me not. ⁸ For he said unto him, Come out of the man, *thou* unclean spirit. ⁹ And he asked him, What *is* thy name? And he answered, saying, My name *is* Legion: for we are many. ¹⁰ And he besought him much that he would not send them away out of the country.

²⁸ When he saw Jesus, he cried out, and fell down before him, and with a loud voice said, What have I to do with thee, Jesus, *thou* Son of God most high? I beseech thee, torment me not. ²⁹ (For he had commanded the unclean spirit to come out of the man. For oftentimes it had caught him: and he was kept bound with chains and in fetters; and he brake the bands, and was driven of the devil into the wilderness.) ³⁰ And Jesus asked him, saying, What is thy name? And he said, Legion: because many devils were entered into him. ³¹ And they besought him that he would not command them to go out into the deep.

³⁰ And there was a good way off from them an herd of many swine feeding. ³¹ So the devils besought him, saying, If thou cast us out, suffer us to go away into the herd of swine. ³² And he said unto them, Go. And when they were come out, they went into the herd of swine: and, behold, the whole herd of swine ran violently down a steep place into the sea, and perished in the waters.ᵉ ³³ And they that kept them fled, and went their ways into the city, and told every thing, and what was befallen to the possessed of the devils. ³⁴ And, behold, the whole city came out to meet Jesus:

¹¹ Now there was there nigh unto the mountains a great herd of swine feeding. ¹² And all the devils besought him, saying, Send us into the swine, that we may enter into them. ¹³ And forthwith Jesus gave them leave. And the unclean spirits went out, and entered into the swine: and the herd ran violently down a steep place into the sea, (they were about two thousand;) and were choked in the sea.ᵉ ¹⁴ And they that fed the swine fled, and told *it* in the city, and in the country. And they went out to see what it was that was done. ¹⁵ And they come to Jesus, and see him that was possessed with the devil, and had the legion, sitting, and

³² And there was there an herd of many swine feeding on the mountain: and they besought him that he would suffer them to enter into them. And he suffered them.

³³ Then went the devils out of the man, and entered into the swine: and the herd ran violently down a steep place into the lake, and were choked.ᵉ

³⁴ When they that fed *them* saw what was done, they fled, and went and told *it* in the city and in the country. ³⁵ Then they went out to see what was done; and came to Jesus, and found the man, out of whom the devils were

---

ᵉ The owners of the swine were probably Jews, for our Lord as yet confined his ministry to that people (Matt. 10. 5, 6); the loss may have been inflicted on them as a punishment for trading in swine. The judgment brought relief to the possessed man, and rid the neighbourhood of a source of terror (Matt. 8. 28). The entrance of the demons into the swine gave *outward* evidence that the powers of darkness were driven forth (*Trench*).

Mark 5.

clothed, and in his right mind : and they were afraid. ¹⁶ And they that saw *it* told them how it befell to him that was possessed with the devil, and *also* concerning the swine.

Matt. 8.

and when they saw him, they besought *him* that he would depart out of their coasts.

Matt. 9.

¹ And he entered into a ship, and passed over, and came into his own city.*f*

Luke 8.

departed, sitting at the feet of Jesus, clothed, and in his right mind : and they were afraid. ³⁵ They also which saw *it* told them by what means he that was possessed of the devils was healed.

¹⁷ And they began to pray him to depart out of their coasts. ¹⁸ And when he was come into the ship, he that had been possessed with the devil prayed him that he might be with him. ¹⁹ Howbeit Jesus suffered him not, but saith unto him, Go home to thy friends, and tell them how great things the Lord hath done for thee, and hath had compassion on thee. ²⁰ And he departed, and began to publish in Decapolis how great things Jesus had done for him : and all *men* did marvel.

³⁷ Then the whole multitude of the country of the Gadarenes round about besought him to depart from them; for they were taken with great fear: and he went up into the ship, and returned back again. ³⁸ Now the man out of whom the devils were departed besought him that he might be with him: but Jesus sent him away, saying, ³⁹ Return to thine own house, and show how great things God hath done unto thee. And he went his way, and published throughout the whole city how great things Jesus had done unto him. ⁴⁰ And it came to pass, that, when Jesus was returned the people *gladly* received him: for they were all waiting for him.

²¹ And when Jesus was passed over again by ship unto the other side, much people gathered unto him: and he was nigh unto the sea.

§ 58. LEVI'S FEAST.*g* DISCOURSE CONCERNING FASTING.—*Capernaum.*

Matt. 9. 10-17.
¹⁰ And it came to pass, as Jesus sat at meat in the house, behold, many publicans and sinners came and sat down with him and his disciples.

¹¹ And when the Pharisees saw *it*, they said unto his disciples, Why

Mark 2. 15-22.
¹⁵ And it came to pass, that as Jesus sat at meat in his house, many publicans and sinners sat also together with Jesus and his disciples : for there were many, and they followed him. ¹⁶ And when the scribes and Pharisees saw him eat with publicans

Luke 5. 29-39.
²⁹ And Levi made him a great feast in his own house: and there was a great company of publicans and of others that sat down with them.

³⁰ But their scribes and Pharisees murmured against his disciples, say-

---

f His own city, i.e., **Capernaum** : see Matt. 4. 13. See in § 34.

g The *call* of Levi or Matthew is placed by the three evangelists immediately after the healing of the paralytic in Capernaum [§§ 34, 35]. Very naturally, too, they all three connect with his call an account of the *feast* which he afterwards made for Jesus. But from Matt. 9. 18 [§ 59] it appears, that while our Lord was reclining and discoursing at

that feast, Jairus comes to beseech him to visit his daughter lying at the point of death. Now this transaction, according to Mark and Luke, did not happen until immediately after the return from the eastern shore of the lake. Hence the narrative of the feast is also to be transferred to this place; and that too with the more certainty, because the twelve appear to have also been present at it.

Matt. 9.

eateth your Master with publicans and sinners?

[12] But when Jesus heard *that*, he said unto them, They that be whole need not a physician, but they that are sick. [13] But go ye and learn what *that* meaneth, I will have mercy, and not sacrifice:[h] for I am not come to call the righteous, but sinners to repentance.[i]

[14] Then came to him the disciples of John,[j] saying, Why do we and the Pharisees fast oft, but thy disciples fast not?

[15] And Jesus said unto them, Can the children of the bridechamber[k] mourn, as long as the bridegroom is with them?

But the days will come, when the bridegroom shall be taken from them, and then shall they fast.

[16] No man putteth a piece of new cloth[l] unto an old garment, for that which is put in to fill it up taketh from the garment; and the rent is made worse.

[17] Neither do men put new wine into

Mark 2.

and sinners, they said unto his disciples, How is it that he eateth and drinketh with publicans and sinners? [17] When Jesus heard *it*, he saith unto them, They that are whole have no need of the physician, but they that are sick: I came not to call the righteous, but sinners to repentance.[i]

[18] And the disciples of John[j] and of the Pharisees used to fast: and they come and say unto him, Why do the disciples of John and of the Pharisees fast, but thy disciples fast not? [19] And Jesus said unto them, Can the children of the bridechamber[k] fast, while the bridegroom is with them? as long as they have the bridegroom with them, they cannot fast. [20] But the days will come, when the bridegroom shall be taken away from them, and then shall they fast in those days.

[21] No man also seweth a piece of new cloth[l] on an old garment: else the new piece that filled it up taketh away from the old, and the rent is made worse.

[22] And no man putteth new wine into old bottles:

Luke 5.

ing, Why do ye eat and drink with publicans and sinners?

[31] And Jesus answering, said unto them, They that are whole need not a physician; but they that are sick. [32] I came not to call the righteous, but sinners to repentance.[i]

[33] And they said unto him, Why do the disciples of John[j] fast often, and make prayers, and likewise *the disciples* of the Pharisees; but thine eat and drink?

[34] And he said unto them, Can ye make the children of the bridechamber[k] fast, while the bridegroom is with them?

[35] But the days will come, when the bridegroom shall be taken away from them, and then shall they fast in those days. [36] And he spake also a parable unto them; No man putteth a piece of a new garment upon an old; if otherwise, then both the new maketh a rent, and the piece that was *taken* out of the new agreeth not with the old. [37] And no man putteth new wine into old bottles:

---

[h] Hos. 6. 6; comp. 1 Sam. 15. 22.
[i] Luke 15. 8–10; 1 Tim. 1. 15.
[j] *The disciples of John.* Many of these did not follow the counsel of their master, by becoming the disciples of Jesus, and acknowledging Him as the Messiah, but remained a distinct sect, with a leaning towards the Pharisees. A very notable trace of this peculiar sect is again found in Acts 19. 3–5.
[k] Comp. Judg. 14. 10, 11.

[l] *New cloth,* properly cloth *unfulled* (ἄγναφος), which is apt to shrink much when wet, and so would rend the old cloth around it. In Luke the illustration is different. Our Lord may have used both. A better rendering of Luke's words would be: "No man putteth a piece of a new garment upon an old garment; but if otherwise, both he cuts the new and the piece from the new does not match the old."

Matt. 9.	**Mark 2.**	**Luke 5.**
old bottles: else the bottles[m] break, and the wine runneth out, and the bottles perish:[n] but they put new wine into new bottles, and both are preserved.	else the new wine doth burst the bottles,[m] and the wine is spilled, and the bottles will be marred:[n] but new wine must be put into new bottles.	else the new wine will burst the bottles,[m] and be spilled, and the bottles shall perish.[n] [38] But new wine must be put into new bottles; and both are preserved. [39] No man also having drunk old *wine* straightway desireth new: for he saith, The old is better.[o]

§ 59. THE RAISING OF JAIRUS' DAUGHTER. THE WOMAN WITH AN ISSUE OF BLOOD.—*Capernaum.*

Matt. 9. 18-26.	**Mark 5.** 22-43.	**Luke 8.** 41-56.
[18] While he spake these things unto them, behold, there came a certain ruler, and worshipped him, saying, my daughter is even now dead: but come and lay thy hand upon her, and she shall live.	[22] And, behold, there cometh one of the rulers of the synagogue, Jairus by name; and when he saw him, he fell at his feet, [23] and besought him greatly, saying, My little daughter lieth at the point of death: *I pray thee,* come and lay thy hands on her, that she may be healed; and she shall live. [24] And *Jesus*	[41] And, behold, there came a man named Jairus, and he was a ruler of the synagogue: and he fell down at Jesus' feet, and besought him that he would come into his house: [42] for he had one only daughter, about twelve years of age, and she lay a dying. But as
[19] And Jesus arose, and followed him, and *so did* his disciples.	went with him; and much people followed him, and thronged him.	he went the people thronged him.
[20] And, behold, a woman, which was diseased[p] with an issue of blood twelve years,	[25] And a certain woman, which had an issue of blood[p] twelve years, [26] and had suffered many things of many physicians, and had spent all that she had, and was nothing bettered, but rather grew worse, [27] when she had heard of Jesus, came in the press behind, and touched his garment. [28] For she said, If I may touch but his clothes, I shall be whole. [29] And straightway the fountain of her blood was dried up; and she felt in *her* body that she was	[43] And a woman having an issue of blood[p] twelve years, which had spent all her living upon physicians, neither could be healed of any,
came behind *him,* and touched the hem of his garment: [21] for she said within herself, If I may but touch his garment, I shall be whole.— [22] And the woman was made whole from that hour.—		[44] came behind *him,* and touched the border of his garment: and immediately her issue of blood stanched.

---

[m] *Bottles,* not of earthenware or glass, but of *skins.*
[n] Comp. Josh. 9. 4. • See in § 37.
[p] *A woman—diseased,* etc. Her disorder, according to the law (Lev. 15. 25–27), defiled by contact; this may account for her timid and stealthy manner of approaching Christ, for her doing no more than touching the hem of his garment, and for her alarm on being discovered.

Mark 5.

healed of that plague. [30] And Jesus, immediately knowing in himself that virtue had gone out of him, turned him about in the press, and said, Who touched my clothes? [31] And the disciples said unto him, Thou seest the multitude thronging thee, and sayest thou, Who touched me? [32] And he looked round about to see her that had done this thing. [33] But the woman fearing and trembling, knowing what was done in her, came and fell down before him, and told him all the truth.

Luke 8.

[45] And Jesus said, Who touched me? When all denied, Peter and they that were with him said, Master, the multitude throng thee and press *thee*, and sayest thou, Who touched me? [46] And Jesus said, Somebody hath touched me: for I perceive that virtue is gone out of me. [47] And when the woman saw that she was not hid, she came trembling, and falling down before him, she declared unto him before all the people for what cause she had touched him, and how she was healed immediately.

Matt. 9.

[22] But Jesus turned him about, and when he saw her, he said, Daughter, be of good comfort; thy faith hath made thee whole.—

Mark 5.

[34] And he said unto her, Daughter, thy faith hath made thee whole; go in peace, and be whole of thy plague. [35] While he yet spake, there came from the ruler of the synagogue's *house certain* which said, Thy daughter is dead: why troublest thou the Master any further? [36] As soon as Jesus heard the word that was spoken, he saith unto the ruler of the synagogue, Be not afraid, only believe.

Luke 8.

[48] And he said unto her, Daughter, be of good comfort; thy faith hath made thee whole; go in peace. [49] While he yet spake, there cometh one from the ruler of the synagogue's *house*, saying to him, Thy daughter is dead; trouble not the Master. [50] But when Jesus heard *it*, he answered him, saying, Fear not: believe only, and she shall be made whole.

[23] And when Jesus came into the ruler's house,

—[38] And he cometh to the house of the ruler of the synagogue. — [37] And he suffered no man to follow him, save Peter, and James, and John the brother of James.—[38] And

[51] And when he came into the house, he suffered no man to go in, save Peter, and James, and John, and the father and the mother of the maiden.

and saw the minstrels and the people making a noise,ᵃ [24] he said unto them, Give place: for the maid is not dead, but sleepeth. And they laughed him to scorn. [25] But when the people were put forth, he went in, and took her by the hand, and the maid arose. [26] And the fame hereof went abroad into all that land.

he seeth the tumult, and them that wept and wailed greatly. [39] And when he was come in, he saith unto them, Why make ye this ado, and weep? the damsel is not dead, but sleepeth. [40] And they laughed him to scorn. But when he had put them all out, he taketh the father and the mother of the damsel, and them that were with him, and entereth in where the damsel was lying. [41] And

[52] And all wept and bewailed her: but he said, Weep not; she is not dead, but sleepeth. [53] And they laughed him to scorn, knowing that she was dead. [54] And he put them all out,

---

ᵃ *Minstrels and people making a noise.* It was customary to have funeral music and | mourning for the dead (comp. 2 Chron. 35. 25; Jer. 9. 17, 18).

Mark 5.

he took the damsel by the hand, and said unto her, Talitha cumi; which is, being interpreted, Damsel, I say unto thee, arise. [42] And straightway the damsel arose, and walked; for she was *of the age* of twelve years. And they were astonished with a great astonishment. [43] And he charged them straitly that no man should know it; and commanded that something should be given her to eat.

Luke 8.

and took her by the hand, and called, saying, Maid, arise. [55] And her spirit came again, and she arose straightway; and he commanded to give her meat. [56] And her parents were astonished: but he charged them that they should tell no man what was done.

60. Two Blind Men healed, and a Dumb Spirit cast out.—*Capernaum?*

Matt. 9. 27-34. [27] And when Jesus departed thence, two blind men followed im,[r] crying, and saying, *Thou* Son of David,[s] have mercy on us. [28] And when he 'as come into the house, the blind men came to him: and Jesus saith unto them, ;elieve ye that I am able to do this? They said unto him, Yea, Lord. [29] Then)uched he their eyes, saying, According to your faith be it unto you. [30] And ıeir eyes were opened; and Jesus straitly charged them, saying, See *that* no man ɪnow *it*. [31] But they, when they were departed, spread abroad his fame in all ıat country.

[32] As they went out, behold, they brought to him a dumb man possessed with a ɜvil. [33] And when the devil was cast out, the dumb spake: and the multitudes ɪarvelled, saying, It was never so seen in Israel. [34] But the Pharisees said, He ɪsteth out devils through the prince of devils.[t]

§ 61. Jesus again at Nazareth, and again Rejected.

Matt. 13. 54-58. [54] And when he ɪas come into his own country, he taught ɪem in their synagogue, insomuch that ɪey were astonished, and said, Whence ɪth this *man* this wisdom, and *these* ɪighty works?

[55] Is not this the carnter's son? is not his mother called ɪary?[u] and his brethren,[v] James, and ɪses, and Simon, and Judas? [56] and his ɪters, are they not all with us? Whence ɪen hath this *man* all these things?

Mark 6. 1-6. [1] And he went out from thence, and came into his own country; and his disciples follow him. [2] And when the sabbath day was come, he began to teach in the synagogue, and many hearing *him* were astonished, saying, From whence hath this *man* these things? and what wisdom *is* this which is given unto him, that even such mighty works are wrought by his hands? [3] Is not this the carpenter, the son of Mary, the brother of James, and Joses, and of Juda, and Simon? and are not his sisters here with us? And they were offended at him. [4] But Jesus said unto them, A prophet is not without

[r] Comp. Matt. 20. 30-34.

[s] *Son of David.* The favourite title among e people for the Messiah; but as it might ɪm to favour the idea of an earthly doɪion, and be liable to abuse, our Lord did ɪ himself use it, but called Himself, instead, ɪe Son of man;" a title never applied to ɪn in His lifetime by others.

[t] See in § 62. [u] Acts 1. 14.

[v] Much has been written to prove that *cousins* must be meant here, and in the like places, but there is no warrant for departing from the obvious sense, that our Lord had brothers and sisters (ver. 56) born of his mother after she became, in the strict sense, Joseph's wife. It is, however, possible that they were children of Joseph by a previous marriage.

Matt. 13.

[97] And they were offended in him. But Jesus said unto them, A prophet is not without honour, save in his own country,[10] and in his own house.[x] [58] And he did not many mighty works there because of their unbelief.

Mark 6.

honour, but in his own country, an among his own kin, and in his ow house. [5] And he could there do n mighty work, save that he laid his hand upon a few sick folk, and healed *them* [6] And he marvelled because of their un belief.—

§ 62. A THIRD CIRCUIT IN GALILEE.[v] THE TWELVE INSTRUCTED AND
SENT FORTH.—*Galilee.*

Matt. 9. 35-38; 10. 1, 5-42; 11. 1. [35] And Jesus went about all the cities and villages, teaching in their synagogues, and preaching the gospel of the kingdom, and healing every sickness and every disease among

Mark 6. 6-13. [6]—An he went round about th villages, teaching.

the people. [36] But when he saw the multitudes, he was moved with compassion on them, because they fainted, and were scattered abroad, as sheep having no shepherd.[z] [37] Then saith he unto his disciples, The harvest truly *is* plenteous,[a] but the labourers *are* few; [38] pray ye therefore the Lord of the harvest, that he will send forth labourers into his harvest.

Matt. 10.

[1] And when he had called unto *him* his twelve disciples, he gave them power *against* unclean spirits, to cast them out, and to heal all manner of sickness and all manner of disease.[b]— [5] These twelve Jesus sent forth, and commanded them, saying,[c] Go not into the way of the Gentiles, and into *any* city of the Samaritans enter ye not: [6] but go rather to the lost sheep[d] of the house of Israel. [7] And as ye go, preach, saying, The kingdom of heaven is at hand. [8] Heal the sick, cleanse the lepers, raise the dead, cast out devils: freely ye have received, freely give.[e] [9] Provide neither gold, nor silver, nor brass in your purses, [10] nor scrip for *your* journey, neither two coats, neither shoes, nor yet staves: for the workman is worthy of his meat.[f] [11] And into whatsoever city or town ye shall enter, inquire who in it is worthy; and there abide till ye go

Mark 6.

[7] And he called *unto him* the twelve, and began to send them forth by two and two; and gave them power over unclean spirits; [8] and commanded them that they should take nothing for *their* journey, save a staff only; no scrip, no bread, no money in *their* purse: [9] but *be* shod with sandals; and not put on two coats. [10] And he said unto them, In what place soever ye enter into an house, there abide till

Luke 9. 1-6.

[1] Then he called h twelve disciples togethe and gave them power an authority over all devil and to cure diseases. [2] A he sent them to prea the kingdom of God, ar to heal the sick.

[3] And h said unto them, Take n thing for *your* journe neither staves, nor scri neither bread, neith money; neither have t coats apiece.

[4] And whatsoev house ye enter into, the abide, and thence depart

---

[v] *His own country.* This means here the place (Nazareth) *where Christ had been brought up.*
[x] Comp. John 4. 44.
[z] Comp. Isa. 53. 6.
[a] Comp. Luke 10. 2.
  Ver. 2-4 in § 40.

[v] See §§ 32, 47.

[c] *Saying.* Very much of what our L. addresses here to the twelve was afterwar spoken also to the seventy, as being app priate to both classes: see Luke 10. in § 81
[d] Matt. 9. 36; 18. 11-13.
[e] Comp. Acts 20. 33-35.
[f] Comp. Luke 10. 7; 1 Tim. 5. 18.

Matt. 10.	Mark 6.	Luke 9.
thence.[s] ¹²And when ye come into an house, salute it. ¹³And if the house be worthy, let your peace come upon it: but if it be not worthy, let your peace return to you. ¹⁴And whosoever shall not receive you, nor hear your words, when ye depart out of that house or city, shake off the dust of your feet.[h] ¹⁵Verily I say unto you, It shall be more tolerable for the land of Sodom and Gomorrha in the day of judgment, than for that city.	¹¹And whosoever shall not receive you, nor hear you, when ye depart thence, shake off the dust under your feet for a testimony against them.[h] Verily I say unto you, It shall be more tolerable for Sodom and Gomorrha in the day of judgment, than for that city.	⁵And whosoever will not receive you, when ye go out of that city, shake off the very dust from your feet for a testimony against them.[h]

¹⁶Behold, I send you forth as sheep in the midst of wolves: be ye therefore wise as serpents,[i] and harmless as doves. ¹⁷But beware of men: for they will deliver you up to the councils, and they will scourge you in their synagogues; ¹⁸and ye shall be brought before governors and kings for my sake, for a testimony against them and the Gentiles. ¹⁹But when they deliver you up, take no thought[j] how or what ye shall speak: for it shall be given you in that same hour what ye shall speak. ²⁰For it is not ye that speak, but the Spirit of your Father which speaketh in you. ²¹And the brother shall deliver up the brother to death, and the father the child: and the children shall rise up against *their* parents, and cause them to be put to death. ²²And ye shall be hated of all *men* for my name's sake: but he that endureth to the end shall be saved. ²³But when they persecute you in this city, flee ye into another: for verily I say unto you, Ye shall not have gone over[k] the cities of Israel, till the Son of man be come. ²⁴The disciple is not above *his* master, nor the servant above his lord. ²⁵It is enough for the disciple that he be as is master, and the servant as his lord. If they have called the master of the house Beelzebub, how much more *shall they call* them of his household?

²⁶Fear them not therefore: for there is nothing covered, that shall not be revealed; and hid that shall not be known. ²⁷What I tell you in darkness, *that* speak ye in light: and what ye hear in the ear, *that* preach ye upon the housetops. ²⁸And fear not them which kill the body,[l] but are not able to kill the soul: but rather fear him[m] which is able to destroy both soul and body in hell. ²⁹Are not two sparrows sold for a farthing? and one of them shall not fall on the ground without your Father. ³⁰But the very hairs of your head are all numbered. ³¹Fear ye not therefore, ye are of more value than many sparrows. ³²Whosoever therefore shall confess me before men, him will I confess also before my Father which is in heaven. ³³But whosoever shall deny me before men, him will I also deny before my Father which is in heaven. ³⁴Think not that I am come[n] to send peace on earth: I came not to send peace, but a sword. ³⁵For I am come to set a man at variance against his father, and the daughter against her mother, and the daughter-

---

[s] Comp. Acts 16. 15: Luke 10. 38–42.
[h] Comp. Acts 13. 51.   [t] Comp. Acts 23. 6.
[j] *Take no thought* is not a good rendering; the word signifies *be not anxious:* even the apostles found it necessary to *think,* though they were freed from *solicitude* by the promise of special assistance (comp. 2 Tim. 4. 16–18) when they had to speak.

[k] *Ye shall not have gone over, etc.* By this language our Lord probably meant that the apostles would not finish evangelizing the towns of Palestine, before he should come to destroy Jerusalem and scatter the nation.
[l] Comp. Dan. 3. 16–18.
[m] Comp. Heb. 12. 28, 29.
[n] Comp. Luke 12. 49–53.

Matt. 10.

in-law against her mother-in-law. [36] And a man's foes *shall be* they of his own household.[o] [37] He that loveth father or mother more than me is not worthy of me: and he that loveth son or daughter more than me is not worthy of me. [38] And he that taketh not his cross,[p] and followeth after me, is not worthy of me. [39] He that findeth his life shall lose it: and he that loseth his life for my sake shall find it.

[40] He that receiveth you receiveth me, and he that receiveth me receiveth him that sent me. [41] He that receiveth a prophet in the name of a prophet shall receive a prophet's reward;[q] and he that receiveth a righteous man in the name of a righteous man shall receive a righteous man's reward. [42] And whosoever shall give to drink unto one of these little ones a cup of cold *water* only in the name of a disciple, verily I say unto you, He shall in no wise lose his reward.

Matt. 11. [1] And it came to pass, when Jesus had made an end of commanding his twelve disciples, he departed thence to teach and to preach in their cities.[r]

Mark 6. 12, 13.	**Luke 9. 6.**
[12] And they went out, and preached that men should repent. [13] And they cast out many devils, and anointed with oil many that were sick, and healed *them*.	[6] And they departed, and went through the towns, preaching the gospel, and healing every where.

§ 63. HEROD HOLDS JESUS TO BE JOHN THE BAPTIST, WHOM HE HAD JUST BEFORE BEHEADED.—*Galilee? Peræa.*

Matt. 14. 1, 2, 6-12.	**Mark 6. 14-16, 21-29.**	**Luke 9. 7-9.**
[1] At that time[s] Herod the tetrarch heard of the fame of Jesus, [2] and said unto his servants, This is John the Baptist; he is risen from the dead; and therefore mighty works do show forth themselves in him.[t]	[14] And king Herod heard *of him;* (for his name was spread abroad:) and he said, That John the Baptist was risen from the dead, and therefore mighty works do show forth themselves in him. [15] Others said, That it is Elias. And others said, That it is a prophet, or as one of the prophets. [16] But when Herod heard *thereof,* he	[7] Now Herod the tetrarch heard of all that was done by him: and he was perplexed, because that it was said of some, that John was risen from the dead; [8] and of some, that Elias had appeared; and of others, that one of the old prophets was risen again. [9] And Herod said, John have I beheaded: but who is this, of who

o Comp. Mic. 7. 6.

p *He that taketh not his cross, etc.* The faithful disciple must be prepared, if necessary, to suffer the punishment of the most disgraced criminals, who had to carry their own cross to the place of execution. In this language our Lord appears to have intimated the manner of his own death.

q Comp. 2 Kings 4. 8-17.   r See in § 44.

s While the twelve are absent preaching in the name of Christ, Herod causes John the Baptist to be beheaded in the castle of Machærus, at the southern extremity of Peræa, near the Dead Sea; Jos. Antiq. 18. 5. 2. In consequence of the preaching of the apostles, Herod hears the fame of Jesus; is conscience-smitten; and says that He is John risen from the dead. The disciples of John come

and tell Jesus; and the twelve also return with the same intelligence; upon which Jesus withdraws from Galilee to the north-eastern coast of the lake, not far from the northern Bethsaida or Julias, which was in the tetrarchy of Philip; Jos. Antiq. 18. 2. All these events seem to have taken place near together. Matthew and Mark narrate the death of the Baptist in explanation of Herod's declaration. The account of his imprisonment is transferred to § 24.

According to John 6. 4, the passover was now at hand, namely, the third during our Lord's ministry. John therefore had lain in prison nearly a year and six months; and was beheaded about three years after entering upon his public ministry. See in § 25.

t Ver. 3-5 in § 24.

Matt. 14.   **Mark 6.**   **Luke 9.**

said, It is John, whom I I hear such things? And beheaded: he is risen from he desired to see him. the dead.—

⁶ But when Herod's birthday ᵘ was kept,ᵛ the daughter of Herodias danced before them, and pleased Herod. ⁷ Whereupon he promised with an oath to give her whatsoever she would ask. ⁸ And she, being before instructed of her mother, said, Give me here John Baptist's head in a charger. ⁹ And the king was sorry: nevertheless for the oath's sake, and them which sat with him at meat, he commanded *it* to be given *her.* ¹⁰ And he sent and beheaded John in the prison. ¹¹ And his head was brought in a charger, and given to the damsel: and she brought *it* to her mother. ¹² And his disciples came, and took up the body, and buried it, and went and told Jesus.ʷ

²¹ And when a convenient day was come, that Herod on his birthday ᵘ made a supper to his lords, high captains, and chief *estates* of Galilee; ²² and when the daughter of the said Herodias came in, and danced, and pleased Herod and them that sat with him, the king said unto the damsel, Ask of me whatsoever thou wilt, and I will give *it* thee. ²³ And he sware unto her, Whatsoever thou shalt ask of me, I will give *it* thee, unto the half of my kingdom. ²⁴ And she went forth, and said unto her mother, What shall I ask? and she said, The head of John the Baptist. ²⁵ And she came in straightway with haste unto the king, and asked, saying, I will that thou give me by and by in a charger the head of John the Baptist. ²⁶ And the king was exceeding sorry; *yet* for his oath's sake, and for their sakes which sat with him, he would not reject her. ²⁷ And immediately the king sent an executioner, and commanded his head to be brought: and he went and beheaded him in the prison, ²⁸ And brought his head in a charger, and gave it to the damsel: and the damsel gave it to her mother. ²⁹ And when his disciples heard *of it,* they came and took up his corpse, and laid it in a tomb.

§ 64. THE TWELVE RETURN,ˣ AND JESUS RETIRES WITH THEM ACROSS THE LAKE. FIVE THOUSAND ARE FED.—*Capernaum. North-east coast of the Sea of Galilee.*

Mark 6. 30-44. ³⁰ And the apostles gathered themselves together unto Jesus, and told him all things, both what they had done, and what they had taught. ³¹ And he said unto them, Come ye yourselves apart into a desert place, and rest awhile: for there were many coming and going, and they had no leisure so much as to eat.

Luke 9. 10-17. ¹⁰ And the apostles when they were returned, told him all they had done.—

Matt. 14. 13-21. ¹³ When Jesus heard *of it,* he departed thence by ship into a desert place ʸ apart: and when the people

Mark 6. ³² And they departed into a desert place ʸ by ship privately. ³³ And the people saw them departing, and

Luke 9. —¹⁰ And he took them, and went aside privately into a desert place ʸ belonging to the city called Bethsaida.

John 6. 1-14. ¹ After these things Jesus went over the sea of Galilee, which is *the sea* of Tiberias. ² And a great multitude

---

ᵘ *Birthday,* rather *birthday festivities,* which lasted more than one day. Thus there was time enough to send even to a distant place for the head of the Baptist.

ᵛ Comp. Gen. 40. 20.

ʷ See in § 64.

ˣ See § 62.

ʸ *Departed thence, etc.:* probably with a view to prevent the rising of the people on His behalf, and also to have quiet communications with His disciples after their return from their first preaching excursion.

Matt. 14.	Mark 6.	Luke 9.	John 6.

had heard *thereof,* they followed him on foot out of the cities.

[14] And Jesus went forth, and saw a great multitude, and was moved with compassion toward them, and he healed their sick.

[15] And when it was evening, his disciples came to him, saying, This is a desert place, and the time is now past ; send the multitude away, that they may go into the villages, and buy themselves victuals.

[16] But Jesus said unto them, They need not depart ; give ye them to eat.

[17] And they say unto him, We have here but five loaves and two fishes. [18] He said, Bring

---

many knew him, and ran afoot thither out of all cities, and outwent them, and came together unto him. [34] And Jesus, when he came out, saw much people, and was moved with compassion toward them, because they were as sheep not having a shepherd : and he began to teach them many things. [35] And when the day was now far spent, his disciples came unto him, and said, This is a desert place, and now the time *is far passed :* [36] send them away, that they may go into the country round about, and into the villages, and buy themselves bread : for they have nothing to eat. [37] He answered and said unto them, Give ye them to eat. And they say unto him, Shall we go and buy two hundred pennyworth of bread, and give them to eat ? [38] He saith unto them, How many loaves have ye ? go and see. And when they knew, they say, Five, and two fishes. [39] And he commanded them to make all sit down by companies

---

[11] And the people, when they knew *it,* followed him : and he received them, and spake unto them of the kingdom of God, and healed them that had need of healing.

[12] And when the day began to wear away, then came the twelve, and said unto him, Send the multitude away, that they may go into the towns and country round about, and lodge, and get victuals : for we are here in a desert place.

[13] But he said unto them, Give ye them to eat. And they said, We have no more but five loaves and two fishes ; except we should go and buy meat for all this people.—

—[14] And he said to his disciples, Make them sit down by fifties in a company.

---

followed him, because they saw his miracles which he did on them that were diseased. [3] And Jesus went up into a mountain, and there he sat with his disciples. [4] And the passover,[a] a feast of the Jews, was nigh. [5] When Jesus then lifted up *his* eyes, and saw a great company come unto him, he

saith unto Philip, Whence shall we buy bread, that these may eat ? [6] And this he said to prove him : for he himself knew what he would do. [7] Philip answered him, Two hundred pennyworth of bread is not sufficient for them, that every one of them may take a little. [8] One of his disciples, Andrew, Simon Peter's brother, saith unto him, [9] There is a lad here, which hath five barley loaves, and two small fishes : but what are they among so many ? [10] And Jesus said, Make the men sit down. Now there was

---

[a] This was the third passover during our Lord's ministry ; but He did not this time go up to Jerusalem to keep the feast : the reason is assigned in John 7. 1.

Matt. 14.	Mark 6.	Luke 9.	John 6.

them hither to me. **19** And he commanded the multitude to sit down on the grass,

and took the five loaves, and the two fishes, and looking up to heaven, he blessed, and brake, and gave the loaves to *his* disciples, and the disciples to the multitude.

20 And they did all eat, and were filled : and they took up of the fragments that remained twelve baskets full.

upon the green grass. **40** And they sat down in ranks, by hundreds, and by fifties. **41** And when he had taken the five loaves and the two fishes, he looked up to heaven, and blessed, and brake the loaves, and gave *them* to his disciples to set before them ; and the two fishes divided he among them all. **42** And they did all eat, and were filled. **43** And they took up twelve baskets full of the fragments, and of the fishes.

15 And they did so, and made them all sit down.

16 Then he took the five loaves and the two fishes, and looking up to heaven, he blessed them, and brake, and gave to the disciples to set before the multitude.

17 And they did eat, and were all filled ; and there was taken up of fragments that remained to them twelve baskets.

much grass in the place.—

11 And Jesus took the loaves ; and when he had given thanks, he distributed to the disciples, and the disciples to them that were set down ; and likewise of the fishes as much as they would.

12 When they were filled, he said unto his disciples, Gather up the fragments that remain, that nothing be lost. **13** Therefore they gathered *them* together, and filled twelve baskets with fragments of the five barley loaves, which remained over and above unto them that had eaten.

21 And they that had eaten were about five thousand men, beside women and children.

44 And they that did eat of the loaves, were about five thousand men.

—**14** For they were about five thousand men.—

—**10** So the men sat down, in number about five thousand. **14** Then those men, when they had seen the miracle that Jesus did, said, This is of a truth that prophet that should come into the world.

§ 65. Jesus Walks upon the Water.—*Night on the Sea of Galilee. Gennesareth.*

Matt. 14. 22, 23. **22** And straightway Jesus constrained [a] his disciples to get into a ship, and to go before him unto the other side, while he sent the multitudes away. **23** And when he had sent the multitudes away he went up into a mountain apart to pray :

Mark 6. 45, 46. **45** And straightway he constrained [a] his disciples to get into the ship, and to go to the other side before unto Bethsaida,[b] while he sent away the people. **46** And when he had sent them away, he departed into a mountain to pray.

---

[a] *Constrained :* implying that the disciples were unwilling to go on the lake without their Master, perhaps because they had some apprehension of the danger which overtook them.

[b] From the region of the northern Bethsaida or Julias, the disciples embark for Bethsaida of Galilee, Mark 6. 45; or for Capernaum, according to John 6. 17. They

land on the plain of Gennesareth, Matt. 14. 34; Mark 6. 53. The next day the multitudes followed in boats to Capernaum seeking for Jesus, and find Him there (John 6. 24, 25, 59). It follows that Capernaum was on or near the plain of Gennesareth; most probably at its north-eastern extremity. See Bibl. Res. in Palestine, III. 238.

Matt. 14.	Mark 6.	John 6.

John 6. 15-20. ¹⁵When Jesus therefore perceived that they would come and take him by force, to make him a king, he departed again into a mountain himself alone. ¹⁶And when even was *now* come, his disciples went down unto the sea, ¹⁷and entered into a ship, and went over the sea toward Capernaum. And it was now dark, and Jesus was not come to them. ¹⁸And the sea arose by reason of a great wind that blew. ¹⁹So when they had rowed about five and twenty or thirty furlongs, they see Jesus walking on the sea, and drawing nigh unto the ship: and they were afraid. ²⁰But he saith unto them, It is I; be not afraid.

Matt. 14. 23-36. ²³And when the evening was come, he was there alone. ²⁴But the ship was now in the midst of the sea, tossed with waves : for the wind was contrary. ²⁵And in the fourth watch of the night ᶜ Jesus went unto them, walking on the sea. ²⁶And when the disciples saw him walking on the sea, they were troubled, saying, It is a spirit; and they cried out for fear. ²⁷But straightway Jesus spake unto them, saying, Be of good cheer; it is I; be not afraid.ᵈ ²⁸And Peter answered him and said, Lord, if it be thou, bid me come unto thee on the water. ²⁹And he said, Come. And when

Mark 6. 47-50. ⁴⁷And when even was come, the ship was in the midst of the sea, and he alone on the land. ⁴⁸And he saw them toiling in rowing; for the wind was contrary unto them : and about the fourth watch of the night ᶜ he cometh unto them, walking upon the sea, and would have passed by them. ⁴⁹But when they saw him walking upon the sea, they supposed it had been a spirit, and cried out :ᵈ ⁵⁰for they all saw him, and were troubled. And immediately he talked with them, and saith unto them, Be of good cheer: it is I; be not afraid.

Peter was come down out of the ship, he walked on the water, to go to Jesus. ³⁰But when he saw the wind boisterous, he was afraid; and beginning to sink, he cried, saying, Lord, save me. ³¹And immediately Jesus stretched forth *his* hand, and caught him, and said unto him, O thou of little faith, wherefore didst thou doubt? ³²And when they were come into the ship, the wind ceased. ³³Then they that were in the ship came and worshipped him, saying, Of a truth thou art the Son of God.ᶠ

Mark 6. 51-56. ⁵¹And he went up unto them into the ship; and the wind ceased : and they were sore amazed in themselves beyond measure, and wondered. ⁵²For they considered not *the miracle* of the loaves : for their heart was hardened.

John 6. 21. ²¹Then they willingly received him into the ship: and immediately the ship was at the land whither they went.ᵉ

³⁴And when they were gone over, they came into the land of Gennesaret. ³⁵And when the men of that place had knowledge of him, they sent out into all that country round

⁵³And when they had passed over, they came into the land of Gennesaret, and drew to the shore. ⁵⁴And when they were come out of the ship, straightway they knew him, ⁵⁵and ran through that whole region round about, and began to carry about in beds those that were sick, where they heard he was. ⁵⁶And whithersoever he

---

ᶜ *Fourth watch,* i.e., about dawn, from three to six in the morning. Our Lord had spent the night in retirement and prayer.

ᵈ Luke 24. 37, 38.
ᵉ See in § 66.
ᶠ Psa. 2. 7; Luke 1. 36 ; Rom. 1. 4.

Matt. 14.	Mark 6.
about, and brought unto him all that were diseased; ³⁶ and besought him that they might only touch the hem of his garment: and *as* many as touched were made perfectly whole.*g*	entered, into villages, or cities, or country, they laid the sick in the streets, and besought him that they might touch if it were but the border of his garment: and as many as touched him were made whole.

§ 66.   OUR LORD'S DISCOURSE TO THE MULTITUDE IN THE SYNAGOGUE AT CAPERNAUM.   MANY DISCIPLES TURN BACK.   PETER'S PROFESSION OF FAITH.—*Capernaum.*

John 6. 22-71; **7.** 1.   ²² The day following, when the people which stood on the other side of the sea saw that there was none other boat there, save that one whereinto his disciples were entered, and that Jesus went not with his disciples into the boat, but *that* his disciples were gone away alone; ²³ (howbeit there came other boats from Tiberias nigh unto the place where they did eat bread, after that the Lord had given thanks:) ²⁴ when the people therefore saw that Jesus was not there, neither his disciples, they also took shipping, and came to Capernaum, seeking for Jesus. ²⁵ And when they had found him on the other side of the sea, they said unto him, Rabbi, when camest thou hither? ²⁶ Jesus answered them and said, Verily, verily, I say unto you, Ye seek me, not because ye saw the miracles, but because ye did eat of the loaves, and were filled. ²⁷ Labour not for the meat which perisheth, but for that meat which endureth unto everlasting life, which the Son of man shall give unto you: for him hath God the Father sealed.*h* ²⁸ Then said they unto him, What shall we do, that we might work the works of God? ²⁹ Jesus answered and said unto them, This is the work of God, that ye believe on him whom he hath sent.*i*

³⁰ They said therefore unto him, What sign showest thou then, that we may see, and believe thee? what dost thou work? ³¹ Our fathers did eat manna in the desert; as it is written,*j* He gave them bread from heaven *k* to eat.*l* ³² Then Jesus said unto them, Verily, verily, I say unto you, Moses gave you not that bread from heaven; but my Father giveth you the true bread from heaven. ³³ For the bread of God is he which cometh down from heaven, and giveth life unto the world.*m* ³⁴ Then said they unto him, Lord, evermore give us this bread. ³⁵ And Jesus said unto them, I am the bread of life: he that cometh to me shall never hunger: and he that believeth on me shall never thirst. ³⁶ But I said unto you, That ye also have seen me, and believe not. ³⁷ All that the Father giveth me shall come to me; and him that cometh to me I will in no wise cast out. ³⁸ For I came down from heaven, not to do mine own will, but the will of him that sent me. ³⁹ And this is the Father's will which hath sent me, that of all which he hath given me I should lose nothing, but should raise it up again at the last day. ⁴⁰ And this

g See in ꝰ 67.

h *Sealed,* that is, sanctioned or accredited as the Messiah, by such wonderful works as the feeding of the five thousand just before: see Acts 2. 22.

i Comp. 1 John 3. 22, 23.

j Psa. 78. 24. Comp. Ex. 16. 15.

k *Bread from heaven.* The manna was so called because of its miraculous supply. That the manna in the wilderness was not a natural production, like what is now found in the

East, is certain, because it corrupted if kept till morning, except on the sabbath, and because on that day it was not sent, but a double quantity on the day before (Ex. 16. 19-30).

l Comp. 1 Cor. 10. 3.

m *Giveth life to the world.* Our Lord's language here and in verse 51 is clearly to be understood not of the *bread* in the *eucharist,* but of the *atonement* which He made in His own *body* on the tree by death.

John 6.

is the will of him that sent me, that every one which seeth the Son, and believeth on him, may have everlasting life: and I will raise him up at the last day.

[41] The Jews then murmured at him, because he said, I am the bread which came down from heaven. [42] And they said, Is not this Jesus, the son of Joseph, whose father and mother we know? how is it then that he saith, I came down from heaven? [43] Jesus therefore answered and said unto them, Murmur not among yourselves. [44] No man can come to me, except the Father which hath sent me draw him: and I will raise him up at the last day. [45] It is written in the prophets,[n] And they shall be all taught of God. Every man therefore that hath heard, and hath learned of the Father, cometh unto me. [46] Not that any man hath seen the Father, save he which is of God, he hath seen the Father. [47] Verily, verily, I say unto you, He that believeth on me hath everlasting life. [48] I am that bread of life. [49] Your fathers did eat manna[o] in the wilderness, and are dead. [50] This is the bread which cometh down from heaven, that a man may eat thereof, and not die. [51] I am the living bread which came down from heaven: if any man eat of this bread, he shall live for ever: and the bread that I will give is my flesh, which I will give for the life of the world.

[52] The Jews therefore strove among themselves, saying, How can this man give us *his* flesh to eat? [53] Then Jesus said unto them, Verily, verily, I say unto you, Except ye eat the flesh of the Son of man, and drink his blood, ye have no life in you. [54] Whoso eateth my flesh, and drinketh my blood, hath eternal life; and I will raise him up at the last day. [55] For my flesh is meat indeed, and my blood is drink indeed. [56] He that eateth my flesh, and drinketh my blood, dwelleth in me, and I in him. [57] As the living Father hath sent me, and I live by the Father: so he that eateth me, even he shall live by me. [58] This is that bread which came down from heaven: not as your fathers did eat manna, and are dead: he that eateth of this bread shall live for ever. [59] These things said he in the synagogue, as he taught in Capernaum.

[60] Many therefore of his disciples, when they had heard *this*, said, This is an hard saying; who can hear it? [61] When Jesus knew in himself that his disciples murmured at it, he said unto them, Doth this offend you? [62] *What* and if ye shall see the Son of man ascend up where he was before? [63] It is the spirit that quickeneth; the flesh profiteth nothing: the words that I speak unto you, *they* are spirit, and they are life. [64] But there are some of you that believe not. For Jesus knew from the beginning who they were that believed not, and who should betray him. [65] And he said, Therefore said I unto you, that no man can come unto me, except it were given unto him of my Father.

[66] From that *time* many of his disciples went back, and walked no more with him. [67] Then said Jesus unto the twelve,[p] Will ye also go away? [68] Then Simon Peter answered him, Lord, to whom shall we go? thou hast the words of eternal life. [69] And we believe and are sure that thou art that Christ,[q] the Son of the living God. [70] Jesus answered them, Have not I chosen you twelve, and one of you is a devil? [71] He spake of Judas Iscariot *the son* of Simon: for he it was that should betray him, being one of the twelve.

John 7. [1] After these things Jesus walked in Galilee: for he would not walk in Jewry, because the Jews sought to kill him.

---

n Isa. 54. 13. Comp. Jer. 31. 33, sq.

o Comp. Ex. 16. 15.

p *The twelve*: mentioned here by John in a manner which assumes their appointment as apostles to be well known, proving this Gospel to be supplementary to the others where that appointment is distinctly recorded: see in ? 40

q Psa. 2. 2–7.

PART V.

FROM THE THIRD [r] PASSOVER DURING OUR LORD'S MINISTRY UN-
TIL HIS FINAL DEPARTURE FROM GALILEE AT THE FESTIVAL
OF TABERNACLES.

TIME: *Six Months.*

§ 67. OUR LORD JUSTIFIES HIS DISCIPLES FOR EATING WITH UNWASHEN
HANDS. PHARISAIC TRADITIONS.—*Capernaum.*

Matt. 15. 1-20.

THEN [s] came to Jesus scribes and Pharisees, which were of Jerusalem,

saying, [2] Why do thy disciples transgress the tradition of the elders? for they wash not their hands when they eat bread. [3] But he answered and said unto them,—[7] Ye hypocrites, well did Esaias prophesy of you, saying, [t] [8] This people draweth nigh unto me with their mouth, and honoureth me with *their* lips; but their heart is far from me. [9] But in vain they do worship me, teaching *for* doctrines the commandments of men.

—[3] Why do ye also transgress the commandment of God by your tradition? [4] for God commanded, saying, [u] Honour thy father and mother: and, He that

Mark 7. 1-23.

[1] Then came together unto him the Pharisees, and certain of the scribes, which came from Jerusalem. [2] And when they saw some of his disciples eat bread with defiled, that is to say, with unwashen, hands, they found fault. [3] For the Pharisees, and all the Jews, except they wash *their* hands oft, eat not, holding the tradition of the elders. [4] And *when they come* from the market, except they wash, they eat not. And many other things there be, which they have received to hold, *as* the washing of cups, and pots, and brasen vessels, and tables. [5] Then the Pharisees and scribes asked him, Why walk not thy disciples according to the tradition of the elders, but eat bread with unwashen hands? [6] He answered and said unto them, Well hath Esaias prophesied of you hypocrites, as it is written, [t] This people honoureth me with *their* lips, but their heart is far from me. [7] Howbeit in vain do they worship me, teaching *for* doctrines the commandments of men. [8] For laying aside the commandment of God, ye hold the tradition of men, *as* the washing of pots and cups: and many other such like things ye do. [9] And he said unto them, Full well ye reject the commandment of God, that ye may keep your own tradition. [10] For Moses said, [u] Honour thy father and thy mother: and, Whoso

---

[r] This passover was not celebrated by our Lord in Jerusalem, because the rulers were seeking to kill Him (John 7. 1), and His time had not yet come (comp. Luke 9. 51); see Note [s] on § 64.

[s] The order of events, as far as to § 79 inclusive, is in accordance with both Matthew and Mark; with whom Luke also coincides, so far as he touches upon the same transactions.
[t] Isa. 29. 13.   [u] Ex. 20. 12: Deut. 5. 16.

Matt. 15.

curseth father or mother, let him die the death.[v] [5] But ye say,[w] Whosoever shall say to *his* father or *his* mother, *It is* a gift, by whatsoever thou mightest be profited by me; [6] and honour not his father or his mother, *he shall be free.*

Thus have ye made the commandment of God of none effect by your tradition.—

[10] And he called the multitude, and said unto them, Hear, and understand : [11] Not that which goeth into the mouth defileth a man; but that which cometh out of the mouth, this defileth a man.

[12] Then came his disciples, and said unto him, Knowest thou that the Pharisees were offended, after they heard this saying ? [13] But he answered and said, Every plant, which my heavenly Father hath not planted, shall be rooted up. [14] Let them alone : they be blind leaders of the blind. And if the blind lead the blind, both shall fall into the ditch. [15] Then answered Peter and said unto him, Declare unto us this parable. [16] And Jesus said, Are ye also yet without understanding ? [17] Do not ye yet understand, that whatsoever entereth in at the mouth goeth into the belly, and is cast out into the draught ?

[18] But those things which proceed out of the mouth come forth from the heart; and they defile the man.[x] [19] For out of the heart proceed evil thoughts, murders, adulteries, fornications, thefts, false witness, blasphemies : [20] these are *the things* which defile a man : but to eat with unwashen hands defileth not a man.

Mark 7.

curseth father or mother, let him die the death :[v] [11] but ye say,[w] If a man shall say to his father or mother, *It is* Corban, that is to say, a gift, by whatsoever thou mightest be profited by me; *he shall be free.* [12] And ye suffer him no more to do aught for his father or his mother ; [13] making the word of God of none effect through your tradition, which ye have delivered: and many such like things do ye. [14] And when he had called all the people *unto him,* he said unto them, Hearken unto me every one *of you,* and understand : [15] There is nothing from without a man, that entering into him can defile him : but the things which come out of him, those are they that defile the man. [16] If any man have ears to hear, let him hear.

[17] And when he was entered into the house from the people, his disciples asked him concerning the parable. [18] And he saith unto them, Are ye so without understanding also ? Do ye not perceive, that whatsoever thing from without entereth into the man, *it* cannot defile him ; [19] because it entereth not into his heart, but into the belly, and goeth out into the draught, purging all meats ? [20] And he said, That which cometh out of the man, that defileth the man.[x] [21] For from within, out of the heart of man, proceed evil thoughts, adulteries, fornications, murders, [22] thefts, covetousness, wickedness, deceit, lasciviousness, an evil eye, [23] blasphemy, pride, foolishness: all these evil things come from within, and defile the man.

---

[v] Ex. 21. 17.
[w] *Ye say, etc.* The meaning of this obscure and elliptical verse may probably be expressed thus,—" Whosoever shall say to his father or mother, ' I make a sacred offering of whatever benefit thou oughtest to receive from me,' he is bound, ye say, by his vow, and shall not honour (that is, support) his parents."

[x] Comp. James 3. 6.

§ 68. The Daughter of a Syrophenician Woman is Healed.
Region of Tyre and Sidon.

Matt. 15. 21-28. [21] Then Jesus went thence, and departed into the coasts of Tyre and Sidon.[y] [22] And, behold, a woman of Canaan came out of the same coasts, and cried unto him, saying, Have mercy on me, O Lord, *thou* Son of David; my daughter is grievously vexed with a devil. [23] But he answered her not a word.[z] And his disciples came and besought him, saying, Send her away; for she crieth after us.[a] [24] But he answered and said, I am not sent but unto the lost sheep of the house of Israel. [25] Then came she and worshipped him, saying, Lord, help me. [26] But he answered and said, It is not meet to take the children's bread, and to cast *it* to dogs. [27] And she said, Truth, Lord : yet the dogs eat of the crumbs which fall from their master's table. [28] Then Jesus answered and said unto her, O woman, great *is* thy faith : be it unto thee even as thou wilt. And her daughter was made whole from that very hour.

Mark 7. 24-30. [24] And from thence he arose, and went into the borders of Tyre and Sidon, and entered into an house, and would have no man know *it :* but he could not be hid. [25] For a *certain* woman, whose young daughter had an unclean spirit, heard of him, and came and fell at his feet : [26] the woman was a Greek, a Syrophenician by nation ; and she besought him that he would cast forth the devil out of her daughter.

[27] But Jesus said unto her, Let the children first be filled : for it is not meet to take the children's bread, and to cast *it* unto the dogs. [28] And she answered and said unto him, Yes, Lord : yet the dogs under the table eat of the children's crumbs. [29] And he said unto her, For this saying go thy way ; the devil is gone out of thy daughter. [30] And when she was come to her house, she found the devil gone out, and her daughter laid upon the bed.

§ 69. A Deaf and Dumb Man healed ; also many others. Four Thousand are Fed.—*The Decapolis.*

Matt. 15. 29-38. [29] And Jesus departed from thence, and came nigh unto the sea of Galilee ; and went up into a mountain, and sat down there.

Mark 7. 31-37 ; 8. 1-9. [31] And again, departing from the coasts of Tyre and Sidon, he came unto the sea of Galilee, through the midst of the coasts of Decapolis.[b] [32] And they bring unto him one that was deaf, and had an impediment in his speech ; and they beseech him to put his hand upon him. [33] And he took him aside from the multitude,

---

[y] Jesus retires from Galilee, first to the region of Tyre and Sidon, then to the Decapolis, and afterwards to the district of Cæsarea Philippi. All these were districts not under the jurisdiction of Herod, whose domain included Galilee and Peræa. Not improbably Jesus may have withdrawn from Galilee at this particular time [as He had done just before, see § 64], because the attention of Herod had been turned to Him after the death of John the Baptist ; and perhaps too on account of Herod's temporary presence in that province by which His own personal danger would naturally be increased. See Note on § 63.

[z] *He answered her not a word :* partly for

the purpose of intimating that His personal ministry on earth was not designed for the heathen ; and partly for a trial of her faith, that its strength might appear, and serve as an example to others.

[a] Comp. Acts 16. 16-18.

[b] The Decapolis was a region including *ten cities* on the S. and S.E. of the lake of Tiberias. Our Lord in returning from Tyre and Sidon had probably passed through Galilee. The feeding of the four thousand obviously took place in the Decapolis ; since Jesus immediately afterwards passes over the lake to Magdala, or Dalmanutha, on its western shore.

Mark 7.

and put his fingers into his ears, and he spit, and touched his tongue; [34] and looking up to heaven, he sighed, and saith unto him, Ephphatha, that is, Be opened. [35] And straightway his ears were opened, and the string of his tongue was loosed, and he spake plain. [36] And he charged them that they should tell

Matt. 15.

[30] And great multitudes came unto him, having with them *those that were* lame, blind, dumb, maimed, and many others, and cast them down at Jesus' feet; and he healed them: [31] insomuch that the multitude wondered, when they saw the dumb to speak, the maimed to be whole, the lame to walk, and the blind to see: and they glorified the God of Israel. [32] Then Jesus called his disciples *unto him*, and said, I have compassion on the multitude, because they continue with me now three days, and have nothing to eat: and I will not send them away fasting, lest they faint in the way. [33] And his disciples say unto him, Whence should we have so much bread in the wilderness, as to fill so great a multitude? [34] And Jesus saith unto them, how many loaves have ye? And they said, Seven, and a few little fishes. [35] And he commanded the multitude to sit down on the ground. [36] And he took the seven loaves and the fishes, and gave thanks, and brake *them*, and gave to his disciples, and the disciples to the multitude.

[37] And they did all eat, and were filled: and they took up of the broken *meat* that was left seven baskets full. [38] And they that did eat were four thousand men, beside women and children.

no man:[c] but the more he charged them, so much the more a great deal they published *it;* [37] and were beyond measure astonished, saying, He hath done all things well: he maketh both the deaf to hear, and the dumb to speak.

Mark 8.

[1] In those days the multitude being very great, and having nothing to eat, Jesus called his disciples *unto him*, and saith unto them, [2] I have compassion on the multitude, because they have now been with me three days, and have nothing to eat: [3] and if I send them away fasting to their own houses, they will faint by the way: for divers of them came from far. [4] And his disciples answered him, From whence can a man satisfy these *men* with bread here in the wilderness? [5] And he asked them, How many loaves have ye? And they said, Seven. [6] And he commanded the people to sit down on the ground: and he took the seven loaves, and gave thanks, and brake, and gave to his disciples to set before *them;* and they did set *them* before the people. [7] And they had a few small fishes: and he blessed, and commanded to set them also before *them.* [8] So they did eat, and were filled: and they took up of the broken *meat* that was left seven baskets. [9] And they that had eaten were about four thousand: and he sent them away.

§ 70. The Jews again require a Sign.[d]—*Near Magdala.*

Matt. 15. 39; **16.** 1-4. [39] And he sent away the multitude, and took ship, and came into the coasts of Magdala.[e]

Matt. 16. [1] The Pharisees also with the Sadducees came, and tempting desired him that he would show them a sign from heaven.[f] [2] He answered and

Mark 8. 10-12. [10] And straightway he entered into a ship with his disciples, and came into the parts of Dalmanutha.[e]

[11] And the Pharisees came forth, and began to question with him, seeking of him a sign from heaven,[f] tempting him.

---

[c] Comp. Matt. 8. 4; 12. 16–20; Mark 8. 26.
[d] See § 49.
[e] *Dalmanutha* was, probably, the name of the district in which the town of *Magdala*

lay, on the west of **Lake** Tiberias. To this town Mary *Magdalene* belonged, as her name signifies.
[f] Comp. Matt. 12. 38–40; Luke 11. 16, 29.

Matt. 16.

said unto them, When it is evening, ye say, *It will be* fair weather: for the sky is red. ³ And in the morning: *It will be* foul weather to-day: for the sky is red and lowering. O *ye* hypocrites, ye can discern the face of the sky; but can ye not *discern* the signs of the times? ⁴ A wicked and adulterous generation seeketh after a sign; and there shall no sign be given unto it, but the sign of the prophet Jonas.

Mark 8.

¹² And he sighed deeply in his spirit, and saith, Why doth this generation seek after a sign? verily I say unto you, There shall no sign be given *g* unto this generation.

§ 71. The Disciples cautioned against the Leaven of the Pharisees, etc.—*N.E. coast of the Sea of Galilee.*

Matt. 16. 4-12. ⁴ And he left them, and departed.

⁵ And when his disciples were come to the other side, they had forgotten to take bread. ⁶ Then Jesus said unto them, Take heed and beware of the leaven *h* of the Pharisees and of the Sadducees. ⁷ And they reasoned among themselves, saying, *It is* because we have taken no bread. ⁸ *Which* when Jesus perceived, he said unto them, O ye of little faith, why reason ye among yourselves, because ye have brought no bread? ⁹ Do ye not yet understand, neither remember the five loaves of the five thousand, and how many baskets ye took up? *i* ¹⁰ Neither the seven loaves of the four thousand, and how many baskets ye took up? *j* ¹¹ How is it that ye do not understand that I spake *it* not to you concerning bread, that ye should beware of the leaven of the Pharisees and of the Sadducees? ¹² Then understood they how that he bade *them* not beware of the leaven of bread, but of the doctrine of the Pharisees and of the Sadducees.

Mark 8. 13-21. ¹³ And he left them, and entering into the ship again departed to the other side.

¹⁴ Now *the disciples* had forgotten to take bread, neither had they in the ship with them more than one loaf. ¹⁵ And he charged them, saying, Take heed, beware of the leaven *h* of the Pharisees, and *of* the leaven of Herod. ¹⁶ And they reasoned among themselves, saying, *It is* because we have no bread. ¹⁷ And when Jesus knew *it*, he saith unto them, Why reason ye, because ye have no bread? perceive ye not yet, neither understand? have ye your heart yet hardened? ¹⁸ having eyes, see ye not? and having ears, hear ye not? and do ye not remember? ¹⁹ When I brake the five loaves among five thousand, how many baskets full of fragments took ye up? They say unto him, Twelve.*i* ²⁰ And when the seven among four thousand, how many baskets full of fragments took ye up? And they said, Seven.*j* ²¹ And he said unto them, How is it that ye do not understand?

§ 72. A Blind Man healed.*k*—*Bethsaida (Julias).*

Mark 8. 22-26. ²² And he cometh to Bethsaida; and they bring a blind man unto him, and besought him to touch him. ²³ And he took the blind man by the hand, and led him out of the town; and when he had spit on his eyes, and put his hands upon him, he asked him if he saw aught. ²⁴ And he looked up, and said, I see men as trees, walking. ²⁵ After that he put *his* hands again upon his eyes, and made him look up: and he was restored, and saw every man clearly. ²⁶ And he sent him away to his house, saying, Neither go into the town, nor tell *it* to any in the town.

---

g There shall no sign be given: meaning such a sign as they desired, i. e., one from heaven.
   h Comp. Luke 12. 1.
i See in ₹ 64.
   j See in ₹ 69.

k This healing of a blind man at the northern Bethsaida, is related only by Mark. It took place on the way from the eastern shore of the lake toward Cæsarea Philippi

§ 73. PETER AND THE REST AGAIN PROFESS THEIR FAITH IN CHRIST.[1]
Region of Cæsarea Philippi.

Matt. 16. 13-20.	Mark 8. 27-30.	Luke 9. 18-21.

[13] When Jesus came into the coasts of Cæsarea Philippi, he asked his disciples, saying, Whom do men say that I the Son of man am? [14] And they said, Some *say that thou art* John the Baptist:[m] some, Elias;[n] and others, Jeremias, or one of the prophets. [15] He said unto them, But whom say ye that I am? [16] And Simon Peter answered and said, Thou art the Christ, the Son of the living God.

[27] And Jesus went out, and his disciples, into the towns of Cæsarea Philippi: and by the way he asked his disciples, saying unto them, Whom do men say that I am? [28] And they answered, John the Baptist:[m] but some *say,* Elias;[n] and others, One of the prophets. [29] And he saith unto them, But whom say ye that I am? And Peter answereth and saith unto him, Thou art the Christ.

[18] And it came to pass, as he was alone praying, his disciples were with him: and he asked them, saying, Whom say the people that I am? [19] They answering said, John the Baptist;[m] but some *say,* Elias;[n] and others *say,* that one of the old prophets is risen again. [20] He said unto them, But whom say ye that I am? Peter answering said, The Christ of God.

[17] And Jesus answered and said unto him, Blessed art thou, Simon Bar-jona: for flesh and blood hath not revealed *it* unto thee, but my Father which is in heaven. [18] And I say also unto thee, That thou art Peter,[o] and upon this rock I will build my church;[p] and the gates of hell shall not prevail against it. [19] And I will give unto thee the keys of the kingdom of heaven: and whatsoever thou shalt bind on earth shall be bound in heaven: and whatsoever thou shalt loose on

earth shall be loosed in heaven. [20] Then charged he his disciples that they should tell no man that he was Jesus the Christ.

	Mark 8.	Luke 9.

[30] And he charged them that they should tell no man of him.

[21] And he straitly charged them, and commanded *them* to tell no man that thing.

§ 74. OUR LORD FORETELLS HIS DEATH, RESURRECTION, AND THE TRIALS OF HIS FOLLOWERS.—*Region of Cæsarea Philippi.*

Matt. 16. 21-28.	Mark 8. 31-38; 9. 1.	Luke 9. 22-27.

[21] From that time forth began Jesus to show unto his disciples, how that he must go unto Jerusalem, and suffer many things of the elders and chief priests and scribes, and be killed, and be raised again the third day. [22] Then Peter took him, and began to rebuke him, saying, Be it far from thee, Lord: this shall not be unto thee. [23] But he turned, and said unto Peter, Get thee behind me, Satan: thou art an offence unto me: for thou savourest not the things that be of God, but those that be of men.

[31] And he began to teach them, that the Son of man must suffer many things, and be rejected of the elders, and *of* the chief priests, and scribes, and be killed, and after three days [q] rise again. [32] And he spake that saying openly. And Peter took him, and began to rebuke him. [33] But when he had turned about and looked on his disciples, he rebuked Peter, saying, Get thee behind me, Satan: for thou savourest not the things that be of God, but the things that be of men.

[22] Saying, The Son of man must suffer many things, and be rejected of the elders and chief priests and scribes, and be slain, and be raised the third day.

---

     [1] See § 66.   [m] Matt. 14. 1, 2.   [n] Mark. 6. 15; Mal. 4. 5.
     [o] John 1. 42.   [p] Eph. 2. 20; Rev. 21. 14.   [q] See Note [1] on § 49.

Matt. 16.

[24] Then said Jesus unto his disciples, If any *man* will come after me, let him deny himself, and take up his cross, and follow me.

[25] For whosoever will save his life shall lose it: and whosoever will lose his life for my sake shall find it.[r] [26] For what is a man profited, if he shall gain the whole world, and lose his own soul? or what shall a man give in exchange for his soul?[s] [27] For the Son of man shall come in the glory of his Father with his angels; and then he shall reward every man according to his works.[t]

[28] Verily I say unto you, There be some[u] standing here, which shall not taste of death, till they see the Son of man coming in his kingdom.

Mark 8.

[34] And when he had called the people *unto him* with his disciples also, he said unto them, Whosoever will come after me, let him deny himself, and take up his cross, and follow me. [35] For whosoever will save his life shall lose it: but whosoever shall lose his life for my sake and the gospel's, the same shall save it.[r] [36] For what shall it profit a man, if he shall gain the whole world, and lose his own soul? [37] or what shall a man give in exchange for his soul?[s] [38] Whosoever therefore shall be ashamed of me and of my words in this adulterous and sinful generation; of him also shall the Son of man be ashamed, when he cometh in the glory of his Father with the holy angels.

Mark 9. [1] And he said unto them, Verily I say unto you, That there be some[u] of them that stand here, which shall not taste of death, till they have seen the kingdom of God come with power.

Luke 9.

[23] And he said to *them* all, If any *man* will come after me, let him deny himself, and take up his cross daily, and follow me.

[24] For whosoever will save his life shall lose it: but whosoever will lose his life for my sake, the same shall save it.[r] [25] For what is a man advantaged, if he gain the whole world, and lose himself, or be cast away?

[26] For whosoever shall be ashamed of me and of my words, of him shall the Son of man be ashamed, when he shall come in his own glory, and *in his* Father's, and of the holy angels.

[27] But I tell you of a truth, there be some[u] standing here, which shall not taste of death, till they see the kingdom of God.

---

§ 75. The Transfiguration. Our Lord's subsequent Discourse with the Three Disciples.—*Region of Cæsarea Philippi.*

Matt. 17. 1-13. [1] And after six days Jesus taketh Peter, James, and John his brother, and bringeth them up into an high mountain apart, [2] and was transfigured before them:

Mark 9. 2-13. [2] And after six days Jesus taketh *with him* Peter, and James, and John, and leadeth them up into an high mountain apart by themselves: and he was trans-

Luke 9. 28-36. [28] And it came to pass about an eight days after these sayings, he took Peter and John and James, and went up into a[v] mountain to pray. [29] And as he prayed,

---

[r] John 12. 25.
[s] Psa. 49. 8.
[t] Rom. 2. 6–11; 2 Cor. 5. 10.
[u] Several of the apostles were alive at the time of Christ's coming to overthrow Jerusalem (A.D. 70), which was the formal end of the "age," the catastrophe of the Jewish dispensation, and a type of the general judgment.
[v] Rather, *the* mountain; i.e., the mountain region above Cæsarea Philippi, some slope or peak of Hermon. The tradition which assigns the transaction to Mount Tabor is without authority.

Matt. 17.	Mark 9.	Luke 9.

and his face did shine as the sun,[w] and his raiment was white as the light. [3] And, behold, there appeared unto them Moses and Elias talking with him.

figured before them. [3] And his raiment became shining, exceeding white as snow; so as no fuller on earth can white them. [4] And there appeared unto them Elias with Moses: and they were talking with Jesus.

the fashion of his countenance was altered,[w] and his raiment was white and glistering. [30] And behold, there talked with him two men, which were Moses and Elias: [31] who appeared in glory,[x] and spake of his decease which he should accomplish at Jerusalem. [32] But Peter and they that were with him were heavy with sleep: and when they were awake, they saw his glory,[y] and the two men that stood with him. [33] And it came to pass, as they departed from him, Peter said unto Jesus, Master, it is good for us to be here: and let us make three tabernacles; one for thee, and one for Moses, and one for Elias: not knowing what he said. [34] While he thus spake, there came a cloud, and overshadowed them: and they feared as they entered into the cloud. [35] And there came a voice out of the cloud, saying,[z] This is my beloved Son: hear him.[a] [36] And when the voice was past, Jesus was found alone. And they kept it close, and told no man in those days any of those things which they had seen.

[4] Then answered Peter, and said unto Jesus, Lord, it is good for us to be here: if thou wilt, let us make here three tabernacles; one for thee, and one for Moses, and one for Elias.

[5] While he yet spake, behold, a bright[v] cloud overshadowed them: and behold a voice out of the cloud, which said,[z] This is my beloved Son, in whom I am well pleased; hear ye him.[a] [6] And when the disciples heard it, they fell on their face, and were sore afraid.[b] [7] And Jesus came and touched them, and said, Arise, and be not afraid. [8] And when they had lifted up their eyes, they saw no man, save Jesus only. [9] And as they came down from the mountain, Jesus charged them, saying, Tell the vision to no man, until the Son of man be risen again from the dead.

[5] And Peter answered and said to Jesus, Master, it is good for us to be here: and let us make three tabernacles; one for thee, and one for Moses, and one for Elias. [6] For he wist not what to say; for they were sore afraid. [7] And there was a cloud that overshadowed them: and a voice came out of the cloud, saying,[z] This is my beloved Son: hear him.[a]

[8] And suddenly, when they had looked round about, they saw no man any more, save Jesus only with themselves.

Mark 9.

[9] And as they came down from the mountain, he charged them that they should tell no man what things they had seen, till the Son of man were risen from the dead. [10] And they kept that saying with themselves, questioning one with another what the rising from the

[10] And his disciples asked him, saying,

---

[w] Exod. 34. 29–35.
[x] 1 Pet. 1. 11; 2 Pet. 1. 17.
[y] This brightness is in contrast with the "blackness, and darkness, and tempest" (Heb. 12. 18) on Mount Sinai; betokening the difference between the two dispensations. The fulfilment of the Law and the Prophets,

and the true glory of Christ, are shown to be connected with His "decease." Hence the close connexion of the Transfiguration with the time when He "began" to speak of His sufferings.
[z] 2 Pet. 1. 17, 18.
[a] Deut. 18. 15, 19.   [b] Rev. 1. 17.

Matt. 17.

Why then say the scribes that Elias must first come ? ¹¹ And Jesus answered and said unto them, Elias truly shall first come, and restore all things.ᶜ ¹² But I say unto you, That Elias is come already,ᵈ and they knew him not, but have done unto him whatsoever they listed. Likewise shall also the Son of man suffer of them. ¹³ Then the disciples understood that he spake unto them of John the Baptist.

Mark 9.

dead should mean. ¹¹ And they asked him, saying, Why say the scribes that Elias must first come ? ¹² And he answered and told them, Elias verily cometh first, and restoreth all things; and how it is written of the Son of man, that he must suffer many things, and be set at nought. ¹³ But I say unto you, That Elias is indeed come, and they have done unto him whatsoever they listed, as it is written of him.

§ 76. The Healing of a Demoniac.—*Region of Cæsarea Philippi.*

Matt. 17. 14-21. ¹⁴ And when they were come to the multitude,

Mark 9. 14-29. ¹⁴ And when he came to *his* disciples, he saw a great multitude about them, and the scribes questioning with them. ¹⁵ And

Luke 9. 37-43. ³⁷ And it came to pass, that on the next day, when they were come down from the hill, much people met him.

straightway all the people, when they beheld him, were greatly amazed, and running to *him* saluted him. ¹⁶ And he asked the scribes, What question ye with them ? ¹⁷ And one of the multitude answered and said, Master,

there came to him a *certain* man, kneeling down to him, and saying, ¹⁵ Lord, have mercy on my son: for he is lunatick, and sore vexed: for ofttimes he falleth into the fire, and oft into the water. ¹⁶ And I brought him to thy disciples, and they could not cure him. ¹⁷ Then Jesus answered and said, O faithless and perverse generation, how long shall I be with you ? how long shall I suffer you ? bring him hither to me.

I have brought unto thee my son, which hath a dumb spirit; ¹⁸ and wheresoever he taketh him, he teareth him: and he foameth, and gnasheth with his teeth, and pineth away: and I spake to thy disciples that they should cast him out: and they could not. ¹⁹ He answereth him, and saith, O faithless generation, how long shall I be with you ? how long shall I suffer you ? bring him unto me. ²⁰ And they brought him unto him: and when he saw him, straightway the spirit tare him; and he fell on the ground, and wallowed foaming. ²¹ And he asked his father, How

³⁸ And, behold, a man of the company cried out, saying, Master, I beseech thee, look upon my son: for he is mine only child. ³⁹ And, lo, a spirit taketh him, and he suddenly crieth out; and it teareth him that he foameth again, and bruising him hardly departeth from him. ⁴⁰ And I besought thy disciples to cast him out; and they could not. ⁴¹ And Jesus answering said, O faithless and perverse generation, how long shall I be with you, and suffer you ? Bring thy son hither. ⁴² And as he was yet a coming, the devil threw him down, and tare *him*.

long is it ago since this came unto him ? and he said, Of a child. ²² And ofttimes it hath cast him into the fire, and into the waters, to destroy him: but if thou canst do any thing, have compassion on us, and help us. ²³ Jesus said unto him, If thou canst believe, all things

---

ᶜ Mal. 4. 5, 6; 1 Kings 18. 17-21, 30-40.   ᵈ See note ʳ on § 13.

Mark 9.

are possible to him that believeth.   ²⁴ And straightway the father of the child cried out, and said with tears, Lord, I believe; help thou mine unbelief.   ²⁵ When

Matt. 17.	Luke 9.

¹⁸ And Jesus rebuked the devil; and he departed out of him: and the child was cured from that very hour.   ¹⁹ Then came the disciples to Jesus apart, and said, Why could not we cast him out?   ²⁰ And Jesus said unto them, Because of your unbelief: for verily I say unto you, If ye have faith as a grain of mustard seed, ye shall say unto this mountain, Remove hence to yonder place; and it shall remove;*ᶠ* and nothing shall be impossible unto you.   ²¹ Howbeit this kind*ᵍ* goeth not out but by prayer and fasting.

Jesus saw that the people came running together, he rebuked the foul spirit, saying unto him, *Thou dumb and deaf spirit,* I charge thee, come out of him, and enter no more into him.   ²⁶ And *the spirit* cried, and rent him sore, and came out of him: and he was as one dead; insomuch that many said, He is dead.   ²⁷ But Jesus took him by the hand, and lifted him up; and he arose.   ²⁸ And when he was come into the house, his disciples asked him privately, Why could not we cast him out?   ²⁹ And he said unto them, This kind*ᵍ* can come forth by nothing, but by prayer and fasting.

And Jesus rebuked the unclean spirit, and healed the child, and delivered him again to his father.   ⁴³ And they were all a-mazed at the mighty power of God.—

---

§ 77. JESUS AGAIN FORETELLS HIS DEATH AND RESURRECTION.ʰ—*Galilee.*

Matt. 17. 22, 23.	Mark 9. 30-32.	Luke 9. 43-45.

²² And while they abode in Galilee,

Jesus said unto them, The Son of man shall be betrayed into the hands of men: ²³ and they shall kill him, and the third day he shall be raised again. And they were exceeding sorry.

³⁰ And they departed thence, and passed through Galilee; and he would not that any man should know *it.*   ³¹ For he taught his disciples, and said unto them, The Son of man shall be delivered into the hands of men, and they shall kill him; and after that he is killed, he shall rise the third day.   ³² But they understood not that saying, and were afraid to ask him.

⁴³ —But while they wondered every one at all things which Jesus did, he said unto his disciples,   ⁴⁴ Let these sayings sink down into your ears: for the Son of man shall be delivered into the hands of men.   ⁴⁵ But they understood not this saying, and it was hid from them, that they perceived it not: and they feared to ask him of that saying.

---

§ 78. THE TRIBUTE-MONEY MIRACULOUSLY PROVIDED.—*Capernaum.*

Matt. 17. 24-27. ²⁴ And when they were come to Capernaum, they that received tribute *ⁱ money* came to Peter, and said, Doth not your master pay tribute? And when they were come into the house, Jesus prevented him,

Mark 9. 33. And he came to Capernaum.—

²⁵ He saith, Yes. And when he was come into the house, Jesus prevented him, saying, What thinkest thou, Simon? of

---

ᶠ Comp. 1 Cor. 13. 2.

ᵍ This kind: probably, this kind of unclean spirits, which could not be cast out without wrestling prayer and self-denial.

ʰ See § 74.

ⁱ *Tribute.* The word used here is the name of a coin (value *two drachms,* that is, fifteen

pence of our money), which was equal to the *half-shekel* of the Jews. It probably stands here for the yearly tax in support of the temple-service (Ex. 30. 13; 2 Chron. 24. 9). The claim for exemption which our Lord makes (ver. 26) may, therefore, be regarded as an indirect declaration that He was the Son of God.

Matt. 17.

whom do the kings of the earth take custom or tribute? of their own children or of strangers? [25] Peter saith unto him, Of strangers. Jesus saith unto him, Then are the children free. [27] Notwithstanding, lest we should offend them, go thou to the sea, and cast an hook, and take up the fish that first cometh up; and when thou hast opened his mouth, thou shalt find a piece of money :*j* that take, and give unto them for me and thee.

---

§ 79. THE DISCIPLES CONTEND WHO SHOULD BE THE GREATEST. JESUS EXHORTS TO HUMILITY, FORBEARANCE, AND BROTHERLY LOVE.—*Capernaum.*

Matt. 18. 1-35. [1] At the same time came the disciples unto Jesus, saying, Who is the greatest in the kingdom of heaven ?*k*

[2] And Jesus called a little child unto him, and set him in the midst of them, [3] and said, Verily I say unto you, Except ye be converted, and become as little children, ye shall not enter into the kingdom of heaven. [4] Whosoever therefore shall humble himself as this little child, the same is greatest in the kingdom of heaven. [5] And whosoever shall receive one such little child in my name receiveth me.

Mark 9. 33-50. [33]—And being in the house he asked them, What was it that ye disputed among yourselves by the way? [34] But they held their peace : for by the way they had disputed among themselves, who *should be* the greatest. [35] And he sat down, and called the twelve, and saith unto them, If any man desire to be first, *the same* shall be last of all, and servant of all. [36] And he took a child, and set him in the midst of them; and when he had taken him in his arms, he said unto them, [37] Whosoever shall receive one of such children in my name, receiveth me : and whosoever shall receive me, receiveth not me, but him that sent me.

Luke 9. 46-50. [46] Then there arose a reasoning among them, which of them should be greatest.*k* [47] And Jesus, perceiving the thought of their heart, took a child, and set him by him, [48] and said unto them, Whosoever shall receive this child in my name receiveth me : and whosoever shall receive me receiveth him that sent me : for he that is least among you all, the same shall be great.

[38] And John answered him, saying, Master, we saw one casting out devils in thy name, and he followeth not us : and we forbad him, because he followeth not us. [39] But Jesus said, Forbid him not: for there is no man which shall do a miracle in my name, that can lightly speak evil of me. [40] For he that is not against us is on our part.*l* [41] For whosoever shall give you a cup of water to drink in my name, because ye belong to Christ, verily I say unto you, he shall not lose his reward.

[49] And John answered and said, Master, we saw one casting out devils in thy name; and we forbad him, because he followeth not with us. [50] And Jesus said unto him, Forbid *him* not: for he that is not against us is for us.*l*

---

j Properly a *stater*, equal to a *shekel*, and exactly the tax for both Christ and Peter.

k Who is the greatest ? The agitation of this question by the twelve was probably occasioned by what had been said to Peter (Matt. 16. 17-19), and by the selection of the three (Matt. 17. 1) to accompany Christ to the mount of transfiguration.

Matt. 12. 30. See in § 80

Matt. 18.

6 But whoso shall offend one of these
little ones which believe in me, it were
better for him that a millstone[m] were
hanged about his neck, and *that* he were
drowned in the depth of the sea. 7 Woe
unto the world because of offences! for
it must needs be that offences come;[n]
but woe to that man by whom the offence
cometh! 8 Wherefore if thy hand[o] or
thy foot offend thee, cut them off, and
cast *them* from thee: it is better for
thee to enter into life halt or maimed,
rather than having two hands or two
feet to be cast into everlasting fire.
9 And if thine eye offend thee, pluck it
out, and cast *it* from thee: it is better
for thee to enter into life with one eye,
rather than having two eyes to be cast
into hell fire.

Mark 9.

42 And whosoever shall offend one of
these little ones that believe in me, it is
better for him that a millstone[m] were
hanged about his neck, and he were
cast into the sea. 43 And if thy hand
offend thee, cut it off: it is better for
thee to enter into life maimed, than
having two hands to go into hell, into
the fire that never shall be quenched:
44 where their worm dieth not, and the
fire is not quenched.[p] 45 And if thy foot
offend thee, cut it off; it is better for
thee to enter halt into life, than having
two feet to be cast into hell, into the fire
that never shall be quenched: 46 where
their worm dieth not, and the fire is not
quenched. 47 And if thine eye offend
thee, pluck it out: it is better for thee
to enter into the kingdom of God with
one eye, than having two eyes to be cast
into hell fire: 48 where their worm dieth not, and the fire is not quenched.
49 For every one shall be salted with fire, and every sacrifice shall be salted
with salt.[q] 50 Salt *is* good: but if the salt have lost his saltness, wherewith
will ye season it? Have salt in yourselves, and have peace one with another.

Matt. 18.

10 Take heed that ye despise not one of these little ones; for I say unto you, That
in heaven their angels do always behold the face of my Father which is in heaven.
11 For the Son of man is come to save that which was lost.[s] 12 How think ye? if
a man have an hundred sheep,[t] and one of them be gone astray, doth he not leave
the ninety and nine, and goeth into the mountains, and seeketh that which is
gone astray? 13 And if so be that he find it, verily I say unto you, he rejoiceth
more of that *sheep*, than of the ninety and nine which went not astray. 14 Even
so it is not the will of your Father which is in heaven, that one of these little ones
should perish. 15 Moreover if thy brother shall trespass against thee, go and tell
him his fault between thee and him alone:[u] if he shall hear thee, thou hast gained
thy brother. 16 But if he will not hear *thee*, *then* take with thee one or two more,
that in the mouth of two or three witnesses every word may be established.[v]
17 And if he shall neglect to hear them, tell *it* unto the church: but if he neglect
to hear the church, let him be unto thee as an heathen man and a publican.[w]
18 Verily I say unto you, Whatsoever ye shall bind on earth shall be bound in
heaven: and whatsoever ye shall loose on earth shall be loosed in heaven.[x] 19 Again
I say unto you, That if two of you shall agree on earth as touching any thing that
they shall ask, it shall be done for them of my Father which is in heaven. 20 For
where two or three are gathered together in my name, there am I in the midst
of them.

---

[m] Properly, *ass millstone* (μύλος ὀνικός), that is, the upper stone of a mill worked by an ass, which was far heavier than that of a hand-mill, Luke 17. 35.

[n] *It must be:* because of human depravity, and for proving and discriminating characters (1 Cor. 11. 19; 1 John 2. 19).

[o] Deut. 13. 6–10.

[p] Isa. 66. 24.

[q] Lev. 2. 13.

[s] Luke 15. 8–10; 1 Tim. 1. 15.

[t] Luke 15. 3–7; Isa. 53. 6.

[u] Lev. 19. 17, 18.

[v] Deut. 19. 15; Heb. 10. 28.

[w] 1 Cor. 5. 11–13; 2 Thess. 3. 6, 14, 15.

[x] Matt. 16. 19.

Matt. 18.

²¹ Then came Peter to him, and said, Lord, how oft shall my brother sin against me, and I forgive him? till seven times? ²² Jesus saith unto him, I say not unto thee, Until seven times: but, Until seventy times seven. ²³ Therefore is the kingdom of heaven likened unto a certain king, which would take account of his servants. ²⁴ And when he had begun to reckon, one was brought unto him, which owed him ten thousand talents.*y* ²⁵ But forasmuch as he had not to pay, his lord commanded him to be sold,*ᶻ* and his wife, and children, and all that he had, and payment to be made. ²⁶ The servant therefore fell down, and worshipped him, saying, Lord, have patience with me, and I will pay thee all. ²⁷ Then the lord of that servant was moved with compassion, and loosed him, and forgave him the debt. ²⁸ But the same servant went out, and found one of his fellowservants, which owed him an hundred pence: and he laid hands on him, and took *him* by the throat, saying, Pay me that thou owest. ²⁹ And his fellowservant fell down at his feet, and besought him, saying, Have patience with me, and I will pay thee all. ³⁰ And he would not: but went and cast him into prison, till he should pay the debt. ³¹ So when his fellowservants saw what was done, they were very sorry, and came and told unto their lord all that was done. ³² Then his lord, after that he had called him, said unto him, O thou wicked servant, I forgave thee all that debt, because thou desiredst me: ³³ shouldest not thou also have had compassion on thy fellowservant, even *ᵃ* as I had pity on thee? ³⁴ And his lord was wroth, and delivered him to the tormentors, till he should pay all that was due unto him. ³⁵ So likewise shall my heavenly Father do also unto you,*ᵇ* if ye from your hearts forgive not every one his brother their trespasses.

§ 80. JESUS GOES UP TO THE FESTIVAL OF TABERNACLES. HIS FINAL DEPARTURE FROM GALILEE. INCIDENTS IN SAMARIA.

John 7. 2–10. ² Now the Jews' feast of tabernacles was at hand.*ᶜ* ³ His *ᵈ* brethren therefore said unto him, Depart hence, and go into Judea, that thy disciples also may see the works that thou doest. ⁴ For *there is* no man *that* doeth any thing in secret, and he himself seeketh to be known openly. If thou do these things, show thyself to the world. ⁵ For neither did his brethren believe in him.*ᶜ* ⁶ Then Jesus said unto them, My time is not yet come: but your time is alway ready. ⁷ The world cannot hate you; but me it hateth, because I testify of it, that the works thereof are evil. ⁸ Go ye up unto this feast: I go not up yet unto this feast; for my time is not yet full come. ⁹ When he had said these words unto them, he abode *still* in Galilee. ¹⁰ But when his brethren were gone up, then went he also up unto the feast, not openly, but as it were in secret.*ᶠ*

---

y Ten thousand talents. This immense sum (reckoning a talent at £187 10s., or at £216, according to some) expresses the incalculable number of our sins against God; and teaches the impossibility of self-justification, and the freeness of the Divine forgiveness.

ᶻ Lev. 25. 39; 2 Kings 4. 1.

ᵃ Eph. 4. 32.

ᵇ James 2. 13.

ᶜ The feast of tabernacles, held in October, during eight days, and so called because the people then dwelt in tents or booths to commemorate the dwelling in the wilderness in tents (Lev. 23. 34–43): and as such was also the *feast of the ingatherings* (somewhat like our *harvest home*), and as such was a

time of high rejoicing (Ex. 23. 16; Deut. 16. 13–15).

ᵈ Our Lord evades the urgency of His relatives: and afterwards goes up to the festival more privately. The journey mentioned in Luke 9. 51 was obviously His last journey from Galilee to Jerusalem; and ver. 53 shows that He was passing on without delay. See Introductory Note to Part vi.

ᶜ Acts 1. 14.

ᶠ In secret, that is, through Samaria instead of Peræa, which was the usual and most frequented though longer route from Galilee to Jerusalem, because the Jews did not like to pass through the country of the Samaritans (see Luke 9. 53; John 4. 9). See in § 83.

Luke 9.

Luke 9. 51–62. [51] And it came to pass, when the time was come that he should be received up, he steadfastly set his face to go to Jerusalem, [52] and sent messengers before his face: and they went and entered into a village of the Samaritans, to make ready for him. [53] And they did not receive him, because his face was as though he would go to Jerusalem.*ᵍ* [54] And when his disciples James and John saw *this*, they said, Lord, wilt thou that we command fire to come down from heaven, and consume them, even as Elias did?*ʰ* [55] But he turned, and rebuked them, and said, Ye know not what manner of spirit ye are of. [56] For the Son of man is not come to destroy men's lives, but to save *them*. And they went to another village. [57] And it came to pass, that, as they went in the way, a certain *man* said unto him, Lord, I will follow thee whithersoever thou goest. [58] And Jesus said unto him, Foxes have holes, and birds of the air *have* nests; but the Son of man hath not where to lay *his* head. [59] And he said unto another, Follow me. But he said, Lord, suffer me first to go and bury my father. [60] Jesus said unto him, Let the dead bury their dead: but go thou and preach the kingdom of God. [61] And another also said, Lord, I will follow thee; but let me first go bid them farewell, which are at home at my house. [62] Jesus said unto him, No man, having put his hand to the plough, and looking back, is fit for the kingdom of God.

§ 81. The Seventy Instructed and sent out.—*Samaria?*

Luke 10. 1–16. [1] After these things *ⁱ* the Lord appointed other seventy also, and sent them two and two before his face into every city and place, whither he himself would come. [2] Therefore said he unto them, The harvest truly *is* great, but the labourers *are* few: pray ye therefore the Lord of the harvest, that he would send forth labourers into his harvest. [3] Go your ways: behold, I send you forth as lambs among wolves. [4] Carry neither purse, nor scrip, nor shoes: and salute no man by the way.*ᵏ* [5] And into whatsoever house ye enter, first say, Peace *be* to this house. [6] And if the son of peace be there, your peace shall rest upon it: if not, it shall turn to you again. [7] And in the same house remain, eating and drinking such things as they give: for the labourer is worthy of his hire. Go not from house to house. [8] And into whatsoever city ye enter, and they receive you, eat such things as are set before you: [9] and heal the sick that are therein, and say unto them, The kingdom of God is come nigh unto you. [10] But into whatsoever city ye enter, and they receive you not, go your ways out into the streets of the same, and say, [11] Even the very dust of your city, which cleaveth on us, we do wipe off against you: notwithstanding be ye sure of this, that the kingdom of God is come nigh unto you. [12] But I say unto you, That it shall be more tolerable in that day for Sodom, than for that city. [13] Woe unto thee, Chorazin! woe unto thee,

---

ᵍ John 4. 9.   *ʰ* 2 Kings 1. 9–14.
ⁱ This specification of time seems to forbid Robinson's order, who considers that the seventy were sent out *before*, and not *after*, the things related in ch. 9. 51–56. He and Greswell suppose that Capernaum was the place, whereas the context, in ch. 9. 52, rather favours Samaria. We have therefore transposed Robinson's §§ 80 and 81. See Supplemental Note, p. 81.

In this transaction, which is recorded only ʙy Luke, who wrote especially for Gentile Christians, the number, the place, and the time, are all significant. Jesus sent forth *seventy*, to indicate that the gospel was to be preached to the heathen nations, which the

Jews of that day set down at that number; just as He had before [see § 62] sent forth the twelve to the tribes of Israel. The *place* is Samaria, representing the heathen world, to which the apostles were at first not allowed to go (Matt. 10. 5, 6). The *time* too is full of meaning: the twelve had been sent,out about the season of the passover, that is, nearly six months before the sending of the seventy, which took place about the feast of tabernacles following; whereby our Lord indicated His pleasure to send the good news first tᴄ the Jews and then to the Gentiles, Luke 24. 47; Acts 3. 26; Rom. 1. 16. See Wieseler's *Synopsis*, sec. 4, p. 298 (Eng. Ed.).

ᵏ 2 Kings 4. 29.

Luke 10.

Bethsaida! for if the mighty works had been done in Tyre and Sidon, which have been done in you, they had a great while ago repented, sitting in sackcloth and ashes.   [14] But it shall be more tolerable for Tyre and Sidon at the judgment, than for you.   [15] And thou, Capernaum, which art exalted to heaven, shalt be thrust down to hell.   [16] He that heareth you heareth me; and he that despiseth you despiseth me; and he that despiseth me despiseth him that sent me.[l]

§ 82.   Ten Lepers Cleansed.—*Samaria ?*

Luke 17. 11-19.   [11] And it came to pass, as he went to Jerusalem, that he passed through the midst of Samaria and Galilee.   [12] And as he entered into a certain village, there met him ten men that were lepers, which stood afar off: [13] and they lifted up *their* voices, and said, Jesus, Master, have mercy on us.   [14] And when he saw *them*, he said unto them, Go shew yourselves unto the priests.[m]   [15] And it came to pass, that, as they went, they were cleansed.   And one of them, when he saw that he was healed, turned back, and with a loud voice glorified God,   [16] and fell down on *his* face at his feet, giving him thanks : and he was a Samaritan.   [17] And Jesus answering said, Were there not ten cleansed? but where *are* the nine.   [18] There are not found that returned to give glory to God, save this stranger.   [19] And he said unto him, Arise, go thy way : thy faith hath made thee whole.[n]

---

[l] See in § 89.
[m] Lev. 13. 2.
[n] The healing of the ten lepers evidently

connects itself with the journey through Samaria, § 80; and is narrated by Luke out of its proper order.

Supplemental Note.

The Mission of the Seventy, § 81. Dr. Robinson thinks, with Greswell, and others, that the Seventy were sent from Capernaum or its neighbourhood, as indicated by Luke 10. 13, 15. The mission would thus be *before* Christ "stedfastly set His face to go to Jerusalem;" the words "after these things" (ch. 10. 1), referring to the general series of events, narrated ch. 9, not to ver. 51, sq., in particular. In fact, the incidents recorded in vers. 57-62, Robinson says, were still earlier, placing them in his Harmony with Matt. 8. 19, 22 in § 56. But in the arrangement here preferred, these incidents are repeated, as having taken place on two several occasions. See § 56, note [e].

Robinson adds, "According to Luke 10. 1, the Seventy were to go to every city and place whither our Lord Himself would come. To what part of the country, then, were they sent ? Not throughout Galilee: for Jesus apparently never returned to that province; and besides, both Himself and the Twelve had already preached in all the towns and villages. Not in Samaria; for He merely passes through that district without making any delay. Possibly into some parts of Judæa,

whither our Lord Himself afterwards came: but more probably along the great valley of the Jordan, and throughout the populous region of Peræa, which our Lord traversed, and where He taught after the festival of dedication, and as He for the last time went up to Jerusalem; see John 10. 40; Matt. 19. 1; Mark 10. 1; Luke 13. 22. In accordance with this view, the return of the Seventy took place in Jerusalem or Judæa, not long before the festival of dedication, § 89; immediately after which festival Jesus withdrew into Peræa to follow up their labours; John 10. 40, sq. See Introd. Note to Part VI."

Our Lord's instructions to the Seventy have a striking resemblance to those given to the Twelve: see in § 62; excepting that the prohibition against going "into the way of the Gentiles," or "into any city of the Samaritans," is significantly withdrawn.

On the whole question of the relation of Luke 9. 51-18. 14 to the other Gospels, see Bishop Ellicott's *Historical Lectures on the Life of our Lord*, Lect. 6, and Godet's *Commentary on the Gospel of St. Luke*, vol. 2, pp. 1-8 (Clark). Godet places the mission of the Seventy in southern Galilee.

PART VI.

THE FEAST OF TABERNACLES, AND THE SUBSEQUENT TRANSACTIONS UNTIL OUR LORD'S ARRIVAL AT BETHANY SIX DAYS BEFORE THE FOURTH PASSOVER.

TIME: *Six Months, less One Week.*

INTRODUCTORY NOTE.

IN this interval of time, from the feast of tabernacles to our Lord's last arrival at Bethany, we encounter one of the most difficult portions of the whole Gospel Harmony.

According to John's narrative, Jesus, after leaving Galilee to go up to the feast of tabernacles in October (John 7. 10), appears not to have returned again to Galilee; but to have spent the time intervening before the festival of dedication in December, probably in Jerusalem, or, when in danger from the Jews, in the neighbouring villages of Judea; John 8. 59; Luke 10. 38, sq. Had Jesus actually returned to Galilee during this interval, it can hardly be supposed that John, who had hitherto so carefully noted our Lord's return thither after each visit to Jerusalem, would have failed to give some hint of it in this case also, either after ch. 8. 59, or after ch. 10. 21. But neither John, nor the other evangelists (unless perhaps Luke in ch. 17. 11), afford any such hint.—Immediately after the festival of dedication, Jesus withdrew from the machinations of the Jews beyond Jordan; whence He was recalled to Bethany by the decease of Lazarus; John 10. 40; 11. 7. He then once more retired to Ephraim; and is found again at Bethany six days before the passover; John 11. 54; 12. 1.

Matthew and Mark contain no allusion at all to the feast of tabernacles; nor do we find any express mention of it in Luke. Yet Luke 9. 51 is most naturally referred to our Lord's journey at that time; and it implies also that this was His final departure from Galilee.[*] Luke and John are therefore here parallel. The circumstances of danger which had induced Jesus during the summer to retire from Galilee in various directions,[p] as well as the approach of the time when "He should be received up," are reasons of sufficient weight to account for His having transferred, at this time, the scene of His ministry

and labours from the north to Jerusalem and Judea, including excursions to Samaria and the country on and beyond the Jordan.

In regard to the transactions during the whole interval of time comprised in this Part, Matthew and Mark are silent, except where they relate that our Lord, after His departure from Galilee, approached Jerusalem for the last time through Peræa and by way of Jericho, where He was followed by multitudes; Matt. 19. 1, 2; 20. 29; Mark 10. 1, 46. With the transactions recorded by these two evangelists during this last approach, Luke also has some things parallel; Luke 18. 15-43. The arrival at Bethany is common to the three; and in this they all accord with John; Matt. 21. 1; Mark 11. 1; Luke 19. 29; John 12. 1, 12, sq.

There exists consequently no difficulty in harmonizing Matthew and Mark, and so much of Luke as is parallel to them (18. 15, sq.), with John. But in Luke, from ch. 9. 51, where Jesus leaves Galilee to ch. 18. 14, where the record again becomes parallel with Matthew and Mark, there is a large body of matter peculiar for the most part to Luke, and relating *prima facie* to the time subsequent to our Lord's departure from Galilee. How is this portion of Luke's Gospel to be arranged and distributed, in order to harmonize with the narrative of John? The difficulty of course does not exist in the case of those harmonists who, like Calvin, Griesbach, and others, attempt to bring together only the first three evangelists.

Those harmonists who have likewise included John's Gospel have hitherto generally *assumed* a return of our Lord to Galilee after the feast of tabernacles; and this avowedly in order to provide a place for this portion of Luke's Gospel. But the manner in which it has been arranged, after all, is exceedingly various. Some, as Le Clerc,[r] insert nearly

---

* See Note on § 80.   p See Note on § 68.   r *Harm. Evang.* p. 264, sq.

the whole during this supposed journey. Others, as Lightfoot, assign to this journey only what precedes Luke 13. 23; and refer the remainder to our Lord's sojourn beyond Jordan, John 10. 40.[r] Greswell[s] maintains that the transactions in Luke 9. 51–18. 14, all belong to the journey from Ephraim (through Samaria, Galilee, and Peræa) to Jerusalem, which he dates in the interval of about four months, between the feast of dedication and our Lord's last passover. Wieseler[t] makes a somewhat different arrangement (intermediate between Robinson and Greswell), according to which, Luke 9. 51–13. 21 relates to the period from Christ's journey from Galilee to the feast of tabernacles till after the feast of dedication (parallel to John 7. 10–10. 42); Luke 13. 22–17. 10 relates to the interval between that time and our Lord's stay at Ephraim (parallel to John 11. 1–54); and Luke 17. 11–18. 14 relates to the journey from Ephraim to Jerusalem, through Samaria, Galilee, and Peræa.

If now we examine more closely the portion of Luke in question (9. 51–18. 14), we perceive, that although an order of time is discoverable in most parts, yet as a whole it is wanting in exact chronological arrangement. This indeed is admitted, at the present day, by all Harmonists, except Greswell.[u] It would seem almost as if, in this portion peculiar to Luke, that evangelist, after recording many of the earlier transactions of Jesus in Galilee, in accordance with Matthew and Mark, had here, upon our Lord's final departure from that province, brought together this new and various matter of his own, relating partly to our Lord's previous ministry in Galilee, partly to this journey, and still more to His subsequent proceedings, until the narrative (in ch. 18. 15) again becomes parallel to the accounts in Matthew and Mark. The transactions narrated in ch. 10. 17–11. 13, have marks of chronological connexion; and the scene of them is obviously Jerusalem or its vicinity.[v] The healing of a demoniac and the consequent blasphemy of the scribes and Pharisees in Luke 11. 14, 15, 17, sq., is parallel with the same events in Matthew and Mark, which these two evangelists describe as having occurred in Galilee.[w] With this passage, again, Luke 11. 37–54 is immediately connected by the words *and as He spake.*[x] The transition to the next chapter (ch. 12) is made by the phrase *in the mean time,* marking proximity of time.[y] And, further, the words introducing Luke 13. 1, show that the conversation there given (ver.

1–9) immediately followed.—The remainder of this portion of Luke, ch. 13. 10–18. 14 (with the exception of ch. 17. 11–19, which probably connects itself with the journey in ch. 9. 51), contains absolutely no definite notation of time or place; nor any thing, indeed, to show that the events happened in the order recorded, or that they did not take place at different times and in different parts of the country. The only passage to which this remark does not perhaps fully apply is ch. 13. 22–35.

For these reasons Robinson has, like Newcome, distributed Luke 9. 51–10. 16, and 11. 14–13. 9 (as also 17. 11–19) in Parts IV., V., as already specified, among the transactions of our Lord's ministry in Galilee, between His second passover and His journey to the feast of tabernacles. The remainder of this whole portion of Luke, viz., ch. 10. 17–11. 13, and 13. 10–17. 10, as also 17. 20–18. 14, remains to be disposed of in the present Part.

With many leading modern commentators, Robinson prefers here to follow the narrative of John, and infers that our Lord did not again return to Galilee after the feast of tabernacles. On this principle, therefore, the present Harmony is constructed. Hence Luke 10. 17–11. 13 is inserted between the feast of tabernacles and that of dedication.[z]

More difficult is it to assign the proper place for Luke 13. 10–17. 10 ; the transactions recorded in which all cluster around or follow ch. 13. 22, where Jesus is represented as travelling leisurely through the cities and villages towards Jerusalem. Now, this journey cannot have been the same with that in Luke 9. 51 and John 7. 10 ; because there Jesus went up privately, while here He is accompanied by multitudes, Luke 14. 25. Nor can it have been a later journey *from Galilee ;* for that in Luke 9. 51 was, probably, the final one. Nor indeed were the Jews accustomed to go up from the country to Jerusalem at the festival of dedication.[a] Besides, Luke 13. 22 stands in connexion with the warning received by our Lord against Herod, ver. 31–33; which under the attendant circumstances cannot well be regarded as having been given in Galilee, and much less in Jerusalem, as Lightfoot supposes.[b] But Herod was lord also of Peræa ; and in that province he had imprisoned and put to death John the Baptist.[c] It would therefore be natural that our Lord, who had been less known in that region, and who now appeared there, followed by multitudes, should receive warning of the danger He was

---

[r] *Chron. Temp. N. T.* Opp. II. pp. 37, 39.

[s] Dissert. xvi., vol. ii.

[t] *Chron. Synopsis,* pp. 292–302.

[u] See Dissert. xvi., vol. ii.

[v] See §§ 86–89 and Notes.

[w] See § 48 and Note.   [x] See § 51 and Note.

[y] See § 52 and Note.

[z] See Notes on §§ 86–89.

[a] See Note on § 91. Lightfoot, *Hor. Heb* on John 19. 22.

[b] *Chron. Temp. N. T.* Opp. II., p. 30.

[c] Joseph. *Ant.* 18. 5. § 2.

thus incurring. Hence this part of Luke (13. 10–17. 10) is here assigned to that period of our Lord's life and ministry which was passed in Peræa after the festival of dedication.

Our Lord first withdrew soon after that festival from the plots of the Jews in Peræa. "He went away again beyond Jordan, into the place where John at first baptized; and there He abode. And many resorted unto Him" and believed; John 10. 40–42. How long Jesus remained in that region before He was recalled by the death of Lazarus, can only be matter of conjecture. In that interval, Lightfoot places all this part of Luke after ch. 13. 22.[d] In this Robinson does not agree; because the language of John does not necessarily imply that our Lord at this time made any journey or circuit in Peræa itself. At least it could not then and there be said of Him in any sense, that "He went through their cities and villages, teaching, and journeying towards Jerusalem," Luke 13. 22; for He had just departed from Jerusalem, and was recalled to Bethany by a special message from the sisters of Lazarus, John 11. 3, 7. All this would seem to imply rather, that Jesus remained during this excursion, at least mainly, in the district "where John had baptized;" so that Martha and Mary knew at once where to send for Him. It follows also as a natural inference, that this first sojourn beyond Jordan could not well have been a long one, nor probably have occupied more than a few weeks out of the four months intervening between the festival of dedication and the passover.

After the raising of Lazarus, Jesus again retired from the machinations of the Jews to "a country near to the wilderness, into a city called Ephraim, and there continued with His disciples," John 11. 54. The evangelist John records nothing more of His movements, until He again appears in Bethany six days before the passover, John 12. 1. But the expression used by John as to His sojourn at Ephraim (κἀκεῖ διέτριβε, *there He passed the time*) does not preclude the idea of excursions from that place, nor of a circuitous route on His return to Bethany and Jerusalem at the passover. Now Matthew, Mark, and Luke affirm expressly, that on this return Jesus went up to Bethany from Jericho; and the two former narrate, as expressly, that in thus reaching Jericho He had come "into the coasts of Judea by the farther side of Jordan," where great multitudes followed Him, and He healed them and taught them, as He was wont; Matt. 19. 1, 2; Mark 10. 1. With all this the language of Luke 13. 22 agrees perfectly: "And He went through the cities and villages, teaching, and journeying towards Jerusalem;" as does also the mention

of the multitudes in Luke 14. 25. With this too accords Luke 13. 31–35, including the warning against Herod and our Lord's reply; as also the touching lamentation over Jerusalem, where Jesus was so soon to perish. With this agrees, further, the fact, that the narrative of Luke subsequent to the portion in question, viz., Luke 18. 15, sq., is parallel with that of Matthew and Mark during the same journey.[e]

Robinson, therefore, comes to the conclusion that Luke 13. 22, with the transactions and discourses of which it forms the nucleus, is to be referred mainly to a journey of our Lord through the populous region of Peræa, on His return to Bethany, after sojourning in Ephraim. There *may* also have been excursions from that city to the neighbouring villages of Judea, or even to the Jordan valley. This city Ephraim is considered by Robinson to be probably identical with Ephron and Ophrah of the Old Testament; and therefore apparently represented by the modern Taiyibeh, situated nearly twenty Roman miles N.N.E. of Jerusalem, and five or six Roman miles N.E. of Bethel, on the borders of the desert which stretches along on the west of the Dead Sea and the valley of Jordan.[f] It occupies a lofty site; and from it one overlooks the adjacent desert, the Jordan with its great valley, and the mountains of Peræa beyond, with the Saracenic castle er-Rŭbŭd, near 'Ajlûn, in the northern part of Peræa, bearing about N.E. Even at the present day the hardy and industrious mountaineers of this place have much intercourse with the valley, and till the rich fields and reap the harvests of Jericho.[g] It was therefore quite natural and easy for our Lord, from this point to cross the valley and the Jordan, and then turn His course towards Jericho and Jerusalem; while at the same time He exercised His ministry among the cities and villages along the valley and in the eastern region.

Robinson has therefore inserted the whole of Luke 13. 11–17. 10 after the mention of our Lord's sojourn at Ephraim, as belonging naturally to that period and to this return-journey through Peræa. And then it only remained to let Luke 17. 20–18. 14 follow directly afterwards; because there is no mark nor authority for placing it anywhere else; and because too it immediately precedes, and thus connects with, that portion of Luke which is subsequently parallel to Matthew and Mark. Not that it is intended by any means to assert that all the events and discourses of our Lord here given are recorded by Luke in their exact chronological order; for this portion of his Gospel presents very much the appearance of a collection of dis-

d See Opp. II. p. 39.   *e* See §§ 105–109.   *f* See Note on § 93.
g See *Bibl. Res. in Palest.* II., pp. 121 and 276.

courses and transactions in themselves disconnected. Yet, as there are no marks nor evidence, internal or external, by which to arrange them differently, it seems hardly advisable, on mere conjecture, to abandon the order in which they have been left to us by Luke himself.

If it be objected that this arrangement crowds too many incidents and discourses into this journey through Peræa, the reply is not difficult. Matthew and Mark confine their previous narratives chiefly to Galilee; and give comparatively little of what took place later in Peræa. Luke, besides recounting the like events in Galilee, has a large amount of matter peculiar to himself, without any definite notation of time and place; and it is therefore not unnatural to suppose that an important portion of it may relate to this last journey. Again, there is room for al-

lowing to this journey in Peræa an interval of time, amply sufficient for all these transactions, and indeed many more. If we assume that our Lord's first sojourn beyond Jordan, His return to Bethany, and the subsequent departure to Ephraim, occupied even two months (which is a large allowance), there still remained nearly two months before the passover, in which to make excursions from Ephraim, and also to traverse leisurely the distance through Peræa to Bethany, requiring in itself, at the utmost, not more than five days of travel. If now we compare the transactions thus spread out over these two months (or not improbably over a longer interval), with those recorded during the following six days next before the passover,[k] we shall hardly be impressed with the idea, that too much in proportion is thus allotted to this journey.

---

§ 83. Jesus at the Feast of Tabernacles. His Public Teaching.
Jerusalem.

John 7. 11-53; 8. 1.

[11] Then the Jews sought him at the feast,[i] and said, Where is he? [12] And there was much murmuring among the people concerning him: for some said, He is a good man: others said, Nay; but he deceiveth the people. [13] Howbeit no man spake openly of him for fear of the Jews.[j] [14] Now about the midst of the feast Jesus went up into the temple, and taught. [15] And the Jews marvelled, saying, How knoweth this man letters, having never learned?[k] [16] Jesus answered them, and said, My doctrine is not mine, but his that sent me. [17] If any man will do[l] his will, he shall know of the doctrine, whether it be of God, or *whether* I speak of myself. [18] He that speaketh of himself seeketh his own glory: but he that seeketh his glory that sent him, the same is true, and no unrighteousness is in him. [19] Did not Moses give you the law, and *yet* none of you keepeth the law? Why go ye about to kill me? [20] The people answered and said, Thou hast a devil: who goeth about to kill thee? [21] Jesus answered and said unto them, I have done one work, and ye all marvel. [22] Moses therefore gave unto you circumcision (not because it is of Moses, but of the fathers); and ye on the sabbath day circumcise a man.[m] [23] If a man on the sabbath day receive circumcision, that the law of Moses should not be broken; are ye angry at me, because I have made a man every whit whole on the sabbath day?[n] [24] Judge not according to the appearance, but judge righteous judgment.

[25] Then said some of them of Jerusalem, Is not this he whom they seek to kill? [26] But, lo, he speaketh boldly, and they say nothing unto him. Do the rulers know indeed that this is the very Christ? [27] Howbeit we know this man whence he is: but when Christ cometh, no man knoweth whence he is. [28] Then cried Jesus in the temple as he taught, saying, Ye both know me, and ye know whence I am: and I am not come of myself, but he that sent me is true, whom ye know not. [29] But I

---

k See Part VII.

i Jesus had now been absent from Jerusalem a year and six months, since His second passover.

j Acts 5. 13.

k Matt. 13. 54.

l *Will do* (θέλῃ ποιεῖν), better rendered *wish to do.*

m Lev. 12. 3.

n John 5. 5-9.

John 7

know him: for I am from him, and he hath sent me. 30 Then they sought to take
him: but no man laid hands on him, because his hour[o] was not yet come.
31 And many of the people believed on him, and said, When Christ cometh, will
he do more miracles than these which this *man* hath done? 32 The Pharisees heard
that the people murmured such things concerning him; and the Pharisees and the
chief priests sent officers to take him. 33 Then said Jesus unto them, Yet a little
while am I with you, and *then* I go unto him that sent me. 34 Ye shall seek me,
and shall not find *me:* and where I am, *thither* ye cannot come. 35 Then said the
Jews among themselves, Whither will he go, that we shall not find him? will he go
unto the dispersed among the Gentiles, and teach the Gentiles? 36 What *manner*
of saying is this that he said, Ye shall seek me, and shall not find *me:* and where I
am, *thither* ye cannot come?
37 In the last day, that great *day* of the feast,[p] Jesus stood and cried, saying, If
any man thirst, let him come unto me, and drink. 38 He that believeth on me, as
the Scripture hath said,[q] out of his belly shall flow rivers of living water. 39 (But
this spake he of the Spirit, which they that believe on him should receive: for the
Holy Ghost was not yet *given;*[r] because that Jesus was not yet glorified.) 40 Many
of the people therefore, when they heard this saying, said, Of a truth this is the
Prophet. 41 Others said, This is the Christ. But some said, Shall Christ come out
of Galilee? 42 Hath not the Scripture said, That Christ cometh of the seed of
David, and out of the town of Bethlehem, where David was?[s] 43 So there was a
division among the people because of him. 44 And some of them would have taken
him; but no man laid hands on him.
45 Then came the officers to the chief priests and Pharisees; and they said unto
them, Why have ye not brought him? 46 The officers answered, Never man spake
like this man. 47 Then answered them the Pharisees, Are ye also deceived? 48 Have
any of the rulers or of the Pharisees believed on him? 49 But this people who
knoweth not the law are cursed. 50 Nicodemus saith unto them, (he that came to
Jesus by night,[t] being one of them,) 51 Doth our law judge *any* man, before it hear
him,[u] and know what he doeth? 52 They answered and said unto him, Art thou
also of Galilee? Search, and look: for out of Galilee ariseth no prophet.
53 And every man went unto his own house. **8.** 1 Jesus went unto the mount of
Olives.

§ 84. THE WOMAN TAKEN IN ADULTERY.—*Jerusalem.*

John 8. 2–11. 2 And early in the morning he came again into the temple, and
all the people came unto him; and he sat down, and taught them. 3 And the
scribes and Pharisees brought unto him a woman taken in adultery; and when they
had set her in the midst, 4 they say unto him, Master, this woman was taken in
adultery, in the very act. 5 Now Moses in the law commanded us, that such should
be stoned:[v] but what sayest thou? 6 This they said, tempting him, that they
might have to accuse him. But Jesus stooped down, and with *his* finger wrote on
the ground, *as though he heard them not.* 7 So when they continued asking him,
he lifted up himself, and said unto them, He that is without sin among you, let him
first cast a stone at her. 8 And again he stooped down, and wrote on the ground.
9 And they which heard *it*, being convicted by *their own* conscience, went out one

---

[o] *His hour*, that is, to suffer and die, John 13. 1.

[p] On the last, the eighth, day of the feast of tabernacles, it was the custom to fetch water from the well of Siloam to be poured on the altar, in the midst of music and loud rejoicings; singing the words (Isa. 12. 3), "With joy shall ye draw water out of the wells of salvation."

[q] Isa. 55. 1; 58. 11. Comp. Isa. 44. 3 Zech. 13. 1; 14. 8.

[r] Comp. Acts 2. 33.

[s] Comp. Psa. 89. 4; 132. 11; Mic. 5. 2.

[t] John 3. 2.

[u] Comp. Deut 19. 16–19.

[v] Lev. 20. 10. Comp. Deut. 22. 21–24.

John 8.

by one, beginning at the eldest, *even* unto the last: and Jesus was left alone, and the woman standing in the midst. [10] When Jesus had lifted up himself, and saw none but the woman, he said unto her, Woman, where are those thine accusers? hath no man condemned thee? She said, No man, Lord. [11] And Jesus said unto her, Neither do I condemn thee: go, and sin no more.

§ 85. FURTHER PUBLIC TEACHING OF OUR LORD. HE REPROVES THE UN-BELIEVING JEWS, AND ESCAPES FROM THEIR HANDS.—*Jerusalem.*

John 8. 12–59. [12] Then spake Jesus again unto them, saying, I am the light of the world: he that followeth me shall not walk in darkness, but shall have the light of life. [13] The Pharisees therefore said unto him, Thou bearest record of thyself; thy record is not true. [14] Jesus answered and said unto them, Though I bear record of myself, *yet* my record is true: for I know whence I came, and whither I go; but ye cannot tell whence I come, and whither I go. [15] Ye judge after the flesh; I judge no man. [16] And yet if I judge, my judgment is true: for I am not alone, but I and the Father that sent me. [17] It is also written in your law,[w] that the testimony of two men is true. [18] I am one that bear witness of myself, and the Father that sent me beareth witness of me. [19] Then said they unto him, Where is thy Father? Jesus answered, Ye neither know me, nor my Father: if ye had known me, ye should have known my Father also. [20] These words spake Jesus in the treasury,[x] as he taught in the temple: and no man laid hands on him; for his hour was not yet come.

[21] Then said Jesus again unto them, I go my way, and ye shall seek me, and shall die in your sins: whither I go, ye cannot come. [22] Then said the Jews, Will he kill himself? because he saith, Whither I go, ye cannot come. [23] And he said unto them, Ye are from beneath; I am from above: ye are of this world; I am not of this world. [24] I said therefore unto you, that ye shall die in your sins: for if ye believe not that I am *he*, ye shall die in your sins. [25] Then said they unto him, Who art thou? And Jesus saith unto them, Even *the same* that I said unto you from the beginning. [26] I have many things to say and to judge of you: but he that sent me is true: and I speak to the world those things which I have heard of him. [27] They understood not that he spake to them of the Father. [28] Then said Jesus unto them, When ye have lifted up[y] the Son of man, then shall ye know that I am *he*, and *that* I do nothing of myself; but as my Father hath taught me, I speak these things. [29] And he that sent me is with me: the Father hath not left me alone; for I do always those things that please him.

[30] As he spake these words, many believed on him. [31] Then said Jesus to those Jews which believed on him, If ye continue in my word, *then* are ye my disciples indeed; [32] and ye shall know the truth, and the truth shall make you free.[z] [33] They answered him, We be Abraham's seed, and were never in bondage to any man: how sayest thou, Ye shall be made free? [34] Jesus answered them, Verily, verily, I say unto you, Whosoever committeth sin is the servant of sin. [35] And the servant abideth not in the house for ever: *but* the Son abideth ever. [36] If the Son therefore shall make you free, ye shall be free indeed.[a] [37] I know that ye are Abraham's seed; but ye seek to kill me, because my word hath no place in you. [38] I speak that which I have seen with my Father: and ye do that which ye have seen with your father. [39] They answered and said unto him, Abraham is our father.

---

[w] Deut. 17. 6. Comp. Deut. 19. 15.

[x] *The treasury* of the temple was in the court of the women, where thirteen large boxes stood for receiving the free-will offerings of the people. These receptacles were called "trumpets," because the openings into them were trumpet-like tubes, wide at the one end and narrow at the other.

[y] Comp. John 3. 14. [z] Rom. 6. 14, 18, 22.

[a] Rom. 8. 2; Gal. 5. 1.

John 8.

Jesus saith unto them, If ye were Abraham's children, ye would do the works of Abraham. [40] But now ye seek to kill me, a man that hath told you the truth, which I have heard of God: this did not Abraham. [41] Ye do the deeds of your father. Then said they to him, We be not born of fornication; we have one Father, *even* God. [42] Jesus said unto them, If God were your Father, ye would love me: for I proceeded forth and came from God; neither came I of myself, but he sent me. [43] Why do ye not understand my speech? *even* because ye cannot hear my word. [44] Ye are of *your* father the devil, and the lusts of your father ye will do. He was a murderer [b] from the beginning, and abode not in the truth, because there is no truth in him. When he speaketh a lie, he speaketh of his own: for he is a liar, and the father of it.[c] [45] And because I tell *you* the truth, ye believe me not. [46] Which of you convinceth me of sin? And if I say the truth, why do ye not believe me? [47] He that is of God heareth God's words:[d] ye therefore hear *them* not, because ye are not of God. [48] Then answered the Jews, and said unto him, Say we not well that thou art a Samaritan, and hast a devil? [49] Jesus answered, I have not a devil; but I honour my Father, and ye do dishonour me. [50] And I seek not mine own glory: there is one that seeketh and judgeth. [51] Verily, verily, I say unto you, If a man keep my saying, he shall never see death. [52] Then said the Jews unto him, Now we know that thou hast a devil. Abraham is dead, and the prophets; and thou sayest, If a man keep my saying, he shall never taste of death. [53] Art thou greater than our father Abraham, which is dead, and the prophets are dead: whom makest thou thyself? [54] Jesus answered, If I honour myself, my honour is nothing: it is my Father that honoureth me; of whom ye say, that he is your God: [55] yet ye have not known him; but I know him: and if I should say, I know him not, I shall be a liar like unto you: but I know him, and keep his saying. [56] Your father Abraham rejoiced to see my day: and he saw *it*, and was glad.[e] [57] Then said the Jews unto him, Thou art not yet fifty years old, and hast thou seen Abraham? [58] Jesus said unto them, Verily, verily, I say unto you, Before Abraham was, I am. [59] Then took they up stones to cast at him: but Jesus hid himself, and went out of the temple, going through the midst of them, and so passed by.[f]

§ 86. A LAWYER INSTRUCTED. LOVE TO OUR NEIGHBOUR DEFINED. PARABLE OF THE GOOD SAMARITAN.—*Near Jerusalem.*

Luke 10. 25–37. [25] And, behold,[g] a certain lawyer stood up, and tempted him, saying, Master, what shall I do to inherit eternal life? [26] He said unto him, What is written in the law? how readest thou? [27] And he answering said,[h] Thou shalt love the Lord thy God with all thy heart, and with all thy soul, and with all thy strength, and with all thy mind; and thy neighbour as thyself. [28] And he said unto him, Thou hast answered right: this do, and thou shalt live.

[29] But he, willing to justify himself,[i] said unto Jesus, And who is my neighbour? [30] And Jesus answering said, A certain *man* went down from Jerusalem to Jericho, and fell among thieves, which stripped him of his raiment, and wounded *him*, and

---

[b] Gen. 3. 4, 5; 1 John 3. 8.
[c] Comp. Acts 5. 3.   [d] 1 John 4. 6.
[e] Gal. 3. 8; Rom. 4. 18–22; Heb. 11. 13.
[f] See in § 90.
[g] Our Lord had left the temple, and apparently the city, John 8. 59. The healing of the blind man (ch. 9. 1–12) occurred later: see Note * on p. 90. While thus absent from the city, and yet in its vicinity, Jesus visits Bethany [see § 87] and is received by

Martha and Mary. That visit is placed by Luke in immediate connexion with the incident of the lawyer and the parable of the Good Samaritan; which therefore are inserted here. The scene of that parable also implies that it was spoken in the vicinity of Jerusalem and Bethany.
[h] Deut. 6. 5; Lev. 19. 18.   Comp. Lev. 18. 5.
[i] Rom. 10. 3

Luke 10.

departed, leaving *him* half dead. 31 And by chance there came down a certain
priest that way: and when he saw him, he passed by on the other side. 32 And
likewise a Levite, when he was at the place, came and looked *on him*, and passed
by on the other side. 33 But a certain Samaritan, as he journeyed, came where he
was: and when he saw him, he had compassion *on him*, and went to *him*, 34 and
bound up his wounds, pouring in oil and wine,[j] and set him on his own beast, and
brought him to an inn, and took care of him. 35 And on the morrow when he
departed, he took out two pence, and gave *them* to the host, and said unto him,
Take care of him; and whatsoever thou spendest more, when I come again, I will
repay thee. 36 Which now of these three, thinkest thou, was neighbour unto him
that fell among the thieves? 37 And he said, He that showed mercy on him. Then
said Jesus unto him, Go, and do thou likewise.

§ 87. Jesus in the House of Martha and Mary.—*Bethany.*

Luke 10. 38–42. 38 Now it came to pass, as they went, that he entered into a
certain village:[k] and a certain woman named Martha[l] received him into her house.
39 And she had a sister called Mary, which also sat at Jesus' feet, and heard his
word. 40 But Martha was cumbered about much serving, and came to him, and
said, Lord, dost thou not care that my sister hath left me to serve alone? bid her
therefore that she help me. 41 And Jesus answered and said unto her, Martha,
Martha, thou art careful and troubled about many things: 42 but one thing is
needful:[m] and Mary hath chosen that good part, which shall not be taken away
from her.[n]

§ 88. The Disciples again[o] taught how to Pray.—*Near Jerusalem.*

Luke 11. 1–13. 1 And it came to pass, that, as he was praying in a certain
place, when he ceased, one of his disciples said unto him, Lord, teach us to pray, as
John also taught his disciples. 2 And he said unto them,[p] When ye pray, say,[q] Our
Father which art in heaven, Hallowed be thy name. Thy kingdom come. Thy
will be done, as in heaven, so in earth. 3 Give us day by day our daily bread.
4 And forgive us our sins; for we also forgive every one that is indebted to us. And
lead us not into temptation; but deliver us from evil.
5 And he said unto them, Which of you shall have a friend, and shall go unto
him at midnight, and say unto him, Friend, lend me three loaves; 6 for a friend
of mine in his journey is come to me, and I have nothing to set before him? 7 And
he from within shall answer and say, Trouble me not: the door is now shut, and
my children are with me in bed; I cannot rise and give thee. 8 I say unto you,
Though he will not rise and give him, because he is his friend, yet because of his
importunity he will rise and give him as many as he needeth. 9 And I say unto
you,[r] Ask, and it shall be given you; seek, and ye shall find; knock, and it shall be
opened unto you. 10 For every one that asketh receiveth; and he that seeketh
findeth; and to him that knocketh it shall be opened. 11 If a son shall ask bread
of any of you that is a father, will he give him a stone? or if *he ask* a fish, will he

---

[j] *Olive oil* mixed with *wine* was, and still is, a means of healing in the East, Isa. 1. 6.

[k] Greswell (Dissert. xvii. vol. ii.), holding the strict chronological order of Luke's narrative, maintains that this village was not Bethany near Jerusalem, but some unknown place in Galilee.

[l] John 11. 1; 12. 1–3.

[m] Matt. 6. 33; John 17. 3.

[n] Psa. 73. 24–26; John 4. 14.

[o] See § 41.

[p] Jesus repeats on this occasion the same model-form of prayer taught in the sermon on the mount, § 41. Luke's order is here retained; as there is no evidence by which to assign any other.

[q] Comp. Matt. 6. 9–13.

[r] Comp. Matt. 7. 7–11.

Luke 11.

for a fish give him a serpent? [12] Or if he shall ask an egg, will he offer him a scorpion? [13] If ye then, being evil, know how to give good gifts unto your children: how much more will *your* heavenly Father give the Holy Spirit to them that ask him?

§ 89. THE SEVENTY RETURN.ᵃ—*Jerusalem?*

Luke 10. 17-24. [17] And the seventy returnedᵗ again with joy, saying, Lord, even the devils are subject unto us through thy name. [18] And he said unto them, I beheld Satan as lightning fall from heaven. [19] Behold, I give unto you power to tread on serpents and scorpions, and over all the power of the enemy: and nothing shall by any means hurt you. [20] Notwithstanding in this rejoice not, that the spirits are subject unto you; but rather rejoice, because your names are writtenᵘ in heaven.

[21] In that hour Jesus rejoiced in spirit, and said, I thank thee, O Father, Lord of heaven and earth, that thou hast hid these things from the wise and prudent, and hast revealed them unto babes: even so, Father; for so it seemed good in thy sight. [22] All things are delivered to me of my Father: and no man knoweth who the Son is, but the Father; and who the Father is, but the Son, and *he* to whom the Son will reveal *him*. [23] And he turned him unto *his* disciples, and said privately, Blessed *are* the eyes which see the things that ye see: [24] for I tell you, that many prophets and kings have desired to see those things which ye see, and have not seen *them;* and to hear those things which ye hear, and have not heard *them*.ᵛ

§ 90. A MAN BORN BLIND IS HEALED ON THE SABBATH. OUR LORD'S SUBSEQUENT DISCOURSES.—*Jerusalem.*

John 9. 1-41; 10. 1-21. [1] And as *Jesus* passed by, he saw a man which was blind from *his* birth.ʷ [2] And his disciples asked him, saying, Master, who did sin, this man, or his parents, that he was born blind? [3] Jesus answered, Neither hath this man sinned, nor his parents: but that the works of God should be made manifest in him. [4] I must work the works of him that sent me, while it is day: the night cometh, when no man can work. [5] As long as I am in the world, I am the light of the world. [6] When he had thus spoken, he spat on the ground, and made clay of the spittle, and he anointed the eyes of the blind man with the clay, [7] and said unto him, Go, washˣ in the pool of Siloam,ʸ (which is by interpretation Sent). He went his way therefore, and washed, and came seeing. [8] The neighbours therefore, and they which before had seen him that he was blind, said, Is not

---

* See § 81.
ᵗ Luke relates the return of the Seventy in immediate connexion with their appointment (Luke 10. 1-16), evidently by anticipation. Their appointment [see § 81] appears to have taken place in Samaria; and they went forth, probably into Samaria, Peræa, and elsewhere, while He proceeded to Jerusalem. Their return to Him, at or near Jerusalem, is therefore here placed as late as may be before the festival of dedication.

ᵘ Comp. Ex. 32. 32; Phil. 4. 3; Rev. 3. 5.
ᵛ See in § 86.
ʷ The discourse in John 10. 1, sq., stands in immediate connexion with the healing of the blind man: see ch. 9. 40. And in the words of our Lord, John 10. 26, spoken at

the festival of dedication, there is a direct allusion to the figurative representation of the shepherd and his sheep in the same discourse. This implies that the same audience was then present, at least in part; and consequently, that the discourse in question had been delivered not long before. For these reasons the healing of the blind man would seem also to have taken place near the beginning of the festival of dedication, or at least not long before.

ˣ Comp. 2 Kings 5. 14.

ʸ *Siloam:* a fountain (with a large basin forming a *pool*) near the walls of Jerusalem on the east, between the city and the brook Kidron.

John 9.

this he that sat and begged ?   ⁹ Some said, This is he : others *said*, He is like him : *but* he said, I am *he*.   ¹⁰ Therefore said they unto him, How were thine eyes opened ?   ¹¹ He answered and said, A man that is called Jesus made clay, and anointed mine eyes, and said unto me, Go to the pool of Siloam, and wash : and I went and washed, and I received sight.   ¹² Then said they unto him, Where is he ?   He said, I know not.

¹³ They brought to the Pharisees him that aforetime was blind.   ¹⁴ And it was the sabbath day when Jesus made the clay, and opened his eyes.   ¹⁵ Then again the Pharisees also asked him how he had received his sight.   He said unto them, He put clay upon mine eyes, and I washed, and do see.   ¹⁶ Therefore said some of the Pharisees, This man is not of God, because he keepeth not the sabbath day. Others said, How can a man that is a sinner do such miracles ?*a*   And there was a division among them.   ¹⁷ They say unto the blind man again, What sayest thou of him, that he hath opened thine eyes ?   He said, He is a prophet.*a*   ¹⁸ But the Jews did not believe concerning him, that he had been blind, and received his sight, until they called the parents of him that had received his sight.   ¹⁹ And they asked them, saying, Is this your son, who ye say was born blind ? how then doth he now see ?   ²⁰ His parents answered them and said, We know that this is our son, and that he was born blind :   ²¹ but by what means he now seeth, we know not ; or who hath opened his eyes, we know not : he is of age ; ask him : he shall speak for himself.   ²² These *words* spake his parents, because they feared the Jews : for the Jews had agreed already, that if any man did confess that he was Christ, he should be put out of the synagogue.   ²³ Therefore said his parents, He is of age ; ask him.

²⁴ Then again called they the man that was blind, and said unto him, Give God the praise :*b* we know that this man is a sinner.   ²⁵ He answered and said, Whether he be a sinner *or no*, I know not : one thing I know, that, whereas I was blind, now I see.   ²⁶ Then said they to him again, What did he to thee ? how opened he thine eyes ?   ²⁷ He answered them, I have told you already, and ye did not hear ; wherefore would ye hear *it* again ? will ye also be his disciples ?   ²⁸ Then they reviled him, and said, Thou art his disciple ; but we are Moses' disciples.   ²⁹ We know that God spake unto Moses : *as for* this *fellow*, we know not from whence he is.   ³⁰ The man answered and said unto them, Why herein is a marvellous thing, that ye know not from whence he is, and *yet* he hath opened mine eyes.   ³¹ Now we know that God heareth not sinners :*c* but if any man be a worshipper of God, and doeth his will, him he heareth.   ³² Since the world began was it not heard that any man opened the eyes of one that was born blind.   ³³ If this man were not of God, he could do nothing.   ³⁴ They answered and said unto him, Thou wast altogether born in sins, and dost thou teach us ?   And they cast him out.

³⁵ Jesus heard that they had cast him out ; and when he had found him, he said unto him, Dost thou believe on the Son of God ?   ³⁶ He answered and said, Who is he, Lord, that I might believe on him ?   ³⁷ And Jesus said unto him, Thou hast both seen him, and it is he that talketh with thee.   ³⁸ And he said, Lord, I believe. And he worshipped him.   ³⁹ And Jesus said, For judgment I am come into this world, that they which see not might see ; and that they which see might be made blind.*d*   ⁴⁰ And *some* of the Pharisees which were with him heard these words, and said unto him, Are we blind also ?   ⁴¹ And Jesus said unto them, If ye were blind ye should have no sin :*e* but now ye say, We see ; therefore your sin remaineth.

---

* John 3. 2.
a John 3. 2 ; 4. 19.
b *Give God the praise*, rather (δὸς δόξαν τῷ Θεῷ) *Give glory to God*, meaning that he should glorify God, not for the miracle, but by telling the truth : it was a way of putting him on his oath : see Josh. 7. 19
c Comp. Prov. 28. 9 ; Isa. 1. 15.
d Isa. 6. 9, 10 ; Matt. 13. 13.
e John 15. 22–24.

John 10.

John 10. [1] Verily, verily, I say unto you, He that entereth not by the door into the sheepfold, but climbeth up some other way, the same is a thief and a robber. [2] But he that entereth in by the door is the shepherd of the sheep. [3] To him the porter openeth; and the sheep hear his voice: and he calleth his own sheep by name, and leadeth them out. [4] And when he putteth forth his own sheep, he goeth before them, and the sheep follow him: for they know his voice. [5] And a stranger will they not follow, but will flee from him: for they know not the voice of strangers. [6] This parable spake Jesus unto them: but they understood not what things they were which he spake unto them.

[7] Then said Jesus unto them again, Verily, verily, I say unto you, I am the door of the sheep. [8] All that ever came before me are thieves and robbers: but the sheep did not hear them. [9] I am the door: *f* by me if any man enter in, he shall be saved, and shall go in and out, and find pasture. [10] The thief cometh not, but for to steal, and to kill, and to destroy: I am come that they might have life, and that they might have *it* more abundantly.*g* [11] I am the good shepherd: the good shepherd giveth his life for the sheep. [12] But he that is an hireling, and not the shepherd, whose own the sheep are not, seeth the wolf coming, and leaveth the sheep, and fleeth:*h* and the wolf catcheth them, and scattereth the sheep. [13] The hireling fleeth, because he is an hireling, and careth not for the sheep. [14] I am the good shepherd, and know my *sheep,i* and am known of mine. [15] As the Father knoweth me, even so know I the Father: and I lay down my life for the sheep. [16] And other sheep I have,*j* which are not of this fold: them also I must bring, and they shall hear my voice; and there shall be one fold,*k and* one shepherd. [17] Therefore doth my Father love me, because I lay down my life, that I might take it again. [18] No man taketh it from me, but I lay it down of myself. I have power to lay it down, and I have power to take it again. This commandment have I received of my Father.

[19] There was a division therefore again among the Jews for these sayings. [20] And many of them said, He hath a devil, and is mad; why hear ye him? [21] Others said, These are not the words of him that hath a devil. Can a devil open the eyes of the blind?*l*

§ 91. JESUS IN JERUSALEM AT THE FESTIVAL OF DEDICATION. HE RETIRES BEYOND JORDAN.—*Jerusalem. Bethabara beyond Jordan.*

John 10. 22–42. [22] And it was at Jerusalem the feast of the dedication,*m* and it was winter. [23] And Jesus walked in the temple in Solomon's porch. [24] Then

---

f John 14. 6; Eph. 2. 18.
g 2 Tim. 1. 10.   *h* Comp. Ez. 34. 3–8.
i 2 Tim. 2. 19.   *j* Comp. Isa. 56. 8.

k One fold: this should be translated *one flock;* the Greek word being ποίμνη, a flock, and not αὐλή, a fold, as in the previous part of the verse. The meaning appears to be this, I have other sheep, not Jews, but among the nations (Gentiles); and there shall be one flock, namely, of true believers, from among both Jews and other nations. Eph. 2. 14–19.

l John 9. 31–33.

m The festival of Dedication (τα ἐγκαινια, *the renewal*) was instituted by Judas Maccabæus to commemorate the purification of the temple and the *renewal* of the temple-worship, after the three years' profanation

by Antiochus Epiphanes. It was held during eight days, commencing on the 25th day of the month Kislev, which began with the new moon of December. See 1 Macc. 4. 52–59; 2 Macc. 10. 5–8. Josephus calls it φῶτα, i.e., festival of *lights* or lanterns, and speaks of it as a season of rejoicing; *Antiq.* 12. 7. 6, 7. It was celebrated by the Jews, not at Jerusalem alone, like the great festivals of the law; but at home, throughout the whole country, by the festive illumination of their dwellings: see Lightfoot, *Hor. Heb.* in Joh. 10. 22.—According to John's narrative, Jesus was now at Jerusalem, not because the Jews were accustomed to go up thither at this festival, but because He had remained in the vicinity since the festival of tabernacles: see Introd. Note to this Part, p. 82.

John 10.

came the Jews round about him, and said unto him, How long dost thou make us to doubt? If thou be the Christ, tell us plainly. ²⁵ Jesus answered them, I told you, and ye believed not: the works that I do in my Father's name, they bear witness of me. ²⁶ But ye believe not, because ye are not of my sheep, as I said unto you. ²⁷ My sheep hear my voice, and I know them, and they follow me: ²⁸ and I give unto them eternal life; and they shall never perish, neither shall any *man* pluck them out of my hand. ²⁹ My Father, which gave *them* me, is greater than all; and no *man* is able to pluck *them* out of my Father's hand. ³⁰ I and *my* Father are one. ³¹ Then the Jews took up stones again to stone him. ³² Jesus answered them, Many good works have I showed you from my Father; for which of those works do ye stone me? ³³ The Jews answered him, saying, For a good work we stone thee not: but for blasphemy; and because that thou, being a man, makest thyself God. ³⁴ Jesus answered them, Is it not written in your law,ⁿ I said, Ye are gods? ³⁵ If he called them gods, unto whom the word of God came, and the Scripture cannot be broken; ³⁶ say ye of him whom the Father hath sanctified, and sent into the world, Thou blasphemest; because I said, I am the Son of God? ³⁷ If I do not the works of my Father, believe me not. ³⁸ But if I do, though ye believe not me, believe the works: that ye may know, and believe, that the Father *is* in me, and I in him. ³⁹ Therefore they sought again to take him:ᵒ but he escaped out of their hand,

⁴⁰ And went away again beyond Jordan into the placeᵖ where John at first baptized; and there he abode. ⁴¹ And many resorted unto him, and said, John did no miracle: but all things that John spake of this man were true. ⁴² And many believed on him there.

§ 92. The Raising of Lazarus.—*Bethany.*

John 11. 1-46. ¹ Now a certain *man* was sick, *named* Lazarus, of Bethany, the town of Mary and her sister Martha. ² (It was *that* Mary which anointed ᵠ the Lord with ointment, and wiped his feet with her hair, whose brother Lazarus was sick.) ³ Therefore his sisters sent unto him, saying, Lord, behold, he whom thou lovest is sick. ⁴ When Jesus heard *that*, he said, This sickness is not unto death, but for the glory of God, that the Son of God might be glorified thereby. ⁵ Now Jesus loved Martha, and her sister, and Lazarus.

⁶ When he had heard therefore that he was sick, he abode two days still in the same place where he was. ⁷ Then after that saith he to *his* disciples, Let us go into Judea again. ⁸ *His* disciples say unto him, Master, the Jews of late sought to stone thee: and goest thou thither again. ⁹ Jesus answered, Are there not twelves hour in the day? If any man walk in the day, he stumbleth not, because he seeth the light of this world. ¹⁰ But if a man walk in the night, he stumbleth, because there is no light in him. ¹¹ These things said he: and after that he saith unto them, Our friend Lazarus sleepeth; but I go, that I may awake him out of sleep. ¹² Then said his disciples, Lord, if he sleep, he shall do well. ¹³ Howbeit Jesus spake of his death: but they thought that he had spoken of taking of rest in sleep. ¹⁴ Then said Jesus unto them plainly, Lazarus is dead. ¹⁵ And I am glad for your sakes that I was not there, to the intent ye may believe; nevertheless let us go unto him. ¹⁶ Then said Thomas, which is called Didymus, unto his fellow-disciples, Let us also go, that we may die with him.

ⁿ Psa. 82. 6. Comp. Ex. 22. 28.

ᵒ Comp. John 8. 59.

ᵖ This place was Bethabara; see John 1. 28. On our Lord's stay here, and also the probable length of it, see Introd. Note to this Part, p. 84.

ᵠ *Which anointed:* i.e., who was known as having done this, from the other Gospels, and the oral information of the apostles and evangelists (see Matt. 26. 13), though John himself does not relate the transaction till the 12th chapter: see § 131.

John 11.

[17] Then when Jesus came, he found that he had *lain* in the grave four days already. [18] Now Bethany was nigh unto Jerusalem, about fifteen furlongs[r] off: [19] and many of the Jews came to Martha and Mary, to comfort them concerning their brother. [20] Then Martha, as soon as she heard that Jesus was coming, went and met him, but Mary sat *still* in the house. [21] Then said Martha unto Jesus, Lord, if thou hadst been here, my brother had not died. [22] But I know, that even now, whatsoever thou wilt ask of God, God will give *it* thee. [23] Jesus said unto her, Thy brother shall rise again. [24] Martha saith unto him, I know[s] that he shall rise again in the resurrection at the last day. [25] Jesus said unto her, I am the resurrection, and the life:[t] he that believeth in me, though he were dead, yet shall he live: [26] and whosoever liveth and believeth in me shall never die. Believest thou this? [27] She saith unto him, Yea, Lord: I believe that thou art the Christ, the Son of God, which should come into the world.

[28] And when she had so said, she went her way, and called Mary her sister secretly, saying, The Master is come, and calleth for thee. [29] As soon as she heard *that*, she arose quickly, and came unto him. [30] Now Jesus was not yet come into the town, but was in that place where Martha met him. [31] The Jews then which were with her in the house, and comforted her, when they saw Mary, that she rose up hastily and went out, followed her, saying, She goeth unto the grave to weep there. [32] Then when Mary was come where Jesus was, and saw him, she fell down at his feet, saying unto him, Lord, if thou hadst been here, my brother had not died. [33] When Jesus therefore saw her weeping, and the Jews also weeping which came with her, he groaned in the spirit,[u] and was troubled, [34] and said, Where have ye laid him? They said unto him, Lord, come and see. [35] Jesus wept. [36] Then said the Jews, Behold how he loved him! [37] And some of them said, Could not this man, which opened the eyes of the blind,[v] have caused that even this man should not have died?

[38] Jesus therefore again groaning in himself cometh to the grave. It was a cave, and a stone lay upon it. [39] Jesus said, Take ye away the stone. Martha, the sister of him that was dead, saith unto him, Lord, by this time he stinketh: for he hath been *dead* four days. [40] Jesus saith unto her, Said I not unto thee, that, if thou wouldest believe, thou shouldest see the glory of God? [41] Then they took away the stone *from the place* where the dead was laid. And Jesus lifted up *his* eyes, and said, Father, I thank thee that thou hast heard me. [42] And I knew that thou hearest me always: but because of the people which stand by I said *it*, that they may believe that thou hast sent me. [43] And when he thus had spoken, he cried with a loud voice, Lazarus, come forth. [44] And he that was dead came forth, bound hand and foot with graveclothes: and his face was bound about with a napkin. Jesus saith unto them, Loose him, and let him go.

[45] Then many of the Jews which came to Mary, and had seen the things which Jesus did, believed on him. [46] But some of them went their ways to the Pharisees, and told them what things Jesus had done.

§ 93. The Counsel of Caiaphas against Jesus. He retires from Jerusalem.—*Jerusalem. Ephraim.*

John 11. 47–54. [47] Then gathered the chief priests and the Pharisees a council, and said, What do we? for this man doeth many miracles. [48] If we let him thus alone, all *men* will believe on him: and the Romans shall come and take away both our place and nation. [49] And one of them, *named* Caiaphas,[w] being the high priest

---

[r] *About fifteen furlongs* (στάδιοι), i.e., about two miles.
[s] Comp. Dan. 12. 2.   [t] 1 Cor. 15. 20–22.

[u] Comp. Mark 7. 34; 8. 12.
[v] John, ch. 9.
[w] John 18. 14; Acts 4. 6.

John 11.

that same year, said unto them, Ye know nothing at all, ⁵⁰ nor consider that it is expedient for us, that one man should die for the people, and that the whole nation perish not. ⁵¹ And this spake he not of himself: but being high priest that year * he prophesied that Jesus should die for that nation; ⁵² and not for that nation only, but that also he should gather together in one the children of God that were scattered abroad. ⁵³ Then from that day forth they took counsel together for to put him to death.

⁵⁴ Jesus therefore walked no more openly among the Jews; but went thence unto a country near to the wilderness, into a city called Ephraim,ᵛ and there continued with his disciples.ᶻ

§ 94. Jesus beyond Jordan is followed by Multitudes. The Healing of the Infirm Woman on the Sabbath.—*Valley of Jordan. Perœa.*

Matt. 19. 1, 2. ¹ And it came to pass, *that* when Jesus had finished these sayings, **he** departed from Galilee, and came into' the coasts of Judea beyond Jordan;ᵃ ²and great multitudes followed him ; and he healed them there.

Mark 10. 1. ¹ And he arose from thence, and cometh into the coasts of Judea by the farther side of Jordan: and the people resort unto him again ; and, as he was wont, he taught them again.ᵇ

Luke 13. 10-21. ¹⁰ And he was teaching in one of the synagogues on the sabbath. ¹¹ And, behold, there **was a woman** which had a spirit of infirmity eighteen years, and was bowed together, and could in no wise lift up *herself.* ¹² And when Jesus saw her, he called *her to him,* and said unto her, Woman, thou art loosed from thine infirmity. ¹³ And he laid *his* hands on her: and immediately she was made straight, and glorified God. ¹⁴ And the ruler of the synagogue answered with indignation, because that Jesus had healed on the sabbath ᴅᴀy, and said unto the people, There are six days in which men ought to work: in them therefore come and be healed, and not on the sabbath day. ¹⁵ The Lord then answered him, and said, *Thou* hypocrite, doth not each one of you on the sabbath loose his ox or *his* ass from the stall, and lead *him* away to watering ? ¹⁶ And ought not this woman, being a daughter of Abraham, whom Satan hath bound,ᶜ lo, these eighteen years, be loosed from this bond on the sabbath day ? ¹⁷ And when he had said these things, all his adversaries were ashamed: and all the people rejoiced for all the glorious things that were done by him.

¹⁸ Then said he, Unto what is the kingdom of God like ? and whereunto shall I resemble it ? ¹⁹ It is like a grain of mustard seed,ᵈ which a man took, and cast into

---

ˣ Comp. Num. ch. 23.

ᵛ As the Sanhedrim had now determined, in accordance with the counsel of Caiaphas, that Jesus should be put to death, He therefore withdrew from Jerusalem into a city called Ephraim, "near to the wilderness," John 11. 54. This place has only recently been identified with any modern site. There is, however, little reason to doubt, that it was the same with the Ephraim or Ephron of 2 Chron. 13. 19, and also with the Ephron of Eusebius and Jerome, nearly twenty Roman miles north of Jerusalem. It lay also near the desert, and corresponds therefore in all these particulars with the modern *Taiyibeh,* a most remarkable and commanding site. See Robinson's *Bibl. Res. in Palest.* II. pp. 121-124.

ᶻ See in § 111.

ᵃ Matthew and Mark, having omitted all mention of our Lord's presence and teaching in Jerusalem at the festivals of Tabernacles and of Dedication, as likewise of the raising of Lazarus and other intervening events, now resume their narrative, by relating, that after Jesus had left Galilee He approached Jerusalem, as the Passover drew nigh, by passing through the country beyond Jordan.

Luke 13. 10-21 is inserted here because it immediately precedes, and is thus connected with, the notice of our Lord's journeying towards Jerusalem in Luke 13. 22.

ᵇ See in § 104.

ᶜ Heb. 2. 14.

ᵈ Matt. 13. 31, 32.

Luke 13.

his garden; and it grew, and waxed a great tree; and the fowls of the air lodged in the branches of it.   **20** And again he said, Whereunto shall I liken the kingdom of God?   **21** It is like leaven,[c] which a woman took and hid in three measures of meal, till the whole was leavened.

§ 95. JESUS GOING TOWARDS JERUSALEM IS WARNED AGAINST HEROD.
Peræa.

Luke 13. 22–35.   **22** And he went[f] through the cities and villages, teaching, and journeying toward Jerusalem.   **23** Then said one unto him, Lord, are there few that be saved?   And he said unto them,   **24** Strive to enter in at the strait gate: for many, I say unto you, will seek to enter in, and shall not be able.[g]   **25** When once the master of the house is risen up, and hath shut to the door, and ye begin to stand without, and to knock at the door, saying, Lord, Lord, open unto us; and he shall answer and say unto you, I know you not whence ye are: **26** Then shall ye begin to say, We have eaten and drunk in thy presence, and thou hast taught in our streets.   **27** But he shall say, I tell you, I know you not whence ye are; depart from me, all *ye* workers of iniquity.   **28** There shall be weeping and gnashing of teeth,[h] when ye shall see Abraham, and Isaac, and Jacob, and all the prophets, in the kingdom of God, and you *yourselves* thrust out.   **29** And they shall come from the east, and *from* the west, and from the north, and *from* the south, and shall sit down in the kingdom of God.   **30** And, behold, there are last which shall be first, and there are first which shall be last.

31 The same day there came certain of the Pharisees, saying unto him, Get thee out, and depart hence: for Herod will kill thee.   **32** And he said unto them, Go ye and tell that fox, Behold, I cast out devils, and I do cures to-day and to-morrow, and the third *day* I shall be perfected.   **33** Nevertheless I must walk to-day, and to-morrow, and the *day* following:[f] for it cannot be that a prophet perish out of Jerusalem.   **34** O Jerusalem, Jerusalem,[j] which killest the prophets, and stonest them that are sent unto thee; how often would I have gathered thy children together, as a hen *doth gather* her brood under *her* wings, and ye would not!   **35** Behold, your house is left unto you desolate: and verily I say unto you, Ye shall not see me, until *the time* come when ye shall say,[k] Blessed *is* he that cometh in the name of the Lord.[l]

§ 96. OUR LORD DINES WITH A CHIEF PHARISEE ON THE SABBATH.—*Peræa.*

Luke 14. 1–24.   **1** And it came to pass, as he went into the house of one of the chief Pharisees to eat bread on the sabbath day, that they watched him.   **2** And, behold, there was a certain man before him which had the dropsy.   **3** And Jesus

---

c Matt. 13. 33.
f For the reasons why Luke 13. 22 is arranged in this connexion, see Introductory Note to this Part.   The lamentation over Jerusalem in ver. 34 arises naturally from the mention of that city in ver. 33. In Matt. 23. 37, sq., the same lamentation is repeated in connexion with our Lord's denunciation of the scribes and Pharisees in Jerusalem. Luke's phrase, *ye shall not see Me*, etc., is explained by the like phrase of Matthew, *ye shall not see Me henceforth*, etc., implying that He was now about to withdraw from the world.
g Rom. 9. 31–33.   *h* Matt. 8. 11, 12.
i Christ was then in Peræa, in Herod's

jurisdiction. His words indicate that He was proceeding leisurely (πορεύεσθαι) toward Jerusalem, and expecting to arrive in about three days, and that He feared nothing from the malice of Herod inasmuch as His "decease was to be accomplished at Jerusalem" (Luke 9. 31), in which blood-guilty city alone could the Messiah be *perfected*, that is, through sufferings, see Heb. 2. 10.   *Out of* Jerusalem; i.e., *anywhere else than* in that city.
j Matt. 23. 37–39.
k This may refer to what was to occur on our Lord's public entry into the city; see Luke 19. 38.
l Psa. 118. 26.

Luke 14.

answering spake unto the lawyers and Pharisees, saying, Is it lawful to heal on the sabbath day? ⁴ And they held their peace. And he took *him*, and healed him, and let him go; ⁵ and answered them, saying, Which of you shall have an ass or an ox fallen into a pit, and will not straightway pull him out on the sabbath day? ⁶ And they could not answer him again to these things.

⁷ And he put forth a parable to those which were bidden, when he marked how they chose out the chief rooms; saying unto them, ⁸ When thou art bidden of any *man* to a wedding, sit not down in the highest room; ᵐ lest a more honourable man than thou be bidden of him; ⁹ and he that bade thee and him come and say to thee, Give this man place; and thou begin with shame to take the lowest room. ¹⁰ But when thou art bidden, go and sit down in the lowest room; that when he that bade thee cometh, he may say unto thee, Friend, go up higher: then shalt thou have worship in the presence of them that sit at meat with thee. ¹¹ For whosoever exalteth himself shall be abased; and he that humbleth himself shall be exalted.

¹² Then said he also to him that bade him, When thou makest a dinner or a supper, call not thy friends, nor thy brethren, neither thy kinsmen, nor *thy* rich neighbours; lest they also bid thee again, and a recompense be made thee. ¹³ But when thou makest a feast, call the poor, the maimed, the lame, the blind: ¹⁴ and thou shalt be blessed; for they cannot recompense thee: for thou shalt be recompensed at the resurrection of the just.

¹⁵ And when one of them that sat at meat with him heard these things, he said unto him, Blessed *is* he that shall eat bread in the kingdom of God. ¹⁶ Then said he unto him,ⁿ A certain man made a great supper, and bade many: ¹⁷ and sent his servant at supper time to say to them that were bidden, Come; for all things are now ready. ¹⁸ And they all with one *consent* began to make excuse. The first said unto him, I have bought a piece of ground, and I must needs go and see it: I pray thee have me excused. ¹⁹ And another said, I have bought five yoke of oxen, and I go to prove them: I pray thee have me excused. ²⁰ And another said, I have married a wife, and therefore I cannot come. ²¹ So that servant came, and showed his lord these things. Then the master of the house being angry said to his servant, Go out quickly into the streets and lanes of the city, and bring in hither the poor, and the maimed, and the halt, and the blind. ²² And the servant said, Lord, it is done as thou hast commanded, and yet there is room. ²³ And the lord said unto the servant, Go out into the highways and hedges, and compel *them* to come in, that my house may be filled. ²⁴ For I say unto you, That none of those men which were bidden shall taste of my supper.

§ 97. WHAT IS REQUIRED OF TRUE DISCIPLES.—*Peræa.*

Luke 14. 25–35. ²⁵ And there went great multitudes with him: and he turned, and said unto them, ²⁶ If any *man* come to me, and hate ᵒ not his father, and mother, and wife, and children, and brethren, and sisters, yea, and his own life also, he cannot be my disciple. ²⁷ And whosoever doth not bear his cross,ᵖ and come after me, cannot be my disciple. ²⁸ For which of you, intending to build a tower, sitteth not down first, and counteth the cost, whether he have *sufficient* to finish it? ²⁹ Lest haply, after he hath laid the foundation, and is not able to finish *it*, all that behold *it* begin to mock him, ³⁰ saying, This man began to build, and was not able to finish. ³¹ Or what king, going to make war against another king, sitteth not down first, and consulteth whether he be able with ten thousand to meet him that cometh against him with twenty thousand? ³² Or else, while the other is yet a great way off, he sendeth an ambassage, and desireth conditions of peace. ³³ So likewise, whosoever

---

ᵐ Prov. 25. 6.
ⁿ Matt. 22. 1–10

ᵒ Deut. 13. 6–10; Matt. 10. 37.
ᵖ Matt. 16. 24.

Luke 14.

he be of you that forsaketh not all that he hath, he cannot be my disciple. [34] Salt *is* good : [q] but if the salt have lost his savour, wherewith shall it be seasoned ? [35] It is neither fit for the land, nor yet for the dunghill ; *but* men cast it out. He that hath ears to hear, let him hear.

§ 98. PARABLE OF THE LOST SHEEP, THE PRODIGAL SON, ETC.—*Peræa.*

Luke 15. 1-32. [1] Then drew near unto him all the publicans and sinners for to hear him. [2] And the Pharisees and scribes murmured, saying, This man receiveth sinners, and eateth with them.

[3] And he spake this parable unto them, saying, [4] What man of you,[r] having an hundred sheep, if he lose one of them, doth not leave the ninety and nine in the wilderness, and go after that which is lost, until he find it ? [5] And when he hath found *it*, he layeth *it* on his shoulders, rejoicing. [6] And when he cometh home, he calleth together *his* friends and neighbours, saying unto them, Rejoice with me ; for I have found my sheep which was lost. [7] I say unto you, that likewise joy shall be in heaven over one sinner that repenteth, more than over ninety and nine just persons, which need no repentance. [8] Either what woman having ten pieces of silver, if she lose one piece, doth not light a candle, and sweep the house, and seek diligently till she find *it* ? [9] And when she hath found *it*, she calleth *her* friends and *her* neighbours together, saying, Rejoice with me ; for I have found the piece which I had lost. [10] Likewise, I say unto you, there is joy in the presence of the angels of God over one sinner that repenteth.

[11] And he said, A certain man had two sons : [12] and the younger of them said to *his* father, Father, give me the portion of goods that falleth *to me*. And he divided unto them *his* living. [13] And not many days after the younger son gathered all together, and took his journey into a far country, and there wasted his substance with riotous living. [14] And when he had spent all, there arose a mighty famine in that land ; and he began to be in want. [15] And he went and joined himself to a citizen of that country ; and he sent him into his fields to feed swine. [16] And he would fain have filled his belly with the husks [s] that the swine did eat : and no man gave unto him.

[17] And when he came to himself, he said, How many hired servants of my father's have bread enough and to spare, and I perish with hunger ! [18] I will arise and go to my father, and will say unto him, Father, I have sinned against heaven, and before thee, [19] and am no more worthy to be called thy son : make me as one of thy hired servants. [20] And he arose, and came to his father. But when he was yet a great way off, his father saw him, and had compassion, and ran, and fell on his neck, and kissed him. [21] And the son said unto him, Father, I have sinned against heaven, and in thy sight, and am no more worthy to be called thy son. [22] But the father said to his servants, Bring forth the best robe, and put *it* on him ; and put a ring on his hand, and shoes on *his* feet : [23] and bring hither the fatted calf, and kill *it* ; and let us eat, and be merry : [24] for this my son was dead, and is alive again ; he was lost, and is found. And they began to be merry.

[25] Now his elder son was in the field : and as he came and drew nigh to the house, he heard music and dancing. [26] And he called one of the servants, and asked what these things meant. [27] And he said unto him, Thy brother is come : and thy father hath killed the fatted calf, because he hath received him safe and sound. [28] And he was angry,[t] and would not go in : therefore came his father out,

---

[q] Matt. 5. 13. [r] Matt. 18. 12.

[s] *The husks* (κεράτια) ; name of the fruit which grows on the carob tree, still used in Palestine as fodder for cattle, and also serving as food for the poorest of the people. Here

the wretched prodigal is not allowed to share even with the swine this mean sustenance, for the master set more value on his herd than on his herdsman.

[t] Comp. Acts 11. 2, 3 ; 13. 45 ; 22. 21, 22

Luke 15.

and intreated him. ²⁹ And he answering said to *his* father, Lo, these many years do I serve thee, neither transgressed I at any time thy commandment : and yet thou never gavest me a kid, that I might make merry with my friends : ³⁰ but as soon as this thy son was come, which hath devoured thy living with harlots, thou hast killed for him the fatted calf. ³¹ And he said unto him, Son, thou art ever with me, and all that I have is thine. ³² It was meet that we should make merry, and be glad : for this thy brother was dead, and is alive again : and was lost, and is found.

§ 99. PARABLE OF THE UNJUST STEWARD.—*Perœa.*

Luke 16. 1–13. ¹ And he said also unto his disciples, There was a certain rich man, which had a steward ; and the same was accused unto him that he had wasted his goods. ² And he called him, and said unto him, How is it that I hear this of thee ? give an account of thy stewardship ; for thou mayest be no longer steward. ³ Then the steward said within himself, What shall I do ? for my lord taketh away from me the stewardship : I cannot dig ; to beg I am ashamed. ⁴ I am resolved what to do, that, when I am put out of the stewardship, they may receive me into their houses. ⁵ So he called every one of his lord's debtors *unto him*, and said unto the first, How much owest thou unto my lord ? ⁶ And he said, An hundred measures of oil. And he said unto him, Take thy bill, and sit down quickly, and write fifty. ⁷ Then said he to another, And how much owest thou ? And he said, An hundred measures of wheat. And he said unto him, Take thy bill, and write fourscore. ⁸ And the lord commended ᵘ the unjust steward, because he had done wisely : for the children of this world ᵛ are in their generation wiser ʷ than the children of light. ⁹ And I say unto you, Make to yourselves friends of the mammon of unrighteousness ; that, when ye fail, they may receive you into everlasting habitations. ¹⁰ He that is faithful in that which is least is faithful also in much ; and he that is unjust in the least is unjust also in much. ¹¹ If therefore ye have not been faithful in the unrighteous mammon, who will commit to your trust the true *riches ?* ¹² And if ye have not been faithful in that which is another man's, who shall give you that which is your own ? ¹³ No servant can serve two masters : for either he will hate the one, and love the other ; or else he will hold to the one, and despise the other. Ye cannot serve God and mammon.

§ 100. THE PHARISEES REPROVED. THE RICH MAN AND LAZARUS.—*Perœa.*

Luke 16. 14–31. ¹⁴ And the Pharisees also,ˣ who were covetous, heard all these things : and they derided him. ¹⁵ And he said unto them, Ye are they which justify yourselves before men ; but God knoweth your hearts ; for that which is highly esteemed among men is abomination in the sight of God.ʸ ¹⁶ The law and the prophets *were* until John : ᶻ since that time the kingdom of God is preached, and every man presseth into it. ¹⁷ And it is easier for heaven and earth to pass, than one tittle of the law to fail. ¹⁸ Whosoever putteth away his wife, and marrieth another, committeth adultery : and whosoever marrieth her that is put away from *her* husband committeth adultery.ᵃ

¹⁹ There was a certain rich man, which was clothed in purple and fine linen, and fared sumptuously every day : ²⁰ and there was a certain beggar named Lazarus, which was laid at his gate, full of sores, ²¹ and desiring to be fed with the crumbs

---

ᵘ *The lord :* not Christ (see ver. 9), but the master. The fraud was not approved, but its policy might be commended by the worldly wise.

ᵛ Psa. 17. 14.
ˣ Matt. 23. 14.
ᶻ Matt. 11. 12, 13.
ᵃ Matt. 5. 32.

ʷ John 12. 36 ; Eph. 5. 8.
ʸ 1 Cor. 1. 26–29.

Luke 16.

which fell from the rich man's table: moreover the dogs came and licked his sores. [12] And it came to pass, that the beggar died, and was carried by the angels into Abraham's bosom: [b] the rich man also died, and was buried; [23] and in hell he lift up his eyes, being in torments, and seeth Abraham afar off, and Lazarus in his bosom. [24] And he cried and said, Father Abraham, have mercy on me, and send Lazarus, that he may dip the tip of his finger in water, and cool my tongue; for I am tormented in this flame. [25] But Abraham said, Son, remember that thou in thy lifetime receivedst thy good things, and likewise Lazarus evil things: but now he is comforted, and thou art tormented. [26] And beside all this, between us and you there is a great gulf fixed: so that they which would pass from hence to you cannot; neither can they pass to us, that *would come* from thence. [27] Then he said, I pray thee therefore, father, that thou wouldest send him to my father's house: [28] for I have five brethren; that he may testify unto them, lest they also come into this place of torment. [29] Abraham saith unto him, They have Moses and the prophets; [c] let them hear them. [30] And he said, Nay, father Abraham: but if one went unto them from the dead, they will repent. [31] And he said unto him, If they hear not Moses and the prophets, [d] neither will they be persuaded, though one rose from the dead.

§ 101. Jesus inculcates Forbearance, Faith, Humility.—*Perœa.*

Luke 17. 1–10. [1] Then said he unto the disciples, It is impossible but that offences will come: [e] but woe *unto him*, through whom they come! [2] It were better for him that a millstone were hanged about his neck, and he cast into the sea, than that he should offend one of these little ones. [3] Take heed to yourselves: If thy brother trespass against thee, rebuke him; and if he repent, forgive him. [4] And if he trespass against thee seven times in a day, and seven times in a day turn again to thee, saying, I repent; thou shalt forgive him. [f]

[5] And the apostles said unto the Lord, Increase our faith. [6] And the Lord said, If ye had faith [g] as a grain of mustard seed, ye might say unto this sycamine tree, Be thou plucked up by the root, and be thou planted in the sea; and it should obey you. [7] But which of you, having a servant plowing or feeding cattle, will say unto him by and by, when he is come from the field, Go and sit down to meat? [8] And will not rather say unto him, Make ready wherewith I may sup, and gird thyself, and serve me, till I have eaten and drunken; and afterward thou shalt eat and drink? [9] Doth he thank that servant because he did the things that were commanded him? I trow not. [10] So likewise ye, when ye shall have done all those things which are commanded you, say, We are unprofitable servants: [h] we have done that which was our duty to do.

§ 102. Christ's Coming will be Sudden.—*Perœa.*

Luke 17. 20–37. [20] And when he was demanded of the Pharisees, when the kingdom of God should come, he answered them and said, The kingdom of God cometh not with observation: [21] neither shall they say, Lo, here! or, lo there! for behold, the kingdom of God is within you. [i] [22] And he said unto the disciples, The days will come, when ye shall desire to see one of the days of the Son of man, and

---

[b] The happiness of heaven is here represented under the idea of a feast, at which the guests reclined on couches in such a manner that the head of the second lay on the *bosom* of the first, see John 13. 23. Hence the posture became an emblem of friendship and intimate fellowship.

[c] John 5. 45–47.

[d] John 12. 10, 11; Acts 5. 30–33.

[e] 1 Cor. 11. 19. [f] Lev. 19. 17, 18.

[g] Matt. 17. 20. [h] Rom. 3. 27.

[i] Rather *among you*, for the kingdom of God was not *within* the Pharisees. But it is *within* all genuine believers, its seat being in the heart; and so it escaped the observation of the worldly-minded Pharisees.

Luke 17.

ye shall not see *it*. [23] And they shall say to you, See here; or, see there: go not after *them*, nor follow *them*. [24] For as the lightning, that lighteneth out of the one *part* under heaven, shineth unto the other *part* under heaven; so shall also the Son of man be in his day. [25] But first must he suffer many things, and be rejected of this generation. [26] And as it was in the days of Noe, so shall it be also in the days of the Son of man. [27] They did eat, they drank, they married wives, they were given in marriage, until the day that Noe entered into the ark, and the flood came, and destroyed them all.[j] [28] Likewise also as it was in the days of Lot; they did eat, they drank, they bought, they sold, they planted, they builded; [29] but the same day that Lot went out of Sodom it rained fire and brimstone from heaven, and destroyed *them* all.[k] [30] Even thus shall it be in the day when the Son of man is revealed.[l] [31] In that day, he which shall be upon the housetop, and his stuff in the house, let him not come down to take it away: and he that is in the field, let him likewise not return back. [32] Remember Lot's wife.[m] [33] Whosoever shall seek to save his life shall lose it; and whosoever shall lose his life shall preserve it. [34] I tell you, in that night there shall be two *men* in one bed; the one shall be taken, and the other shall be left. [35] Two *women* shall be grinding together; the one shall be taken, and the other left. [36] Two *men* shall be in the field; the one shall be taken, and the other left. [37] And they answered and said unto him, Where, Lord? And he said unto them, Wheresoever the body *is*, thither will the eagles be gathered together.[n]

§ 103. The importunate Widow. The Pharisee and Publican.
Perœa.

Luke 18. 1–14. [1] And he spake a parable unto them *to this end*, that men ought always *to* pray,[o] and not to faint; [2] saying, There was in a city a judge, which feared not God, neither regarded man: [3] And there was a widow in that city; and she came unto him, saying, Avenge me of mine adversary. [4] And he would not for a while: but afterward he said within himself, Though I fear not God, nor regard man; [5] yet because this widow troubleth me, I will avenge her, lest by her continual coming she weary me. [6] And the Lord said, Hear what the unjust judge saith. [7] And shall not God avenge his own elect,[p] which cry day and night unto him, though he bear long with them? [8] I tell you that he will avenge them speedily. Nevertheless when the Son of man cometh, shall he find faith on the earth?

[9] And he spake this parable unto certain which trusted in themselves that they were righteous, and despised others: [10] Two men went up into the temple to pray; the one a Pharisee, and the other a publican. [11] The Pharisee stood and prayed thus with himself, God, I thank thee, that I am not as other men *are*, extortioners, unjust, adulterers, or even as this publican. [12] I fast twice in the week,[q] I give tithes of all that I possess. [13] And the publican, standing afar off, would not lift up so much as *his* eyes towards heaven, but smote upon his breast, saying, God be merciful to me a sinner.[r] [14] I tell you, this man went down to his house justified *rather* than the other: for every one that exalteth himself shall be abased; and he that humbleth himself shall be exalted.[s]

---

j Gen. 7. 4, 7.
l 2 Thess. 1. 7.
n Job 39. 30; Matt. 24. 28.
o Rom. 12. 12; Eph. 6. 18; 1 Thess. 5. 17.
p Rev. 6. 10.
q The Pharisee shows his self-righteousness not only by asserting his avoidance of other men's vices and crimes, but by reciting his

k Gen. 19. 15.
m Gen. 19. 26.

works of supererogation, namely, the *two fasts* each week and the paying of *tithes* on *all* that he acquired (κτῶμαι), neither of which was enjoined in the law.

r To me a sinner, rather *the sinner;* that is, a notable or very great sinner, or the one just pointed at with contempt by the Pharisee.

s See in ¿ 105.

§ 104. Precepts respecting Divorce.[t]—*Peræa*

Matt. 19. 3–12. [3] The Pharisees also came unto him, tempting him, and saying unto him, Is it lawful for a man to put away his wife for every cause?

[4] And he answered and said unto them, Have ye not read, that he which made *them* at the beginning made them male and female,[u] [5] and said, For this cause shall a man leave father and mother, and shall cleave to his wife; and they twain shall be one flesh.[v] [6] Wherefore they are no more twain, but one flesh. What therefore God hath joined together, let not man put asunder. [7] They say unto him, Why did Moses then command to give a writing of divorcement, and to put her away?[w] [8] He saith unto them, Moses because of the hardness of your hearts suffered you to put away your wives: but from the beginning it was not so. [9] And I say unto you, Whosoever shall put away his wife, except *it be* for fornication, and shall marry another,

Mark 10. 2–12. [2] And the Pharisees came to him, and asked him, Is it lawful for a man to put away *his* wife? tempting him. [3] And he answered and said unto them, What did Moses command you? [4] And they said, Moses suffered to write a bill of divorcement, and to put *her* away.[t] [5] And Jesus answered and said unto them, For the hardness of your heart he wrote you this precept. [6] But from the beginning of the creation God made them male and female.[u] [7] For this cause shall a man leave his father and mother, and cleave to his wife; [8] and they twain shall be one flesh: so then they are no more twain, but one flesh.[v] [9] What therefore God hath joined together, let not man put asunder. [10] And in the house his disciples asked him again of the same *matter*. [11] And he saith unto them, Whosoever shall put away his wife, and marry another, committeth adultery against her. [12] And if a woman shall put away her husband, and be married to another, she committeth adultery.

committeth adultery: and whoso marrieth her which is put away doth commit adultery. [10] His disciples say unto him, If the case of the man be so with *his* wife, it is not good to marry [11] But he said unto them, All! *men* cannot receive this saying, save *they* to whom it is given. [12] For there are some eunuchs, which were so born from *their* mother's womb: and there are some eunuchs, which were made eunuchs of men: and there be eunuchs, which have made themselves eunuchs for the kingdom of heaven's sake. He that is able to receive *it*, let him receive *it*.

§ 105. Jesus Receives and Blesses Little Children.—*Peræa.*

Matt. 19. 13–15. [13] Then were there brought unto him little children, that he should put *his* hands on them, and pray: and the disciples rebuked them. [14] But Jesus said, Suffer little children, and forbid them not, to come unto me: for of such is the

Mark 10. 13–16. [13] And they brought young children to him, that he should touch them: and *his* disciples rebuked those that brought *them*. [14] But when Jesus saw *it*, he was much displeased, and said unto them, Suffer the little children to come unto me,

Luke 18. 15–17. [15] And they brought unto him also infants, that he would touch them: but when *his* disciples saw *it*, they rebuked them. [16] But Jesus called them *unto him*, and said, Suffer little children to come unto me, and forbid them not: for of such

---

[t] This section properly precedes § 105, where Luke is again parallel with Matthew and Mark.

[t] Deut. 24. 1.
[v] Gen. 2. 24.
[w] Deut. 24. 1.

[u] Gen. 1. 27.

Matt. 19.	**Mark 10.**	**Luke 18.**

kingdom of heaven.*ˣ* ¹⁵And he laid *his* hands on them, and d parted thence.

and forbid them not: for of such is the kingdom of God.*ˣ* ¹⁵Verily I say unto you, Whosoever shall not receive the kingdom of God as a little child, he shall not enter therein. ¹⁶And he took them up in his arms, put *his* hands upon them, and bl ssed them.

is the kingdom of God.*ˣ* ¹⁷Verily I say unto you, Whosoever shall not receive the kingdom of God as a little child shall in no wise enter therein.

§ 106. The Rich Youth. Labourers in the Vineyard.—*Peræa.*

Matt. 19. 16–30; **20.** 1–16. ¹⁶And behold, one c ame and said unto him, Good Master, what good thing shall I do, that I may have eternal life?

¹⁷And he said unto him, Why callest thou me good? *there is* none good but one, *that is,* God: but if thou wilt enter into life,*ʸ* keep the comm ndments.*ᶻ* ¹⁸He saith unto him, Which? Jesus said, *ᵃ*Thou shalt do no murder, Thou shalt not commit adultery, Thou shalt not steal, Thou shalt not bear false witness, ¹⁹Honour thy father and *thy* mother . and, Thou shalt love thy neighbour as thyself. ²⁰The young man saith unto him, All these things have I kept from my youth up : what lack I yet? ²¹Jesus said unto him, If thou wilt be perfect, go *and* sell that thou hast, and giv to the poor, and thou shalt have treasure in heaven : and come *and* follow me.

²²But when the young man heard that

Mark 10. 17–31. ¹⁷And when he was gone forth into the way, there came one running, and kneeled to him, and asked him, Good Master, what shall I do that I may inherit eternal life? ¹⁸And Jesus said unto him, Why callest thou me good? *there is* none good but one, *that is,* God. ¹⁹Thou knowest the commandments,*ᵃ* Do not commit adultery, Do not kill, Do not steal, Do not bear false witness, Defraud not, Honour thy father and mother.

²⁰And he answered and said unto him, Master, all these have I observed from my youth. ²¹Then Jesus beholding him, loved him, and said unto him, One thing thou lackest: go thy way, sell whatsoever thou hast, and give to the poor, and thou shalt have treasure in heaven : and come, take up the cross, and follow me. ²²And he was sad at that saying, and went away

Luke 18. 18–30. ¹⁸And a certain ruler asked him, saying, Good Master, what shall I do to inherit eternal life?

¹⁹And Jesus said unto him, Why callest thou me good? none *is* good, save one, *that is,* God. ²⁰Thou knowest the commandments,*ᵃ* Do not commit adultery, Do not kill, Do not steal, Do not bear false witness, Honour thy father and thy mother.

²¹And he said, All these have I kept from my youth up.

²²Now when Jesus heard these things, he said unto him, Yet lackest thou one thing: sell all that thou hast, and distribute unto the poor, and thou shalt have treasure in heaven : and come, follow me.

²³And when he heard this, he was very

ˣ Matt. 18. 3; 1 Cor. 14. 20.
ʸ The design of our Lord in thus addressing the young ruler, was to bring him to a knowledge of his sinfulness (see Rom. 3. 20), and

then to lead him to embrace the gospel (see ver. 21).
ᶻ Lev. 18. 5; Rom. 10. 5.
ᵃ Ex. 20. 12, sq.; Lev. 19. 8.

Matt. 19.	Mark 10.	Luke 18.

saying, he went away sorrowful: for he had great possessions. [23] Then said Jesus unto his disciples, Verily, I say unto you, That a rich man shall hardly enter into the kingdom of heaven.

grieved: for he had great possessions. [23] And Jesus looked round about, and saith unto his disciples, How hardly shall they that have riches enter into the kingdom of God! [24] And the disciples were astonished at his words. But Jesus answereth again, and saith unto them, Children, how hard is it for them that trust in riches to enter into the kingdom of God! [25] It is easier for a camel to go through the eye of a needle,[b] than for a rich man to enter into the kingdom of God. [26] And they were astonished out of measure, saying among themselves, Who then can be saved? [27] And Jesus looking upon them saith, With men *it is* impossible, but not with God: for with God all things are possible.[c]

sorrowful: for he was very rich. [24] And when Jesus saw that he was very sorrowful, he said, How hardly shall they that have riches enter into the kingdom of God!

[24] And again I say unto you, It is easier for a camel to go through the eye of a needle,[b] than for a rich man to enter into the kingdom of God. [25] When his disciples heard *it*, they were exceedingly amazed, saying, Who then can be saved? [26] But Jesus beheld *them*, and said unto them, With men this is impossible; but with God all things are possible.[c]

[25] For it is easier for a camel to go through a needle's eye,[b] than for a rich man to enter into the kingdom of God. [26] And they that heard *it* said, Who then can be saved?

[27] And he said, The things which are impossible with men are possible with God.[c]

[27] Then answered Peter and said unto him, Behold, we have forsaken all, and followed thee; what shall we have therefore? [28] And Jesus said unto them, Verily I say unto you, That ye which have followed me, in the regeneration when the Son of man shall sit in the throne of his glory,[d] ye also shall sit upon twelve thrones, judging the twelve tribes of Israel.[e] [29] And every one that hath forsaken houses, or brethren, or sisters, or father, or mother, or wife, or children, or lands, for my name's sake, shall receive an

[28] Then Peter began to say unto him, Lo, we have left all, and have followed thee.

[29] And Jesus answered and said, Verily I say unto you, There is no man that hath left house, or brethren, or sisters, or father, or mother, or wife, or children, or lands, for my sake, and the gospel's, [30] but he shall receive an hundredfold now in this time, houses, and brethren, and sisters, and mothers, and children, and lands, with persecutions;

and in

[28] Then Peter said, Lo, we have left all, and followed thee.

[29] And he said unto them, Verily I say unto you, There is no man that hath left house, or parents, or brethren, or wife, or children, for the kingdom of God's sake, [30] who shall not receive manifold more in this present time,

and in the

---

[b] This proverb is still used in the East.
[c] Gen. 18. 14; Luke 1. 37; 3. 8.
[d] Dan. 7. 13, 14; Rev. 3. 21.
[e] Luke 22. 28–30.

Matt. 19.	Mark 10.	Luke 18.
hundredfold, and shall inherit everlasting life. ³⁰ But many *that are* first shall be last; and the last *shall* be first.*f*	the world to come eternal life. ³¹ But many *that are* first shall be last; and the last first.*f*	world to come life **everlasting**.*f*

Matt. 20. ¹ For the kingdom of heaven is like unto a man *that is* an householder, which went out early in the morning *g* to hire labourers into his vineyard. ² And when he had agreed with the labourers for a penny a day, he sent them into his vineyard. ³ And he went out about the third hour, and saw others standing idle in the market-place, ⁴ and said unto them; Go ye also into the vineyard, and whatsoever is right I will give you. And they went their way. ⁵ Again he went out about the sixth and ninth hour, and did likewise. ⁶ And about the eleventh hour he went out, and found others standing idle, and saith unto them, Why stand ye here all the day idle? ⁷ They say unto him, Because no man hath hired us. He saith unto them, Go ye also into the vineyard; and whatsoever is right, *that* shall ye receive. ⁸ So when even was come, the lord of the vineyard saith unto his steward, Call the labourers, and give them *their* hire, beginning from the last unto the first. ⁹ And when they came that *were hired* about the eleventh hour, they received every man a penny. ¹⁰ But when the first came, they supposed that they should have received more; and they likewise received every man a penny. ¹¹ And when they had received *it*, they murmured against the good man of the house, ¹² saying, These last have wrought *but* one hour, and thou hast made them equal unto us, which have borne the burden and heat of the day. ¹³ But he answered one of them, and said, Friend, I do thee no wrong: didst thou not agree with me for a penny? ¹⁴ Take *that* thine *is*, and go thy way: I will give unto this last, even as unto thee. ¹⁵ Is it not lawful for me to do what I will with mine own? Is thine eye evil,*h* because I am good? ¹⁶ So the last shall be first, and the first last: for many be called, but few chosen.*i*

§ 107. JESUS A THIRD TIME*j* FORETELLS HIS DEATH AND RESURRECTION.
Peræa.

Matt. 20. 17-19.	Mark 10. 32-34.	Luke 18. 31-34.
¹⁷ And Jesus going up to Jerusalem took the twelve disciples apart in the way, and said unto them,	³² And they were in the way going up to Jerusalem; and Jesus went before them: and they were amazed; and as they followed, they were afraid. And he took again the twelve, and began to tell them what things should happen unto him, ³³ *saying*, Behold, we go up to Jerusalem; and the Son of man shall be delivered unto the chief	³¹ Then he took *unto him* the twelve, and said unto them,
¹⁸ Behold, we go up to Jerusalem; and the Son of man shall be betrayed unto the chief priests and		Behold, we go up to Jerusalem, and all things that are written by the prophets concerning

f Rom. 9. 30–33. See in ? § 107.
g *Early in the morning*, that is, about six o'clock or sunrise, from which time the Jews counted the hours of the day, so that their 3rd hour answered nearly to our 9, their 6th to our 12, their 9th to our 3 p.m., and their 11th to our 5 p.m. This parable was obviously spoken in reference to the question of Peter

(Matt. 19. 27), *What shall we have therefore?* and with the view to repress a mercenary spirit in the apostles' breasts. Those called into the kingdom later, *e.g.*, the Gentiles, were to have an equal place in its privileges.
h Deut. 28. 54.
i Matt. 22. 11–14.
j See § 74 and 77.

Matt. 20.	Mark 10.	Luke 18.
unto the scribes, and they shall condemn him to death, ¹⁹ and shall deliver him to the Gentiles to mock, and to scourge, and to crucify *him:* and the third day he shall rise again.	priests, and unto the scribes, and they shall condemn him to death, and shall deliver him to the Gentiles: ³⁴ and they shall mock him, and shall scourge him, and shall spit upon him, and shall kill him: and the third day he shall rise again.	the Son of man shall be accomplished. ³² For he shall be delivered unto the Gentiles, and shall be mocked, and spitefully entreated, and spitted on; ³³ and they shall scourge *him,* and put him to death: and the third day he shall rise again. ³⁴ And they understood none of these

things:*k* and this saying was hid from them, neither knew they the things which were spoken.

§ 108. James and John make their ambitious Request.—*Peræa.*

Matt. 20. 20–28. ²⁰ Then came to him the mother *l* of Zebedee's children with her sons, worshipping *him,* and desiring a certain thing of him. ²¹ And he said unto her, What wilt thou? She saith unto him, Grant that these my two sons may sit, the one on thy right hand, and the other on the left, in thy kingdom. ²² But Jesus answered and said, Ye know not what ye ask. Are ye able to drink of the cup *m* that I shall drink of, and to be baptized with the baptism that I am baptized with? *n* They say unto him, We are able. ²³ And he saith unto them, Ye shall drink indeed of my cup,*o* and be baptized with the baptism that I am baptized with: but to sit on my right hand, and on my left, is not mine to give, but *it shall be given to them* for whom it is prepared of my Father. ²⁴ And when the ten heard *it,* they were moved with indignation against the two brethren. ²⁵ But Jesus called them *unto him,* and said, Ye know that the princes of the Gentiles exercise dominion over them, and they that are great exercise authority upon them. ²⁶ But it shall be not so among you: but whosoever will be great among you, let him be your minister; ²⁷ and whoso-

Mark 10. 35–45. ³⁵ And James and John, the sons of Zebedee, come unto him, saying, Master, we would that thou shouldest do for us whatsoever we shall desire. ³⁶ And he said unto them, What would ye that I should do for you? ³⁷ They said unto him, Grant unto us that we may sit, one on thy right hand, and the other on thy left hand, in thy glory. ³⁸ But Jesus said unto them, Ye know not what ye ask: can ye drink of the cup *m* that I drink of? and be baptized with the baptism that I am baptized with? *n* ³⁹ And they said unto him, We can. And Jesus said unto them, Ye shall indeed drink of the cup that I drink of;*o* and with the baptism that I am baptized withal shall ye be baptized: ⁴⁰ but to sit on my right hand and on my left hand is not mine to give; but *it shall be given to them* for whom it is prepared. ⁴¹ And when the ten heard *it,* they began to be much displeased with James and John. ⁴² But Jesus called them *to him,* and saith unto them, Ye know that they which are accounted to rule over the Gentiles exercise lordship over them; and their great ones exercise authority upon them. ⁴³ But so shall it not be among you: but who-

---

k They understood not, &c. They probably fancied that our Lord's declaration was only a figurative representation of the difficulties and obstacles He was to meet with; and they hoped that He would, on the approaching festival, take to Himself the kingdom (see Matt. 20. 21, and Luke 19. 11); which indeed He did, but in a way wholly different from their apprehension and expectation.

l In Matthew it is the mother of James and John (by name *Salome,* as appears from Matt. 27. 56, compared with Mark 15. 40; see § 156) who makes the request; in Mark it is the two disciples themselves: see Note on § 42.

m Psa. 75. 8.

n Psa. 42. 7; Luke 12. 50.

o Acts 12. 2.; Rev. 1. 9.

Matt. 20.

ever will be chief among you, let him be your servant: [28] even as the Son of man came not to be ministered unto, but to minister, and to give his life[p] a ransom for many.[q]

Mark 10.

soever will be great among you, shall be your minister: [44] and whosoever of you will be the chiefest, shall be servant of all. [45] For even the Son of man came not to be ministered unto, but to minister, and to give his life[p] a ransom for many.[q]

§ 109. The Healing of Two[r] Blind Men near Jericho.

Matt. 20. 29–34. [29] And as they departed from Jericho, a great multitude followed him. [30] And, behold, two blind men sitting by the way side,

when they heard that Jesus passed by, cried out, saying, Have mercy on us, O Lord, *thou* Son of David. [31] And the multitude re-

Mark 10. 46–52. [46] And they came to Jericho; and as he went out of Jericho with his disciples and a great number of people, blind Bartimeus, the son of Timeus, sat by the highway side begging. [47] And when he heard that it was Jesus of Nazareth, he began to cry out, and say, Jesus, *thou* Son of David, have mercy on me. [48] And

Luke 18. 35–43; **19.** 1. [35] And it came to pass, that as he was come nigh unto Jericho, a certain blind man sat by the way side begging: [36] and hearing the multitude pass by, he asked what it meant.

[37] And they told him, that Jesus of Nazareth passeth by. [38] And he cried, saying, Jesus,

---

p Isa. 53. 10, 11; 1 Tim. 2. 6.

q *To give His life a ransom for many.* A clear proof, from Christ's own mouth, of the vicarious and atoning character of His death.

r Mark and Luke here speak of *one* blind man; Matthew of *two*. The case is similar to that of the demoniacs of Gadara: see Note on § 57.

More difficult is it to harmonize the accounts as to the *place* where the miracle was wrought. Matthew and Mark narrate it as having occurred when Jesus was *departing* from Jericho; while Luke seems to describe it as happening during his *approach* to the city. Several ways of solving this difficulty have been proposed.

1. The language of Mark is, "they came to Jericho." This, it is said, may be understood as implying that Jesus remained some days at least in Jericho; and that the miracle may have been wrought, not when he was *finally* leaving Jericho for Jerusalem, but when He was *occasionally* going out *of*, and returning *to*, Jericho. So Newcome, *Harm.* Note on § 108.

2. The Greek verb here used may, it is said, signify not only *to draw nigh*, but also *to be nigh*. Hence, the language of Luke may include also the idea expressed by Matthew and Mark, that is, while He was *still near* the city. So Grotius, *Comm. in Matt.* 20. 30. It is very doubtful whether this definition can be fully sustained by classic authority. Yet in the New Testament and Septuagint there are several passages which go to imply such a usage of the Greek word. Thus Luke 19. 29, compared with Matt. 21. 1. So Phil. 2. 3, *he was nigh unto death.* The usage of the LXX. is still more definite; e.g. of Naboth's vineyard, 1 Kings 21. 2, *because it is near unto my house.* Also Deut. 21. 3, *the city next [nigh] unto the slain man*, ver. 6; 22. 2; and trop. Jer. 23. 23; Ruth 2. 20; 2 Sam. 19. 42. These instances seem sufficient to bear out the proposed interpretation in Luke; which is also adopted by Le Clerc, Doddridge, Pilkington, and others.—Nor is this method of explanation "made useless for the purpose of reconciling the evangelists, by Luke 19. 1," as Newcome asserts. In connexion with Jericho, Luke first of all relates this striking miracle; then goes back and mentions that Jesus "entered and passed through Jericho;" and lastly records the visit to the house of Zaccheus, apparently within the city. Luke 19. 1, therefore, is not more at variance with this view respecting the miracle than it is with the visit to Zaccheus. It is a passing announcement of a general fact, in connexion with which other more important circumstances are related, not indeed in the order of time, but partly by anticipation.

3. Less probable than either of the above is the solution of Lightfoot (*Chron. Tempor.* in N.T. Opp. II. p. 42) and others, who assume that Jesus healed one blind man before entering the city, and another on departing from it. This solution is, however, strongly advocated by Greswell (*Dissert.* xxii. vol. ii.), and also regarded with favour by Wieseler (*Chron. Synops.* p. 303).

Matt. 20.	Mark 10.	Luke 18.
buked them, because they should hold their peace: but they cried the more, saying, Have mercy on us, O Lord, *thou* Son of David. [32] And Jesus stood still, and called them, and	many charged him that he should hold his peace: but he cried the more a great deal, *Thou* Son of David, have mercy on me. [49] And Jesus stood still, and commanded him to be called. And they call the blind man, saying unto him, Be of good comfort, rise; he calleth thee. [50] And he, casting away his garment, rose, and came to Jesus. [51] And Jesus answered and	*thou* Son of David, have mercy on me. [39] And they which went before rebuked him, that he should hold his peace: but he cried so much the more, *Thou* Son of David, have mercy on me. [40] And Jesus stood, and commanded him to be brought unto him:
said, What will ye that I shall do unto you? [33] They say unto him, Lord, that our eyes may be opened. [34] So Jesus had compassion *on them*, and touched their eyes: and immediately their eyes received sight, and they followed him.*	said unto him, What wilt thou that I should do unto thee? The blind man said unto him, Lord, that I might receive my sight. [52] And Jesus said unto him, Go thy way; thy faith hath made thee whole. And immediately he received his sight, and followed Jesus in the way.*	and when he was come near, he asked him, saying, [41] What wilt thou that I shall do unto thee? And he said, Lord, that I may receive my sight. [42] And Jesus said unto him, Receive thy sight: thy faith hath saved thee. [43] And immediately he received his sight, and followed him, glorifying God: and all the people, when they saw *it*, gave praise unto God.

Luke 19.   [1] And *Jesus* entered and passed through Jericho.

§ 110. The Visit to Zaccheus. Parable of the Ten Pounds.
Jericho.

Luke 19. 2-28. [2] And, behold, *there was* a man named Zaccheus, which was the chief among the publicans, and he was rich. [3] And he sought to see Jesus, who he was; and could not for the press, because he was little of stature. [4] And he ran before, and climbed up into a sycomore tree to see him; for he was to pass that *way*. [5] And when Jesus came to the place, he looked up, and saw him, and said unto him, Zaccheus, make haste, and come down; for to-day I must abide at thy house. [6] And he made haste, and came down, and received him joyfully. [7] And when they saw *it*, they all murmured, saying, That he was gone to be guest with a man that is a sinner. [8] And Zaccheus stood, and said unto the Lord; Behold, Lord, the half of my goods I give to the poor; and if I have taken anything from any man by false accusation, I restore *him* fourfold.[f] [9] And Jesus said unto him, This day is salvation come to this house, forsomuch as he also is a son of Abraham. [10] For the Son of man is come to seek and to save that which was lost.

[11] And as they heard these things, he added and spake a parable, because he was nigh to Jerusalem, and because they thought that the kingdom of God should

---

* See in § 112.

[f] Probably, because the Roman law exacted a fourfold restitution from publicans who were convicted of extortion in collecting the taxes. But according to the Jewish law, if a defrauder wished of his own accord, or on his own confession, to make restitution, he was not required to restore more than the amount defrauded, and a fifth part in addition; see Numb. 5. 6, 7.

Luke 19.

immediately appear.ᵘ ¹²He said therefore, A certain nobleman went into a far country to receive for himself a kingdom, and to return. ¹³And he called his ten servants, and delivered them ten pounds,ᵛ and said unto them, Occupy till I come. ¹⁴But his citizens hated him, and sent a message after him, saying, We will not have this *man* to reign over us. ¹⁵And it came to pass, that when he was returned, having received the kingdom, then he commanded these servants to be called unto him, to whom he had given the money, that he might know how much every man had gained by trading. ¹⁶Then came the first, saying, Lord, thy pound hath gained ten pounds. ¹⁷And he said unto him, Well, thou good servant; because thou hast been faithful in a very little, have thou authority over ten cities. ¹⁸And the second came, saying, Lord, thy pound hath gained five pounds. ¹⁹And he said likewise to him, Be thou also over five cities. ²⁰And another came, saying, Lord, behold, *here is* thy pound, which I have kept laid up in a napkin: ²¹for I feared thee, because thou art an austere man: thou takest up that thou layedst not down, and reapest that thou didst not sow. ²²And he saith unto him, Out of thine own mouth will I judge thee, *thou* wicked servant. Thou knewest that I was an austere man, taking up that I laid not down, and reaping that I did not sow: ²³wherefore then gavest not thou my money into the bank, that at my coming I might have required mine own with usury? ²⁴And he said unto them that stood by, Take from him the pound, and give *it* to him that hath ten pounds. ²⁵(And they said unto him, Lord, he hath ten pounds.) ²⁶For I say unto you, That unto every one which hath shall be given; and from him that hath not, even that he hath shall be taken away from him. ²⁷But those mine enemies, which would not that I should reign over them, bring hither, and slay *them* before me.

²⁸And when he had thus spoken, he went before, ascending up to Jerusalem.

§ 111. JESUS ARRIVES AT BETHANY SIX DAYS BEFORE THE PASSOVER.
Bethany.

John 11. 55–57; 12. 1, 9–11. ⁵⁵And the Jews' passover was nigh at hand: and many went out of the country up to Jerusalem before the passover, to purify themselves. ⁵⁶Then sought they for Jesus, and spake among themselves, as they stood in the temple, What think ye, that he will not come to the feast? ⁵⁷Now both the chief priests and the Pharisees had given a commandment, that, if any man knew where he were, he should show *it*, that they might take him.

John 12. ¹Then Jesus six days before the passover ʷ came to Bethany, where Lazarus was which had been dead,ˣ whom he raised from the dead.ʸ⁻⁹ Much people of the Jews therefore knew that he was there: and they came not for Jesus' sake only, but that they might see Lazarus also, whom he had raised from the dead. ¹⁰But the chief priests consulted that they might put Lazarus also to death; ¹¹because that by reason of him many of the Jews went away, and believed on Jesus.

ᵘ Comp. Acts 1. 6.

ᵛ *Ten pounds.* What is here rendered *pound* (μνᾶ, *mina*) is reckoned to be equal to £3 2*s.* 6*d.* of our money.

ʷ *Six days before the passover* is equivalent to the "sixth day" before that festival; see Note on ‡ 49. As our Lord ate the paschal supper on the evening following Thursday (which evening was reckoned by the Jews as a part of Friday), the sixth day before it was

Saturday, or the Jewish sabbath, provided we reckon *exclusively*, as Greswell shows we ought, *Dissert.* i. p. 8, vol. iii. On that day, then, Jesus came to Bethany.

John 12. 2–8, where the supper at Bethany is described, is postponed in accordance with the order of Matthew and Mark. See Note on ‡ 131 in the Appendix.

ˣ John 11. 1, 43.

ʸ For var. 2–8 see ‡ 131.

PART VII.

OUR LORD'S PUBLIC ENTRY INTO JERUSALEM, AND THE SUBSEQUENT TRANSACTIONS BEFORE THE FOURTH PASSOVER.

TIME: *Five Days.*

INTRODUCTORY NOTE.

THE Jewish day of twenty-four hours was reckoned from sunset to sunset; as is still the case in Oriental countries. The paschal lamb was killed on the fourteenth day of Nisan towards sunset; and was eaten the same evening, after the fifteenth day of Nisan had begun.[a] Our Lord was crucified on the day before the Jewish sabbath, that is, on Friday; and as, according to the view maintained in this *Harmony* (see Introduction to Part VIII.), He had eaten the passover on the preceding evening, it follows that the fourteenth of Nisan fell that year on Thursday, reckoned from the preceding sunset. Hence, the sixth day (reckoning *exclusively*) before the passover, when Jesus came to Bethany, was the Jewish sabbath, or our Saturday;[a] and the transactions of the following week, comprised in Parts VII. and VIII., may be distributed according to the following schedule; which agrees in the main with the *Schema* of Lightfoot[b] and with the arrangement of Wieseler.[c]

SCHEDULE OF DAYS.

Day of Nisan.	Day of Week.		
9.	7.	SAT.	*reckoned from preceding sunset.* The Jewish sabbath. Jesus arrives at Bethany, John 12. 1.
10.	1.	SUND.	*from preced. sunset.* Jesus makes His public entry into Jerusalem, § 112; and returns at night to Bethany, Mark 11. 11.—On this day the paschal lamb was to be selected, Ex. 12. 3.
11.	2.	MOND.	*from preced. sunset.* Jesus goes to Jerusalem; on His way the incident of the barren fig-tree. He cleanses the temple, § 113; and again returns to Bethany, Mark 11. 19.
12.	3.	TUESD.	*from preced. sunset.* As Jesus returns to the city; on the way the disciples see the fig-tree withered, Mark 11. 20. Our Lord discourses in the temple, §§ 115–126; takes leave of it; and, when on the mount of Olives, on His way to Bethany, foretells His coming to destroy the city, and proceeds to speak also of His final coming to judgment, §§ 127–130.
13.	4.	WEDN.	*from preced. sunset.* The rulers conspire against Christ. On the eve of this day (i.e., the evening following Tuesday), our Lord had partaken of the supper at Bethany; where Mary anointed Him, and where Judas laid his plan of treachery, which he made known to the chief priests in the course of this day.—Jesus remained this day at Bethany.
14.	5.	THURSD.	*from preced. sunset.* Jesus sends two disciples to the city to make ready the passover. He Himself repairs thither in the afternoon, in order to eat the paschal supper at evening.
15.	6.	FRID.	*from preced. sunset.* At evening, in the very beginning of the fifteenth of Nisan, Jesus partakes of the paschal supper; institutes the Lord's supper; is betrayed and apprehended; §§ 133–143. He is brought first before Caiaphas, and then in the morning before Pilate; is condemned, crucified, and before sunset laid in the sepulchre; §§ 144–158.
16.	7.	SAT.	The Jewish sabbath. Our Lord rests in the sepulchre.
17.	1.	SUND.	Jesus rises from the dead at early dawn; see § 159 and Note.

---

[a] Ex. 12. 6, 8, and Introd. Note to Part VIII.

[a] See Note *v* on 111.

[b] See *Hor. Heb.* in Joh. 12. 2.

[c] *Chron. Synop.* p. 357–378.

§ 112. Our Lord's Public Entry into Jerusalem.—*Bethany, Jerusalem.*
First Day of the Week.

John 12. 12–19. [12] On the next day *d* much people that were come to the feast, when they heard that Jesus was coming to Jerusalem,—

Matt. 21. 1–11, 14–17.
And when they drew nigh unto Jerusalem, and were come to Bethphage, unto the mount of Olives, then sent Jesus two disciples, *2* saying unto them, Go into the village over against you, and straightway ye shall find an ass tied, and a colt with her: loose *them*, and bring *them* unto me.

3 And if any *man* say aught unto you, ye shall say, The Lord hath need of them; and straightway he will send them.—*6* And the disciples went, and did as Jesus commanded them,

7 and brought the ass, and the colt, and put on them their clothes, and they set *him* thereon.

Matt. 21. *4* All this was done, that it might be fulfilled which was spoken by the prophet, saying,*e* *5* Tell ye the daughter of Sion, Behold, thy king cometh unto thee, meek, and sitting upon an ass, and a colt the foal of an ass.—*8* And a very great multitude

Mark 11. 1–11. *1* And when they came nigh to Jerusalem, unto Bethphage and Bethany, at the mount of Olives, he sendeth forth two of his disciples, *2* and saith unto them, Go your way into the village over against you: and as soon as ye be entered into it, ye shall find a colt tied, whereon never man sat; loose him, and bring *him*. *3* And if any man say unto you, Why do ye this? say ye that the Lord hath need of him; and straightway he will send him hither. *4* And they went their way, and found the colt tied by the door without in a place where two ways met; and they loose him. *5* And certain of them that stood there said unto them, What do ye, loosing the colt ? *6* And they said unto them even as Jesus had commanded: and they let them go. *7* And they brought the colt to Jesus, and cast their garments on him; and he sat upon him.

Luke 19. 29–44.
29 And it came to pass, when he was come nigh to Bethphage and Bethany, at the mount called *the mount* of Olives, he sent two of his disciples, *30* saying, Go ye into the village over against *you ;* in the which at your entering ye shall find a colt tied, whereon yet never man sat: loose him, and bring *him hither.* *31* And if any man ask you, Why do ye loose *him ?* thus shall ye say unto him, Because the Lord hath need of him. *32* And they that were sent went their way, and found even as he had said unto them. *33* And as they were loosing the colt, the owners thereof said unto them, Why loose ye the colt ? *34* And they said, The Lord hath need of him.

35 And they brought him to Jesus: and they cast their garments upon the colt, and they set Jesus thereon.

John 12. *14* And Jesus, when he had found a young ass, sat thereon ; as it is written,*e* *15* Fear not, Daughter of Sion : behold, thy King cometh, sitting on an ass's colt.—

Mark 11. *8* And many spread their garments in

Luke 19. *36* And as he went, they spread their

---

d On the next day, that is, after the arrival at Bethany, not after the supper in Simon's house (see § 131). This was the 10th of Nisan, on which day the paschal lamb was set apart (Ex. 12. 3). Might not our Lord's choice of this day for making His public entry into Jerusalem and the temple have reference to the fact, that He Himself was the true Passover which was then to be slain for us (1 Cor. 5. 7) ?   *e* Zech. 9. 9.

Matt. 21.	Mark 11.	Luke 19.	John 12.
spread their garments in the way;[i] others cut down branches from the trees, and strawed *them* in the way. [9] And the multitudes that went before, and that followed, cried,	the way:[i] and others cut down branches off the trees, and strawed *them* in the way. [9] And they that went before, and they that followed, cried, saying,	clothes in the way. [37] And when he was come nigh, even now at the descent of the mount of Olives, the whole multitude of the disciples began to rejoice and praise God with a loud voice for all the mighty works that they had seen; [38] Saying, Blessed	[13]*j* took branches of palm trees, and went forth to meet him,
saying, Hosanna to the Son of David: Blessed *is* he that cometh in the name of the Lord;[k] Hosanna in the highest.	Hosanna, Blessed *is* he that cometh in the name of the Lord:[k] [10] Blessed *be* the kingdom of our father David, that cometh in the name of the Lord: Hosanna in the highest.	*be* the King that cometh in the name of the Lord:[k] peace in heaven, and glory in the highest.[l]	and cried, Hosanna: Blessed *is* the King of Israel that cometh in the name of the Lord.[k]

John 12. [16] These things understood not his disciples at the first: but when Jesus was glorified, then remembered[m] they that these things were written of him, and *that* they had done these things unto him. [17] The people therefore that was with him when he called Lazarus out of his grave, and raised him from the dead, bare record.[n] [18] For this cause the people also met him, for that they heard that he had done this miracle. [19] The Pharisees therefore said among themselves, Perceive ye how ye prevail nothing? behold, the world is gone after him.

Luke 19. [39] And some of the Pharisees from among the multitude said unto him, Master, rebuke thy disciples. [40] And he answered and said unto them, I tell you that, if these should hold their peace, the stones would immediately cry out. [41] And when he was come near, he beheld the city, and wept over it, [42] saying, If thou hadst known, even thou, at least in this thy day, the things *which belong* unto thy peace! but now they are hid from thine eyes. [43] For the days shall come upon thee, that thine enemies shall cast a trench about thee, and compass thee round, and keep thee in on every side, [44] and shall lay thee even with the ground, and thy children within thee; and they shall not leave in thee one stone upon another; because thou knewest not the time of thy visitation.[o]

Matt. 21. [10] And when he was come into Jerusalem, all the city was moved, saying, Who is this? [11] And the multitude said, This is Jesus the prophet[p] of Nazareth of Galilee.—[14] And the blind and the lame came to him in the temple; and he healed them. [15] And when the chief priests and scribes saw the wonderful things that he did, and the children crying in the temple, and saying, Hosanna to the Son of David; they were sore displeased, [16] and said unto him, Hearest thou what these say? And Jesus saith unto them, Yea; have ye never read,[q] Out of the mouths of babes and sucklings thou hast perfected praise?

Mark 11. [11] And Jesus entered into Jerusalem, and into the temple; and when he had looked round about upon all things,—

---

i A custom observed in honour and welcome for a king: 2 Kings 9. 13.
j For connection see beginning of section.
k Psa. 118. 25.
l Luke 2. 14.
m John 14. 26.
o Luke 1. 68, 78.
p Luke 7. 16.
q Psa. 8. 2.
n John 11. 43.

Matt. 21.

[17] And he left them, and went out of the city into Bethany; and he lodged there.

Mark 11.

—[11] And now the eventide was come, he went out unto Bethany with the twelve.

§ 113. BARREN FIG TREE. CLEANSING THE TEMPLE.—*Bethany, Jerusalem.*
Second Day of the Week.

Matt. 21. 12, 13, 18, 19. [18] Now in the morning [r] as he returned into the city, he hungered. [19] And when he saw a fig tree [s] in the way, he came to it, and found nothing thereon, but leaves only, and said unto it, Let no fruit grow on thee henceforward for ever. And presently the fig tree withered away.—

Mark 11. 12–19. [12] And on the morrow, when they were come from Bethany, he was hungry: [13] and seeing a fig tree [s] afar off having leaves, he came, if haply he might find any thing thereon; and when he came to it, he found nothing but leaves; for the time of figs was not *yet.* [14] And Jesus answered and said unto it, No man eat fruit of thee hereafter for ever. And his disciples heard *it.*

Matt. 21. [12] And Jesus went into the temple of God, [u] and cast out all them that sold and bought in the temple, and overthrew the tables of the moneychangers, and the seats of them that sold doves, [v]

Mark 11. [15] And they come to Jerusalem: and Jesus went into the temple, [u] and began to cast out them that sold and bought in the temple, and overthrew the tables of the moneychangers, and the seats of them that sold doves; [v] [16] and would not suffer that any man should carry *any* vessel through the temple. [17] And he taught, saying unto them, Is it not written, [w] My house shall be called of all nations the house of prayer? but ye have made it a den of thieves. [18] And the scribes and chief priests heard *it,* and sought how they might destroy him: for they feared him, because all the people was astonished at his doctrine. [19] And when even was come, he went out of the city.

Luke 19. 45–48. [45] And he went into the temple, [u] and began to cast out them that sold therein, and them that bought; [v]

[13] And said unto them, It is written, [w] My house shall be called the house of prayer; but ye have made it a den of thieves.

[46] saying unto them, It is written, [w] My house is the house of prayer: but ye have made it a den of thieves. [47] And he taught daily in the temple. But the chief priests and the scribes and the chief of the people sought to destroy him, [48] and could not find what they might do: for all the people were very attentive to hear him.

Luke 21. 37, 38. [37] And in the daytime he was teaching in the temple; and at night he went out, and abode in the mount that is called *the mount* of Olives. [38] And all the people came early in the morning to him in the temple, for to hear him.

---

[r] See Note on § 21.
Luke 21. 37, 38 is inserted here, because in Luke's order it is only retrospective; being placed after our Lord's discourses on the mount of Olives, when He had already taken leave of the temple, to which He returned no more.

[s] *A fig tree.* On mount Olivet, over which our Lord was passing, there grew not only olives but also fig trees, as the name of the place, Bethphage, indicates, for it signifies *house of figs.*
[u] John 2. 13–17.   [v] Deut. 14. 24–26.
[w] Isa. 56. 7; Jer. 7. 11.

§ 114. The Barren Fig Tree Withers Away.—*Between Bethany and Jerusalem.*

Third Day of the Week.

Matt. 21. 20–22. [20] And when the disciples saw *it*, they marvelled, saying, How soon is the fig tree withered away! [21] Jesus answered and said unto them, Verily I say unto you, If ye have faith, and doubt not, ye shall not only do this *which is done* to the fig tree, but also if ye shall say unto this mountain,[y] Be thou removed, and be thou cast into the sea; it shall be done. [22] And all things, whatsoever ye shall ask in prayer, believing, ye shall receive.

Mark 11. 20–26. [20] And in the morning,[x] as they passed by, they saw the fig tree dried up from the roots. [21] And Peter calling to remembrance saith unto him, Master, behold, the fig tree which thou cursedst is withered away. [22] And Jesus answering saith unto them, Have faith in God. [23] For verily I say unto you, That whosoever shall say unto this mountain,[y] Be thou removed, and be thou cast into the sea; and shall not doubt in his heart, but shall believe that those things which he saith shall come to pass; he shall have whatsoever he saith. [24] Therefore I say unto you, What things soever ye desire, when ye pray, believe that ye receive *them*, and ye shall have *them*. [25] And when ye stand praying, forgive, if ye have aught against any: that your Father also which is in heaven may forgive you your trespasses. [26] But if ye do not forgive, neither will your Father which is in heaven forgive your trespasses.[z]

§ 115. Christ's Authority. Parable of the Two Sons.—*Jerusalem.*

Third Day of the Week.

Matt. 21. 23–32. [23] And when he was come into the temple, the chief priests and the elders of the people came unto him as he was teaching, and said, By what authority[a] doest thou these things?[b] and who gave thee this authority? [24] And Jesus answered and said unto them, I also will ask you one thing, which if ye tell me, I in like wise will tell you by what authority I do these things. [25] The baptism of John, whence was it? from heaven, or of

Mark 11. 27–33. [27] And they come again to Jerusalem: and as he was walking in the temple, there come to him the chief priests, and the scribes, and the elders, [28] and say unto him, By what authority[a] doest thou these things?[b] and who gave thee this authority to do these things? [29] And Jesus answered and said unto them, I will also ask of you one question, and answer me, and I will tell you by what authority I do these things. [30] The baptism of John, was *it* from heaven, or of men?

Luke 20. 1–8. [1] And it came to pass, *that* on one of those days, as he taught the people in the temple, and preached the gospel, the chief priests and the scribes came upon *him* with the elders, [2] and spake unto him, saying, Tell us, by what authority doest thou these things?[b] or who is he that gave thee this authority? [3] And he answered and said unto them, I will also ask you one thing: and answer me:

[4] The baptism of John, was it from heaven, or of men? [5] And they

---

[x] The account of the withering away of the fig tree might well in itself be connected with the preceding Section. But according to Mark 11. 20, this occurrence took place on the subsequent day.

| 1 Cor. 13. 2.
[z] Matt. 6. 15.
[a] Comp. Acts 4. 7.
[b] *Doest thou these things:* meaning particularly the clearing of the temple; see § 113.

Matt. 21.

men? And they reasoned with themselves, saying, If we shall say, From heaven; he will say unto us, Why did ye not then believe him? 26 But if we shall say, Of men; we fear the people; for all hold John as a prophet.c

27 And they answered Jesus, and said, We cannot tell. And he said unto them, Neither tell I you by what authority I do these things.

28 But what think ye? A *certain* man had two

Mark 11.

answer me. 31 And they reasoned with themselves, saying, If we shall say From heaven; he will say, Why then did ye not believe him? 32 But if we shall say, Of men; they feared the people: for all *men* counted John, that he was a prophet indeed.c 33 And they answered and said unto Jesus, We cannot tell. And Jesus answering saith unto them, Neither do I tell you by what authority I do these things.

Luke 20.

reasoned with themselves, saying, If we shall say, From heaven; he will say, Why then believed ye him not? 6 But and if we say, Of men; all the people will stone us: for they be persuaded that John was a prophet.c 7 And they answered, that they could not tell whence *it was.* 8 And Jesus said unto them, Neither tell I you by what authority I do these things.

sons; and he came to the first, and said, Son, go work to-day in my vineyard. 29 He answered and said, I will not: but afterward he repented, and went. 30 And he came to the second, and said likewise. And he answered and said, I *go,* sir: and went not. 31 Whether of them twain did the will of *his* father? They say unto him, The first. Jesus saith unto them, Verily I say unto you, That the publicans and harlots go into the kingdom of God before you. 32 For John came unto you in the way of righteousness, and ye believed him not: but the publicans and the harlots believed him:d and ye, when ye had seen *it,* repented not afterward, that ye might believe him.

◊ 116. PARABLE OF THE WICKED HUSBANDMEN.—*Jerusalem.*
Third Day of the Week.

Matt. 21. 33-46.

33 Hear another parable; There was a certain householder, which planted a vineyard,e and hedged it round about, and digged a winepress in it, and built a tower, and let it out to husbandmen, and went into a far country: 34 and when the time of the fruit drew near, he sent his servants to the husbandmen, that they might receive the fruits of it. 35 And the husbandmen took his servants, and beat one,f and killed another,g and stoned another.h 36 Again, he sent other servants more than

Mark 12. 1-12.

1 And he began to speak unto them by parables. A *certain* man planted a vineyard,e and set an hedge about *it,* and digged *a place for* the winefat, and built a tower, and let it out to husbandmen, and went into a far country. 2 And at the season he sent to the husbandmen a servant, that he might receive from the husbandmen of the fruit of the vineyard. 3 And they caught *him,* and beat him,f and sent *him* away empty. 4 And again he sent unto them another servant;

Luke 20. 9-19.

9 Then began he to speak to the people this parable; A certain man planted a vineyard,e and let it forth to husbandmen, and went into a far country for a long time.

10 And at the season he sent a servant to the husbandmen, that they should give him of the fruit of the vineyard: but the husbandmen beat him, and sent *him* away empty.

11 And again he sent another servant: and they

---

c Matt. 14. 5; John 5. 35.

d Luke 7. 29, 30.   e Isa. 5. 1-4.

f Jer. 37. 15; 38. 6.   g Jer. 26. 20-23.

h 2 Chron. 24. 21.

Matt. 21.	Mark 12.	Luke 20.
the first: and they did unto them likewise. 37 But last of all he sent unto them his son,[i] saying, They will reverence my son. 38 But when the husbandmen saw the son, they said among themselves, This is the heir; come, let us kill him, and let us seize on his inheritance. 39 And they caught him, and cast *him* out of the vineyard, and slew *him.* 40 When the lord of the vineyard cometh, what will he do unto those husbandmen? 41 They say unto him, He will miserably destroy those wicked men, and will let out *his* vineyard unto other husbandmen, which shall render him the fruits in their seasons. 42 Jesus saith unto them, Did ye never read in the Scriptures,[j] The stone which the builders rejected, the same is become the head of the corner: this is the Lord's doing, and it is marvellous in our eyes? 43 Therefore say I unto you, The kingdom of God shall be taken from you, and given to a nation bringing forth the fruits thereof.[k] 44 And whosoever shall fall on this stone shall be broken: but on whomsoever it shall	and at him they cast stones, and wounded *him* in the head, and sent *him* away shamefully handled. 5 And again he sent another, and him they killed, and many others; beating some, and killing some. 6 Having yet therefore one son, his wellbeloved,[1] he sent him also last unto them, saying, They will reverence my son. 7 But those husbandmen said among themselves, This is the heir; come, let us kill him, and the inheritance shall be our's. 8 And they took him, and killed *him,* and cast *him* out of the vineyard. 9 What shall therefore the lord of the vineyard do? He will come and destroy the husbandmen, and will give the vineyard unto others. 10 And have ye not read this Scripture;[j] The stone which the builders rejected is become the head of the corner: 11 this was the Lord's doing, and it is marvellous in our eyes?	beat him also, and entreated *him* shamefully, and sent *him* away empty. 12 And again he sent a third: and they wounded him also, and cast *him* out. 13 Then said the Lord of the vineyard, What shall I do? I will send my beloved son:[i] it may be they will reverence *him* when they see him. 14 But when the husbandmen saw[1] him, they reasoned among themselves, saying, This is the heir; come, let us kill him, that the inheritance may be our's. 15 So they cast him out of the vineyard, and killed *him.* What therefore shall the lord of the vineyard do unto them? 16 He shall come and destroy these husbandmen, and shall give the vineyard to others. And when they heard *it,* they said, God forbid. 17 And he beheld them, and said, What is this then that is written, The stone which the builders rejected, the same is become the head of the corner? 18 Whosoever shall fall upon that stone shall be broken; but on whomso-

---

His only and beloved Son. This is very striking and important, as showing how Christ made an essential distinction between Himself and all former messengers of God; they were but servants, while He stood in | the wholly peculiar relation of Son to God, that is, He was a Divine person: comp. Heb. 1. 1-3, and 3. 5, 6.
  j Psa. 118. 22.
  k Comp. Acts 13. 46-48.

Matt. 21.	Mark 12.	Luke 20.
all, it will grind him to powder.[l] [45] And when the chief priests and Pharisees had heard his parables, they perceived that he spake of them. [46] But when they sought to lay hands on him, they feared the multitude, because they took him for a prophet.	[12] And they sought to lay hold on him, but feared the people: for they knew that he had spoken the parable against them: and they left him, and went their way.	ever it shall fall, it will grind him to powder. [19] And the chief priests and the scribes the same hour sought to lay hands on him; and they feared the people: for they perceived that he had spoken this parable against them.

§ 117. PARABLE OF THE MARRIAGE OF THE KING'S SON.—*Jerusalem.*
Third Day of the Week.

Matt. 22. 1–14. [1] And Jesus answered and spake unto them again by parables, and said, [2] The kingdom of heaven is like unto a certain king,[m] which made a marriage for his son, [3] and sent forth his servants to call them that were bidden to the wedding: and they would not come.[n] [4] Again, he sent forth other servants, saying, Tell them which are bidden, Behold, I have prepared my dinner: my oxen and *my* fatlings *are* killed, and all things *are* ready: come unto the marriage. [5] But they made light of *it*, and went their ways, one to his farm, another to his merchandise: [6] and the remnant took his servants, and entreated *them* spitefully, and slew *them*. [7] But when the king heard *thereof*, he was wroth: and he sent forth his armies, and destroyed those murderers, and burned up their city. [8] Then saith he to his servants, The wedding is ready, but they which were bidden were not worthy. [9] Go ye therefore into the highways, and as many as ye shall find, bid to the marriage. [10] So those servants went out into the highways, and gathered together all as many as they found, both bad and good: and the wedding was furnished with guests. [11] And when the king came in to see the guests, he saw there a man which had not on a wedding garment: [12] And he saith unto him, Friend, how camest thou in hither not having a wedding garment? And he was speechless. [13] Then said the king to the servants, Bind him hand and foot, and take him away, and cast *him* into outer darkness: [o] there shall be weeping and gnashing of teeth. [14] For many are called, but *few* are chosen. [p]

§ 118. INSIDIOUS QUESTION OF THE PHARISEES AND HERODIANS.—*Jerusalem.*
Third Day of the Week.

Matt. 22. 15–22.	Mark 12. 13–17.	Luke 20. 20–26.
[15] Then went the Pharisees, and took counsel how they might entangle him in *his* talk. [16] And they sent out unto him their disciples with the Herodians,[q] saying, Master, we know that thou art true, and teachest the way of God in truth, neither carest thou for any	[13] And they send unto him certain of the Pharisees and of the Herodians,[q] to catch him in *his* words. [14] And when they were come, they say unto him, Master, we know that thou art true, and carest for no man: for thou regardest not the person of	[20] And they watched *him*, and sent forth spies, which should feign themselves just men, that they might take hold of his words, that so they might deliver him unto the power and authority of the governor. [21] And they asked him, saying, Master, we know

---

[l] Comp. Isa. 15; Zech. 12. 3; Dan. 2. 34, 35, 44.
[m] Luke 14. 16–18; Rev. 19. 6–9.

[n] John 5. 40; Rom. 10. 16–21.
[o] Matt. 8. 12.   [p] Matt. 20. 16.
[q] See Note *s* on § 38.

Matt. 22.	Mark 12.	Luke 20.

man: for thou regardest not the person of men. [17] Tell us therefore, What thinkest thou? Is it lawful to give tribute unto Cæsar, or not? [18] But Jesus perceived their **wickedness,** and said, Why tempt ye me, *ye* hypocrites? [19] show me the tribute money. And they brought unto him a penny.* [20] And he saith unto them, Whose *is* this image and superscription? [21] They say unto him, Cæsar's. Then saith he unto them, Render therefore unto Cæsar the things which are Cæsar's,* and unto God the things that are God's.† [22] When they had heard *these words,* they marvelled, and left him, and went their way.

men, but teachest the way of God in truth:

Is it lawful to give tribute to Cæsar, or not? [15] Shall we give, or shall we not give? But he, knowing their hypocrisy, said unto them, Why tempt ye me? bring me a penny, that I may see *it.* [16] And they brought *it.* And he saith unto them, Whose *is* this image and superscription? And they said unto him, Cæsar's. [17] And Jesus answering said unto them, Render to Cæsar the things that are Cæsar's,* and to God the things that are God's.† And they marvelled at him.

that thou sayest and teachest rightly, neither acceptest thou the person *of any,* but teachest the way of God truly: [22] Is it lawful for us to give tribute unto Cæsar, or no? [23] But he perceived their craftiness, and said unto them, Why tempt ye me? [24] Show me a penny. Whose image and superscription hath it? They answered and said, Cæsar's. [25] And he said unto them, Render therefore unto Cæsar the things which be Cæsar's,* and unto God the things which be God's. [26] And they could not take hold of his words before the people: and they marvelled at his answer, and held their peace.

§ 119. Insidious Question of the Sadducees: the Resurrection.
Jerusalem.
Third Day of the Week.

Matt. 22. 23-33.	Mark 12. 18-27.	Luke 20. 27-40.

[23] The same day came to him the Sadducees, which say that there is no resurrection, and asked him,

[24] saying, Master, Moses said,˵ If a man die, having no children, his brother shall marry his wife, and raise up seed unto his brother.

[25] Now there were with us seven brethren: and the first, when he had married a wife, deceased, and, having no issue, left his wife unto his brother: [26] likewise the second also,

[18] Then come unto him the Sadducees, which say there is no resurrection; and they asked him, saying, [19] Master, Moses wrote unto us,˵ If a man's brother die, and leave *his* wife *behind him,* and leave no children, that his brother should take his wife, and raise up seed unto his brother. [20] Now there were seven brethren: and the first took a wife, and dying left no seed. [21] And the second took her, and died, neither left he any seed: and the third like-

[27] Then came to him certain of the Sadducees, which deny that there is any resurrection; and they asked him, [28] saying, Master, Moses wrote unto us,˵ If any man's brother die, having a wife, and he die without children, that his brother should take his wife, and raise up seed unto his brother. [29] There were therefore seven brethren: and the first took a wife, and died without children. [30] And the second took her to wife, and he died childless. [31] And the third took her

---

* *A penny:* the Roman *denarius* (equal to 7½*d.* of our money) was the coin in which the tribute (or rather poll-tax, *census*) had to be paid.

* Rom. 13. 7.

† Dan. 3. 16-18; 6. 10-13; Acts 5. 29.

˵ Deut. 25. 5.   Comp. Gen. 38. 8.

Matt. 22.

and the third, unto the seventh. ²⁷ And last of all the woman died also.

²⁸ Therefore in the resurrection whose wife shall she be of the seven ? for they all had her. ²⁹ Jesus answered and said unto them, Ye do err, not knowing the Scriptures, nor the power of God.

³⁰ For in the resurrection they neither marry, nor are given in marriage, but are as the angels of God in heaven.

³¹ But as touching the resurrection of the dead, have ye not read *v* that which was spoken unto you by God, saying,*w* ³² I am the God of Abraham, and the God of Isaac, and the God of Jacob ? God is not the God of the dead, but of the living. ³³ And when the multitude heard *this*, they were astonished at his doctrine.

Mark 12.

wise. ²² And the seven had her, and left no seed : last of all the woman died also.

²³ In the resurrection therefore, when they shall rise, whose wife shall she be of them ? for the seven had her to wife. ²⁴ And Jesus answering said unto them, Do ye not therefore err, because ye know not the Scriptures, neither the power of God ? ²⁵ For when they shall rise from the dead, they neither marry, nor are given in marriage : but are as the angels which are in heaven.

²⁶ And as touching the dead, that they rise : have ye not read in the book of Moses,*v* how in the bush God spake unto him, saying, I *am* the God of Abraham, and the God of Isaac, and the God of Jacob ? ²⁷ He is not the God of the dead, but the God of the living : ye therefore do greatly err.

Luke 20.

and in like manner the seven also : and they left no children, and died. ³² Last of all the woman died also. ³³ Therefore in the resurrection whose wife of them is she ? for seven had her to wife. ³⁴ And Jesus answering said unto them, The children of this world marry, and are given in marriage : ³⁵ but they which shall be accounted worthy to obtain that world, and the resurrection from the dead, neither marry, nor are given in marriage : ³⁶ neither can they die any more : for they are equal unto the angels ; and are the children of God, being the children of the resurrection. ³⁷ Now that the dead are raised, even Moses *v* showed at the bush,*w* when he calleth the Lord the God of Abraham, and the God of Isaac, and the God of Jacob. ³⁸ For he is not a God of the dead, but of the living : for all live unto him. ³⁹ Then certain of the scribes answering said, Master, thou hast well said. ⁴⁰ And after that they durst not ask him any *question at all.*

§ 120. THE TWO GREAT COMMANDMENTS.—*Jerusalem.*

Third Day of the Week.

Matt. 22. 34–40. ³⁴ But when the Pharisees had heard that he had put the Sadducees to silence, they were gathered together. ³⁵ Then one of them, *which was* a lawyer, asked *him a question*, tempting him, and saying, ³⁶ Master,

Mark 12. 28–34. ²⁸ And one of the scribes came, and having heard them reasoning together, and perceiving that he had answered them well, asked him, Which is the first commandment of all ? ²⁹ And Jesus answered him, The first of

---

v Our Lord, in dealing with the Sadducees, takes his proof from the Pentateuch, because to that alone they allowed Divine authority. He meets them on their own ground, saying, " *even* Moses showed," etc. In other books of the Old Testament we find ampler and clearer proof, e.g., Dan. 12. 2, 3 ; Hos. 13. 14.

w Ex. 3. 6. *The Bush*, means here the *section* so called.

Matt. 22.

which is the great commandment in the law? [37] Jesus said unto him,[w] Thou shalt love the Lord thy God with all thy heart, and with all thy soul, and with all thy mind. [38] This is the first and great commandment. [39] And the second is like unto it,[x] Thou shalt love thy neighbour as thyself. [40] On these two commandments hang all the law and the prophets.

Mark 12.

all the commandments is,[w] Hear, (Israel; The Lord our God is one Lord [30] and thou shalt love the Lord thy Go with all thy heart, and with all thy soul and with all thy mind, and with all thy strength: this is the first command ment. [31] And the second is like, namely this,[x] Thou shalt love thy neighbour a thyself. There is none other command ment greater than these. [32] And the scribe said unto him, Well, Master, thou hast said the truth: for there is one God; and there is none other but he [33] and to love him with all the heart, and with all the understanding, and with all the soul, and with all the strength, and to love his neighbour as himself, i more than all whole burnt offerings and sacrifices.[v] [34] And when Jesus saw that he answered discreetly, he said unto him, Thou art not far from the kingdom of God. And no man after that durst ask him any question.

§ 121. How is Christ the Son of David?—*Jerusalem.*

Third Day of the Week.

Matt. 22. 41–46.

[41] While the Pharisees were gathered together, Jesus asked them, saying, [42] What think ye of Christ? whose son is he? They say unto him, The Son of David. [43] He saith unto them, How then doth David in spirit[z] call him Lord, saying,[a] [44] The Lord said unto my Lord, Sit thou on my right hand, till I make thine enemies thy footstool?[b] [45] If David then call him Lord, how is he his son? [46] And no man was able to answer him a word, neither durst any man from that day forth ask him any more questions.

Mark 12. 35–37.

[35] And Jesus answered and said, while he taught in the temple, How say the scribes that Christ is the Son of David?

[36] For David himself said[z] by the Holy Ghost,[a] The Lord said to my Lord, Sit thou on my right hand, till I make thine enemies thy footstool.[b]

[37] David therefore himself calleth him Lord; and whence is then his son? And the common people heard him gladly.

Luke 20. 41–44.

[41] An he said unto them, How say they that Christ i David's son?

[42] And David himself saith in the book of Psalms,[a] The Lord said unto my Lord, Sit thou on my right hand [43] till I make thine enemies thy footstool.[b]

[44] David therefore calleth him Lord, how is he then his son?

§ 122. Warnings against the Evil Example of the Scribes and Pharisees.—*Jerusalem.*

Third Day of the Week.

Mark 12. 38, 39.

[38] And he said unto them in his doctrine, Beware of the scribes, which love to go in long clothing,

Luke 20. 45, 46.

[45] Then in the audience of all the people he said unto his disciples, [46] Beware of the scribes,

---

[w] Deut. 6. 4, 5.   [z] Lev. 19. 18; Luke 10. 29–37.   [y] 1 Sam. 15. 22; Mic. 6. 6–8.
[s] 2 Sam. 23. 2.   [a] Psa. 110. 1.   [b] Comp. Acts 2. 34, 35; 1 Cor. 15. 25

Mark 12.

and *love* salutations in the market-places, **39** and the chief seats in the synagogues, and the uppermost rooms at feasts.

Luke 20.

which desire to walk in long robes, and love greetings in the markets, and the highest seats in the synagogues, and the chief rooms at feasts.

Matt. 23. 1-12. **1** Then spake Jesus to the multitude, and to his disciples, **2** saying, The scribes and the Pharisees sit in Moses' seat: **3** all therefore whatsoever they bid you observe, *that* observe and do; but do not ye after their works: for they say, and do not.*d* **4** For they bind heavy burdens and grievous to be borne, and lay *them* on men's shoulders; but they *themselves* will not move them with one of their fingers. **5** But all their works they do for to be seen of men: they make broad their phylacteries,*e* and enlarge the borders of their garments, **6** and love *f* the uppermost rooms at feasts, and the chief seats in the synagogues, **7** and greetings in the markets, and to be called of men, Rabbi, Rabbi. **8** But be not ye called Rabbi: for one is your Master, *even* Christ; and all ye are brethren. **9** And call no *man* your father upon the earth: for one is your Father, which is in heaven. **10** Neither be ye called masters: for one is your Master, *even* Christ. **11** But he that is greatest among you shall be your servant. **12** And whosoever shall exalt himself shall be abased; and he that shall humble himself shall be exalted.*g*

§ 123. WOES AGAINST THE SCRIBES AND PHARISEES. LAMENTATION OVER JERUSALEM.—*Jerusalem.*

Third Day of the Week.

Matt 23. 13-39.

14 Woe unto you,*h* scribes and Pharisees, hypocrites! for ye devour widows' houses, and for a pretence make long prayer: therefore ye shall receive the greater damnation.—**13** But woe unto you, scribes and

Mark 12. 40.

40 Which devour widows' houses, and for a pretence make long prayers: these shall receive greater damnation.

Luke 20. 47.

47 Which devour widows' houses, and for a show make long prayers: the same shall receive greater damnation.

Pharisees, hypocrites: for ye shut up *i* the kingdom of heaven against men: for ye neither go in *yourselves*, neither suffer ye them that are entering to go in.*j*—**15** Woe unto you, scribes and Pharisees, hypocrites! for ye compass sea and land to make one proselyte, and when he is made, ye make him twofold more the child of hell than yourselves.

16 Woe unto you, *ye* blind guides, which say, Whosoever shall swear by th temple, it is nothing; but whosoever shall swear by the gold of the temple, he i a debtor! **17** *Ye* fools and blind: for whether is greater, the gold, or the temple tha*i* sanctifieth the gold?*k* **18** And, Whosoever shall swear by the altar, it is nothing; but whosoever sweareth by the gift that is upon it, he is guilty. **19** *Ye* fools and blind: for whether *is* greater, the gift, or the altar that sanctifieth the gift?*l*

---

c Neh. 8. 4-8.   *d* Rom. 2. 17-24.
e *Phylacteries* (φυλακτήρια, from φυλάσσω, *to keep* or *guard*) were strips of parchment, inscribed with the passages in Deut. 6. 4-9; 11. 13-21; Ex. 13. 2-16, worn at prayer on the forehead and the left arm (according to a literal understanding of Ex. 13. 9), either as mementos to remind the wearer to *keep* the law, or as charms to *guard* him from evil. Such things are still used by the Jews,

and go by the Hebrew name, *tephillin* (*prayers*).
f Luke 14. 7-11.
g Job 22. 29; Prov. 29. 23; Isa. 57. 15; 1 Pet. 5. 5.
h In Matthew, verses 13 and 14 are transposed, as in the best editions of the Greek.
i Luke 11. 52.   *j* 1 Thess. 2. 15, 16.
k Ex. 30. 29.
l Ex. 29. 37.

Matt. 23.

[20] Whoso therefore shall swear by the altar, sweareth by it, and by all things thereon. [21] And whoso shall swear by the temple, sweareth by it, and by him that dwelleth therein. [22] And he that shall swear by heaven, sweareth by the throne of God, and by him that sitteth thereon.

[23] Woe unto you, scribes and Pharisees, hypocrites! for ye pay tithe [m] of mint and anise and cummin, and have omitted the weightier *matters* of the law, judgment, mercy, and faith: these ought ye to have done, and not to leave the other undone. [24] *Ye* blind guides, which strain at [n] a gnat, and swallow a camel. [25] Woe unto you, scribes and Pharisees, hypocrites! for ye make clean the outside of the cup and of the platter, but within they are full of extortion and excess. [26] *Thou* blind Pharisee, cleanse first that *which is* within the cup and platter, that the outside of them may be clean also. [27] Woe unto you, scribes and Pharisees, hypocrites! for ye are like unto whited sepulchres, which indeed appear beautiful outward, but are within full of dead *men's* bones, and of all uncleanness. [28] Even so ye also outwardly appear righteous unto men, but within ye are full of hypocrisy and iniquity.

[29] Woe unto you, scribes and Pharisees, hypocrites! because ye build the tombs of the prophets, and garnish the sepulchres of the righteous, [30] and say, If we had been in the days of our fathers, we would not have been partakers with them in the blood of the prophets. [31] Wherefore ye be witnesses unto yourselves, that ye are the children of them which killed the prophets. [32] Fill ye up then the measure of your fathers. [33] *Ye* serpents, *ye* generation of vipers, how can ye escape the damnation of hell? [34] Wherefore, behold, I send unto you prophets,[o] and wise men, and scribes: and *some* of them ye shall kill and crucify; and *some* of them shall ye scourge in your synagogues, and persecute *them* from city to city: [35] that upon you may come all the righteous blood shed upon the earth, from the blood of righteous Abel unto the blood of Zacharias son of Barachias,[p] whom ye slew between the temple and the altar.[q] [36] Verily I say unto you, All these things shall come upon this generation.

[37] O Jerusalem, Jerusalem,[r] *thou* that killest the prophets, and stonest them which are sent unto thee, how often would I have gathered thy children together, even as a hen gathereth her chickens under *her* wings, and ye would not! [38] Behold, your house is left unto you desolate.[s] [39] For I say unto you, Ye shall not see me henceforth, till ye shall say, Blessed *is* he that cometh in the name of the Lord.[t]

§ 124. THE WIDOW'S MITE.—*Jerusalem.*

Third Day of the Week.

Mark 12. 41–44.	Luke 21. 1–4.
[41] And Jesus sat over against the treasury,[u] and beheld how the people cast money into the treasury:[v] and many that were rich cast in much. [42] And there came a certain	[1] And he looked up, and saw the rich men casting their gifts into the treasury.[v] [2] And he saw also a certain poor widow casting in thither two mites.

[m] Luke 11. 42.   1 Sam. 15. 22; Mic. 6. 6–8.

[n] Rather, "strain *out*," by filtration.

[o] Comp. Luke 11. 49–51.

[p] *Zacharias son of Barachias.* The name of the father here creates some difficulty, because in 2 Chron. 24. 20 we find another name, *Jehoiada.* Various solutions of this difficulty have been proposed. It is possible that the father's name might be known in both forms, the words having substantially the same import (Jehoiada, i.e., *whom Jeho-*

vah knows or *cares for*; Barachiah, i.e., *whom Jehovah blesses*). After this manner, for example, king Uzziah (i.e., *strength of Jehovah*, 2 Chron. 26. 1) was called also Azariah (i.e., *whom Jehovah helps*, 2 Kings 14. 21).   [q] Gen. 4. 8; 2 Chron. 24. 20–22.

[r] Luke 13. 34, 35.

[s] Psa. 69. 25; Jer. 12. 7; 22. 5.

[t] Psa. 118. 26.

[u] *The treasury :* on this see Note *u* on § 85.

[v] 2 Kings 12. 9.

Mark 12.	Luke 21.
poor widow, and she threw in two mites, which make a farthing. ⁴³ And he called *unto him* his disciples, and saith unto them, Verily I say unto you, That this poor widow hath cast more in, than all they which have cast into the treasury: ⁴⁴ for all *they* did cast in of their abundance; but she of her want did cast in all that she had,ʷ *even* all her living.	³ And he said, Of a truth I say unto you, that this poor widow hath cast in more than they all: ⁴ for all these have of their abundance cast in unto the offerings of God: but she of her penury hath cast in all the living that she had.ʷ

§ 125. CERTAIN GREEKS DESIRE TO SEE JESUS.—*Jerusalem.*
Third Day of the Week.

John 12. 20–36. ²⁰ And there were certain Greeksˣ among them that came up to worship at the feast: ²¹ the same came therefore to Philip, which was of Bethsaida of Galilee, and desired him, saying, Sir, we would see Jesus. ²² Philip cometh and telleth Andrew: and again Andrew and Philip tell Jesus. ²³ And Jesus answered them, saying, The hour is come, that the Son of man should be glorified. ²⁴ Verily, verily, I say unto you, Except a corn of wheat fall into the ground and die, it abideth alone: but if it die,ʸ it bringeth forth much fruit. ²⁵ He that loveth his life shall lose it; and he that hateth his life in this world shall keep it unto life eternal.ᶻ ²⁶ If any man serve me, let him follow me; and where I am, there shall also my servant be: if any man serve me, him will *my* Father honour. ²⁷ Now is my soul troubled;ᵃ and what shall I say? Father, save me from this hour: but for this causeᵇ came I unto this hour. ²⁸ Father, glorify thy name. Then came there a voice from heaven, *saying,* I have both glorified *it,* and will glorify *it* again. ²⁹ The people therefore, that stood by, and heard *it,* said that it thundered: others said, An angel spake to him. ³⁰ Jesus answered and said, This voice came not because of me, but for your sakes. ³¹ Now is the judgment of this world: now shall the prince of this world be cast out. ³² And I, if I be lifted up from the earth, will draw all menᶜ unto me. ³³ This he said, signifying what death he should die. ³⁴ The people answered him, We have heard out of the law that Christ abideth for ever:ᵈ and how sayest thou, The Son of man must be lifted up? who is this Son of man? ³⁵ Then Jesus said unto them, Yet a little while is the light with you. Walk while ye have the light, lest darkness come upon you: for he that walketh in darkness knoweth not whither he goeth. ³⁶ While ye have light, believe in the light, that ye may be the children of light. These things spake Jesus, and departed, and did hide himself from them.

§ 126. REFLECTIONS UPON THE UNBELIEF OF THE JEWS – *Jerusalem.*
Third Day of the Week.

John 12. 37–50. ³⁷ But though he had done so many miracles before them, yet they believed not on him: ³⁸ that the saying of Esaias the prophet might be fulfilled which he spake,ᵉ Lord, who hath believed our report? and to whom hath the arm of

---

ʷ 2 Cor. 8. 1–3.
ˣ This incident of the Greeks is inserted here on the third day of the week, rather than on the first, because of John 12. 36; which implies that Jesus afterwards appeared no more in public as a teacher. He immediately takes leave of the temple.
ʸ 1 Cor. 15. 36.   ᶻ Matt. 10. 39.
ᵃ Luke 12. 50.

ᵇ *For this cause, etc.* : i.e., in order to die as the sacrifice for sin.
ᶜ i.e., not Jews alone. Our Lord takes occasion from the presence of the Greeks (ver. 20) to announce the comprehension of the Gentiles in His work of redemption.
ᵈ 2 Sam. 7. 13; Psa. 89. 29, 36; 110. 4; Dan. 7. 14.
ᵉ Isa. 53. 1.

John 12.

the Lord been revealed? [39] Therefore they could not believe, because that Esaias said again,/ [40] He hath blinded their eyes, and hardened their heart; that they should not see with *their* eyes, nor understand with *their* heart, and be converted, and I should heal them. [41] These things said Esaias, when he saw his glory,*g* and spake of him.*h* [42] Nevertheless among the chief rulers also many believed on him; but because of the Pharisees they did not confess *him*, lest they should be put out of the synagogue:*i* [43] for they loved the praise of men more than the praise of God.

[44] Jesus cried and said, He that believeth on me, believeth not on me, but on him that sent me. [45] And he that seeth me seeth him that sent me. [46] I am come a light into the world, that whosoever believeth on me should not abide in darkness. [47] And if any man hear my words, and believe not, I judge him not: for I came not to judge the world, but to save the world.*j* [48] He that rejecteth me, and receiveth not my words, hath one that judgeth him: the word that I have spoken, the same shall judge him in the last day. [49] For I have not spoken of myself; but the Father which sent me, he gave me a commandment, what I should say, and what I should speak. [50] And I know that his commandment is life everlasting: whatsoever I speak therefore, even as the Father said unto me, so I speak.*k*

§ 127.   JESUS, ON TAKING LEAVE OF THE TEMPLE, FORETELLS ITS DESTRUCTION AND THE PERSECUTION OF HIS DISCIPLES.—*Jerusalem. Mount of Olives.*

Third Day of the Week.

Matt. 24. 1–14. [1] And Jesus went out,*l* and departed from the temple: and his disciples came to *him* for to show him the buildings of the temple. [2] And Jesus said unto them, See ye not all these things? verily I say unto you, There shall not be left here one stone upon another, that shall not be thrown down. [3] And as he sat upon the mount of Olives, the disciples came unto him privately, saying, Tell us, when shall these things be? and what	Mark 13. 1–13. [1] And as he went out of the temple, one of his disciples saith unto him, Master, see what manner of stones and what buildings *are here*! [2] And Jesus answering said unto him, Seest thou these great buildings? there shall not be left one stone upon another, that shall not be thrown down. [3] And as he sat upon the mount of Olives over against the temple, Peter and James and John and Andrew asked him privately, [4] Tell us, when shall these things	Luke 21. 5–19. [5] And as some spake of the temple, how it was adorned with goodly stones and gifts, he said, [6] *As for* these things which ye behold, the days will come, in the which there shall not be left one stone upon another, that shall not be thrown down. [7] And they asked him, saying, Master, but when shall these things be? and what sign *will there be* when these

---

f Isa. 6. 10.

g When he saw His glory, etc. This passage, when compared with Isa. 6. 1, 3, 5, furnishes a most striking proof of Christ's Divinity; for it declares Him to be even *Jehovah*, whose glory the prophet saw in the temple, and concerning whom he spoke in that chapter.

   h Isa. 6. 1, sq.   *i* John 9. 22.
   j John 3. 17.   *k* See in § 134.

l Our Lord takes leave of the temple, to which He returns no more; at the same time foretelling its impending destruction. On

His way to Bethany, He seats Himself for a time upon the mount of Olives, over against the temple, where the city was spread out before Him as on a map; and here four of His disciples put to Him the question, "When shall these things be?" According to Matthew they add, "and what shall be the sign of thy coming, and of the end of the world?" They still believed, like the other Jews, that the Messiah was to go forth as a temporal prince, to subvert the then existing order of things, to subdue all nations, and reign in peace and splendour over the world: see Luke 24. 21; Acts 1. 6.

Matt. 24.

shall be the sign of thy coming, and of the end of the world ? ⁴ And Jesus answered and said unto them, Take heed that no man deceive you. ⁵ For many shall come in my name, saying, I am Christ;ᵐ and shall deceive many. ⁶ And ye shall hear of wars and rumours of wars: see that ye be not troubled:ⁿ for all *these things* must come to pass, but the end is not yet. ⁷ For nation shall rise against nation, and kingdom against kingdom: and there shall be famines, and pestilences, and earthquakes, in divers places. ⁸ All these *are* the beginning of sorrows.

Mark 13.

be ? and what *shall be* the sign when all these things shall be fulfilled ? ⁵ And Jesus answering them began to say, Take heed lest any *man* deceive you: ⁶ for many shall come in my name, saying, I am *Christ;*ᵐ and shall deceive many. ⁷ And when ye shall hear of wars and rumours of wars, be ye not troubled:ⁿ for *such things* must needs be: but the end *shall* not *be* yet. ⁸ For nation shall rise against nation, and kingdom against kingdom: and there shall be earthquakes in divers places, and there shall be famines and troubles: these *are* the beginnings of sorrows.

Luke 21.

things shall come to pass ? ⁸ And he said, Take heed that ye be not deceived: for many shall come in my name, saying, I am *Christ ;*ᵐ and the time draweth near: go ye not therefore after them. ⁹ But when ye shall hear of wars and commotions, be not terrified:ⁿ for these things must first come to pass; but the end *is* not by and by. ¹⁰ Then said he unto them, Nation shall rise against nation, and kingdom against kingdom: ¹¹ and great earthquakes shall be in divers places, and famines, and pestilences; and fearful sights and great signs shall there be from heaven.

Mark 13.

But take heed to yourselves: for they shall deliver you up to councils; and in the synagogues ye shall be beaten: and ye shall be brought before rulers and kings for my sake, for a testimony against them.—¹¹ But when they shall lead *you*, and deliver you up, take no thought beforehand what ye shall speak, neither do ye premeditate:° but whatsoever shall be given you in that hour, that speak ye: for it is not ye that speak, but the Holy Ghost.

Luke 21.

¹² But before all these, they shall lay their hands on you, and persecute *you*, delivering *you* up to the synagogues, and into prisons, being brought before kings and rulers for my name's sake. ¹³ And it shall turn to you for a testimony. ¹⁴ Settle *it* therefore in your hearts, not to meditate° before what ye shall answer: ¹⁵ for I will give you a mouth and wisdom, which all your adversaries shall not be able to gainsay nor resist.

Matt. 24.

⁹ Then shall they deliver you up to be afflicted, and shall kill you: and ye shall be hated of all nations for my name's sake. ¹⁰ And then shall many be offended, and shall betray one another, and shall hate one another. ¹¹ And many false prophets shall rise, and shall deceive many. ¹² And because iniquity shall abound, the love of many

Mark 13.

¹² Now the brother shall betray the brother to death, and the father the son; and children shall rise up against *their* parents, and shall cause them to be put to death. ¹³ And ye shall be hated of all *men* for my name's sake:

Luke 21.

¹⁶ And ye shall be betrayed both by parents, and brethren, and kinsfolks, and friends; and *some* of you shall they cause to be put to death.

¹⁷ And ye shall be hated of all *men* for my name's sake.

ᵐ Comp. Acts 5. 36, 37; 8. 9, 10.　　ⁿ Comp. Isa. 8. 11–14.　　° Matt. 10. 19, 20.

Matt. 24.	Mark 13.	Luke 21.

shall wax cold.ᴾ ¹³ But he that shall endure unto the end, the same shall be saved.ᵠ ¹⁴ And this gospel of the kingdom shall be preached in all the world for a witness unto all nations; and then shall the end come.

but he that shall endure unto the end, the same shall be saved.ᵠ— ¹⁰ And the gospel must first be published among all nations.—

¹⁸ But there shall not an hair of your head perish. ¹⁹ In your patience possess ye your souls.

§ 128. The Signs of Christ's coming to Destroy Jerusalem and put an End to the Jewish State and Dispensation.—*Mount of Olives.*

Third Day of the Week.

Matt. 24. 15–42.	Mark 13. 14–37.	Luke 21. 20–36.

¹⁵ When ye therefore shall see the abomination of desolation,ʳ spoken of by Daniel the prophet,ˢ stand in the holy place, (whoso readeth, let him understand:) ¹⁶ then let them which be in Judea flee into the mountains: ¹⁷ let him which is on the housetop not come down to take any thing out of his house: ¹⁸ neither let him which is in the field return back to take his clothes.

¹⁹ And woe unto them that are with child, and to them that give suck in those days! ²⁰ But pray ye that your flight be not in the winter, neither on the sab-

¹⁴ But when ye shall see the abomination of desolation, spoken of by Daniel the prophet,ˢ standing where it ought not, (let him that readeth understand,) then let them that be in Judea flee to the mountains: ¹⁵ and let him that is on the housetop not go down into the house, neither enter *therein*, to take any thing out of his house: ¹⁶ and let him that is in the field not turn back again for to take up his garment. ¹⁷ But woe to them that are with child, and to them that give suck in those days! ¹⁸ And pray ye that your flight be not in the winter. ¹⁹ For *in* those days shall be

²⁰ And when ye shall see Jerusalem compassed with armies, then know that the desolation thereof is nigh. ²¹ Then let them which are in Judea flee to the mountains; and let them which are in the midst of it depart out; and let not them that are in the countries enter thereinto. ²² For these be the days of vengeance, that all things which are written may be fulfilled.

²³ But woe unto them that are with child, and to them that give suck, in those days! for there shall be great distress in the land, and wrath upon this people. ²⁴ And they shall

---

ᴾ Comp. 2 Tim. 3. 1–5.
ᵠ Rev. 2. 10
ʳ That the *abomination of desolation,* Matt. 24. 15, etc., refers to the Roman armies by which Jerusalem was destroyed, is shown by Luke 21. 20.

The figurative language of these verses is similar to that of many passages in the Old Testament which refer to civil commotions and historical events. See Isa. 13. 9, sq.; 19. 1, 5, sq.; 34. 2, 4, sq.; Ezek. 32. 2, 7; Psa. 18. 7–14; 68. 1, sq., etc. Further, Luke 21. 28 shows that these verses cannot refer to the general judgment of the great and final day; and the same appears also from the limitation

to *this generation,* in Matt. 24. 34, and the parallel passages.

Matt. 24. 36–42 connects itself directly with what precedes, see ver. 36; and refers likewise to the overthrow of the Jewish nation and dispensation. Comp. Luke 17. 20–37. But with ver. 42 of Matthew all direct reference to the Jewish catastrophe terminates. This appears from the nature of the language; and from the fact, that thus far both Mark and Luke give parallel reports; while at this point their report cease, and all that follows belongs to Matthew alone. This goes to show that at this point a new topic is introduced.

ˢ Dan. 9. 27.

Matt. 24.

bath day :[t] 21 for then shall be great tribulation, such as was not since the beginning of the world to this time, no, nor ever shall be. 22 And except those days should be shortened, there should no flesh be saved : but for the elect's sake those days shall be shortened. 23 Then if any man shall say unto you, Lo, here *is* Christ, or there; believe *it* not.[u] 24 For there shall arise false Christs, and false prophets, and shall show great signs and wonders;[v] insomuch that, if *it were* possible, they shall deceive the very elect.[w] 25 Behold, I have told you before. 26 Wherefore if they shall say unto you, Behold, he is in the desert; go not forth: behold, *he is* in the secret chambers; believe *it* not. 27 For as the lightning cometh out of the east, and shineth even unto the west; so shall also the coming of the Son of man be.[x] 28 For wheresoever the carcase is, there will the eagles be gathered together.[y]

29 Immediately after the tribulation of those days shall the sun be darkened, and the moon shall not give her light, and the stars shall fall from heaven, and the powers of the heavens shall be shaken :[z] 30 and then shall appear the sign of the Son of man in heaven : and then shall all the tribes of the earth mourn, and they shall see the Son of man coming in the clouds of heaven with power and great glory.[a] 31 And he shall send his angels with a great sound of a trumpet, and they shall gather together his

Mark 13.

affliction, such as was not from the beginning of the creation which God created unto this time, neither shall be. 20 And except that the Lord had shortened those days, no flesh should be saved : but for the elect's sake, whom he hath chosen, he hath shortened the days. 21 And then if any man shall say to you, Lo, here *is* Christ; or, lo, *he is* there; believe *him* not :[u] 22 for false Christs and false prophets shall rise, and shall show signs and wonders,[v] to seduce, if *it were* possible, even the elect.[w] 23 But take ye heed: behold, I have foretold you all things.

Mark 13.

24 But in those days, after that tribulation, the sun shall be darkened, and the moon shall not give her light, 25 and the stars of heaven shall fall, and the powers that are in heaven shall be shaken.[z]

26 And then shall they see the Son of man coming in the clouds with great power and glory.[a] 27 And then shall he send his angels, and shall gather together his elect from the four

Luke 21.

fall by the edge of the sword, and shall be led away captive into all nations; and Jerusalem shall be trodden down of the Gentiles, until the times of the Gentiles be fulfilled.

Luke 21.

25 And there shall be signs in the sun, and in the moon, and in the stars; and upon the earth distress of nations, with perplexity; the sea and the waves roaring; 26 men's hearts failing them for fear, and for looking after those things which are coming on the earth: for the powers of heaven shall be shaken.[z] 27 And then shall they see the Son of man coming in a cloud with power and great glory.[a] 28 And when these things begin to come to pass, then look up, and lift up your heads; for

---

[t] *Nor on the Sabbath:* probably because the Jews were accustomed to go only a short distance on that day, which distance they called a *sabbath day's journey*, reckoned about a mile. Compare Ex. 16. 29; Acts 1. 12.
[u] Luke 17. 23.

[v] 2 Thess. 2. 9–11; Rev. 13. 13.
[w] John 10. 28, 29.
[x] Luke 17. 24.
[y] Luke 17. 37; Job 39. 30.
[z] Isa. 13. 9, 10; Joel 3. 15.
[a] Dan. 7. 13, 14.

Matt. 24.	Mark 13.	Luke 21.
elect from the four winds, from one end of heaven to the other.	winds, from the uttermost part of the earth to the uttermost part of heaven.	your redemption draweth nigh.
³² Now learn a parable of the fig tree: When his branch is yet tender, and putteth forth leaves, ye know that summer *is* nigh: ³³ so likewise ye, when ye shall see all these things, know that it is near, *even* at the doors. ³⁴ Verily I say unto you, This generation *b* shall not pass, till all these things be fulfilled.*c* ³⁵ Heaven and earth shall pass away, but my words shall not pass away. ³⁶ But of that day and hour knoweth no *man*, no not the angels of heaven, but my Father only.	²⁸ Now learn a parable of the fig tree: When her branch is yet tender, and putteth forth leaves, ye know that summer is near: ²⁹ so ye in like manner, when ye shall see these things come to pass, know that it is nigh, *even* at the doors. ³⁰ Verily, I say unto you, That this generation *b* shall not pass till all these things be done.*c* ³¹ Heaven and earth shall pass away: but my words shall not pass away. ³² But of that day and *that* hour knoweth no man, no, not the angels which are in heaven, neither the Son, but the Father.	²⁹ And he spake to them a parable: Behold the fig tree, and all the trees; ³⁰ when they now shoot forth, ye see and know of your own selves that summer is now nigh at hand. ³¹ So likewise ye, when ye see these things come to pass, know ye that the kingdom of God is nigh at hand. ³² Verily I say unto you, This generation *b* shall not pass away, till all be fulfilled.*c* ³³ Heaven and earth shall pass away: but my words shall not pass away.

Matt. 24.

³⁷ But as the days of Noe *were,a* so shall also the coming of the Son of man be. ³⁸ For as in the days that were before the flood they were eating and drinking, marrying and giving in marriage, until the day that Noe entered into the ark, ³⁹ and knew not until the flood came, and took them all away; so shall also the coming of the Son of man be. ⁴⁰ Then shall two be in the field; the one shall be taken, and the other left. ⁴¹ Two *women shall be* grinding at the mill; the one shall be taken, and the other left.

	Mark 13.	Luke 21.
	³³ Take ye heed, watch and pray: for ye know not when the time is. ³⁴ *For the Son of man is* as a man taking a far journey, who left his house, and gave authority to his servants, and to every man his work, and commanded the porter to watch.	³⁴ And take heed to yourselves, lest at any time your hearts be overcharged with surfeiting, and drunkenness, and cares of this life, and *so* that day come upon you unawares. ³⁵ For as a snare shall it come on all them that dwell on the face of the whole earth. ³⁶ Watch ye therefore, and

Matt. 24.

¹² Watch therefore: for ye   ³⁵ Watch ye therefore:

---

b These words cannot be understood of the Jewish nation or the human race. The meaning is, that the men of that age should not all die (see Matt. 16. 28, in § 74) before the prophecy would be accomplished, which began to come to pass thirty-seven years after its utterance, in the destruction of Jerusalem, which event the apostle John outlived by about thirty years. The full accomplishment took place, perhaps, in the complete scattering of the Jews about fifty years later under Adrian.
c Matt. 16. 28.
d Gen. 7. 1–13; Luke 17. 26, 27.

Matt. 24.	Mark 13.	Luke 21.
know not what hour your Lord doth come.	for ye know not when the master of the house cometh, at even, or at midnight, or at the cockcrowing, or in the morning: ³⁶ lest coming suddenly he find you sleeping. ³⁷ And what I say unto you, I say unto all, Watch.	pray always, that ye may be accounted worthy to escape all these things that shall come to pass, and to stand before the Son of man.

§ 129. Christ's Coming at the Day of Judgment. Exhortation to Watchfulness. Parables: The Ten Virgins; The Five Talents.

Mount of Olives.—Third Day of the Week.

Matt. 24. 43–51; 25. 1–30. ⁴³ But know this, that if the good man of the house had known in what watch the thief would come, he would have watched, and would not have suffered his house to be broken up. ⁴⁴ Therefore be ye also ready:^e for in such an hour as ye think not the Son of man cometh. ⁴⁵ Who then is a faithful and wise servant, whom his lord hath made ruler over his household, to give them meat in due season? ⁴⁶ Blessed *is* that servant, whom his lord when he cometh shall find so doing. ⁴⁷ Verily, I say unto you, That he shall make him ruler over all his goods. ⁴⁸ But and if that evil servant shall say in his heart, My lord delayeth his coming;^f ⁴⁹ and shall begin to smite *his* fellowservants, and to eat and drink with the drunken; ⁵⁰ the lord of that servant shall come in a day when he looketh not for *him*, and in an hour that he is not aware of, ⁵¹ and shall cut him asunder, and appoint *him* his portion with the hypocrites: there shall be weeping and gnashing of teeth.

Matt. 25. ¹ Then shall the kingdom of heaven be likened unto ten virgins, which took their lamps, and went forth to meet the bridegroom. ² And five of them were wise, and five *were* foolish. ³ They that *were* foolish took their lamps, and took no oil with them: ⁴ but the wise took oil in their vessels with their lamps. ⁵ While the bridegroom tarried, they all slumbered and slept. ⁶ And at midnight there was a cry made, Behold, the bridegroom cometh; go ye out to meet him. ⁷ Then all those virgins arose, and trimmed their lamps. ⁸ And the foolish said unto the wise, Give us of your oil; for our lamps are gone out. ⁹ But the wise answered, saying, Not so ; lest there be not enough for us and you: but go ye rather to them that sell, and buy for yourselves. ¹⁰ And while they went to buy, the bridegroom came ; and they that were ready went in with him to the marriage: and the door was shut. ¹¹ Afterward came also the other virgins, saying, Lord, Lord, open to us.^g ¹² But he answered and said, Verily I say unto you, I know you not. ¹³ Watch therefore, for ye know neither the day nor the hour wherein the Son of man cometh.

¹⁴ For *the kingdom of heaven is* as a man travelling ^h into a far country, *who* called his own servants, and delivered unto them his goods. ¹⁵ And unto one he gave five talents, to another two, and to another one ; to every man according to his several ability ; and straightway took his journey. ¹⁶ Then he that had received the five talents went and traded with the same, and made *them* other five talents. ¹⁷ And likewise he that *had received* two, he also gained other two. ¹⁸ But he that had received one went and digged in the earth, and hid his lord's money. ¹⁹ After a long time the lord of those servants cometh, and reckoneth with them. ²⁰ And so he that had received five talents came and brought other five talents, saying,

---

^e 1 Thess. 5. 1–6,   ^f 2 Pet. 3. 3, 4.   ^g Luke 13. 25, 26.   ^h Luke 19. 12–28

Matt. 25.

Lord, thou deliveredst unto me five talents: behold, I have gained beside them five talents more. [31] His lord said unto him, Well done, *thou* good and faithful servant: thou hast been faithful over a few things, I will make thee ruler over many things: enter thou into the joy of thy lord. [22] He also that had received two talents came and said, Lord, thou deliveredst unto me two talents: behold, I have gained two other talents beside them. [23] His lord said unto him, Well done, good and faithful servant; thou hast been faithful over a few things, I will make thee ruler over many things: enter thou into the joy of thy lord. [24] Then he which had received the one talent came and said, Lord, I knew thee that thou art an hard man, reaping where thou hast not sown, and gathering where thou hast not strawed: [25] and I was afraid, and went and hid thy talent in the earth: lo, *there* thou hast *that is* thine. [26] His lord answered and said unto him, *Thou* wicked and slothful servant, thou knewest *i* that I reap where I sowed not, and gather where I have not strawed: [27] thou oughtest therefore to have put my money to the exchangers, and *then* at my coming I should have received mine own with usury. [28] Take therefore the talent from him, and give *it* unto him which hath ten talents. [29] For unto every one that hath shall be given, and he shall have abundance: but from him that hath not shall be taken away even that which he hath. [30] And cast ye the unprofitable servant into outer darkness: there shall be weeping and gnashing of teeth.

§ 130. SCENES ON THE JUDGMENT DAY.—*Mount of Olives.*
Third Day of the Week.

Matt. 25. 31–46. [31] When the Son of man *j* shall come in his glory, and all the holy angels with him, then shall he sit upon the throne of his glory: [32] and before him shall be gathered all nations: and he shall separate them one from another, as a shepherd divideth *his* sheep from the goats: [33] and he shall set the sheep on his right hand, but the goats on the left.

[34] Then shall the King say unto them on his right hand, Come, ye blessed of my Father, inherit the kingdom prepared for you from the foundation of the world: [35] for I was an hungred, and ye gave me meat: I was thirsty, and ye gave me drink: I was a stranger, and ye took me in: [36] naked, and ye clothed me: I was sick, and ye visited me: I was in prison, and ye came unto me. [37] Then shall the righteous answer him, saying, Lord, when saw we thee an hungred, and fed *thee ?* or thirsty, and gave *thee* drink ? [38] When saw we thee a stranger, and took *thee* in ? or naked, and clothed *thee ?* [39] or when saw we thee sick, or in prison, and came unto thee ? [40] And the King shall answer and say unto them, Verily I say unto you, Inasmuch as ye have done *it* unto one of the least of these my brethren, ye have done *it* unto me.

[41] Then shall he say also unto them on the left hand, Depart from me, ye cursed, into everlasting fire, prepared for the devil and his angels: [42] for I was an hungred, and ye gave me no meat: I was thirsty, and ye gave me no drink: [43] I was a stranger, and ye took me not in: naked, and ye clothed me not: sick, and in prison, and ye visited me not. [44] Then shall they also answer him, saying, Lord, when saw we thee an hungred, or athirst, or a stranger, or naked, or sick, or in prison, and did not minister unto thee ? [45] Then shall he answer them, saying, Verily I say unto you, Inasmuch as ye did *it* not to one of the least of these, ye did *it* not to me. [46] And these shall go away into everlasting punishment: but the righteous into life eternal.*k*

---

i Thou knewest: better interrogatively, *Didst thou know ?* Was such thy opinion? Then "out of thine own mouth will I judge thee" (according to the parallel in Luke 19.

22); for thy opinion ought to have led to a different conduct.

j Comp. Dan. 7. 13, 14.

k Dan. 12. 2; John 5. 29; Rom. 2. 7–9.

§ 131. THE RULERS CONSPIRE. THE SUPPER AT BETHANY. TREACHERY OF JUDAS.—*Jerusalem. Bethany.*

Fourth Day of the Week.

Matt. 26. 1-16. [1] And it came to pass, when Jesus had finished all these sayings, he said unto his disciples, [2] Ye know that after two days is *the feast of* the passover, and the Son of man is betrayed to be crucified. [3] Then assembled[l] together the chief priests, and the scribes, and the elders of the people, unto the palace of the high priest, who was called Caiaphas, [4] and consulted[l] that they might take Jesus by subtilty, and kill *him.* [5] But they said, Not on the feast *day,*[m] lest there be an uproar among the people. [6] Now when Jesus was in Bethany, in the house of Simon the leper,

[7] There came unto him a woman having an alabaster box of very precious ointment, and poured it on his head,[o] as he sat *at meat.* [8] But when his disciples[p] saw *it,* they had indignation, saying, To what purpose *is* this waste? [9] for this ointment might have been sold for

Mark 14. 1-11. [1] After two days was *the feast of* the passover, and of unleavened bread: and the chief priests and the scribes

sought how they might take him by craft, and put *him* to death. [2] But they said, Not on the feast *day,* lest there be an uproar of the people. [3] And being in Bethany in the house of Simon the leper, as he sat at meat,

there came a woman having an alabaster box of ointment of spikenard very precious; and she brake the box, and poured *it* on his head.[o] [4] And there were some[p] that had indignation within themselves, and said, Why was this waste of the ointment made? [5] for it

Luke 22. 1-6. [1] Now the feast of unleavened bread drew nigh, which is called the passover. [2] And the chief priests and the scribes

sought how they might kill him; for they feared the people.

John 12. 2-8.

[2] There they made him a supper;[n] and Martha served: but Lazarus was one of them that sat at the table with him. [3] Then took Mary a pound of ointment of spikenard, very costly, and anointed the feet[o] of Jesus, and wiped his feet with her hair: and the house was filled with the odour of the ointment. [4] Then saith one of his disciples, Judas Iscariot,[p] Simon's son, which should betray

---

[l] Psa. 2. 2.

[m] *Not on the feast.* This counsel was soon abandoned by the rulers, owing to the unexpected offer of Judas quietly to betray Jesus into their hands. See at the end of this Section.

[n] On the date of this supper, see Note to ¿ 131, in the Appendix. John 12. 1 is in ¿ 111.

[o] *Christ's head* was anointed according to Matthew and Mark, and his *feet* according to John: but there is no contradiction in these statements, since both actions are con-

sistent, though both are not mentioned by one evangelist; unless indeed they be so in John 11. 2.

[p] *The disciples, or some* of them, were indignant; but, according to John's account, it was *Judas* that found fault. He was actuated by a base motive; and probably his dissatisfaction led others, who did not know his real feelings, to show uneasiness at the seeming waste of the ointment, not being able fully to appreciate the affection of Mary in this memorable deed.

Matt. 24.	Mark 15.	John 12.
much, and given to the poor.	might have been sold for more than three hundred pence, and have been given to the poor. And they murmured against her.	him, ⁵ Why was not this ointment sold for three hundred pence. and given to the poor ? ⁶ This he said, not that he cared for the poor; but because he was a thief, and had the bag, and bare what was put therein. ⁷ Then said Jesus, Let her alone : against the day of my burying hath she kept this. ⁸ For the poor always ye have with you; but me ye have not always.
¹⁰ When Jesus understood *it*, he said unto them, Why trouble ye the woman ? for she hath wrought a good work upon me. ¹¹ For ye have the poor always with you; but me ye have not always. ¹² For in that she hath poured this ointment on my body, she did *it* for my burial. ¹³ Verily I say unto you, Wheresoever this gospel shall be preached in the whole world, *there* shall also this, that this woman hath done, be told for a memorial of her.*q*	⁶ And Jesus said, Let her alone ; why trouble ye her ? she hath wrought a good work on me. ⁷ For ye have the poor with you always, and whensoever will ye may do them good : but me ye have not always. ⁸ She hath done what she could : she is come aforehand to anoint my body to the burying. ⁹ Verily I say unto you, Wheresoever this gospel shall be preached throughout the whole world, *this* also that she hath done shall be spoken of for a memorial of her.*q*	
		Luke 22.
¹⁴ Then one of the twelve, called Judas Iscariot, went unto the chief priests, ¹⁵ and said *unto them*, What will ye give me, and I will deliver him unto you ? And they covenanted with him for thirty pieces of silver.*r* ¹⁶ And from that time he sought opportunity to betray him.	¹⁰ And Judas Iscariot, one of the twelve, went unto the chief priests, to betray him unto them. ¹¹ And when they heard *it*, they were glad, and promised to give him money. And he sought how he might conveniently betray him.	³ Then entered Satan into Judas surnamed Iscariot, being of the number of the twelve. ⁴ And he went his way, and communed with the high priests and captains, how he might betray him unto them. ⁵ And they were glad, and covenanted to give him money. ⁶ And he promised, and sought opportunity to betray him unto them in the absence of the multitude.

q In John 11. 2, we find a striking illustration of the fulfilment of this saying. See note on the verse, § 92.
r Comp. Matt. 27. 9; Ex. 21. 32. The "piece of silver" was no doubt equivalent to the *shekel*, or the Greek *stater*, in weight about equal to our half-crown, although in purchasing power considerably more. The sum, it will be seen from the passage in Exodus, was anciently the price of a *slave*. See Zech. 11. 13; and compare note on Matt. 27. 9, § 151. The way in which the different evangelists supplement one another in the record of this transaction is very remarkable. Luke, who makes no mention of the supper in Simon's house, simply says that "Satan entered into Judas," without further accounting for his malignant deed at that par-

ticular time. Matthew and Mark imply that Judas went straight from that supper to the chief priests, but assign no special motive for his doing so. John alone shows that Judas had been personally and pointedly reproved by our Lord at the table, thus accounting for his exasperation at that particular time. That there had been no previous understanding between Judas and our Lord's enemies appears from the fact that the latter had just before been compassing His death in another way; Matt. 26. 3, 4. The priests did not go to Judas, he went to them : the incident at the feast being but the spark that inflamed a disposition already secretly malignant (John 6. 70), as well as covetous. See John 12. 6; where some propose to render the word translated *bare* as *embezzled*.

PART VIII.

THE FOURTH PASSOVER; OUR LORD'S PASSION; ACCOMPANYING EVENTS TILL THE END OF THE JEWISH SABBATH.

INTRODUCTORY NOTE—THE PASSOVER.

As the events of our Lord's passion were intimately connected with the celebration of the passover, it seems proper here to bring together, in one view, those circumstances relating to that festival, which may illustrate the sacred history.

I. *Time of killing the paschal lamb.* The paschal lamb (or kid, Ex. 12. 5) was to be selected on the tenth day of the first month, Ex. 12. 3. On the fourteenth day of the same month (called Abib in the Pentateuch, and later Nisan, Deut. 16. 1; Esth. 3. 7), the lamb thus selected was to be killed, at a point of time designated by the expression, *between the two evenings* (as in the marginal reading of our version), Ex. 42. 6; Lev. 23. 5; Num. 9. 3, 5; or, as is elsewhere said, *at evening about the going down of the sun,* Deut. 16. 6. The same phrase, *between the two evenings,* is put for the time of the daily evening sacrifice, Ex. 29. 39, 41; Num. 28. 4. The time thus marked was regarded by the Samaritans and Karaites as being the interval between sunset and deep twilight; whilst the Pharisees and Rabbinists held the first evening to commence with the declining sun, and the second evening with the setting sun. Hence, according to the latter, the paschal lamb was to be killed in the interval between the ninth and eleventh hour, equivalent to our three and five o'clock. That this was the practice among the Jews in the time of our Lord, appears from the testimony of Josephus.[s] The daily evening sacrifice was offered at the ninth hour, or three o'clock p.m.[t]

The true time, then, of killing the passover was between the ninth and eleventh hour, near the close of the fourteenth day of Nisan.

II. *Time of eating the passover.* This was to be done the same night. "And they shall eat the flesh in that night, roast with fire, and unleavened bread, and with bitter herbs shall they eat it," Ex. 12. 8. The Hebrews in Egypt ate the first passover, and struck the blood of the victims on their door-posts, on the evening before the last great plague; at midnight the Lord smote all the first-born; and in the morning the people broke up from Rameses on their march, viz. "on the fifteenth day of the first month, on the morrow after the passover," Num. 33. 3.

It hence appears very definitely, that the paschal lamb was to be slain in the afternoon of the fourteenth day of the month; and was eaten some time after the sunset which began the fifteenth day.

III. *Festival of unleavened bread.* From Ex. 12. 17, 18 (comp. Num. 28. 17) it appears that the festival of unleavened bread began strictly with the passover meal, at or after sunset following the fourteenth day, and continued until sunset at the end of the twenty-first day.[u]

It was customary for the Jews, on the fourteenth day of Nisan, to cease from labour at or before midday, to put away all leaven out of their houses, and to slay the paschal lamb towards the close of the day.[v] Hence, in popular usage, the fourteenth day came to be reckoned as the beginning or first day of the festival;[w] and Josephus also says that the festival was celebrated for eight days.[x]

It is hardly necessary to remark that, in consequence of the close mutual relation between the passover and the festival of unleavened bread, these terms are often used interchangeably, especially in Greek, for the whole festival.[y]

IV. *Other paschal sacrifices.*

1. In Num. 28. 18–25 it is prescribed that on the first and last days of the festival, the fifteenth and twenty-first of Nisan, there should be a holy convocation, in which "no manner of servile work" should be done. And on each of the seven days, besides the ordinary daily sacrifices of the sanctuary,

---

[s] Jos. B. J. 6. 9. 3.
[t] Jos. *Ant.* 14. 4. 3. See Acts 3. 1.
[u] Comp. Jos. *Ant.* 3. 10. 5.
[v] See above, and Note on § 132.

[w] See Matt. 26. 17; Mark 14. 12.
[x] See Note on § 132.
[y] See Luke 22. 1; John 6. 4; Acts 12. 3, 4; Jos. *Ant.* 2. 1. 3.

there was to be "a burnt-offering unto the Lord; two young bullocks, and one ram, and seven lambs of the first year;" also a meat-offering, and "one goat for a sin-offering." The first and last days of the festival, therefore, were each a day of convocation and *rest*, and hence were strictly *sabbaths.*

2. On the morrow after this first day of rest or sabbath, that is, on the sixteenth day of Nisan, the first-fruits of the harvest were offered, together with a lamb as a burnt-offering; Lev. 23. 10–12. This rite is expressly assigned by Josephus, in like manner, to the second day of the festival, the sixteenth of Nisan.[c] The grain offered was barley; this being the earliest ripe, and its harvest occurring a week or two earlier than that of wheat.[d] Until this offering was made, no husbandman could begin his harvest; nor might any one eat of the new grain, Lev. 23. 14.

3. There was also another sacrifice connected with the passover, known among the later Hebrews as the *Chagigah,* or *festival,* of which there are traces likewise in the Old Testament. It was a festive thank-offering (Engl. Vers. *peace-offering*), made by private individuals or families, in connexion with the passover, but distinct from the appointed public offerings of the temple. Such voluntary sacrifices or free-will offerings were provided and regulated by the Mosaic law. The fat only was burned on the altar (Lev. 3. 3, 9, 14); the priest had for his portion the breast and the right shoulder (Lev. 7. 29–34; 10. 14); and the remainder was eaten by the bringer with his family and friends in a festive manner, on the same or the next day (Lev. 7. 16–18; 22. 29, 30; Deut. 12. 17, 18, 27; 27. 7). These private sacrifices were often connected with the public festivals, both in honour of the same, and as a matter of convenience; Num. 10. 10; Deut. 14. 26; 16. 11, 14.[e] They might be eaten in any clean place within the city (Lev. 10. 14; Deut. 16. 11, 14); but those only might partake of them, as likewise of the passover, who were themselves ceremonially clean; Num. 18. 11–13; John 11. 55[f] Hence, being a sacrifice connected with a festival, these private free-will offerings were themselves called, by the later Hebrews, by the name *Chagigah,* i.e., *a festival.* There was, however, some difference of opinion among them as to the particular day of the paschal festival on which the Chagigah ought to be offered, whether on the fourteenth or fifteenth day

of Nisan; but the weight of authority was greatly in favour of the fifteenth day. Yet the later accounts of the mode of celebrating the paschal supper seem to imply that a Chagigah was ordinarily connected with that meal. Indeed, mention is made of a "Chagigah of the fourteenth day," so called in distinction from the more important and formal ceremonial Chagigah of the passover festival; which latter was not regularly offered until the fifteenth day, when the paschal supper had already been eaten. The former was then a mere voluntary oblation of thanksgiving, made for the purpose of enlarging and diversifying the passover meal.[g]

V. *The paschal supper.* That the Jews in the course of ages had neglected some of the original precepts, and also introduced various additional ceremonies, is evident from the manner in which our Lord celebrated the supper, as narrated by the evangelists. What all these additions were we have no specific historical account from contemporary writers; yet the precepts preserved in the Mishna (compiled in the third century from earlier traditions), probably refer to the most important of them, and serve to throw light upon some of the circumstances connected with the institution of the Lord's supper.[h]

According to these authorities, four cups of red wine, usually mingled with one fourth part of water, were drunk during the meal, and served to mark its progress. The *first* was merely preliminary, in connexion with a blessing invoked upon the day and upon the wine; and this corresponds to the cup mentioned in Luke 22. 17. Then followed ablutions, and the bringing in of bitter herbs, the unleavened bread, the roasted lamb, and also the Chagigah of the fourteenth day, and a broth or sauce made with spices. After this followed the instructions to the son, etc., respecting the passover; and the first part of the *Hallel,* or song of praise (Psalms 113, 114), was repeated. The *second* cup was now drunk. Next came the blessing upon each kind of food, and the guest partook of the meal reclining; the paschal lamb being eaten last. Thanks were then returned, and the *third* cup drunk, called *the cup of blessing.*[i] The remainder of the *Hallel* (Psalms 115–118) was now repeated, and the *fourth* cup drunk; which was ordinarily the end of the celebration. Sometimes a *fifth* cup might be added, after repeating the great *Hallel* (Psalms 120–137).

[c] *Antiq.* 3. 10. 5.
[d] Jos. ib. *Bibl. Res. in Palest.* II. p. 99.
[e] Comp. 1. Sam. 1. 3–5, 24, 25; 2. 12–16, 19.
[f] Comp. Numb. 9. 10–13; 2 Chron. 30. 18. Jos. B. J. 6. 9. 3.
[g] See Lightfoot, *Ministerium Templi,* 13. 4. Ib. c. 14. Reland, *Antiqq. Sac.* 4. 2. 2.

[h] See Lightfoot, *Minist. Templi,* c. 13. *Hor. Heb.* in Matt. 26. 26. 27. Werner, *de poculo Benedict.* in Ugolini Thesaur. T. XXX. See also *Bibliotheca Sacra,* August 1845 (article by Dr. Robinson on the Passover), p. 411, sq.
[i] Comp. 1 Cor. 10. 16.

The institution of the Lord's supper probably took place at the close of the proper meal, immediately before the third cup, or cup of blessing, which would seem to have made part of it.[j]

VI. *Did our Lord, the night in which He was betrayed, eat the passover with His disciples?* Had we only the testimony of the first three evangelists, not a doubt upon this question could ever arise. Their language[k] is full, explicit, and decisive, to the effect that our Lord's last meal with His disciples was the regular and ordinary paschal supper of the Jews, introducing the festival of unleavened bread, on the evening after the fourteenth day of Nisan. Mark says expressly, 14. 12, *when* THEY *killed the passover;* which, whether the subject *they* refer to the Jews or be indefinite, implies at least the regular and ordinary time of killing the paschal lamb. Luke's language is, if possible, still stronger in 22. 7: "Then came the day of unleavened bread, *when the passover* MUST *be killed,* i.e., according to law and custom. This marks of course the fourteenth day of Nisan; and on that same evening our Lord and His disciples sat down to that same passover meal, which had thus by His own appointment been prepared for them, and of which Jesus speaks expressly as the passover, Luke 22. 15. Philologically considered, there cannot be a shadow of doubt that Matthew, Mark, and Luke intended to express, and do express, in the plainest terms, their testimony to the fact, that Jesus regularly partook of the ordinary and legal passover meal, on the evening after the fourteenth of Nisan, at the same time with all the Jews.

When, however, we turn to the Gospel of John, we seek in vain in this evangelist for any trace of the paschal supper, as such, in connexion with our Lord at that time. John narrates indeed (ch. 13) our Lord's last meal with His disciples; which the attendant and subsequent circumstances show to have been the same with that which the other evangelists describe as the passover. Upon just that point, however, John is silent; but from this silence the inference can never be rightfully drawn, that this last meal was *not* the passover; any more than John's similar silence in respect to the Lord's supper warrants the conclusion that no such rite was ever instituted. John, as all admit, wrote his Gospel as a supplement to the others; and hence, in speaking of this meal, he narrates only such circumstances as had not been fully set forth by the other evangelists. He does not describe this meal as being the passover, nor make any mention of the eucharist, because this had been done, in both cases, in the most explicit manner, by Matthew, Mark, and Luke. In this way the difference in the two reports of the same occasion is satisfactorily accounted for.

But there are a few expressions in John's Gospel, in connexion with this meal, and especially with our Lord's passion, which taken together might, at first view, and if we had only John, seem to imply that on Friday, the day of our Lord's crucifixion, the regular and legal passover had not yet been eaten, but was still to be eaten on the evening after that day.

The point of the whole inquiry relates simply to the time of the passover. According to all the four evangelists, our Lord was crucified on Friday, the day before the Jewish sabbath; and His last meal with His disciples took place on the preceding evening, the same night in which He was betrayed. The simple question, therefore, at issue is, Did this Friday fall upon the fifteenth day of Nisan, or upon the fourteenth? Or, in other words, did our Lord on the evening before His crucifixion eat the passover, as is testified by the first three evangelists; or was the passover still to be eaten on the evening of that day, as John might seem to imply? The second of these alternatives is supported by Greswell, Tischendorf, and others,[l] who maintain, from certain expressions in John, that the proper passover was eaten on the evening after our Lord was crucified, and that therefore His paschal supper with the disciples had been celebrated one day in anticipation of the regular time; but the first is advocated by Wieseler,[m] as well as by Robinson.

This question has been more or less a subject of discussion in the church ever since the earliest centuries; chiefly with a view to harmonize the difficulties. It is only in recent years that the alleged difference between John and the other evangelists has been urged to the extreme of attempting to make it irreconcilable.

John obviously wrote his Gospel as supplementary to the other three. He had them then before him, and was acquainted with their contents. He was aware that the other three evangelists had testified to the fact, that Jesus partook of the passover with His disciples. Did John believe that their testimony on this point was wrong; and did he mean to correct it? If so, we should naturally expect to find some notice of the correction along with the mention of the meal itself, which John describes, as well as they. Indeed, that would have been the appropriate and only fitting place for such a correction. But John has nothing of the kind; and we are therefore authorised to maintain, that it was not John's purpose thus and there

---

[j] Comp. 1 Cor. 10. 16.
[k] See § 132.

[l] *Dissert.* iv. vol. iii.
[m] *Chron. Synopsis,* pp. 313–352.

to correct or contradict the testimony of the other evangelists; and if not there, then much less by mere implication in other places and connexions.

Let us examine the passages referred to in John's Gospel, and see whether they require to be so understood or interpreted, as to present any appearance of discrepancy. They are the following:—

(A.) John 13. 1, "*Before the feast of the passover.*" This form of expression, it is said, shows that our Lord's last meal with His disciples took place *before* the passover; and could not, therefore, itself have been the paschal supper.

But we must here take into account the meaning of the Greek word thus rendered *feast*, the true and only proper signification of which is *festival*; that is, it implies everywhere a yearly day or days of festive commemoration; never a single meal or entertainment. So in Num. 28. 16, 17, where the *paschal supper*, prepared on the fourteenth of Nisan and eaten at evening, is distinguished from the *festival* (English version, *feast*), which began on the fifteenth, and continued for seven days.[a]

In this view, the phrase in question does not mean "before the paschal supper," but "before the festival of the passover," i.e., of unleavened bread (Luke 22. 1). It is equivalent, therefore, to the English *festival-eve*, and here marks the evening immediately before the *festival* proper, of seven days' continuance; on which evening, during the (paschal) supper, our Lord "manifested His love for His disciples unto the end," by the touching symbolical act of washing their feet.

It is, therefore, evident that this passage does not sustain the inference attempted to be drawn from it.

(B.) John 18. 28, "and they themselves (the Jews) went not into the judgment-hall, lest they should be defiled; *but that they might eat the passover.*" From this last phrase it has been inferred that the Jews were expecting to partake of the paschal supper the ensuing evening; and of course had not eaten it already.

Thus has been met by the suggestion (Prof. Plumptre, in Ellicott's *New Testament for English Readers*) that the Jews were intending to eat the passover the same night, but deferred it until a later hour; just, in fact, before daybreak. This view is at least worth consideration, and yet the words of the evangelist do not need the explanation.

For, to bring out the inference we are discussing, the phrase "to eat the passover" must be taken in the most limited sense, "to eat the paschal supper." This certainly cannot be necessary, unless the context re-

quires such a limitation: which is not the case here.

The word *passover*, in the New Testament, is found in no less than three main significations: (a) *The paschal lamb*, Mark 14. 12; Luke 22. 7; 1 Cor. 5. 7. (b) *The paschal meal*, Matt. 26. 18, 19; Luke 22. 8, 13; Heb. 11. 28. (c) *The paschal festival*, comprising the seven days of unleavened bread, Luke 22. 1; 2. 41, comp. 43; Matt. 26. 2; John 2. 13; 6. 4; 11. 55, etc.—As now there is nothing in the circumstances or context of John 18. 28 to limit the meaning of the word *passover* in itself either to the paschal lamb or paschal meal, we certainly are not bound by any intrinsic necessity so to understand it here in the phrase "to eat the passover." If, on the other hand, we adopt for it in this place the wider sense of *paschal festival*, two modes of interpretation are admissible, either of which leaves no room for the above inference.

1. By modifying the force of the verb *to eat*, so as to make the phrase, "to eat the passover," equivalent to the more common expression, "*to keep* or *celebrate* the passover." Precisely this form of expression occurs in the Hebrew, in 2 Chron. 30. 22; literally, "*and they did eat the festival seven days;*" where the English version has it "*throughout* the feast seven days." The Septuagint translates correctly according to the sense, though not according to the letter: "*and they fulfilled* (kept) *the festival of unleavened bread seven days.*"

2. Or we may assign to the word *passover* (paschal festival), the sense of *paschal sacrifices*; that is, the voluntary peace-offerings and thank-offerings made in the temple during the paschal festival, and more especially on the fifteenth of Nisan; called, in later times, the *Chagigah*.[b] A like metonymy is found in Psa. 118. 27: "Bind the sacrifice (festival offering, lit., *festival*) with cords." See too Ex. 23. 18; Mal. 2. 3. The same metonymy is assumed by some in the passage above quoted, 2 Chron. 30. 22; which they then render thus, "and they did eat the festival *offerings* seven days."

It is manifest that both the above methods of interpretation are founded on fair analogies; and that either of them relieves us from the necessity of referring the phrase in question to the paschal supper, and thus removes the alleged difficulty. The chief priests and other members of the Sanhedrim, on the morning of the first day of the festival, were unwilling to defile themselves by entering beneath the roof of the Gentile procurator; since in that way they would have been debarred from partaking of the sacrificial offerings and banquets, which were customary on that day in the temple and

---

[a] See further, Luke 2. 41; 22. 1.   [b] See p. 134.

elsewhere; and in which they, from their station, were entitled and expected to participate.

This view receives some further confirmation from the circumstance, that the defilement which the Jews would thus have contracted by entering the dwelling of a heathen, could only have belonged to that class of impurities from which a person might be cleansed the same day by ablution; the *ablutions of a day,* so called by the Talmudists.[p] If now *the passover* in John 18. 28 was truly the mere paschal supper, and was not to take place until the evening after the day of the crucifixion, then this defilement of a day could have been no bar to their partaking of it; for at evening they were, or might be, clean. Their scruple, therefore, in order to be well founded, could have had reference only to the *Chagigah,* or paschal sacrifices offered during the same day before evening.

(c.) John 19. 14, "and it was *the preparation of the passover,* about the sixth hour." Does this "preparation" refer, as usual, to the Jewish sabbath, which actually occurred the next day? or does it here refer to the festival of the passover as such, and as distinct from the sabbath? It is only on the latter supposition that the passage can be made, in any way, to conflict with the testimony of the other evangelists.

This "preparation" is defined by Mark (15. 42) to be "the day before the sabbath," i.e., the *fore-sabbath,* the day or hours immediately preceding the weekly sabbath, and devoted to preparation for that sacred day. No trace of any such observance is found in the Old Testament; though the strictness of the Mosaic law respecting the sabbath, which forbade the kindling of fire and of course the preparation of food on that day (Ex. 35. 2, 3; comp. 16. 22–27), would very naturally lead to the subsequent introduction of such a custom; as we find it in the times of the New Testament. In the still later Hebrew of the Talmudists, it bore the specific appellation of *eve,* as being the *eve of the sabbath.*[q] The Greek word "preparation" is also everywhere translated by the like Syriac form for *eve,* in the Syriac version of the New Testament.

Primarily and strictly this "preparation" or "eve" would seem to have commenced not earlier than the ninth hour (or three o'clock p.m.) of the preceding day; as is implied perhaps in the decree of Augustus in favour of the Jews; where it is directed that they shall not be held to give pledges on the sabbath, nor during the preparation before the same, *after the ninth hour.*[r] But in process of time, the same Hebrew word for "eve" or "preparation," came in popular usage to be the distinctive name for the *whole day* before the Jewish sabbath, i.e., for the sixth day of the week, or Friday. The same was the case in Syriac; and we know, too, that the corresponding word in Arabic for *eve,* was likewise an ancient name for Friday.[s] It appears, then, that among the Jews, Syrians, and Arabs, the common word for *eve,* to which corresponded the Greek word "preparation," meaning the preparation of the weekly sabbath, became at an early date a current appellation for the sixth day of the week. That is, Friday was known as the *preparation* or *fore-sabbath;* just as in German the usual name for Saturday is now Sonnabend, i.e., "eve of Sunday."

In the later Talmudists, a *passover-eve* is likewise spoken of.[u] But what this could well have been, so long as the passover (paschal supper) continued to be regularly celebrated at Jerusalem, it is difficult to perceive. The *eve* before the passover *festival* could have included, at most, only the evening and the few hours before sunset at the close of the fourteenth of Nisan; as in the primary usage in respect to the *fore-sabbath,* as we have just seen. But according to all usage of language, both in the Old and New Testament, those hours and that evening were part and parcel of the *passover festival itself,* and not its preparation; unless indeed the paschal meal and its accompaniments be called the preparation of the subsequent festival of seven days; which again is contrary to all usage. It would seem most probable, therefore, that this mode of expression did not arise until after the destruction of the temple and the consequent cessation of the regular and legal passover-meal, when of course the seven days of unleavened bread became the main festival.

But even admitting that a passover-eve did exist in the time of our Lord, still the expression could in no legitimate way be so far extended as to include more than a few hours before sunset. It could not have commenced apparently before the ninth hour, when they began to kill the paschal lamb.[v] On the other hand, the Hebrew term for *eve,* for which the Greek "preparation" stands in the New Testament, was employed, as we have seen, as a specific name in popular usage for the whole sixth day of the week or Friday, not only by the Jews, but also by the Syrians and Arabs. Hence, when John

---

[p] See Lev. 15. 5, sq.; 17. 15; 22. 6, 7; Num. 19. 7, sq. Lightfoot, *Hor. Heb.* on Joh. 18. 28.

[q] Buxtorf, *Lex.* col. 1659.

[r] See Jos. *Ant.* 16. 6. 2.

[s] Buxtorf, *Lex.* col. 1659. Scaliger, *Emend. Temp.* vi. p. 569.

[t] See Golius, *Arab. Lexicon,* p. 1551. Freytag, iii. p. 130.

[u] Buxtorf, *Lex.* col. 1765. [v] See p. 133.

here says, *it was the preparation of the passover, and about the sixth hour,* there is a twofold difficulty in referring his language to a preparation or *eve* of the regular passover; *first,* because apparently no such eve or preparation did or could well then exist; and, *secondly,* because, it being then the sixth hour or mid-day, the eve or time of preparation (supposing it to exist) had not yet come, and the language was therefore inapplicable. But if John be understood as speaking of the weekly preparation or fore-sabbath, which was a common name for the whole of Friday, then the mention of the sixth hour was natural and appropriate.

We come then to the conclusion, that if John, like Mark in ch. 15. 42, had here defined the phrase in question, he would probably have written on this wise: " and it was the preparation of the passover," that is, the *fore-sabbath* of the passover, implying that it was the paschal Friday, the day of preparation or *fore-sabbath* which occurred during the paschal festival; in other words, " the Friday of the passover week." In a similar manner Ignatius writes, " sabbath of the passover ;"[w] and Socrates also, " sabbath of the festival."[x] And further, in the only other two instances where John uses the word " preparation" he applies to this very same day of our Lord's crucifixion, and in this very same sense of the weekly preparation preceding the weekly sabbath; John 19. 31, 42.

(D.) John 19. 31, " for that sabbath day was an high day." Here, as is alleged, it is the coincidence of the first festival day with the sabbath that made the latter a " high" or more properly a " great" day. This would certainly be the effect of such a coincidence; but the sabbath of the passover would also be still a " great" day, even when it fell upon the second day of the festival. The last day of the festival of tabernacles is called " that great day," though in itself not more sacred than the first day, John 7. 37 ; comp. Lev. 23. 33–36. So the *calling of assemblies,* Isa. 1. 13, is rendered " a great day" by the Seventy, implying that in their estimation any day of solemn convocation was a great day.

The sabbath, then, upon which the sixteenth of Nisan or second day of the festival fell, might be called " great" or " high" for various reasons. *First,* as the sabbath of

the great national festival, when all Israel was gathered before the Lord. *Secondly,* as the day when the first-fruits were presented with solemn rites in the temple; a ceremony paramount in its obligations even to the sabbath.[y] *Thirdly,* because on that day they began to reckon the fifty days until the festival of Pentecost, Lev. 23. 15, sq.

In all these circumstances there is certainly enough to warrant the epithet " great" as applied to the sabbath on which the sixteenth of Nisan might fall, as compared with other sabbaths.—There exists, therefore, no necessity, and indeed no reason, for supposing that John by this language meant to describe the sabbath in question as coincident with the first paschal day or fifteenth of Nisan.

The preceding four passages are those mainly urged against the consistency of John with the other evangelists. One or two other considerations are also sometimes brought forward.

(E.) John 13. 27–30. Here the words, "Buy that we have need of *against the feast* [festival]" having been spoken apparently near the close of the meal, imply, as some suppose, that the *passover* meal was yet to come. But this, again, is to mistake the *festival* for the *paschal supper,* a signification which is quite foreign to the word.[z] The disciples thought Judas was to buy the things necessary for the *festival* on the fifteenth and following days. If now our Lord's words were spoken on the evening preceding and introducing the fifteenth of Nisan, they were appropriate; for some haste was necessary, since it was already quite late to make purchases for the next day. But if they were uttered on the evening preceding and introducing the fourteenth of Nisan, they were not thus appropriate; for then a whole day was yet to intervene before the festival. This passage therefore confirms, rather than contradicts, the testimony of the other evangelists.

(F.) There remains the objection, sometimes brought forward, that a public judicial act, like that by which Jesus was condemned and executed, was unlawful upon the sabbath and on all great festival days.[a] This consideration has, at first view, some weight, and has been often and strenuously urged; yet it is counterbalanced by several circumstances which very greatly weaken its force.

The execution itself took place under Roman

[w] Ep. ad Phil. c. 13.
[x] Hist. Ecc. V. 22.
[y] See p. 134. Lightfoot, *Hor. Heb.* on Joh. 19. 31. Reland *Antiqq. Sac.* 4. 2. 4. p. 227.
[z] See p. 135.
[a] See Lightfoot, *Hor. Heb.* on Matt. 27. 1, and Tischendorf, who says, " It is incredible that on the fifteenth of Nisan, the first day of the paschal feast, a day which the law

commanded to be kept as a sabbath of peculiar sacredness, Jesus should not only have been apprehended by an armed crowd, and hurried from tribunal to tribunal, but even hung upon the cross. The Talmudical tradition," adds Tischendorf, " represents the death of Jesus to have occurred on the fourteenth of Nisan," *Synopsis Evangelica,* p. xlvii.

authority; and therefore does not here come into account. And as to the proceedings of the Sanhedrim, even admitting that the prohibitory precepts already existed, at this early time (which is very doubtful), yet there are in the Talmud other precepts, of equal antiquity and authority, which actually direct and regulate the meeting and action of that body on the sabbath and on festival days.[b] But besides all this, the chief priests and Pharisees and scribes, who composed the Sanhedrim, are everywhere denounced by our Lord as hypocrites, "who say, and do not; who bind heavy burdens upon others, but themselves touch them not with one of their fingers;" Matt. 23. 1, sq. Such men, in their rage against Jesus, would hardly have been restrained even by their own precepts. They professed likewise, and perhaps some of them believed, that they were doing God service; and regarded the condemnation of Jesus as a work of religious duty, paramount to the obligations of any festival. Nor are other examples of such a procedure by any means wanting. We learn from John 10. 22, 31, that on the festival of dedication, as Jesus was teaching in the temple, "the Jews took up stones to stone him." On the day after the crucifixion, which, as all agree, was a sabbath and a "great day," the Sanhedrim applied to Pilate for a watch; and themselves caused the sepulchre to be sealed, and the watch to be set, Matt. 27. 62, sq. A stronger instance still is recorded in John 7. 32, 37, 44, 45; where it appears that on the last *great* day of the festival of tabernacles, the Sanhedrim having sent out officers to seize Jesus, "some of them would have taken Him, but no man laid hands on Him;" so that the officers returned without Him to the Sanhedrim, and were in consequence censured by that body. The circumstances show conclusively, that on this last great day of that festival, the Sanhedrim were in session, and waiting for Jesus to be brought before them as a prisoner. Nor was it merely a casual or packed meeting, but one regularly convened; for Nicodemus was with them, ver. 50.

And finally, according to Matt. 26. 3-5, the Sanhedrim, when afterwards consulting to take Jesus and put Him to death, decided not to do it on the festival. Why? because it would be unlawful? Not at all; but simply "lest there should be an uproar among the people." But when, through the treachery of Judas, this danger was avoided, the occasion was too opportune not to be gladly seized upon even on a great festival day. These considerations, taken together, seem to sweep away the whole force of this objection.

Such, then, is a general review of the passages and arguments, on the strength of which the alleged discrepancy between John and the other evangelists in respect to this passover has usually been maintained. There is nothing in the language of John, or in the attendant circumstances, which upon fair interpretation requires or permits us to believe, that the beloved disciple either intended to correct, or has in fact corrected or contradicted, the explicit and unquestionable testimony of Matthew, Mark, and Luke.

---

§ 132. PREPARATION FOR THE PASSOVER.—*Bethany. Jerusalem.*

Fifth Day of the Week.

Matt. 26. 17-19.	Mark 14. 12-16.	Luke 22. 7-13.
[17] Now the first *day* of the *feast of* unleavened bread[c] the disciples came to Jesus, saying unto him, Where wilt thou that we prepare for thee to eat the passover?	[12] And the first day of unleavened bread, when they killed the passover, his disciples said unto him, Where wilt thou that we go and prepare that thou mayest eat the passover?	[7] Then came the day of unleavened bread, when the passover must be killed. [8] And he sent Peter and John, saying, Go and prepare us the passover, that we may eat. [9] And

---

[b] Wieseler's *Chronological Synopsis*, pp. 331-333.

[c] "The first day of unleavened bread" is here the fourteenth of Nisan; on which day, at, or before noon, the Jews were accustomed to cease from labour and put away all leaven out of their houses; Ex. 12. 15-17. Light-

foot, Opp. I. p. 728, sq. *Hor. Heb.* on Mark 14. 12. On that day towards sunset the paschal lamb was killed; and was eaten the same evening, after the fifteenth of Nisan had begun; at which time, strictly, the festival of unleavened bread commenced, which continued seven days. In popular

Matt. 26.	**Mark 14.**	**Luke 22.**
		they said unto him, Where wilt thou that we prepare ?
¹⁸ And he said, Go into the city to	¹³ And he sendeth forth two of his disciples, and saith unto them, Go ye into the city, and there shall meet you a man bearing a pitcher of water: follow him. ¹⁴ And wheresoever he shall go in, say	¹⁰ And he said unto them, Behold, when ye are entered into the city, there shall a man meet you, bearing a pitcher of water; follow him into the house where he entereth in. ¹¹ And ye shall
such a man, and say unto him, The Master saith, My time is at hand; I will keep the passover at thy house with my disciples.	ye to the goodman of the house, The Master saith, Where is the guest-chamber, where I shall eat the passover with my disciples? ¹⁵ And he will show you a large upper room furnished *and* prepared: there make ready	say unto the goodman of the house, The Master saith unto thee, Where is the guestchamber, where I shall eat the passover with my disciples? ¹² And he shall show you a large upper room furnished: there make ready. ¹³ And
¹⁹ And the disciples did as Jesus had appointed them; and they made ready the passover.	for us. ¹⁶ And his disciples went forth, and came into the city, and found as he had said unto them: and they made ready the passover.	they went, and found as he had said unto them: and they made ready the passover.

§ 133. THE PASSOVER MEAL.ᵈ CONTENTION AMONG THE TWELVE.
Jerusalem.

Evening introducing the Sixth Day of the Week.

| **Matt. 26.** 20. Now when the even ᵉ was come, he sat down with the twelve. | **Mark 14.** 17. And in the evening ᵉ he cometh with the twelve. | **Luke 22.** 14–18, 24–30. ¹⁴ And when the hour ᵉ was come, he sat down, and the twelve apostles with him. ¹⁵ And |

---

usage, however, the fourteenth day, being thus a day of preparation, was spoken of as belonging to the festival, and therefore is here called the "first" day. That such a usage was common, appears also from Josephus; who, having in one place expressly fixed the commencement of the festival of unleavened bread on the fifteenth of Nisan (*Antiq.* 3. 10. 5), speaks, nevertheless, in another passage, of the fourteenth as the day of that festival; *Wars,* 5. 3. 1. Comp. *Ant.* 11. 4. 8.

In this way, further, the same historian could say, that the festival was celebrated for *eight* days, *Ant.* 2. 15. 1.

On this fifth day of the week, as the circumstances show, our Lord, after sending Peter and John to the city to prepare the passover, Himself followed them thither with the other disciples, probably towards

evening. (On the Passover in general, **see** Introductory Note.)

ᵈ The order of the transactions during the paschal supper appears to have been the following: The taking of their places at table; the contention; the first cup of wine; the washing of the disciples' feet and reproof (§§ 133, 134); the pointing out of the traitor (§ 135); the foretelling of Peter's denial (§ 136); institution of the Lord's supper (§ 137), etc. Luke's order differs from that of Matthew and Mark, in placing by anticipation the institution of the eucharist before the pointing out of the traitor. He was apparently led to this by the mention of the first cup of wine, ver. 17, 18. Afterwards he returns and narrates the previous circumstances.

ᵉ About six o'clock: from three to five the paschal lamb was killed.

Luke 22.

he said unto them, With desire I have desired to eat this passover with you before I suffer: [16] for I say unto you, I will not any more eat thereof, until it be fulfilled in the kingdom of God. [17] And he took the cup,*f* and gave thanks, and said, Take this, and divide *it* among yourselves: [18] for I say unto you, I will not drink of the fruit of the vine, until the kingdom of God shall come.*g*—

[24] And there was also a strife *h* among them,*i* which of them should be accounted the greatest. [25] And he said unto them, The kings of the Gentiles exercise lordship over them; and they that exercise authority upon them are called benefactors. [26] But ye *shall* not *be* so: but he that is greatest among you, let him be as the younger; and he that is chief, as he that doth serve. [27] For whether *is* greater, he that sitteth at meat, or he that serveth? *is* not he that sitteth at meat? but I am among you as he that serveth. [28] Ye are they which have continued with me in my temptations. [29] And I appoint unto you a kingdom, as my Father hath appointed unto me;*j* [30] that ye may eat and drink at my table in my kingdom, and sit on thrones judging the twelve tribes of Israel.

§ 134. Jesus washes *k* the Feet of His Disciples.—*Jerusalem.*

Evening introducing the Sixth Day of the Week.

John 13. 1-20. [1] Now before the feast of the passover, when Jesus knew that his hour was come that he should depart out of this world unto the Father, having loved his own which were in the world, he loved them unto the end. [2] And supper being ended, the devil having now put *l* into the heart of Judas Iscariot, Simon's son, to betray him; [3] Jesus knowing that the Father had given all things into his hands, and that he was come from God, and went to God; [4] he riseth from supper, and laid aside his garments; and took a towel, and girded himself. [5] After that he poureth water into a bason, and began to wash the disciples' feet, and to wipe *them* with the towel wherewith he was girded.

[6] Then cometh he to Simon Peter: and Peter said unto him, Lord, dost thou wash my feet? [7] Jesus answered and said unto him, What I do thou knowest not now; but thou shalt know hereafter. [8] Peter saith unto him, Thou shalt never wash my feet. Jesus answered him, If I wash thee not, thou hast no part with me. [9] Simon Peter saith unto him, Lord, not my feet only, but also *my* hands and *my* head. [10] Jesus saith to him, He that is washed needeth not save to wash *his* feet, but is clean every whit: and ye are clean, but not all. [11] For he knew who should betray him; therefore said he, Ye are not all clean.

[12] So after he had washed their feet, and had taken his garments, and was set

---

f See Introductory Note, p. 134.

g See § 137.

h The contention among the disciples had apparently occurred quite recently, perhaps even in the guest-chamber while taking their places at the table. That they were prone to yield to such a spirit is evident from the instances recorded in § 79, and also § 108. Our Lord on this solemn occasion reproves them; especially by the touching act of washing their feet; see § 134.—The verb *was* (Luke 22. 24) is to be taken as the pluperfect: see Note on §.145.

i Comp. Matt. 20. 25–28. *j* Phil. 2. 9–11.

k The washing of the disciples' feet by their Lord and Master was an impressive lesson, that they should live in harmony and love and humility one with another. The

occasion of this act was their previous contention, as related by Luke in § 133. Compare Luke 24. 26, sq., with John 13. 16, sq. John's narrative is supplementary to that of Luke; and therefore he does not speak of the contention itself, because the latter had already described it.

On the phrase *before the feast of the passover*, ver. 1, see above in Introductory Note, p. 136.—The phrase *supper being ended* (δείπνου γενομένου), ver. 2, ought to be rendered "supper being come," or "during supper;" see ver. 4 and ver. 12. The time of the action was probably after they had taken their places at table, and before they had partaken of the proper meal; perhaps between the first and second cups of wine.

l Acts 5. 3.

John 13.

down again, he said unto them, Know ye what I have done to you ? [13] Ye call me Master and Lord : and ye say well ; for *so* I am. [14] If I then, *your* Lord and Master, have washed your feet : ye also ought to wash one another's feet.[m] [15] For I have given you an example, that ye should do as I have done to you. [16] Verily, verily, I say unto you, The servant is not greater than his lord, neither he that is sent greater than he that sent him. [17] If ye know these things, happy are ye if ye do them. [18] I speak not of you all : I know whom I have chosen : but that the Scripture may be fulfilled,[n] He that eateth bread with me hath lifted up his heel against me. [19] Now I tell you before it come, that, when it is come to pass, ye may believe that I am *he.* [20] Verily, verily, I say unto you, He that receiveth whomsoever I send receiveth me ; and he that receiveth me receiveth him that sent me.

§ 135. Jesus points out the Traitor. Judas withdraws.—*Jerusalem.*

Evening introducing the Sixth Day of the Week.

Matt. 26. 21-25. [21] And as they did eat, he said, Verily I say unto you, that one of you shall betray me.

[22] And they were exceeding sorrowful, and began every one of them to say unto him, Lord, is it I ?

Mark 14. 18-21. [18] And as they sat and did eat, Jesus said, Verily I say unto you, One of you which eateth with me shall betray me. [19] And they began to be sorrowful, and to say unto him one by one, *Is* it I ? and another *said,* Is it I ?

Luke 22. 21-23. [21] But, behold, the hand of him that betrayeth me *is* with me on the table.—

[23] And they began to inquire among themselves, which of them it was that should do this thing.

John 13. 21-35. [21] When Jesus had thus said, he was troubled in spirit, and testified, and said, Verily, verily, I say unto you, that one of you shall betray me. [22] Then the disciples looked one on another, doubting of whom he spake. [23] Now there was leaning on Jesus' bosom one of his disciples, whom Jesus loved. [24] Simon Peter therefore beckoned to him, that he should ask who it should be of whom he spake. [25] He then lying on Jesus' breast saith unto him, Lord, who is it ? [26] Jesus answered, He it is, to whom I shall give a sop, when I have dipped *it.*—

Matt. 26.
[23] And he answered and said, He that dippeth *his* hand with me in the dish, the same shall betray me. [24] The Son of man goeth as it is written of him : but woe unto that man by whom the Son of man is betrayed ! it had been good for that man if he had not been born. [25] Then Judas, which betrayed him, answered and said, Master, is it I ? He said unto him, Thou hast said.

Mark 14.
[20] And he answered and said unto them, *It is* one of the twelve, that dippeth with me in the dish. [21] The Son of man indeed goeth, as it is written of him : but woe to that man by whom the Son of man is betrayed ! good were it for that man if he had never been born.

Luke 22.
[22] And truly the Son of man goeth, as it was determined : but woe unto that man by whom he is betrayed !

John 13.
—[26] And when he had dipped the sop, he gave *it* to Judas Iscariot, *the son* of Simon. [27] And after the sop Satan entered into

---

[m] Rom. 12. 10.   [n] Psa. 41. 9.

John 13.

him. Then said Jesus unto him, That thou doest, do quickly. ²⁸ Now no man at the table knew for what intent he spake this unto him. ²⁹ For some *of them* thought, because Judas had the bag, that Jesus had said unto him, Buy *those things* that we have need of against the feast; ᑫ or, that he should give something to the poor. ³⁰ He then having received the sop went immediately out: ʳ and it was night. ³¹ Therefore, when he was gone out, Jesus said, Now is the Son of man glorified, and God is glorified in him. ³² If God be glorified in him, God shall also glorify him in himself, and shall straightway glorify him. ³³ Little children, yet a little while I am with you. Ye shall seek me: and as I said unto the Jews,ˢ Whither I go, ye cannot come; so now I say to you. ³⁴ A new commandment ᵗ I give unto you, That ye love one another; as I have loved you, that ye also love one another. ³⁵ By this shall all *men* know that ye are my disciples, if ye have love one to another.ᵘ

§ 136. Jesus Foretells the Fall of Peter, and the Dispersion of the Twelve.—*Jerusalem.*

Evening introducing the Sixth Day of the Week.

John 13. 36–38. ³⁶ Simon Peter said unto him, Lord, whither goest thou? Jesus answered him, Whither I go, thou canst not follow me now; but thou shalt follow me afterwards.ᵛ ³⁷ Peter said unto him, Lord, why cannot I follow thee now? I will lay down my life for thy sake.

| **Matt. 26. 31–35.** ³¹ Then saith Jesus unto them, All ye shall be offended because of me this night: for it is written,ʷ I will smite the shepherd, and the sheep of the flock shall be scattered abroad. ³² But after I am risen again, I will go before you into Galilee.ˣ ³³ Peter answered and said unto him, Though all *men* shall be offended because of thee, *yet* will I never be offended. | **Mark 14.** 27–31. ²⁷ And Jesus saith unto them, All ye shall be offended because of me this night: for it is written,ʷ I will smite the shepherd, and the sheep shall be scattered. ²⁸ But after that I am risen, I will go before you into Galilee.ˣ ²⁹ But Peter said unto him, Although all shall be offended, yet *will* not I. |

Luke 22. 31–38. ³¹ And the Lord said, Simon, Simon, behold, Satan hath desired *to have* you, that he may sift *you* as wheat: ³² but I have prayed for thee, that thy faith fail not: and when thou art converted, strengthen thy brethren. ³³ And he said unto him, Lord, I am ready to go with thee, both into prison, and to death.

| **Matt. 26.** ³⁴ Jesus said unto him,ʸ Verily I say unto thee, That this night, before the | **Mark 14.** ³⁰ And Jesus saith unto him,ʸ Verily I say unto thee, That this day, *even* | **Luke 22.** ³⁴ And he said,ʸ I tell thee, Peter, the cock shall not crow this day, before that | **John 13.** ³⁸ Jesus answered him,ʸ Wilt thou lay down thy life for my sake? |

ᑫ On the sense of *feast* here, see above in Introductory Note, p. 136.

ʳ *Went immediately out.* Judas therefore was not present at the Lord's supper, which was instituted at the close of the paschal meal. This is the obvious conclusion, at least, from the account of John, in connexion with the statements of Matthew and Mark; and it is the view taken by most harmonists and commentators. It might appear, however, from Luke's account (ch. 22. 19–21) that Judas was present; but the whole force of this proof depends on the chronological regularity of this Gospel. We have seen

that it does not always follow the order of time (see Note on ᑫ 1).

ˢ John 7. 33. 34.   ᵗ 1 John 2. 8–11; 4. 21.

ᵘ 1 John 3. 10.   ᵛ 2 Pet. 1. 14.

ʷ Zech. 13. 7.   ˣ John 21. 1.

ʸ This foretelling of Peter's fall took place, according to Luke (ch. 22. 39) and John (ch. 18. 1), *before* the departure to the mount of Olives; but according to Matthew (ch. 26. 30) and Mark (ch. 14. 26), it occurred *during* that departure. This difference may be explained by simply supposing that our Lord touched on the subject *twice;* before setting out, and while on the way.

Matt. 26.	Mark 14.	Luke 22.	John 13.
cock crow, thou shalt deny me thrice. ³⁶ Peter said unto him, Though I should die with thee, yet will I not deny thee. Likewise also said all the disciples.	in this night, before the cock crow twice, thou shalt deny me thrice.ᶻ ³¹ But he spake the more vehemently, If I should die with thee, I will not deny thee in any wise. Likewise also said they all.	thou shalt thrice deny that thou knowest me.	Verily, verily, I say unto thee, The cock shall not crow, till thou hast denied me thrice.

Luke 22.

³⁵ And he said unto them, When I sent you without purse, and scrip, and shoes, lacked ye any thing? And they said, Nothing. ³⁶ Then said he unto them, But now, he that hath a purse, let him take *it*, and likewise *his* scrip: and he that hath no sword, let him sell his garment and buy one. ³⁷ For I say unto you, that this that is written must yet be accomplished in me,ᵃ And he was reckoned among the transgressors: for the things concerning me have an end. ³⁸ And they said, Lord, behold, here *are* two swords. And he said unto them, It is enough.

§ 137. THE LORD'S SUPPER.ᵇ—*Jerusalem.*
Evening introducing the Sixth Day of the Week.

Matt. 26. 26-29.	Mark 14. 22-25.	Luke 22. 19, 20.	1 Cor. 11. 23-25.
²⁶ And as they were eating, Jesus took bread, and blessed *it*, and brake *it*, and gave *it* to the disciples, and said, Take, eat; this is my body.	²² And as they did eat, Jesus took bread, and blessed and brake *it*, and gave to them, and said, Take, eat: this is my body.	¹⁹ And he took bread, and gave thanks, and brake *it*, and gave unto them, saying, This is my body which is given for you: this do in remembrance of me.	²³ The Lord Jesus—took bread: ²⁴ and when he had given thanks, he brake *it*, and said, Take, eat: this is my body, which is broken for you: this do in remembrance of me.
²⁷ And he took the cup, and gave thanks, and gave *it* to them, saying, Drink ye all of it; ²⁸ for this is my blood of the new testament,ᶜ which is shed for many for the remission	²³ And he took the cup, and when he had given thanks, he gave *it* to them: and they all drank of it. ²⁴ And he said unto them, This is my blood of the new testament,ᶜ which	²⁰ Likewise also the cup after supper, saying, This cup *is* the new testament in my blood,ᵈ which is shed for you.	²⁵ After the same manner also *he* took the cup, when he had supped, saying, This cup is the new testament in my blood:ᵈ this do ye, as oft as ye drink *it*, in remembrance of me.

ᶻ Mark here says, "Before the cock crow *twice;*" the other evangelists have simply, "Before the cock crow;" see Note on § 144.

ᵃ Isa. 53. 12.

ᵇ The institution of the Lord's supper took place obviously at the close of the passover meal, and in connexion with the "cup of blessing," or third cup, which terminated the meal proper; comp. 1 Cor. 10. 16, and see p. 134 above. With this view accords the expression, *after supper* of Luke 22. 20 and 1 Cor. 11. 25. Matthew and Mark speak

of Jesus as breaking the bread *as they were eating*, which implies nothing more than "during the meal," while they were *yet* eating; and does not require the institution of the bread to be separated from that of the cup.

ᶜ *New testament:* better rendered "This is My blood of the *new covenant,*" evidently referring to the words of Moses in Exodus 24. 8, "Behold the *blood of the covenant* which the Lord hath made with you."

ᵈ Heb. 9. ¹¹–22.

Matt. 26.

of sins. ²⁹ But I say unto you, I will
not drink henceforth of this fruit of
the vine,*e* until that day when I drink
it new with you in my Father's kingdom.*f*

Mark 14.

is shed for many. ²⁵ Verily I say unto
you, I will drink no more of the fruit of
the vine,*e* until that day that I drink it
new in the kingdom of God.

§ 138. Jesus comforts His Disciples. The Holy Spirit promised.
Jerusalem.

Evening introducing the Sixth Day of the Week.

John 14. 1–31. ¹ Let not your heart be troubled: ye believe in God,*g* believe
also in me. ² In my Father's house are many mansions: if *it were* not so, I would
have told you. I go to prepare a place for you. ³ And if I go and prepare a place
for you, I will come again, and receive you unto myself; that where I am, *there* ye
may be also. ⁴ And whither I go ye know, and the way ye know.
⁵ Thomas saith unto him, Lord, we know not whither thou goest; and how can
we know the way? ⁶ Jesus saith unto him, I am the way, the truth, and the life:
no man cometh unto the Father, but by me. ⁷ If ye had known me, ye should have
known my Father also: and from henceforth ye know him, and have seen him.
⁸ Philip saith unto him, Lord, show us the Father, and it sufficeth us. ⁹ Jesus
saith unto him, Have I been so long time with you, and yet hast thou not known
me, Philip? he that hath seen me hath seen the Father; and how sayest thou
then, Show us the Father? ¹⁰ Believest thou not that I am in the Father, and
the Father in me? the words that I speak unto you I speak not of myself: but
the Father that dwelleth in me, he doeth the works. ¹¹ Believe me that I *am* in
the Father, and the Father in me: or else believe me for the very works' sake.
¹² Verily, verily, I say unto you, He that believeth on me, the works that I do
shall he do also; and greater *works* than these shall he do; because I go unto my
Father. ¹³ And whatsoever ye shall ask in my name, that will I do, that the Father
may be glorified in the Son. ¹⁴ If ye shall ask any thing in my name, I will do *it*.
¹⁵ If ye love me, keep my commandments.*h* ¹⁶ And I will pray the Father, and he
shall give you another Comforter, that he may abide with you for ever; ¹⁷ *even* the
Spirit of truth; whom the world cannot receive, because it seeth him not, neither
knoweth him: but ye know him; for he dwelleth with you, and shall be in you.
¹⁸ I will not leave you comfortless: I will come to you. ¹⁹ Yet a little while, and
the world seeth me no more; but ye see me: because I live, ye shall live also.*i*
²⁰ At that day ye shall know that I *am* in my Father, and ye in me, and I in you.
²¹ He that hath my commandments, and keepeth them, he it is that loveth me: and
he that loveth me shall be loved of my Father, and I will love him, and will manifest
myself to him.
²² Judas saith unto him, not Iscariot, Lord, how is it that thou wilt manifest
thyself unto us, and not unto the world? ²³ Jesus answered and said unto him,
If a man love me, he will keep my words: and my Father will love him, and we
will come unto him,*j* and make our abode with him. ²⁴ He that loveth me not
keepeth not my sayings: and the word which ye hear is not mine, but the Father's
which sent me.
²⁵ These things have I spoken unto you, being *yet* present with you. ²⁶ But the
Comforter, *which is* the Holy Ghost, whom the Father will send in my name, he
shall teach you all things,*k* and bring all things to your remembrance, whatsoever

---

e Comp. Acts 10. 41.   *f* See ? 142.
g *Ye believe in God, etc.*: as if He had
said, Ye trust in God though *unseen*, in like
manner trust in Me when I shall be no longer
visibly present with you.

h 1 John 5. 3.
i Col. 3. 3; 1 Cor. 15. 20.   *j* Rev. 3. 20.
k *He shall teach you all things, etc.* The
plenary inspiration of the apostles is here set
forth as consisting in two things, viz., the

John 14.

I have said unto you.[l] [27] Peace I leave with you, my peace [m] I give unto you: not as the world giveth, give I unto you. Let not your heart be troubled, neither let it be afraid. [28] Ye have heard how I said unto you, I go away, and come *again* unto you. If ye loved me, ye would rejoice, because I said, I go unto the Father: for my Father is greater than I.[n] [29] And now I have told you before it come to pass, that, when it is come to pass, ye might believe. [30] Hereafter I will not talk much with you: for the prince of this world cometh, and hath nothing in me. [31] But that the world may know that I love the Father; and as the Father gave me commandment, even so I do. **Arise, let us go hence.**[o]

§ 139. Christ the True Vine. His Disciples hated by the World.
Jerusalem.
Evening introducing the Sixth Day of the Week.

John 15. 1-27. [1] I am the true vine, and my Father is the husbandman. [2] Every branch in me that beareth not fruit he taketh away: and every *branch* that beareth fruit, he purgeth it, that it may bring forth more fruit. [3] Now ye are clean through the word which I have spoken unto you. [4] Abide in me, and I in you. As the branch cannot bear fruit of itself, except it abide in the vine; no more can ye, except ye abide in me. [5] I am the vine, ye *are* the branches: He that abideth in me, and I in him, the same bringeth forth much fruit: for without me ye can do nothing. [6] If a man abide not in me, he is cast forth as a branch, and is withered; and men gather them, and cast *them* into the fire, and they are burned. [7] If ye abide in me, and my words abide in you, ye shall ask what ye will, and it shall be done unto you. [8] Herein is my Father glorified, that ye bear much fruit, so shall ye be my disciples. [9] As the Father hath loved me, so have I loved you: continue ye in my love. [10] If ye keep my commandments, ye shall abide in my love; even as I have kept my Father's commandments, and abide in his love. [11] These things have I spoken unto you, that my joy might remain in you, and *that* your joy might be full. [12] This is my commandment, That ye love one another, as I have loved you. [13] Greater love hath no man than this, that a man lay down his life for his friends. [14] Ye are my friends, if ye do whatsoever I command you. [15] Henceforth I call you not servants; for the servant knoweth not what his lord doeth: but I have called you friends; for all things that I have heard of my Father I have made known unto you. [16] Ye have not chosen me, but I have chosen you, and ordained you, that ye should go and bring forth fruit, and *that* your fruit should remain: that whatsoever ye shall ask of the Father in my name, he may give it you. [17] These things I command you, that ye love one another. [18] If the world hate you, ye know that it hated me before *it hated* you. [19] If ye were of the world, the world would love his own: but because ye are not of the world, but I have chosen you out of the world, therefore the world hateth you. [20] Remember the word that I said unto you,[p] The servant is not greater than his lord. If they have persecuted me, they will also persecute you; if they have kept my saying, they will keep your's also. [21] But all these things will they do unto you for my name's sake,[q] because they know not him that sent me. [22] If I had not come

---

direct teaching of the Spirit in conveying new truths to their minds, and the quickening of their memories in recalling truths they had heard.
[l] Comp. 1 John 2. 27. [m] Phil. 4. 7.
[n] Comp. 1 Cor. 11. 3; 15. 24-28.
[o] *Arise, let us go hence.* Jesus and the eleven now prepare to set out from the supper room, to proceed to the mount of Olives:

see § 142. But what John relates in chapters 15-17 occurred most likely before they actually quitted the house. [p] Matt. 10. 24.
[q] *For My name's sake.* This means that the disciples should suffer persecution, not merely because they are named after Christ, but because they possess His spirit and bear His image, so as to be His representatives in the world.

John 15.

and spoken unto them, they had not had sin : but now they have no cloke for their sin. ²³ He that hateth me hateth my Father also. ²⁴ If I had not done among them the works which none other man did, they had not had sin : but now have they both seen and hated both me and my Father. ²⁵ But *this cometh to pass,* that the word might be fulfilled that is written in the law,ʳ They hated me without a cause. ²⁶ But when the Comforter is come, whom I will send unto you from the Father, *even* the Spirit of truth, which proceedeth from the Father, he shall testify of me : ²⁷ and ye also shall bear witness, because ye have been with me from the beginning.ᵃ

§ 140. PERSECUTION FORETOLD. FURTHER PROMISE OF THE HOLY SPIRIT. PRAYER IN THE NAME OF CHRIST.—*Jerusalem.*

Evening introducing the Sixth Day of the Week.

John 16. 1–33. ¹ These things have I spoken unto you, that ye should not be offended. ² They shall put you out of the synagogues : yea, the time cometh, that whosoever killeth you will think that he doeth God service.ᵗ ³ And these things will they do unto you, because they have not known the Father, nor me. ⁴ But these things have I told you, that when the time shall come, ye may remember that I told you of them. And these things I said not unto you at the beginning, because I was with you. ⁵ But now I go my way to him that sent me ; and none of you asketh me, Whither goest thou ? ⁶ But because I have said these things unto you, sorrow hath filled your heart. ⁷ Nevertheless I tell you the truth ; It is expedient for you that I go away : for if I go not away, the Comforter will not come unto you ; but if I depart, I will send him unto you. ⁸ And when he is come, he will reprove the world of sin, and of righteousness, and of judgment : ⁹ of sin, because they believe not on me ; ¹⁰ of righteousness, because I go to my Father, and ye see me no more ; ¹¹ of judgment, because the prince of this world is judged. ¹² I have yet many things to say unto you, but ye cannot bear them now.ᵘ ¹³ Howbeit when he, the Spirit of truth, is come, he will guide you into all truth : for he shall not speak of himself ; but whatsoever he shall hear, *that* shall he speak : and he will show you things to come. ¹⁴ He shall glorify me : for he shall receive of mine, and shall show *it* unto you. ¹⁵ All things that the Father hath are mine : therefore said I, that he shall take of mine, and shall show *it* unto you. ¹⁶ A little while, and ye shall not see me : and again, a little while, and ye shall see me, because I go to the Father.

¹⁷ Then said *some* of his disciples among themselves, What is this that he saith unto us, A little while, and ye shall not see me : and again, a little while, and ye shall see me : and, Because I go to the Father ? ¹⁸ They said therefore, What is this that he saith, A little while ? we cannot tell what he saith. ¹⁹ Now Jesus knew that they were desirous to ask him, and said unto them, Do ye inquire among yourselves of that I said, A little while, and ye shall not see me : and again, a little while, and ye shall see me ? ²⁰ Verily, verily, I say unto you, That ye shall weep and lament, but the world shall rejoice : and ye shall be sorrowful, but your sorrow shall be turned into joy. ²¹ A woman when she is in travail hath sorrow, because her hour is come : but as soon as she is delivered of the child, she remembereth no more the anguish, for joy that a man is born into the world. ²² And ye now therefore have sorrow :ᵛ but I will see you again, and your heart shall rejoice, and your joy no man taketh from you. ²³ And in that day ye shall ask me nothing. Verily, verily, I say unto you, Whatsoever ye shall ask the Father in my name, he will

---

ʳ Psa. 69. 4. ˢ Acts 1. 21, 22; Luke 1. 1, 2. ᵗ Acts 26. 9–11.
ᵘ Mark 4. 33. ᵛ Luke 24. 40, 41.

John 16.

give *it* you. ²⁴ Hitherto have ye asked nothing in my name:ʷ ask, and ye shall receive, that your joy may be full. ²⁵ These things have I spoken unto you in proverbs: but the time cometh, when I shall no more speak unto you in proverbs, but I shall show you plainly of the Father. ²⁶ At that day ye shall ask in my name: and I say not unto you, that I will pray the Father for you: ²⁷ for the Father himself loveth you, because ye have loved me, and have believed that I came out from God. ²⁸ I came forth from the Father, and am come into the world: again, I leave the world, and go to the Father. ²⁹ His disciples said unto him, Lo, now speakest thou plainly, and speakest no proverb. ³⁰ Now are we sure that thou knowest all things, and needest not that any man should ask thee: by this we believe that thou camest forth from God. ³¹ Jesus answered them, Do ye now believe? ³² Behold, the hour cometh, yea, is now come, that ye shall be scattered, every man to his own, and shall leave me alone:ˣ and yet I am not alone, because the Father is with me. ³³ These things have I spoken unto you, that in me ye might have peace. In the world ye shall have tribulation:ʸ but be of good cheer; I have overcome the world.ᶻ

§ 141. Christ's last Prayer with His Disciples.—*Jerusalem.*

Evening introducing the Sixth Day of the Week.

John 17. 1–24. ¹ These words spake Jesus, and lifted up his eyes to heaven, and said, Father, the hour is come; glorify thy Son, that thy Son also may glorify thee: ² as thou hast given him power over all flesh, that he should give eternal life to as many as thou hast given him. ³ And this is life eternal, that they might know thee the only true God, and Jesus Christ, whom thou hast sent. ⁴ I have glorified thee on the earth: I have finished the work which thou gavest me to do. ⁵ And now, O Father, glorify thou me with thine own self with the glory which I had with thee before the world was.

⁶ I have manifested thy name unto the men which thou gavest me out of the world: thine they were, and thou gavest them me; and they have kept thy word. ⁷ Now they have known that all things whatsoever thou hast given me are of thee. ⁸ For I have given unto them the words which thou gavest me; and they have received *them*, and have known surely that I came out from thee, and they have believed that thou didst send me. ⁹ I pray for them: I pray not for the world, but for them which thou hast given me; for they are thine. ¹⁰ And all mine are thine, and thine are mine; and I am glorified in them. ¹¹ And now I am no more in the world, but these are in the world, and I come to thee. Holy Father, keep through thine own name those whom thou hast given me, that they may be one, as we *are*. ¹² While I was with them in the world, I kept them in thy name: those that thou gavest me I have kept, and none of them is lost, but the son of perdition: that the Scripture might be fulfilled.ᵃ ¹³ And now come I to thee; and these things I speak in the world, that they might have my joy fulfilled in themselves. ¹⁴ I have given them thy word; and the world hath hated them, because they are not of the world, even as I am not of the world. ¹⁵ I pray not that thou shouldest take them out of the world, but that thou shouldest keep them from the evil. ¹⁶ They are not of the

---

ʷ *Ye shall ask Me nothing,* v. 23; i.e. Ye shall ask Me *no more questions,* of doubt or unsatisfied curiosity; as those in 14. 5, 22; 16. 17; etc. The word *ask* is different in the two parts of the verse. And when Christ adds, *Hitherto have ye asked nothing in My name,* He does not imply that the disciples had previously exercised no faith whatever in Him as Mediator, but that they did not distinctly comprehend the nature and importance of His mediation, until after the completion of the work of redemption.

ˣ Matt. 26. 56.
ʸ 1 Thess. 3. 3, 4; 2 Tim. 3. 12.
ᶻ Rom. 8. 37.
ᵃ Psa. 41. 9; 109. 8, 17; Acts 1. 16–20.

John 17.

world, even as I am not of the world. ¹⁷ Sanctify [b] them through thy truth: thy word is truth. ¹⁸ As thou hast sent me into the world, even so have I also sent them into the world. ¹⁹ And for their sakes I sanctify myself,[c] that they also might be sanctified through the truth.

²⁰ Neither pray I for these alone, but for them also which shall believe on me through their word; ²¹ that they all may be one; as thou, Father, *art* in me, and I in thee, that they also may be one in us: that the world may believe that thou hast sent me. ²² And the glory which thou gavest me I have given them; that they may be one, even as we are one: ²³ I in them, and thou in me, that they may be made perfect in one; and that the world may know that thou hast sent me, and hast loved them, as thou hast loved me.

²⁴ Father, I will that they also, whom thou hast given me, be with me where I am; that they may behold my glory, which thou hast given me: for thou lovedst me before the foundation of the world. ²⁵ O righteous Father, the world hath not known thee: but I have known thee, and these have known that thou hast sent me. ²⁶ And I have declared unto them thy name, and will declare *it:* that the love wherewith thou hast loved me may be in them, and I in them.

§ 142. The Agony [d] in Gethsemane.—*Mount of Olives.*

Evening introducing the Sixth Day of the Week.

Matt. 26. 30, 36 – 46.	Mark 14. 26, 32 – 42.	Luke 22. 39– 46.	John 18. 1.
³⁰ And when they had sung [e] an hymn, they went out into the mount of Olives. —³⁶ Then cometh Jesus with them unto a place called Gethsemane,[f] and saith unto the disciples, Sit ye here, while I go and pray yonder.	²⁶ And when they had sung [e] an hymn, they went out into the mount of Olives. —³² And they came to a place which was named Gethsemane: and he saith to his disciples, Sit ye here, while I shall pray.	³⁹ And he came out, and went, as he was wont, to the mount of Olives; and his disciples also followed him. ⁴⁰ And when he was at the place, he said unto them, Pray that ye enter not into temptation.	¹ When Jesus had spoken these words he went forth with his disciples over the brook Cedron, where was a garden, into the which he entered, and his disciples.

Matt. 26.	Mark 14.
³⁷ And he took with him Peter and the two sons of Zebedee, and began to be	³³ And he taketh with him Peter and James and John, and began to be sore

---

[b] Eph. 4. 21–24; 5. 26.

[c] *i.e.* prepare and present myself as a sacrifice.

[d] Matthew relates that our Lord went away *thrice* and prayed. Mark speaks of His going away twice only, but mentions His coming again the *third* time, ver. 41; and therefore accords with Matthew. According to Luke, Jesus goes away and prays, and an angel strengthens Him; after which He prays the "more earnestly," ver. 44. The three evangelists, therefore, agree.

[e] On this *singing*, see Introductory Note, p. 134.

[f] The present garden of Gethsemane, situated between the brook Kidron and the foot of Olivet, may be regarded as the real scene of the Lord's agony. It was, probably, an olive plantation, for the name, *Gethsemane*, signifies an *oil-press*. The present, however, is supposed to be but a part of the ancient garden; for it is only about fifty paces square, which is too small to satisfy all the conditions of the narrative. (See Luke 22. 41.) It is probable that the ancient garden occupied some of the space now covered by similar enclosures adjacent, which contain olive trees of the same age and character as Gethsemane, which exhibits eight that are certainly very old; probably standing ever since Christ was there. See Kitto's *Ancient Jerusalem,* p. 184 (Religious Tract Society).

Matt. 26.

sorrowful and very heavy.[g] **38** Then saith he unto them, My soul is exceeding sorrowful, even unto death: tarry ye here, and watch with me.

Mark 14.

amazed, and to be very heavy;[g] **34** and saith unto them, My soul is exceeding sorrowful unto death: tarry ye here, and watch.

Matt. 26.

39 And he went a little further, and fell on his face, and prayed,

saying, O my Father, if it be possible, let this cup pass from me: nevertheless not as I will, but as thou *wilt.*[h]

Mark 14.

35 And he went forward a little, and fell on the ground, and prayed that, if it were possible, the hour might pass from him. **36** And he said, Abba, Father, all things *are* possible unto thee; take away this cup from me: nevertheless not what I will, but what thou wilt.[h]

Luke 22.

41 And he was withdrawn from them about a stone's cast, and kneeled down, and prayed, **42** saying, Father, if thou be willing remove this cup from me: nevertheless not my will, but thine, be done.[h] **43** And there appeared an angel unto him from heaven strengthening him. **44** And being in an agony he prayed more earnestly: and his sweat was as it were great drops of blood falling down to the ground. **45** And when he rose up from prayer, and was come to his disciples, he found them sleeping for sorrow, **46** and said unto them, Why sleep ye? rise and pray, lest ye enter into temptation.

40 And he cometh unto the disciples, and findeth them asleep, and saith unto Peter, What, could ye not watch with me one hour? **41** Watch and pray, that ye enter not into temptation: the spirit indeed *is* willing, but the flesh *is* weak.[j]

37 And he cometh, and findeth them sleeping, and saith unto Peter, Simon, sleepest thou? couldest not thou watch one hour? **38** Watch ye and pray, lest ye enter into temptation. The spirit truly *is* ready, but the flesh *is* weak.[j]

Matt. 26.

42 He went away again the second time, and prayed, saying, O my Father, if this cup may not pass away from me, except I drink it, thy will be done. **43** And he came and found them asleep again: for their eyes were heavy. **44** And he left them, and went away again, and prayed the third time,[k] saying the same words. **45** Then cometh he to his disciples, and saith unto them, Sleep on now, and take *your* rest:[l] behold, the hour is at hand, and the Son of man is betrayed into the hands of sinners. **46** Rise, let us be going: behold, he is at hand that doth betray me.

Mark 14.

39 And again he went away, and prayed and spake the same words. **40** And when he returned, he found them asleep again, (for their eyes were heavy,) neither wist they what to answer him.

41 And he cometh the third time, and saith unto them, Sleep on now, and take *your* rest:[l] it is enough, the hour is come; behold, the Son of man is betrayed into the hands of sinners. **42** Rise up, let us go; lo, he that betrayeth me is at hand.

---

[g] Heb. 5. 7; John 12. 27.
[h] Phil. 2. 6–8; Heb. 5. 8.
[i] Heb. 5. 7.
[j] Rom. 7. 18–25.

[k] Comp. 2 Cor. 12. 8.
[l] Greswell and Robinson understand these words interrogatively; thus, *Do ye sleep on still and take rest?*

§ 143. JESUS BETRAYED, AND MADE PRISONER.—*Gethsemane.*

Evening introducing the Sixth Day of the Week.

John 18. 2–12. ² And Judas also, which betrayed him, knew the place: for Jesus ofttimes resorted thither with his disciples. ³ Judas then, having received a band *of men* and officers from the chief priests and Pharisees, cometh thither with lanterns and torches and weapons.

Matt. 26. 47–56.	Mark 14. 43–52.	Luke 22. 47–53.
⁴⁷ And while he yet spake, lo, Judas, one of the twelve, came, and with him a great multitude with swords and staves, from the chief priests and elders of the people.	⁴³ And immediately, while he yet spake, cometh Judas, one of the twelve, and with him a great multitude with swords and staves, from the chief priests and the scribes and the elders.	⁴⁷ And while he yet spake, behold a multitude, and he that was called Judas, one of the twelve, went before them.

John 18.

⁴ Jesus therefore, knowing all things that should come upon him, went forth, and said unto them, Whom seek ye? ⁵ They answered him, Jesus of Nazareth. Jesus saith unto them, I am *he*. And Judas also, which betrayed him, stood with them. ⁶ As soon then as he had said unto them, I am *he*, they went backward, and fell to the ground. ⁷ Then asked he them again, Whom seek ye? And they said, Jesus of Nazareth. ⁸ Jesus answered, I have told you that I am *he* : if therefore ye seek me, let these go their way: ⁹ that the saying might be fulfilled, which he spake," Of them which thou gavest me have I lost none.

Matt. 26.	Mark 14.	Luke 22.	John 18.
⁴⁸ Now he that betrayed him gave them a sign, saying, Whomsoever I shall kiss, that same is he: hold him fast. ⁴⁹ And forthwith he came to Jesus, and said, Hail, Master; and kissed him. ⁵⁰ And Jesus said unto him, Friend,° wherefore art thou come? Then came they, and laid hands on Jesus, and took him. ⁵¹ And, behold, one of them which were with Jesus stretched out *his* hand, and drew his sword, and struck a servant of the	⁴⁴ And he that betrayed him had given them a token, saying, Whomsoever I shall kiss, that same is he; take him, and lead *him* away safely. ⁴⁵ And as soon as he was come, he goeth straightway to him, and saith, Master, Master; and kissed him. ⁴⁶ And they laid their hands on him, and took him. ⁴⁷ And one of them that stood by drew a sword, and smote a servant of the high priest, and cut off his ear.	—⁴⁷ and drew near unto Jesus to kiss him. ⁴⁸ But Jesus said unto him, Judas, betrayest thou the Son of man with a kiss? ⁴⁹ When they which were about him saw what would follow, they said unto him, Lord, shall we smite with the sword? ⁵⁰ And one of them smote the servant of the high priest, and cut off his right ear. ⁵¹ And Jesus answered and said,	—¹² Then the band and the captain and officers of the Jews took Jesus, and bound him. — ¹⁰ Then Simon Peter having a sword drew it, and smote the high priest's servant, and cut off his right ear.

° Comp. John 17. 12; 6, 39.

° *Friend* is here too strong a term, for the original word denotes a mere *companion* or *acquaintance*, without implying respect or affection. Where our Lord calls (as in John 15. 15) His faithful disciples *friends*, another word (φίλοι) is employed, which denotes attachment.

Matt. 26.

high priest's, and smote off his ear. [52] Then said Jesus unto him, Put up again thy sword into his place: for all they that take the sword shall perish with the sword.[p] [53] Thinkest thou that I cannot now pray to my Father, and he shall presently give me more than twelve legions of angels? [54] But how then shall the Scriptures be fulfilled, that thus it must be?[q] [55] In that same hour said Jesus to the multitudes, Are ye come out as against a thief with swords and staves for to take me? I sat daily with you teaching in the temple, and ye laid no hold on me. [56] But all this was done, that the Scriptures of the prophets might be fulfilled. Then all the disciples forsook him, and fled.[r]

Luke 22.

Suffer ye thus far. And he touched his ear, and healed him.

John 18.

The servant's name wa Malchus. [11] Then sai Jesus unto Peter, Put u thy sword into the sheath the cup which my Fathe hath given me, shall I no drink it?

Mark 14.

[48] And Jesus answered and said unto them, Are ye come out, as against a thief, with swords and *with* staves to take me? [49] I was daily with you in the temple teaching, and ye took me not: but the Scriptures must be fulfilled. [50] And they all forsook him, and fled.

Luke 22.

[52] Then Jesus said unt the chief priests, and cap tains of the temple, an the elders, which wer come to him, Be ye com out, as against a thie with swords and staves [53] When I was daily wit you in the temple, y stretched forth no hand against me: but this i your hour, and the powe of darkness.

Mark 14.

[51] And there followed him a certain young man, having a linen cloth cast abou *his* naked *body;* [52] and the young men laid hold on him: and he left the liner cloth, and fled from them naked.

§ 144. JESUS BEFORE CAIAPHAS.[s] PETER THRICE DENIES HIM.—*Jerusalem.*

Night introducing the Sixth Day of the Week.

Matt. 26. 57, 58, 69–75. [57] And they that had laid hold on Jesus led	Mark 14. 53, 54, 66–72. [53] And they led Jesus away to the high priest:	Luke 22. 54–62. [54] Then took they him, and led him, and brought	John 18. 13–18, 25–27. [13] An they led him awa to Annas first; fo

[p] Gen. 9. 6.
[q] Luke 24. 44–46.   [r] John 16. 32.
[s] An Oriental house is usually built around a quadrangular interior court; into which there is a passage through the front part of the house, closed next the street by a heavy folding gate, with a smaller wicket for single persons. The interior court, often paved or flagged, and open to the sky, is the *hall* (αὐλή), mentioned in the following section, where the attendants made a fire; and the passage from the street to this court, is the *porch* (προαύλιον or πυλών). The place where Jesus stood before the high priest may have been an open room or place of audience on

the ground floor; such rooms, open in front being customary. It was close upon th court; for Jesus heard all that was going or around the fire; and turned and looked upor Peter; Luke 22. 61.

Peter's *first* denial took place at the fire ir the middle of the court (αὐλή), on his being questioned by the female porter.—Peter then according to Matthew and Mark, retreats into the passage leading to the street (πυλών προαύλιον), where he is again questioned, and makes his *second* denial. Luke and John do not specify the place. The evange lists differ in their statements here, as to the person who now questioned him. Mark says

Matt. 26.	**Mark 14.**	**Luke 22.**	**John 18.**
him away to Caiaphas the high priest, where the scribes and the elders were assembled.	and with him were assembled all the chief priests and the elders and the scribes.	him into the high priest's house.—	he was *t* father-in-law to Caiaphas, which was the high priest that same year. ¹⁴ Now Caiaphas was he, which gave counsel to the Jews, that it was expedient that one man should die for the people.*u* ¹⁵ And
⁵⁸ But Peter followed him afar off unto the high priest's palace,—	⁵⁴ And Peter followed him afar off, even into the palace of the high priest :—	—And Peter followed afar off.	Simon Peter followed Jesus, and *so did* another disciple : that disciple was known unto to the high priest, and went in with Jesus into the palace of the high priest. ¹⁶ But Peter stood at the door without. Then went out that other disciple, which was known unto the high priest, and spake unto her that kept the door, and brought in Peter.—
—⁵⁸ and went in, and sat with the servants, to see the end.*v*—	—⁵⁴ And he sat with the servants, and warmed himself by the fire.— ⁶⁶ And as Peter was beneath in the palace, there cometh one of the maids of the high priest;	⁵⁵ And when they had kindled a fire in the midst of the hall, and were sat down together, Peter sat down among them.	¹⁸ And the servants and officers stood there, who had made a fire of coals; for it was cold : and they warmed themselves : and Peter stood with them, and warmed himself.—
⁶⁹ Now Peter sat	⁶⁷ And when she	⁵⁶ But a certain	¹⁷ Then saith the

---

the same maid saw him again, and began to question him, ver. 69; Matthew has, another maid, ver. 71; Luke writes another person, or another man, ver. 58; while John uses the indefinite form, *they said*. As; according to Matthew (ver. 70) and Mark (ver. 69), there were several persons present, Peter may have been interrogated by several.— The *third* denial took place an hour after, probably near the fire, or at least within the court, where our Lord and Peter could see each other; Luke 22. 61. Here Matthew and Mark speak of several interrogators, Luke has, *some other man*, and John specifies the servant of the high priest.

The three denials are here placed together for convenience, although during the intervals between them the examination of Jesus was going on before the high priest; the progress of which is given in § 145.

t For he was, etc. The reason for taking our Lord first to Annas was, perhaps, this, that he was known from his family relation to share the views and feelings of his son-in-law, Caiaphas, whose avowed purpose to seek the death of Jesus is mentioned in the next verse.

u John 11. 50.

v Ver. 59–68 in § 145.

Matt. 26.

without in the palace : and a damsel came unto him, saying, Thou also wast with Jesus of Galilee. ⁷⁰ But he denied before *them* all, saying, I know not what thou sayest. ⁷¹ And when he was gone out into the porch, another *maid* saw him, and said unto them that were there, This *fellow* was also with Jesus of Nazareth. ⁷² And again he denied with an oath, I do not know the man.

⁷³ And after a while came unto *him* they that stood by, and said to Peter, Surely thou also art *one* of them ; for thy speech bewrayeth thee. ⁷⁴ Then began he to curse and to swear, *saying*, I know not the man. And immediately the cock crew.

Mark 14.

saw Peter warming himself, she looked upon him, and said, And thou also wast with Jesus of Nazareth. ⁶⁸ But he denied, saying, I know not, neither understand I what thou sayest. And he went out into the porch ; and the cock crew. ⁶⁹ And a maid saw him again, and began to say to them that stood by, This is *one* of them. ⁷⁰ And he denied it again.

And a little after, they that stood by said again to Peter, Surely thou art *one* of them : for thou art a Galilean, and thy speech agreeth *thereto*. ⁷¹ But he began to curse and to swear, *saying*, I know not this man of whom ye speak. ⁷² And the second time*ᵂ* the cock crew.

Luke 22.

maid beheld him as he sat by the fire, and earnestly looked upon him, and said, This man was also with him. ⁵⁷ And he denied him, saying, Woman, I know him not. ⁵⁸ And after a little while another saw him, and

said, Thou art also of them. And Peter said, Man, I am not.

⁵⁹ And about the space of one hour after another confidently affirmed, saying, Of a truth this *fellow* also was with him : for he is a Galilean. ⁶⁰ And Peter said, Man, I know not what thou sayest. And immediately, while he yet spake, the cock crew.

John 18.

damsel that kept the door unto Peter, Art not thou also *one* of this **man's** disciples ? He **saith**, I am not.—

²⁵ And Simon Peter stood and warmed himself. They said therefore unto

him, Art not thou also *one* of his disciples ? He denied *it*, and said, I am not.

²⁶ One of the servants of the high priest, being *his* kinsman whose ear Peter cut off, saith, Did not I see thee in the garden with him ? ²⁷ Peter then denied again :

and immediately the cock crew.

Matt. 26.

⁷⁵ And Peter remembered the word of Jesus, which said unto him, Before the cock crow, thou shalt deny me thrice. And he went out, and wept bitterly.

Mark 14.

⁷² And Peter called to mind the word that Jesus said unto him, Before the cock crow twice, thou shalt deny me thrice. And when he thought thereon, he wept.

Luke 22.

⁶¹ And the Lord turned, and looked upon Peter. And Peter remembered the word of the Lord, how he had said unto him, Before the cock crow, thou shalt deny me thrice. ⁶² And Peter went out, and wept bitterly.

ᵂ Mark relates that the cock crowed *twice*, ver. 68, 72; the others speak only of his crowing *once*. This accords also with their respective accounts of our Lord's prophecy; see § 136. The cock often crows irregularly about midnight or not long after; and again always and regularly about the third hour or day-break. When therefore "the cock-crow-

ing" is spoken of alone, this last is always meant. Hence the name *cock-crowing*, for the third watch of the night, which ended at the third hour after midnight; Mark 13. 35. Mark therefore here relates more definitely; while the other evangelists speak in more general terms.

§ 145. Jesus before Caiaphas and the Sanhedrim. He declares Himself to be the Christ; is condemned and mocked.—*Jerusalem.*

Early Morning of the Sixth Day of the Week.

John 18. 19-24. [19] The high priest then asked y Jesus of his disciples, and of his doctrine. [20] Jesus answered him, I spake openly to the world; I ever taught in the synagogue, and in the temple, whither the Jews always resort; and in secret have I said nothing. [21] Why askest thou me? ask them which heard me, what I have said unto them: behold, they know what I said. [22] And when he had thus spoken, one of the officers which stood by struck Jesus with the palm of his hand, saying, Answerest thou the high priest so? [23] Jesus answered him, If I have spoken evil, bear witness of the evil: but if well, why smitest thou me? [24] Now Annas had sent him bound unto Caiaphas the high priest.

Luke 22. 63-71. [66] And as soon as it was day, the elders of the people and the chief priests and the scribes came together, and led him into their council,—

Matt. 26. 59-68. [59] Now the chief priests, and elders, and all the council, sought false witness z against Jesus, to put him to death; but found none: [60] yea though many false witnesses came, *yet* found they none. At the last came two false witnesses, [61] and said,

This *fellow* said, I am able to destroy the temple of God, and to build it in three days.a

[62] And the high priest arose, and said unto him, Answerest thou nothing? what *is it which* these witness against thee? [63] But Jesus held his peace.

And the high priest answered and said unto him, I adjure thee by the living God, that thou tell us whether thou be the Christ, the Son of God. [64] Jesus saith unto him, Thou hast said: nevertheless I say unto you, Hereafter shall ye see the Son of man sitting on the right hand of power, and coming in the clouds of heaven. [65] Then the high priest rent his clothes,

Mark 14. 55-65. [55] And the chief priests and all the council sought for witness z against Jesus to put him to death; and found none. [56] For many bare false witness against him, but their witness agreed not together. [57] And there arose certain, and bare false witness against him, saying, [58] We heard him say, I will destroy this temple that is made with hands, and within three days I will build another made without hands.a [59] But neither so did their witness agree together. [60] And the high priest stood up in the midst, and asked Jesus, saying, Answerest thou nothing? what *is it which* these witness against thee? [61] But

he held his peace, and answered nothing.b Again the high priest asked him, and said unto him, Art thou the Christ, the Son of the Blessed? [62] And Jesus said, I am: and ye shall see the Son of man sitting on the right hand of power, and coming in the clouds of heaven.

[63] Then the high priest rent his clothes, and saith,

Luke 22.

—saying, [67] Art thou the Christ? tell us. And he said unto them, If I tell you, ye will not believe: [68] and if I also ask *you*, ye will not answer me, nor let *me* go. [69] Hereafter shall the Son of man sit on the right hand of the power of God. Then said they all, Art thou then the Son of God? And he said unto them,

y This examination by Caiaphas, John 18. 19-23, took place soon after Peter's first denial; see § 144. Not improbably the high priest again withdrew, after having sent off messengers to convoke the Sanhedrim, which met at early dawn, Luke 22. 66.—Luke 22. 63-65 is transposed, in accordance with Matthew and Mark.

z Comp. Acts 6. 11-13.
a Comp. John 2. 19.   b Isa. 53. 7.

Matt. 26.

saying, He hath spoken blasphemy; what further need have we of witnesses? behold, now ye have heard his blasphemy. [65] What think ye? They answered and said, He is guilty of death.[c] [67] Then did they spit in his face,[d] and buffeted him; and others smote *him* with the palms of their hands, [68] saying, Prophesy unto us, thou Christ, Who is he that smote thee?

Mark 14.

What need we any further witnesses? [64] Ye have heard the blasphemy: what think ye? And they all condemned him to be guilty of death.[c]

[65] And some began to spit on him, and to cover his face, and to buffet him, and to say unto him, Prophesy: and the servants did strike him with the palms of their hands.

Luke 22.

Ye say that I am. [71] And they said, What need we any further witness? for we ourselves have heard of his own mouth.—

[63] And the men that held Jesus mocked him, and smote *him*. [64] And when they had blindfolded him, they struck him on the face, and asked him, saying, Prophesy, who is it that smote thee? [65] And many other things blasphemously spake they against him.

§ 146. **The Sanhedrim lead Jesus to Pilate.**—*Jerusalem.*

Early Morning of the Sixth Day of the Week.

Matt. 27. 1, 2, 11-14.

[1] When the morning was come, all the chief priests and elders of the people took counsel against Jesus to put him to death: [2] and when they had bound him, they led *him* away, and delivered him to Pontius Pilate the governor.[g]

Mark 15. 1-5.

[1] And straightway in the morning the chief priests held a consultation with the elders and scribes and the whole council, and bound Jesus, and carried *him* away, and delivered *him* to Pilate.

Luke 23. 1-5.

[1] And the whole multitude of them arose, and led him unto Pilate.

[2] And they began to accuse him, saying, We found this *fellow* perverting the nation, and forbidding to give tribute to Cæsar,

John 18. 28-38.

[28] Then led they Jesus from Caiaphas unto the hall of judgment:[e] and it was early; and they themselves went not into the judgment hall, lest they should be defiled; but that they might eat the passover.[f] [29] Pilate then went out unto them, and said, What accusation bring ye against this man? [30] They answered and said unto him, If he were not a malefactor, we would not have delivered him up unto thee. [31] Then said Pilate unto them, Take ye him, and judge him according to your law. The Jews therefore said unto him, It is not lawful for us to put any man to death: [32] that the saying of Jesus might be fulfilled, which he spake,[h] signifying what death he should die. [33] Then Pilate

---

[c] Comp. Lev. 24. 16; John 19. 7.
[d] Isa. 50. 6.
[e] Rather the *prætorium*, the residence of the Roman governor.

[f] On the meaning of *passover* in this place see Introductory Note, p. 130.
[g] See § 151.
[h] John 12. 32, 33; Matt. 20. 19

Matt. 27.	Mark 15.	Luke 23.	John 18.
[11] And Jesus stood before the governor: and the governor asked him, saying, Art thou the King of the Jews ?—	[2] And Pilate asked him, Art thou the King of the Jews ?	saying that he himself is Christ a King. [3] And Pilate asked him, saying, Art thou the King of the Jews ?—	entered into the judgment hall again, and called Jesus, and said unto him, Art thou the King of the Jews ? [34] Jesus answered him, Sayest

thou this thing of thyself, or did others tell it thee of me ? [35] Pilate answered, Am I a Jew ? Thine own nation and the chief priests have delivered thee unto me : what hast thou done ? [36] Jesus answered, My kingdom is not of this world : if my kingdom were of this world, then would my servants fight, that I should not be delivered to the Jews : but now is my kingdom not from hence.

Matt. 27.	Mark 15.	Luke 23.	[37] Pilate therefore said unto him, Art thou a king then ? Jesus answered,
—[11] And Jesus said unto him, Thou sayest.	—[2] And he answering said unto him, Thou sayest *it*.	—[3] And he answered him and said, Thou sayest *it*.	Thou sayest that I am a king. To

this end was I born, and for this cause came I into the world, that I should bear witness unto the truth. Every one that is of the truth heareth my voice. [38] Pilate saith unto him, What is truth ? And when he had said this, he went out again unto the Jews, and saith unto them, I find in him no fault *at all*.

Matt. 27.	Mark 15.
[12] And when he was accused of the chief priests and elders, he answered nothing. [13] Then said Pilate unto him, Hearest thou not how many things they witness against thee ? [14] And he answered him to never a word ;[j] insomuch that the governor marvelled greatly.[k]	[3] And the chief priests accused him of many things : but he answered nothing. [4] And Pilate asked him again, saying, Answerest thou nothing ? behold how many things they witness against thee. [5] But Jesus yet answered nothing ;[j] so that Pilate marvelled.

Luke 23.

[4] Then said Pilate to the chief priests and *to* the people, I find no fault in this man. [5] And they were the more fierce, saying, He stirreth up the people, teaching throughout all Jewry, beginning from Galilee to this place.

§ 147. Jesus before Herod.—*Jerusalem.*

Sixth Day of the Week.

Luke 23. 6-12. [6] When Pilate heard of Galilee, he asked whether the man were a Galilean. [7] And as soon as he knew that he belonged unto Herod's jurisdiction, he sent him to Herod, who himself also was at Jerusalem at that time. [8] And when Herod saw Jesus, he was exceeding glad : for he was desirous to see him of a long *season*,[l] because he had heard many things of him ; and he hoped to have seen some miracle done by him. [9] Then he questioned with him in many words ; but he answered him nothing. [10] And the chief priests and scribes stood and vehemently accused him. [11] And Herod with his men of war set him at

---

[j] Isa. 53. 7.   [k] See § 148.   [l] Luke 9. 9.

Luke 23.

nought, and mocked *him*, and arrayed him in a gorgeous robe,ᵐ and sent him again to Pilate. ¹²And the same day Pilate and Herod were made friends together: for before they were at enmity between themselves.

§ 148. PILATE SEEKS TO RELEASE JESUS. THE JEWS DEMAND BARABBAS.
Jerusalem.
Sixth Day of the Week.

Luke 23. 13–25. ¹³And Pilate, when he had called together the chief priests and the rulers and the people, ¹⁴said unto them, Ye have brought this man unto me, as one that perverteth the people: and, behold, I, having examined *him* before you, have found no fault in this man touching those things whereof ye accuse him: ¹⁵no, nor yet Herod: for I sent you to him; and, lo, nothing worthy of death is done unto him. ¹⁶I will therefore chastise him, and release *him*.

Matt. 27. 15–26.	Mark 15. 6–15.	Luke 23.	John 18. 39, 40.
¹⁵Now at *that* feast the governor was wont to release unto the people a prisoner, whom they would.	⁶Now at *that* feast he released unto them one prisoner, whomsoever they desired.	¹⁷(For of necessity he must release one unto them at the feast.)	³⁹But ye have a custom, that I should release unto you one at the passover.—

Matt. 27.	Mark 15.
¹⁶And they had then a notable prisoner, called Barabbas. ¹⁷Therefore when they were gathered together,	⁷And there was *one* named Barabbas, *which lay* bound with them that had made insurrection with him, who had committed murder in the insurrection. ⁸And the multitude crying aloud began to desire *him to do* as he had ever done unto them.

Matt. 27.	Mark 15.	John 18.
Pilate said unto them, Whom will ye that I release unto you? Barabbas, or Jesus which is called Christ? ¹⁸For he knew that for envy they had delivered him. ¹⁹When he was set down on the judgment seat, his wife sent unto him, saying, Have thou nothing to do with that just man: for I have suffered many things this day in a dream because of him.	⁹But Pilate answered them, saying, Will ye that I release unto you the King of the Jews? ¹⁰For he knew that the chief priests had delivered him for envy.	—³⁹Will ye therefore that I release unto you the King of the Jews?

Matt. 27.	Mark 15.	Luke 23.	John 18.
²⁰But the chief priests and elders persuaded the multitude that they	¹¹But the chief priests moved the people, that he should rather re-	¹⁸And they cried out all at once, saying, Away with this *man*, and release	⁴⁰Then cried they all again, saying, Not this man, but Barabbas. Now

---

ᵐ *Gorgeous robe.* The Greek (λαμπράν) favours the idea that the robe was *white*, which was the royal colour among the Hebrews. Comp. Matt. 6. 28, 29. But the imperial colour among the Romans was *purple*, and hence that was the colour of the robe in which the soldiers of Pilate arrayed Jesus in their mockery of Him.

Matt. 27.

should ask Barabbas, and destroy Jesus. [21] The governor answered and said unto them, Whether of the twain will ye that I release unto you? They said, Barabbas. [22] Pilate saith unto them, What shall I do then with Jesus which is called Christ? *They* all say unto him, Let him be crucified. [23] And the governor said, Why, what evil hath he done? But they cried out the more, saying, Let him be crucified.

Mark 15.

lease Barabbas unto them.

Mark 15.

[12] And Pilate answered and said again unto them, What will ye then that I shall do *unto him* whom ye call the King of the Jews? [13] And they cried out again, Crucify him. [14] Then Pilate said unto them, Why, what evil hath he done? And they cried out the more exceedingly, Crucify him.

Luke 23.

unto us Barabbas: [19] (who for a certain sedition made in the city, and for murder, was cast into prison.) [20] Pilate therefore, willing to release Jesus, spake again to them. [21] But they cried, saying, Crucify *him*, crucify him. [22] And he said unto them the third time, Why, what evil hath he done? I have found no cause of death in him: I will therefore chastise him, and let *him* go. [23] And they were instant with loud voices, requiring that he might be crucified. And the voices of them and of the chief priests prevailed.

John 18.

Barabbas was a robber.

Matt. 27.

[24] When Pilate saw that he could prevail nothing, but *that* rather a tumult was made, he took water, and washed[n] *his* hands before the multitude, saying, I am innocent of the blood of this just person: see ye *to it*. [25] Then answered all the people, and said, His blood *be* on us,[o] and on our children. [26] Then released he Barabbas unto them.—

Mark 15.

[15] And *so* Pilate, willing to content the people, released Barabbas unto them.—

Luke 23..

[24] And Pilate gave sentence that it should be as they required. [25] And he released unto them him

that for sedition and murder was cast into prison. whom they had desired;[p] but he delivered Jesus to their will.

§ 149. PILATE DELIVERS UP JESUS. HE IS SCOURGED AND MOCKED.
Jerusalem.

Sixth Day of the Week.

Matt. 27. 26–30.

—[26] And when he had scourged Jesus, he delivered *him* to be crucified. [27] Then the soldiers of the governor took Jesus into the common hall, and gathered unto him the whole band *of soldiers*. [28] And they stripped him, and put on him a scarlet

Mark 15. 15–19.

—[15] And *he* delivered Jesus, when he had scourged *him*, to be crucified. [16] And the soldiers led him away into the hall, called Prætorium; and they call together the whole band. [17] And they clothed him with purple,[q] and platted

John 19. 1–3.   [1] Then Pilate therefore took Jesus, and scourged *him*.

[2] And the soldiers platted a crown of thorns, and put *it* on his head, and they put on him a purple robe,[q]

---

n Comp. Deut. 21. 6, 7; Psa. 26. 6.
o Acts 5. 28.
p Acts 3. 14.
q The *scarlet robe* of Matt. 27. 28, and the

purple robe of John 19. 2, are put for the *paludamentum* or military cloak worn by officers. The terms *crimson* and *purple* seem to be nearly synonymous.

Matt. 27.	Mark 15.	John 19.
robe. [29] And when they had platted a crown of thorns, they put *it* upon his head, and a reed in his right hand: and they bowed the knee before him, and mocked him, saying, Hail, King of the Jews! [30] And they spit upon him, and took the reed, and smote him on the head.[r]	a crown of thorns, and put it about his *head*, [18] and began to salute him, Hail, King of the Jews! [19] And they smote him on the head with a reed, and did spit upon him, and bowing *their* knees worshipped him.	[3] and said, Hail, King of the Jews! and they smote him with their hands.

§ 150. PILATE, AFTER AGAIN SEEKING TO RELEASE JESUS, DELIVERS HIM TO BE CRUCIFIED.—*Jerusalem.*

Sixth Day of the Week.

John 19. 4–16. [4] Pilate therefore went forth again, and saith unto them, Behold, I bring him forth to you, that ye may know that I find no fault in him. [5] Then came Jesus forth, wearing the crown of thorns, and the purple robe. And *Pilate* saith unto them, Behold the man! [6] When the chief priests therefore and officers saw him, they cried out, saying, Crucify *him*, crucify *him*. Pilate saith unto them, Take ye him, and crucify *him*: for I find no fault in him. [7] The Jews answered him, We have a law, and by our law he ought to die, because he made himself the Son of God. [8] When Pilate therefore heard that saying, he was the more afraid; [9] and went again into the judgment hall, and saith unto Jesus, Whence art thou? But Jesus gave him no answer.[s] [10] Then saith Pilate unto him, Speakest thou not unto me? knowest thou not that I have power to crucify thee, and have power to release thee? [11] Jesus answered, Thou couldest have no power *at all* against me, except it were given thee from above: therefore he that delivered me unto thee hath the greater sin. [12] And from thenceforth Pilate sought to release him: but the Jews cried out, saying, If thou let this man go, thou art not Cæsar's friend: whosoever maketh himself a king speaketh against Cæsar. [13] When Pilate therefore heard that saying, he brought Jesus forth, and sat down in the judgment seat in a place that is called the Pavement, but in the Hebrew, Gabbatha.[t] [14] And it was the preparation of the passover,[u] and about the sixth hour: and he

---

[r] Comp. Mic. 5. 1.   [s] Isa. 53. 7.

[t] *Gabbatha* (i.e. literally *the back*), or the *pavement*, was a space between the castle of Antonia and the western corner of the temple, where the *ridge* of the rock or hill was *paved* with smooth stones (Josephus, Bell. Jud. 5. 5, 8). Here, in full view of the temple and before the Jewish multitudes, Pilate took his place on the judgment seat, to deliver to death Jesus, though he held Him to be innocent.

[u] On the phrase, *preparation of the passover*, ver. 14, see the Introductory Note, Part viii.—In the same verse the expression, *about the sixth hour*, does not accord with the *third hour* of Mark 15. 25; see in § 153. But the *third hour* of Mark, as the hour of the crucifixion, is sustained by the whole

course of the transactions and circumstances; as also by the fact stated by Matthew, Mark, and Luke, that the darkness commenced at the *sixth* hour, after Jesus had already for some time hung upon the cross; see § 155, init. The reading, *sixth*, in John is therefore probably an error of transcription for *third*. Indeed, this last reading is found in two of the best manuscripts (*Cod. Bezæ* and *Cod. Reg.* 62), as well as several other authorities; so that its external weight is marked by Griesbach as nearly or quite equal to that of the common reading.—The suggestion of Greswell and many other commentators, that John here computes the sixth hour from midnight, is however worthy of regard. If this be admitted, it would throw light upon John 1. 40; 4. 6, (reckoning from noon).

John 19.

saith unto the Jews, Behold your King! [15] But they cried out, Away with *him*, away with *him*, crucify him. Pilate saith unto them, Shall I crucify your King? The chief priests answered, We have no king but Cæsar. [16] Then delivered he him therefore unto them to be crucified.—

§ 151. JUDAS REPENTS AND HANGS HIMSELF.—*Jerusalem.*

Sixth Day of the Week.

Matt. 27. 3-10. [3] Then Judas,[v] which had betrayed him, when he saw that he was condemned, repented himself, and brought again the thirty pieces of silver to the chief priests and elders, [4] saying, I have sinned in that I have betrayed the innocent blood. And they said, What *is that* to us? see thou *to that.* [5] And he cast down the pieces of silver in the temple, and departed, and went and hanged himself. [6] And the chief priests took the silver pieces, and said, It is not lawful for to put them into the treasury, because it is the price of blood. [7] And they took counsel, and bought with them the potter's field, to bury strangers in. [8] Wherefore that field was called, The field of blood, unto this day. [9] Then was fulfilled that which was spoken by Jeremy the prophet,[w] saying, And they took the thirty pieces of silver, the price of him that was valued, whom they of the children of Israel did value; [10] and gave them for the potter's field, as the Lord appointed me.

Acts 1. 18, 19.

[18] Now this man purchased a field with the reward of iniquity; and falling headlong, he burst asunder in the midst, and all his bowels gushed out. [19] And it was known unto all the dwellers in Jerusalem; insomuch as that field is called in their proper tongue, Aceldama, that is to say, The field of blood.

§ 152. JESUS IS LED AWAY TO BE CRUCIFIED.[x]—*Jerusalem.*

Sixth Day of the Week.

Matt. 27. 31-34.	Mark 15. 20-23.	John 19. 16, 17.
[31] And after that they had mocked him, they took the robe off from him, and put his own raiment on him, and led him away to crucify *him.* [32] And as they came out, they found a man of Cyrene, Simon by name: him they compelled to bear his cross.[x]	[20] And when they had mocked him, they took off the purple from him, and put his own clothes on him, and led him out to crucify him. [21] And they compel one Simon, a Cyrenian, who passed by, coming out of the country, the father of Alexander and Rufus, to bear his cross.[x]	—[16] And they took Jesus, and led *him* away. [17] And he bearing his cross—
		Luke 23. 26-33.
		[26] And as they led him away, they laid hold upon one Simon, a Cyrenian, coming out of the country, and on him they laid the cross, that he might bear *it* after Jesus.[x] [27] And

---

[v] Judas repented, it would seem, as soon as he saw that Jesus was delivered over to be crucified. Till then he had hoped, perhaps, to enjoy the reward of his treachery, without involving himself in the guilt of his Master's blood.

In Acts 1. 18 *purchased* is to be understood, *he gave occasion to purchase,* was the occasion of purchasing. For such a usage, see Heb. 2. 10; Matt. 27. 60; John 3. 22, comp. 4. 1, 2; Rom. 14. 15; 1 Cor. 7. 16; 1 Tim. 4. 16, etc.

[w] Zech. 11. 12, sq. Comp. Jer. 32. 6, sq.

[x] Jesus bore His cross at first; but He being probably faint from exhaustion, Simon was compelled to bear it after Him.

The *vinegar mingled with gall* of Matthew 27. 34 is the same with the *wine mingled with myrrh* of Mark 15. 23, viz., cheap acid wine mingled with myrrh. Such a drink was given to persons about to be executed, in order to stupefy them. See Lightfoot, *Hor. Heb.* on Matt. 27. 34.

Luke 23.

there followed him a great company of people, and of women, which also bewailed and lamented him. ²⁸ But Jesus turning unto them said, Daughters of Jerusalem, weep not for me, but weep for yourselves, and for your children. ²⁹ For, behold, the days are coming, in the which they shall say, Blessed *are* the barren, and the wombs that never bare, and the paps which never gave suck.ʸ ³⁰ Then shall they begin to say to the mountains, Fall on us; and to the hills, Cover us.ᶻ ³¹ For if they do these things in a green tree, what shall be done in the dry? ³² And there were also two other, malefactors, led with him to be put to death.

Matt. 27.	Mark 15.	Luke 23.	John 19.
³³ And when they were come unto a place called Golgotha,ᵃ that is to say, A place of a skull,	²² And they bring him unto the place Golgotha,ᵃ which is, being interpreted, The place of a skull.	³³ And when they were come to the place, which is called Calvary.ᵃ—	—¹⁷ went forth into a place called *the place* of a skull, which is called in the Hebrew Golgotha: ᵃ—

Matt. 27.

³⁴ they gave him vinegar to drink mingled with gall: and when he had tasted *thereof,* he would not drink.

Mark 15.

²³ And they gave him to drink wine mingled with myrrh: but he received *it* not.

§ 153. The Crucifixion.—*Jerusalem.*

Sixth Day of the Week.

Mark 15. 24–28. ²⁵ And it was the third hour, and they crucified him. —²⁷ And with him they crucify two thieves: the one on his right hand, and the other on his left. ²⁸ And the Scripture was fulfilled, which saith,ᶜ And he was numbered with the transgressors.—

Matt. 27.		Luke 23.	John 19.

Matt. 27. 35–38. ³⁸ Then ᵇ were there two thieves crucified with him, one on the right hand, and another on the left.—

Luke 23. 33, 34, 38. —³³ There they crucified him, and the malefactors, one on the right hand and the other on the left. ³⁴ Then said Jesus, Father, forgive them; for they know not what they do.

John 19. 18–24. —¹⁹ Where they crucified him, and two other with him, on either side one, and Jesus in the midst.—

³⁵ And they crucified him, and parted his garments,—

³⁴ And when they had crucified him, they parted his garments,—

And they parted his raiment,—

²³ Then the soldiers, when they had crucified Jesus, took his garments, and made four parts, to every soldier a part; and also *his* coat: now the coat was without seam, woven from the top throughout. ²⁴ They said therefore among themselves,

---

ʸ Comp. Isa. 54. 1.   ᶻ Hos. 10. 8.
ᵃ *Golgotha,* the Hebrew form, κρανίον Greek, *Calvaria* Latin, whence our *Calvary,* was the place of public execution, lying *outside* of Jerusalem (John 19. 17; Matt. 27. 32), and near the city, on the side of some

public road (John 19. 20; Matt. 27. 39); but more is not known certainly concerning it.
ᵇ Various slight transpositions in the verses are made in this Section, in order to present their parallelism to the eye.
ᶜ Isa. 53. 12.

Matt. 27.	Mark 15.	Luke 23.	John 19.
casting lots : that it might be fulfilled which was spoken by the prophet,[d] They parted my garments among them, and upon my vesture did they cast lots. [35] And sitting down they watched him there; [37] and set up over his head his accusation written, THIS IS JESUS THE KING OF THE JEWS.[e]	casting lots upon them, what every man should take.— [26] And the superscription of his accusation was written over, THE KING OF THE JEWS.[e]	—and cast lots. [38] And a superscription also was written over him in letters of Greek, and Latin, and Hebrew, THIS IS THE KING OF THE JEWS.[e]	Let us not rend it, but cast lots for it, whose it shall be : that the Scripture might be fulfilled, which saith,[d] They parted my raiment among them, and for my vesture they did cast lots. These things therefore the soldiers did.— [19] And Pilate wrote a title, and put *it* on the cross. And the writing was, JESUS OF NAZARETH THE KING OF THE JEWS.[e]

John 19.

[20] This title then read many of the Jews : for the place where Jesus was crucified was nigh to the city : and it was written in Hebrew, *and* Greek, *and* Latin. [21] Then said the chief priests of the Jews to Pilate, Write not, The King of the Jews; but that he said, I am King of the Jews. [22] Pilate answered, What I have written I have written.

§ 154.   THE JEWS MOCK JESUS. HE COMMENDS HIS MOTHER TO JOHN.
Jerusalem.

Sixth Day of the Week.

Matt. 27. 39–44.	Mark 15. 29–32.
[39] And they that passed by reviled him, wagging their heads, [40] and saying, Thou that destroyest the temple, and buildest *it* in three days, save thyself. If thou be the Son of God, come down from the cross. [41] Likewise also the chief priests mocking *him*, with the scribes and elders, said, [42] He saved others; himself he cannot save. If he be the King of Israel, let him now come down from the cross, and we will believe him. [43] He trusted in God; let him deliver him now, if he will	[29] And they that passed by railed on him, wagging their heads, and saying, Ah, thou that destroyest the temple, and buildest *it* in three days, [30] save thyself, and come down from the cross. [31] Likewise also the chief priests mocking said among themselves with the scribes, He saved others; himself he cannot save. [32] Let Christ the King of Israel descend now from the cross, that we may see and believe.

Luke 23. 35–37, 39–43. [35] And the people stood beholding. And the rulers also with them derided *him*, saying, He saved others; let him save himself, if he be Christ, the chosen of God. [36] And the soldiers also mocked him, coming to him, and offering him vinegar,[f] and saying, [37] If thou be the king of the Jews, save

---

[d] Psa. 22. 18.   [e] On the difference in titles, see Note [m] on § 14.   [f] See Note [n], § 155.

Matt. 27.	**Mark 15.**	**Luke 23.**
have him: *g* for he said, I am the Son of God. [44] The thieves also, which were crucified with him, cast the same in his teeth.*h*	And they that were crucified with him reviled him.*h*	thyself.—[39] And one of the malefactors which were hanged railed on him, saying, If thou be Christ, save thyself and us.*h* [40] But the other answering re-

buked him, saying, Dost not thou fear God, seeing thou art in the same condemnation? [41] And we indeed justly; for we receive the due reward of our deeds: but this man hath done nothing amiss. [42] And he said unto Jesus, Lord, remember me when thou comest into thy kingdom. [43] And Jesus said unto him, Verily I say unto thee, To-day *i* shalt thou be with me in paradise.*j*

John 19. 25–27. [25] Now there stood by the cross of Jesus his mother, and his mother's sister, Mary the *wife* of Cleophas, and Mary Magdalene. [26] When Jesus therefore saw his mother, and the disciple standing by, whom he loved, he saith unto his mother, Woman, behold thy son! [27] Then saith he to the disciple, Behold thy mother! And from that hour that disciple took her unto his own *home.*

§ 155. DARKNESS PREVAILS. CHRIST EXPIRES ON THE CROSS.—*Jerusalem.*

Sixth Day of the Week.

Matt. 27. 45–50.	**Mark 15.** 33–37.	**Luke 23.** 44–46.
[45] Now from the sixth hour there was darkness over all the land unto the ninth hour. [46] And about the ninth hour Jesus cried with a loud voice, saying, Eli, Eli,*k* lama sabach- thani? that is to say, My God, my God, why hast thou forsaken me?*l* [47] Some of them that stood there, when they heard *that,* said, This *man* calleth for Elias. [48] And straightway one of them ran, and took a sponge, and filled it with vinegar,*n*	[33] And when the sixth hour was come, there was darkness over the whole land until the ninth hour. [34] And at the ninth hour Jesus cried with a loud voice, saying, Eloi, Eloi,*k* lama sabach- thani? which is, being in- terpreted, My God, my God, why hast thou for- saken me? [35] And some of them that stood by, when they heard *it,* said, Behold, he calleth Elias. [36] And one ran and filled a sponge full of vinegar,*n* and put *it* on a reed, and	[44] And it was about the sixth hour, and there was a darkness over all the earth until the ninth hour. [45] And the sun was dark- ened.—
		John 19. 28–30. [28] After this, Jesus know- ing that all things were now accomplished, that the Scripture might be ful- filled,*m* saith, I thirst. [29] Now there was set a vessel full of vinegar;*n* and they filled a sponge with vine- gar, and put *it* upon hyssop, and put *it* to his mouth.

g Comp. Psa. 22. 7, 8.

h According to Matthew and Mark, both the malefactors reviled Jesus; while, accord- ing to Luke, one was penitent. In the former the plural is put for the singular. This is often done. So Matt. 26. 8, comp. John 12. 4; Matt. 2. 20; 9. 8; Mark 7. 17, comp. Matt. 15. 15; Mark 5. 31, comp. Luke 8. 45; Matt. 24. 1, comp. Mark 13. 1; John 19. 29, comp. Matt. 27. 48, &c.

In John 19. 25, the marginal reading of the English version is the proper one, viz., *Clopas* instead of *Cleophas.* It is strictly a Greek form of a Hebrew name, which is else- where represented by *Alpheus.*—The *Cleopas* of Luke 24. 18 is a different name, of regular

Greek derivation, and belongs to another person.

i 2 Cor. 5. 9.

j 2 Cor. 12. 4; Rev. 2. 7.

k In Matt. 27. 46, *Eli* is the Hebrew for *my God;* and in Mark 15. 34, *Eloi* is the corresponding Aramæan word for the same.

l Psa. 22. 1. *m* Comp. Psa. 69. 21.

n The *vinegar,* in Matt. 27. 48, and the parallel verses, is here the *posca* or common drink of the Roman soldiers, namely, cheap acid wine, mingled with water. In Matthew and Mark the sponge is said to be put upon a reed; in John, upon hyssop. Here, probably, a *stalk* or *stem* of hyssop is to be understood; the cross not being of any great height.

Matt. 27.

and put *it* on a reed, and gave him to drink. [49] The rest said, Let be, let us see whether Elias will come to save him.

Mark 15.

gave him to drink, saying, Let alone; let us see whether Elias will come to take him down.

Matt. 27.	Mark 15.	Luke 23.	John 19.
[50] Jesus, when he had cried again with a loud voice, yielded up the ghost.	[37] And Jesus cried with a loud voice, and gave up the ghost.	[46] And when Jesus had cried with a loud voice, he said, Father, into thy hands I commend my spirit: and having said thus, he gave up the ghost.	[30] When Jesus therefore had received the vinegar, he said, It is finished: and he bowed his head, and gave up the ghost.

§ 156. THE VEIL OF THE TEMPLE RENT, AND GRAVES OPENED. JUDGMENT OF THE CENTURION. THE WOMEN AT THE CROSS.—*Jerusalem.*

Sixth Day of the Week.

Matt. 27. 51-56.	Mark 15. 38-41.	Luke 23. 45, 47-49.
[51] And, behold, the veil of the temple was rent in twain from the top to the bottom; [o] and the earth did quake, and the rocks rent; [52] and the graves were opened; and many bodies of the saints which slept arose, [53] and came out of the graves after his resurrection, and went into the holy city, and appeared unto many. [54] Now when the centurion, and they that were with him, watching Jesus, saw the earthquake, and those things that were done, they feared greatly, saying, Truly this was the Son of God. [55] And many women [p] were there beholding afar off, which followed Jesus from Galilee, ministering unto him: [q] [56] among which was Mary Magdalene, and Mary the mother of James and Joses, and the mother of Zebedee's children.	[38] And the veil of the temple was rent in twain from the top to the bottom. [39] And when the centurion, which stood over against him, saw that he so cried out, and gave up the ghost, he said, Truly this man was the Son of God. [40] There were also women [p] looking on afar off: among whom was Mary Magdalene, and Mary the mother of James the less and of Joses, and Salome; [41] (who also, when he was in Galilee, followed him, and ministered unto him;) [q] and many other women which came up with him unto Jerusalem.	[45] —And the veil of the temple was rent in the midst. [o]— [47] Now when the centurion saw what was done, he glorified God, saying, Certainly this was a righteous man. [48] And all the people that came together to that sight, beholding the things which were done, smote their breasts, and returned. [49] And all his acquaintance, and the women [p] that followed him from Galilee, stood afar off, beholding these things.

---

[o] Comp. Heb. 10. 19–22.

[p] Matt. 27. 55, 56, and the parallel places, **refer** to a later point of time than John 19.

25, sq. Mary and the other women had now retired to a distance from the scene of suffering.   [q] Luke 8. 3.

§ 157. THE TAKING DOWN FROM THE CROSS. THE BURIAL.—*Jerusalem.*

Sixth Day of the Week.

John 19. 31–42. [31] The Jews therefore, because it was the preparation, that the bodies should not remain upon the cross[r] on the sabbath day, (for that sabbath day[s] was an high day,) besought Pilate that their legs might be broken, and *that* they might be taken away. [32] Then came the soldiers, and brake the legs of the first, and of the other which was crucified with him. [33] But when they came to Jesus, and saw that he was dead already, they brake not his legs: [34] but one of the soldiers with a spear pierced his side, and forthwith came thereout blood and water. [35] And he that saw *it* bare record, and his record is true: and he knoweth that he saith true, that ye might believe. [36] For these things were done, that the Scripture should be fulfilled,[t] A bone of him shall not be broken. [37] And again another Scripture saith,[u] They shall look on him whom they pierced.

Matt. 27. 57–61.	**Mark 15. 42–47.**	**Luke 23. 50–56.**	**John 19.**
[57] When the even was come, there came a rich man of Arimathea, named Joseph, who also himself was Jesus' disciple:	[42] And now when the even was come, because it was the preparation, that is, the day before the sabbath, [43] Joseph of Arimathea, an honourable counsellor, which also waited for the kingdom of God, came, and went in boldly unto Pilate, and craved the body of Jesus. [44] Pilate marvelled[w] if he were already dead: and calling *unto him* the centurion, he asked him whether he had been any while dead. [45] And when he knew *it* of the centurion, he gave the body to Joseph. [46] And he bought fine linen, and took him down, and wrapped him in	[54] And that day was the preparation, and the sabbath drew on.[v]— [50] And, behold, *there was* a man named Joseph, a counsellor; *and he was* a good man, and a just: [51] (the same had not consented to the counsel and deed of them;) *he was* of Arimathea, a city of the Jews: who also himself waited for the kingdom of God. [52] This *man* went unto Pilate, and begged the body of Jesus. [53] And he took it down, and wrapped it in linen, and laid it in a sepulchre	[38] And after this Joseph of Arimathea, being a disciple of Jesus, but secretly for fear of the Jews, besought Pilate that he might take away the body of Jesus: and Pilate gave *him* leave. He came therefore, and took the body of Jesus. [39] And there came also Nicodemus, which at the first came to Jesus by night, and brought a mixture of myrrh and aloes, about an hundred pound *weight*. [40] Then took they the body of Jesus,
[58] he went to Pilate, and begged the body of Jesus. Then Pilate commanded the body to be delivered. [59] And when Joseph had taken the body, he wrapped it in a clean linen cloth, [60] and laid it in his own new			

---

[r] Deut. 21. 22, 23.

[s] On the phrase *that sabbath day was an high day*, see Introductory Note, p. 138.

[t] Ex. 12. 46; Psa. 34. 20.

[u] Zech. 12. 10. Comp. Psa. 22. 16, 17.

[v] It was according to custom among the Jews that the bodies of persons publicly executed should be taken down and buried before sunset.

[w] *Pilate marvelled, etc.* The tortures of crucifixion did not cause a speedy death. The narrative strikingly teaches us that our Lord's death was hastened on by a mysterious cause, which was the withdrawal of the Father's presence from Him, when He laid on Him the iniquities of us all, and made His soul an offering for sin (Isa. 53. 6, 10). See also 2 Cor. 5. 21.

Matt. 27.	Mark 15.	Luke 23.	John 19.
tomb,ˣ which he had hewn out in the rock: and he rolled a great stone to the door of the sepulchre, and departed.	the linen, and laid him in a sepulchre which was hewn out of a rock, and rolled a stone unto the door of the sepulchre.	that was hewn in stone, wherein never man before was laid.—	and wound it in linen clothes with the spices, as the manner of the Jews is to bury. ⁴¹ Now in the place where he was crucified there was a garden;

and in the garden a new sepulchre, wherein was never man yet laid. ⁴² There laid they Jesus therefore because of the Jews' preparation *day ;* for the sepulchre was nigh at hand.

Matt. 27.	Mark 15.	Luke 23.
⁶¹ And there was Mary Magdalene, and the other Mary, sitting over against the sepulchre.	⁴⁷ And Mary Magdalene and Mary *the mother* of Joses beheld where he was laid.	⁵⁵ And the women also, which came with him from Galilee, followed after, and beheld the sepulchre, and how his body was laid. ⁵⁶ And they returned, and prepared spices and ointments; and rested the sabbath day according to the commandment.ʸ

§ 158. The Watch at the Sepulchre.—*Jerusalem.*

Seventh Day of the Week, or Sabbath.

Matt. 27. 62-66. ⁶² Now the next day, that followed the day of preparation, the chief priests and Pharisees came together unto Pilate, ⁶³ saying, Sir, we remember that that deceiver said, while he was yet alive, After three days ᶻ I will rise again.ᵃ ⁶⁴ Command therefore that the sepulchre be made sure until the third day, lest his disciples come by night, and steal him away, and say unto the people, He is risen from the dead: so the last error shall be worse than the first. ⁶⁵ Pilate said unto them, Ye have a watch: go your way, make *it* as sure as you can. ⁶⁶ So they went, and made the sepulchre sure, sealing the stone, and setting a watch.

ˣ Isa. 53. 9.   ʸ Ex. 20. 10.
ᶻ See Matt. 12. 40: "the Son of man shall be *three days and three nights* in the heart of the earth. In reality, He was laid in the grave on the evening of Friday, and arose early on Sunday—a space of about 36 hours. It must be remembered (1) that the Hebrews customarily spoke of "a day" as though complete when only a small part of it had been occupied by a given transaction. The days were thus Friday, Saturday, and Sunday. Compare the German idiom in which the phrase *nach drei Tagen,* "after three days," denotes "the day after to-morrow." "On the third day" (Matt. 20. 19; Mark 10. 34; Luke 18. 33, etc.) is in like manner equivalent to "after three days," ver. 63 above. (2) The "night" is included with the "day" (so the Greek νυχθήμερον, a day of twenty-four hours), the phrase *three days and three nights* thus being used generally and indefinitely for *three days* simply, as in 1 Sam. 30. 12, 13.

ᵃ Matt. 20. 19.

PART IX.

OUR LORD'S RESURRECTION, HIS SUBSEQUENT APPEARANCES, AND HIS ASCENSION.

Time: *Forty Days.*

INTRODUCTORY NOTE.

A FULL discussion upon this part of the gospel history, embracing a review of the main difficulties in the way of harmonizing the accounts of the four evangelists, was published by Dr. Robinson in the *Bibliotheca Sacra*, for Feb., 1845, p. 162, sq. To this the student is referred for a more complete examination of the subject.

More of these apparent difficulties are found in this short portion of the Gospels than in almost all the rest. This has its cause in the circumstance that each writer here records only what appertained to his own particular purpose or experience. Thus many of the minor and connecting facts have not been preserved; and the data are therefore wanting to make out a full and complete harmony of all the accounts, without an occasional resort to something of hypothesis.

The general results of the investigations upon which we are now entering may be presented in the following summary view of the events and circumstances connected with our Lord's resurrection and ascension, in the order of their occurrence.

The resurrection took place at or before early dawn on the first day of the week; when there was an earthquake, and an angel descended and rolled away the stone from the sepulchre and sat upon it; so that the keepers became as dead men from terror. At early dawn, the same morning, the women who had attended on Jesus, namely, Mary Magdalene, Mary the mother of James, Joanna, Salome, and others, went out with spices to the sepulchre in order further to embalm the Lord's body. They inquired among themselves who should remove for them the stone which closed the sepulchre. On their arrival they found the stone already taken away. The Lord had risen. The women, knowing nothing of all that had taken place, were amazed; they entered the tomb, and found not the body of the Lord, and were greatly perplexed. At this time Mary Magdalene, impressed with the idea

that the body had been stolen away, left the sepulchre and the other women, and ran to the city to tell Peter and John.

The other women remained still in the tomb; and immediately two angels appeared, who announced to them that Jesus was risen from the dead, and gave them a charge in His name for the apostles. They went out quickly from the sepulchre, and proceeded in haste to the city to make this known to the disciples. On the way Jesus met them, permitted them to embrace His feet, and renewed the charge to the apostles. The women related these things to the disciples; but their words seemed to them as idle tales, and they believed them not.

Meantime Peter and John had run to the sepulchre, and entering in had found it empty. But the orderly arrangement of the grave-clothes and of the napkin convinced John that the body had not been removed either by violence or by friends; and the germ of a belief sprang up in his mind that the Lord had risen. The two returned to the city. Mary Magdalene, who had again followed them to the sepulchre, remained standing and weeping before it; and looking in, she saw two angels sitting. Turning round she saw Jesus; who gave to her also a solemn charge for His disciples.

The further sequence of events, consisting chiefly of our Lord's appearances, presents comparatively few difficulties. The various manifestations which the Saviour made of Himself to His disciples and others, as recorded by the evangelists and Paul, may accordingly be arranged and enumerated as follows:—

1. To the women returning from the sepulchre. Reported only by Matthew. See ¿ 162.
2. **To Mary Magdalene, at the sepulchre. By John and Mark. ¿ 164.**
3. To Peter, perhaps early in the afternoon. By Luke and Paul. ¿ 166.
4. To the two disciples going to Emmaus,

towards evening. By Luke and Mark. § 166.

5. To the apostles (except Thomas) assembled at evening. By Mark, Luke, John, and Paul. § 167.

   N.B. These five appearances all took place at or near Jerusalem, upon the first day of the week, or the Lord's day, the same day on which the Lord arose.

6. To the apostles, Thomas being present, eight days afterwards at Jerusalem, i.e., again on the Lord's day. Only by John. § 168.

7. To seven of the apostles on the shore of the Lake of Tiberias. Only by John. § 169.

8. To the eleven apostles, and to five hundred other brethren, on a mountain in Galilee. By Matthew and Paul. § 170.

9. To James, probably at Jerusalem. Only by Paul. § 171.

10. To the eleven at Jerusalem, immediately before the ascension. By Luke in Acts, and by Paul. § 171.

Then follows the ascension. § 172.

§ 159. MORNING OF THE RESURRECTION.—*Jerusalem.*

First Day of the Week.

Mark 16. 1. And when the sabbath was past,[b] Mary Magdalene, and Mary the *mother* of James, and Salome, had bought sweet spices, that they might come and anoint him.

Matt. 28. 2-4. [2] And, behold, there was a great earthquake: for the angel of the Lord descended from heaven, and came and rolled back the stone from the door, and sat upon it. [3] His countenance was like lightning, and his raiment white as snow: [4] and for fear of him the keepers did shake, and became as dead *men.*

§ 160. VISIT OF THE WOMEN[c] TO THE SEPULCHRE. MARY MAGDALENE RETURNS.—*Jerusalem.*

First Day of the Week.

Matt. 28. 1.	Mark 16. 2-4.	Luke 24. 1-3.	John 20. 1, 2.
In the end of the sabbath, as it began to dawn toward the first *day* of the week, came Mary Magdalene, and the	[2] And very early in the morning the first *day* of the week, they came unto the sepulchre at the rising of the	[1] Now upon the first *day* of the week, very early in the morning, they came unto the sepulchre, bringing the spices	[1] The first *day* of the week cometh Mary Magdalene early, when it was yet dark, unto the sepulchre,—

[b] The women had rested on the seventh day, according to Luke 23. 56; and the sabbath being past, Mark relates (ver. 1) that they brought spices to anoint the body. This purchase would seem to have been made in the evening after the sabbath; since Mark proceeds in ver. 2 to narrate what they did early the next morning. In that case Luke (23. 56) speaks of the spices by way of anticipation.—Or we may, with Wieseler, obviate every difficulty by supposing that the preparation of the spices commenced indeed at the time given by Luke, but was not completed till after the sabbath, according to Mark.

The angel had descended and the earthquake had taken place, before the arrival of the women. Our Lord therefore had arisen

from the tomb at or before early dawn. See Note to § 160 in the Appendix.—Verses 2–4 of Matthew are here transposed into their natural order. As they stand in Matthew, the verbs must be read as in the pluperfect, "*had* been" and "*had* rolled away." See Note on § 145.

The body of our Lord was laid in the sepulchre before sunset on Friday; and He rose early on the morning of Sunday. He therefore rose on the third day; having lain in the tomb during one whole day, and a part of two others; in all not far from thirty-six hours. On the expressions, *the third day* and *after three days,* see Note on § 158.

[c] On the time of the women's visit, see Note to § 160 in the Appendix.

Matt. 28.	**Mark 16.**	**Luke 24.**
other Mary to see the sepulchre.	sun. ³ And they said among themselves, Who shall roll us away the stone from the door of the sepulchre?	which they had prepared, and certain *others* with them.

Mark 16.	**Luke 24.**	**John 20.**
⁴ And when they looked, they saw that the stone was rolled away: for it was very great.	² And they found the stone rolled away from the sepulchre. ³ And they entered in, and found not the body of the Lord Jesus.	— and seeth the stone taken away from the sepulchre. ² Then she runneth, and cometh to Simon Peter, and to the other disciple, whom Jesus loved,

and saith unto them, They have taken away the Lord out of the sepulchre, and we know not where they have laid him.

§ 161. VISION OF ANGELS *d* IN THE SEPULCHRE.—*Jerusalem.*

First Day of the Week.

	Mark 16. 5-7.	**Luke 24.** 4-8.
Matt. 28. 5-7. ⁵ And the angel answered and said unto the women, Fear not ye: for I know that ye seek Jesus, which was crucified. ⁶ He is not here: for he is risen, as he said. Come, see the place where the Lord lay. ⁷ And go quickly, and tell his disciples that he is risen from the dead; and, behold, he goeth before you into Galilee; there shall ye see him :*f* lo, I have told you.	⁵ And entering into the sepulchre, they saw a young man sitting on the right side, clothed in a long white garment; and they were affrighted. ⁶ And he said unto them, Be not affrighted: ye seek Jesus of Nazareth, which was crucified: he is risen; he is not here: behold the place where they laid him. ⁷ But go your way, tell his disciples and Peter that he goeth before you into Galilee: there shall ye see him, as he said unto you.*f*	⁴ And it came to pass, as they were much perplexed thereabout, behold, two men stood by them in shining garments: ⁵ and as they were afraid, and bowed down *their* faces to the earth, they said unto them, Why seek ye the living among the dead? ⁶ He is not here, but is risen: remember how he spake unto you when he was yet in Galilee, saying,*e* The Son of man must be delivered into the hands of sinful men, and be crucified, and the third day rise again. ⁸ And they remembered his words.

---

d Luke speaks of two angels, Matthew and Mark of only one; see Note on § 57.—Mark says he was sitting; Luke speaks of them apparently while still standing, ver. 4. But ἐφίστημι, in its appropriate and acknowledged usage, is *to appear suddenly, to be suddenly present,* without reference to its etymology. Comp. Luke 2. 9; Acts 12. 7.

In Matthew, the angel addresses the women apparently while still sitting on the stone outside of the sepulchre; in Mark and Luke, on the contrary, the conversation takes place in the sepulchre. But although Matthew does not speak of the women as entering the tomb, yet, in ver. 8, he describes them as *coming out* of it; so that of course his account too implies that the interview took place within the tomb, as narrated by Mark and Luke.

In recording the charge sent by the angels to the apostles, Matthew and Mark dwell more upon Galilee, and Luke more upon the Lord's previous announcement of His resurrection.

e Luke 9. 22.
f Matt. 26. 32; Mark 14. 28.

§ 162. The Women return to the City. Jesus meets them.*—*Jerusalem.*
First Day of the Week.

Matt. 28. 8–10. ⁸ And they departed quickly from the sepulchre with fear and great joy; and did run to bring his disciples word. ⁹ And as they went to tell his disciples, behold, Jesus met them, saying, All hail. And they came and held him by the feet, and worshipped him. ¹⁰ Then said Jesus unto them, Be not afraid: go tell my brethren ʰ that they go into Galilee, and there shall they see me.

Mark 16. 8. And they went out quickly, and fled from the sepulchre; for they trembled and were amazed: neither said they any thing to any *man :* for they were afraid.

Luke 24. 9–11. ⁹ And *they* returned from the sepulchre, and told all these things unto the eleven, and to all the rest. ¹⁰ It was Mary Magdalene, and Joanna, and Mary *the mother* of James, and other *women that were* with them, which told these things unto the apostles. ¹¹ And their words seemed to them as idle tales, and they believed them not.

§ 163. Peter and John run to the Sepulchre.—*Jerusalem.*
First Day of the Week.

John 20. 3–10. ³ Peter therefore went forth, and that other disciple,ⁱ and came to the sepulchre. ⁴ So they ran both together: and the other disciple did outrun Peter, and came first to the sepulchre.

Luke 24. 12. Then arose Peter, and ran unto the sepulchre; and stooping down, he beheld the linen clothes laid by themselves,—

⁵ And he stooping down, *and looking in,* saw the linen clothes lying; yet went he not in. ⁶ Then cometh Simon Peter following him, and went into the sepulchre, and seeth the linen clothes lie, ⁷ and the napkin, that was about his head, not lying with the linen clothes, but wrapped together in a place by itself. ⁸ Then went in also that other disciple, which came first to the sepulchre, and he saw, and believed. ⁹ For as yet

---

ᵍ It is evident that Mary Magdalene was not with the other women when Jesus thus met them on their return. John 20. 2, and Note on § 164.

ʰ Comp. Matt. 12. 50.

ⁱ Mary Magdalene had gone to Peter and John only; who would seem to have lodged by themselves in a different part of the city. The other women went apparently to the rest of the disciples. What therefore is here said of John (ver. 8), that "he saw and believed," is not at variance with ver. 9, nor yet with Luke 24. 11. What was it that John thus believed? Not the mere report of Mary Magdalene, that the body had been taken away; for so much he must have known and believed when he stooped down and looked into the sepulchre. His belief must have been of something more and greater. The grave-clothes lying orderly in their place,

and the napkin folded together by itself, made it evident that the tomb had not been rifled, nor the body stolen; for these garments and the spices would have been of more value to thieves than a naked corpse; at least, thieves would not have taken the pains thus to fold the garments together. The same circumstances showed also that the body had not been removed by friends; for they would not thus have left the grave-clothes behind. All these considerations excited in the mind of John the germ of a belief that Jesus was risen from the dead. He believed *because* he saw; "*for* as yet they knew not the Scripture," ver. 9. He now began to recall and understand our Lord's repeated declaration, that He was to rise again on the third day; a declaration on which they had already acted in setting a watch. In this way, **the** apparent want of connexion between verses 8 and 9 disappears.

Luke 24.

—and departed, wondering in himself at that which was come to pass.

John 20.

they knew not the Scripture, *j* that he must rise again from the dead. ¹⁰ Then the disciples went away again unto their own home.

§ 164. OUR LORD IS SEEN BY MARY MAGDALENE *k* AT THE SEPULCHRE. *Jerusalem.*

First Day of the Week.

John 20. 11–18. ¹¹ But Mary stood without at the sepulchre weeping: and as she wept, she stooped down, *and looked* into the sepulchre, ¹² and seeth two angels in white sitting, the one at the head, and the other at the feet, where the body of Jesus had lain. ¹³ And they say unto her, Woman, why weepest thou? She saith unto them, Because they have taken away my Lord, and I know not where they have laid him. ¹⁴ And when she had thus said, she turned herself back, and saw Jesus standing, and knew not that it was Jesus. ¹⁵ Jesus saith unto her, Woman, why weepest thou? whom seekest thou? She, supposing

Mark 16. 9–11. ⁹ Now when *Jesus* was risen early the first *day* of the week, he appeared first to Mary Magdalene, out of whom he had cast seven devils.

him to be the gardener, saith unto him, Sir, if thou have borne him hence, tell me where thou hast laid him, and I will take him away. ¹⁶ Jesus saith unto her, Mary. She turned herself, and saith unto him, Rabboni; which is to say, Master. ¹⁷ Jesus saith unto her, Touch me not; for I am not yet ascended to my Father: but go to my brethren, and say unto them, I ascend unto my Father, and your Father; and *to* my God, and your God. ¹⁸ Mary Magdalene came and told the disciples that she had seen the Lord, and *that* he had spoken these things unto her.

Mark 16.

¹⁰ *And* she went and told them that had been with him, as they mourned and wept. ¹¹ And they, when they had heard that he was alive, and had been seen of her, believed not.

§ 165. REPORT OF THE WATCH.—*Jerusalem.*

First Day of the Week.

Matt. 28. 11–15. ¹¹ Now when they were going, behold, some of the watch came into the city, and showed unto the chief priests all the things that were done.

j Psa. 16. 10; Acts 2. 25–31.

k Mary Magdalene now manifestly sees the angels for the first time; and this circumstance also goes to show that she had left the other women at the sepulchre before the angels appeared to them.

A main difficulty occurs here in fixing the order of time between our Lord's appearance to Mary Magdalene and that to the other women in § 162. This arises from the use of the word *first*, in Mark 16. 9, which seems to imply that this appearance to Mary Magdalene was the first of all: *he appeared first to Mary Magdalene.* Yet the whole course of events and circumstances shows conclusively that Jesus had previously appeared to the other women. We are therefore compelled,

and that in accordance with good and ordinary usage, to regard *first* as put here not absolutely, but *relatively.* That is to say, Mark narrates three and only three appearances of our Lord; of *these three* that to Mary Magdalene takes place *first*, and that to the assembled disciples the same evening occurs *last*, Mark 16. 14, where our translators have used the word *afterward*, which is less correct. Now as the word for *last* is here put relatively, and does not exclude the subsequent appearances of our Lord to Thomas and in Galilee; so too *first* stands here relatively, and does not exclude the previous appearance to the other women. In this way the whole difficulty in the case before us vanishes.

Matt. 28.

[12] And when they were assembled with the elders, and had taken counsel, they gave large money unto the soldiers, [13] saying, Say ye, His disciples came by night, and stole him *away* while we slept. [14] And if this come to the governor's ears, we will persuade him, and secure you. [15] So they took the money, and did as they were taught: and this saying is commonly reported among the Jews until this day.

§ 166. OUR LORD IS SEEN BY PETER.[1] THEN BY TWO DISCIPLES ON THE WAY TO EMMAUS.—*Emmaus.*

First Day of the Week.

Luke 24. 13-35. [13] And, behold, two of them went that same day to a village called Emmaus, which was from Jerusalem *about* threescore furlongs.

Mark 16. 12, 13. [12] After that he appeared in another form unto two of them, as they walked, and went into the country.

[14] And they talked together of all these things which had happened. [15] And it came to pass, that, while they communed *together* and reasoned,[m] Jesus himself drew near, and went with them. [16] But their eyes were holden that they should not know him. [17] And he said unto them, What manner of communications *are* these that ye have one to another, as ye walk, and are sad? [18] And the one of them, whose name was Cleopas, answering said unto him, Art thou only a stranger in Jerusalem, and hast not known the things which are come to pass there in these days? [19] And he said unto them, What things? And they said unto him, Concerning Jesus of Nazareth, which was a prophet mighty in deed and word before God and all the people: [20] and how the chief priests and our rulers delivered him to be condemned to death, and have crucified him. [21] But we trusted that it had been he which should have redeemed Israel: and beside all this, to-day is the third day since these things were done. [22] Yea, and certain women also of our company made us astonished, which were early at the sepulchre; [23] and when they found not his body, they came, saying, that they had also seen a vision of angels, which said that he was alive. [24] And certain of them which were with us went to the sepulchre, and found *it* even so as the women had said: but him they saw not. [25] Then he said unto them, O fools, and slow of heart to believe all that the prophets have spoken: [26] ought not Christ to have suffered these things, and to enter into his glory? [27] And beginning at Moses and all the prophets, he expounded unto them in all the Scriptures the things concerning himself. [28] And they drew nigh unto the village, whither they went: and he made as though he would have gone further. [29] But they constrained him, saying, Abide with us: for it is toward evening, and the day is far spent. And he went in to tarry with them. [30] And it came to pass, as he sat at meat with them, he took bread, and blessed *it*, and brake, and gave to them. [31] And their eyes were opened, and they knew him; and he vanished out of their sight. [32] And they said one to another, Did not our heart burn within us, while he talked with us by the way, and while he opened to us the Scriptures? [33] And they rose up the same hour, and returned

---

[1] This appearance of our Lord to Peter is mentioned only by Paul and by Luke, ver. 34. It had not taken place when the two disciples left Jerusalem for Emmaus; or at least they had not heard of it. It had occurred when they returned; and that long enough before to have been fully reported to all the disciples and believed by them. It may perhaps have happened about the time the two disciples set off, or shortly afterwards.

[m] *Reasoned,* or rather *disputed,* i.e., concerning the Messiahship of Jesus. On this point they, in their unbelief, felt great perplexity, owing to His dying, and that without having effected the political deliverance of Israel, which they thought was sure to be done by the Messiah.

Mark 16.

Luke 24.

to Jerusalem, and found the eleven gathered together, and them that were with them, [31] saying, The Lord is risen indeed, and hath appeared to Simon.[r] [35] And they told what things *were done* in the way, and how he was known of them in breaking of bread.

[13] And they went and told *it* unto the residue: neither believed they them.

---

§ 167.　Jesus appears in the midst,[s] Thomas being absent.—*Jerusalem.***

Evening following the First Day of the Week, or the Lord's Day.

Mark　16.　14 – 18.
[14] Afterward he appeared unto the eleven as they sat at meat, and upbraided them with their unbelief and hardness of heart, because they believed not them which had seen him after he w[)] is risen

1 Cor. 15. 5.—And that he was seen of Cephas; then of the twelve.

Luke　24.　36 – 49.
[36] And as they thus spake, Jesus himself stood in the midst of them, and saith unto them, Peace *be* unto you. [37] But they were terrified and affrighted,

John 20. 19-23. [19] Then the same day at evening, being the first *day* of the week, when the doors were shut where the disciples were assembled for fear of the Jews, came Jesus and stood in the midst, and saith unto them, Peace *be* unto you.

Luke 24.

and supposed that they had seen a spirit.[t] [38] And he said unto them, Why are ye troubled? and why do thoughts arise in your hearts? [39] Behold my hands and my feet, that it is I myself; handle me, and see; for a spirit hath not flesh and bones, as ye see me have. [40] And when he had thus spoken, he showed them *his* hands and *his* feet. [41] And while they yet believed not for joy, and wondered, he said unto them, Have ye here any meat? [42] And they gave him a piece of a broiled fish, and of an honeycomb. [43] And he took *it*, and did eat before them.[u] [44] And he said unto them, These *are* the words which I spake unto you, while I was yet with you,[v] that all things must be fulfilled, which were written in the law of Moses,[w] and *in* the prophets, and *in* the psalms, concerning me. [45] Then opened he their understanding,[x] that they

John 20.

[20] And when he had so said, he showed unto them *his* hands and his side. Then were the disciples glad, when they saw the Lord.

---

[r] 1 Cor. 15. 5.

[s] When the disciples beheld their risen Lord, they thought they saw a spirit. Jesus reassures them; and presents to them indubitable evidence, that the same body of flesh and bones which had been crucified and laid in the sepulchre was now risen and alive before them.

Then follows our Lord's charge and commission to the eleven apostles, delivered to them here in private; and distinct from the public and more general commission recorded in Matt. 28. 19, 20.—As a symbol of this commission to them in particular, and of the

power which they should shortly receive through the Spirit, "he breathed on them, and said, Receive ye the Holy Ghost," John 20. 22.

[t] Comp. Matt. 14. 26; Acts 12. 15.

[u] Acts 10. 41.　[v] Comp. Luke 18. 31.

[w] *Law of Moses—prophets—psalms.* These three designations express the *three divisions* of the Old Testament, according to the Jewish classification.

[x] This place, and the similar one in verse 27 of this chapter, are weighty, as proofs that the apostles had explicit intimations from the Saviour respecting the interpretation of the Old Testament.

Luke 24.

might understand the Scriptures, [46] and said unto them, Thus it is written, and thus it behoved Christ to suffer, and to rise from the dead the third day: [47] and that repentance and remission of sins should be preached in his name among all nations, beginning at Jerusalem.[v] [48] And ye are witnesses of these things.[z]

Mark 16.	Luke 24.	John 20.
[15] And he said unto them, Go ye into all the world, and preach the gospel to every creature. [16] He that believeth and is baptized shall be saved; but he that believeth not shall be damned.	[49] And, behold, I send the promise of my Father upon you: but tarry ye in the city of Jerusalem,[a] until ye be endued with power from on high.	[21] Then said Jesus to them again, Peace *be* unto you: as *my* Father hath sent me, even so send I you.

[17] And these signs shall follow them that believe; In my name shall they cast out devils; they shall speak with new tongues;[b] they shall take up serpents;[c] [18] and if they drink any deadly thing, it shall not hurt them; they shall lay hands on the sick,[d] and they shall recover.[e]

John 20.

[22] And when he had said this, he breathed on *them*, and saith unto them, Receive ye the Holy Ghost: [23] whose soever sins ye remit, they are remitted unto them; *and* whose soever *sins* ye retain, they are retained.

§ 168. Jesus appears in the midst, Thomas being present.—*Jerusalem.*

Evening following the First Day of the Week, next after the Resurrection.

John 20. 24–29. [24] But Thomas, one of the twelve, called Didymus, was not with them when Jesus came. [25] The other disciples therefore said unto him, We have seen the Lord. But he said unto them, Except I shall see in his hands the print of the nails, and put my finger into the print of the nails, and thrust my hand into his side, I will not believe. [26] And after eight days again his disciples were within, and Thomas with them: *then* came Jesus, the doors being shut, and stood in the midst, and said, Peace *be* unto you. [27] Then saith he to Thomas, Reach hither thy finger, and behold my hands; and reach hither thy hand, and thrust *it* into my side: and be not faithless, but believing. [28] And Thomas answered and said unto him, My Lord and my God. [29] Jesus saith unto him, Thomas, because thou hast seen me, thou hast believed: blessed *are* they that have not seen, and *yet* have believed.[f]

§ 169. The Apostles go away into Galilee. Jesus shows Himself to nine of them at the Sea of Tiberias.—*Galilee.*

Matt. 28. 16. [16] Then the eleven disciples went away into Galilee.—

John 21. 1–24. [1] After these things Jesus showed himself again to the disciples at the sea of Tiberias; and on this wise showed he *himself.* [2] There were together Simon Peter, and Thomas called Didymus, and Nathanael of Cana in Galilee, and the *sons* of Zebedee, and two other of his disciples. [3] Simon Peter saith unto them, I go a fishing. They say unto him, We also go with thee. They went forth, and entered into a ship immediately; and that night they caught nothing. [4] But when the morning was now come, Jesus stood on the shore: but the disciples knew not that it was Jesus. [5] Then Jesus saith unto them, Children, have ye any meat? They answered him,

---

[v] Acts 3. 26. [x] John 15. 27; Acts 1. 8. [c] Acts 28. 5. [d] James 5. 14, 15.
[z] Acts 1. 4. [b] Acts 2. 4; 1 Cor. 13. 1. [e] See § 172. 1 Peter 1. 8.

John 21.

No. ⁶ And he said unto them, Cast the net on the right side of the ship, and ye shall find. They cast therefore, and now they were not able to draw it for the multitude of fishes. ⁷ Therefore that disciple whom Jesus loved saith unto Peter, It is the Lord. Now when Simon Peter heard that it was the Lord, he girt *his* fisher's coat *unto him*, (for he was naked,) and did cast himself into the sea. ⁸ And the other disciples came in a little ship; (for they were not far from land, but as it were two hundred cubits,) dragging the net with fishes. ⁹ As soon then as they were come to land, they saw a fire of coals there, and fish laid thereon, and bread. ¹⁰ Jesus saith unto them, Bring of the fish which ye have now caught. ¹¹ Simon Peter went up, and drew the net to land full of great fishes, an hundred and fifty and three: and for all there were so many, yet was not the net broken. ¹² Jesus saith unto them, Come *and* dine. And none of the disciples durst ask him, Who art thou ? knowing that it was the Lord. ¹³ Jesus then cometh, and taketh bread and giveth them, and fish likewise. ¹⁴ This is now the third time *g* that Jesus showed himself to his disciples, after that he was risen from the dead.

¹⁵ So when they had dined, Jesus saith to Simon Peter, Simon, *son* of Jonas, lovest thou me more than these ? *h* He saith unto him, Yea, Lord; thou knowest that I love thee. ¹⁶ He saith unto him, Feed my lambs. He saith to him again the second time, Simon, *son* of Jonas, lovest thou me ? He saith unto him, Yea, Lord; thou knowest that I love thee. He saith unto him, Feed my sheep. ¹⁷ He saith unto him the third time,*i* Simon, *son* of Jonas, lovest thou me ? Peter was grieved because he said unto him the third time, Lovest thou me ? And he said unto him, Lord, thou knowest all things; thou knowest that I love thee. Jesus saith unto him, Feed my sheep.*j* ¹⁸ Verily, verily, I say unto thee, When thou wast young, thou girdedst thyself, and walkedst whither thou wouldest: but when thou shalt be old, thou shalt stretch forth thy hands, and another shall gird thee, and carry *thee* whither thou wouldest not. ¹⁹ This spake he, signifying by what death he should glorify God.*k* And when he had spoken this, he saith unto him, Follow me. ²⁰ Then Peter, turning about, seeth the disciple whom Jesus loved following; which also leaned on his breast at supper,*l* and said, Lord, which is he that betrayeth thee ? ²¹ Peter seeing him saith to Jesus, Lord, and what *shall* this man *do* ? ²² Jesus saith unto him, If I will that he tarry till I come, what *is that* to thee ? Follow thou me. Then went this saying abroad among the brethren, that that disciple should not die: yet Jesus said not unto him, He shall not die; but, If I will that he tarry till I come,*m* what *is that* to thee ?

²³ This is the disciple which testifieth of these things, and wrote these things: nd we know that his testimony is true.

---

g This appearance of our Lord to the seven disciples at the Lake of Galilee, is shown to have preceded that upon the mountain by John 21. 14. It was his *third* appearance to the *apostles* (see §§ 167, 168), but the *seventh* in all. (See Introductory Note to this Part.) They were now waiting the appointed time, to meet Jesus upon a certain mountain, Matt. 28. 16.

h Comp. Matt. 26. 33.

i *The third time.* There can be no doubt that our Lord sought Peter's confession *thrice*, because the denial had been *thrice* repeated. Peter, before the hour of his trial and his fall, professed to have more love to his Master than the others had (Mark 14. 29; John 13. 37), but now he claims no pre-eminence nor institutes any comparison, being content simply to declare with meekness his sincere love.

j This threefold charge is in effect the public restoration to Peter of his apostolic commission. He had already appeared to him *in private*, no doubt to assure the repentant disciple of His forgiving love. See 1 Pet. 5. 1.

k 2 Pet. 1. 14.

l John 13. 23-25.

m *That he tarry till I come.* The apostle John was alive when Christ came to destroy Jerusalem (A.D. 70), and died a natural death about A.D. 100. But Peter was, according to the intimation in verse 19, put to death as a martyr, probably in Rome, A.D. 67.

§ 170. Jesus meets His Apostles and about five hundred Brethren on a Mountain in Galilee.

Matt. 28. 16 - 20. —[16] Into a mountain where [n] Jesus had appointed them.[o] [17] And when they saw him, they worshipped him: but some doubted. [18] And Jesus came and spake unto them, saying, All power is given unto me in heaven and in earth.[p]

1 Cor. 15. 6. [6] After that, he was seen of above five hundred brethren at once; of whom the greater part remain unto this present, but some are fallen asleep.

[19] Go ye therefore, and teach all nations,[q] baptizing them in the name of the Father, and of the Son, and of the Holy Ghost: [20] teaching [r] them to observe all things whatsoever I have commanded you: and, lo, I am with you always, *even* unto the end of the world. Amen.

§ 171. Our Lord is seen of James; then of all the Apostles.[s]

Jerusalem.

1 Cor. 15. 7. After that, he was seen of James; then of all the apostles.

Acts 1. 3-8. [3] To whom also he showed himself alive after his passion by many infallible proofs, being seen of them forty days, and speaking of the things pertaining to the kingdom of God: [4] and, being assembled together with *them*, commanded them [t] that they should not depart from Jerusalem, but wait for the promise of the Father, which, *saith he*, ye have heard of me. [5] For John truly baptized with water; but ye shall be baptized with the Holy Ghost not many days hence.

---

[n] Matt. 26. 32.

[o] The set time had now come; and the eleven disciples went away into the mountain, "where Jesus had appointed them." It would seem probable that this time and place had been appointed of our Lord for a solemn and more public interview, not only with the eleven, but with all His disciples in Galilee; and that therefore it was on this same occasion, when, according to Paul, "He was seen of about five hundred brethren at once." That the interview in Matthew was not confined to the eleven alone, seems evident from the fact that "some doubted;" for this could hardly be supposed true of any of the eleven, after what had already happened to them in Jerusalem and Galilee. The appearance to the five hundred must at any rate be referred to Galilee; for even after our Lord's ascension, the number of the names in Jerusalem were together only about a hundred and twenty, Acts 1. 15. And further, Paul in enumerating the appearances of Jesus, in 1 Cor. 15. 5-8, specifies only those to *apostles*, with this single exception; which therefore seems of itself to imply that the eleven also were here included. Robinson therefore, with many leading commentators, regards the interviews thus described by Matthew and Paul as identical. He here takes leave on earth of those among whom He had lived and laboured longest; and repeats to all His disciples in public the solemn charge which

He had already given in private to the apostles: "Go ye therefore and teach all nations;—and lo, I am with you always, even unto the end of the world."

[p] Acts 2. 36; Phil. 2. 9, 10.

[q] John 4. 1; Mark 16. 15, 16; Acts 2. 38-41.

[r] Acts 2. 42.

[s] Luke relates, in Acts 1. 3, that Jesus showed Himself alive to the apostles "after His passion, by many infallible proofs, being seen of them forty days, and speaking of the things pertaining to the kingdom of God." This would seem to imply interviews and communications as to which we have little more than this very general notice. One of these may have been the appearance to James, probably "the Lord's brother," mentioned by Paul only (1 Cor. 15. 7). It may be referred with most probability to Jerusalem after the return of the apostles from Galilee. It is observable that our Lord's brethren did not believe in Him before His death, John 7. 5; but after His resurrection they are found among His followers, Acts 1. 14. See note § 50.

Afterwards, our Lord again, according to Paul, "was seen of all the apostles." This was apparently an appointed meeting; the same which Luke speaks of in Jerusalem, immediately before the ascension. It was of course the Lord's last interview with His apostles.

[t] Luke 24. 49.

Acts 1.

⁶ When they therefore were come together, they asked of him, saying, Lord, wilt thou at this time restore again the kingdom to Israel? ⁷ And he said unto them, It is not for you to know the times or the seasons, which the Father hath put in his own power. ⁸ But ye shall receive power, after that the Holy Ghost is come upon you: and ye shall be witnesses ᵘ unto me both in Jerusalem, and in all Judea, and in Samaria, and unto the uttermost part of the earth.

§ 172. THE ASCENSION.—*Bethany.*

Luke 24. 50–53. ⁵⁰ And he led them out as far as to Bethany,ᵛ and he lifted up his hands, and blessed them.

Mark 16. 19, 20. ¹⁹ So then after the Lord had spoken unto them, he was received up into heaven, and sat on the right hand of God.	**Luke 24.** ⁵¹ And it came to pass, while he blessed them, he was parted from them, and carried up into heaven.	**Acts 1. 9–12.** ⁹ And when he had spoken these things, while they beheld he was taken up; and a cloud received him out of their sight. ¹⁰ And while they looked stedfastly to-

ward heaven as he went up, behold, two men stood by them in white apparel; ¹¹ which also said, Ye men of Galilee, why stand ye gazing up into heaven? this same Jesus, which is taken up from you into heaven, shall so come in like manner as ye have seen him go into heaven.

Luke 24. ⁵² And they worshipped him, and returned to Jerusalem with great joy: ⁵³ and were continually in the temple, praising and blessing God. Amen.

¹² Then returned they unto Jerusalem from the mount called Olivet, which is from Jerusalem a sabbath day's journey.

Mark 16. ²⁰ And they went forth, and preached every where, the Lord working with *them*, and confirming the word with signs following. Amen.

§ 173. CONCLUSION OF JOHN'S GOSPEL.

John 20. 30, 31. ³⁰ And many other signs truly did Jesus in the presence of his disciples, which are not written in this book: ³¹ but these are written, that ye might believe that Jesus is the Christ, the Son of God; and that believing ye might have life through his name.

John 21. ²⁵ And there are also many other things which Jesus did, the which, if they should be written every one, I suppose that even the world itself could not contain the books that should be written. Amen.

ᵘ John 15. 27.

ᵛ During the preceding discourse, Acts 1. 7, 8, or in immediate connexion with it, our Lord leads the apostles out *as far as to Bethany*, and lifting up His hands He blessed them, Luke 24. 50. This act of blessing must be understood as having taken place at or near Bethany. Our Lord's ascension, then, took place at or near Bethany. Indeed, the sacred writer could hardly have found words to express the fact more definitely; and a doubt on this point could never have suggested itself but for the language of the same writer in Acts 1. 12, where he related that after the ascension the disciples "returned unto Jerusalem from the mount called Olivet." Luke obviously did not mean to contradict himself; and the most that this expression can be made to imply is, that from Bethany where their Lord had ascended, the disciples returned to Jerusalem by a path across the mount.

Indeed, Bethany is described in the New Testament as connected with, or as a part of, the mount of Olives, Mark 11. 1; Luke 19. 29. And further, where Matthew and Mark speak of Jesus, as going out at evening from Jerusalem to lodge at *Bethany*, Luke says that He spent the nights going out into the *mount of Olives*. See Matt. 21. 17; Mark 11. 11, 19, 20; Luke 21. 37. This serves to show that Luke uses the terms *Bethany* and *mount of Olives* interchangeably, and almost as synonymous.

APPENDIX.

Note to ₹ 7.—THE TIME OF THE NATIVITY.

THE precise year of our Lord's birth is uncertain. According to Matt. 2. 1-6, He was born during the lifetime of Herod the Great, and not long before his death. Herod died in the year of Rome (A.U.) 750, just before the passover: see Jos. *Antiq.* 17. 8. 1, and 17. 9. 3. This has been verified by calculating the eclipse of the moon, which happened just before his death: Jos. *Ant.* 17. 6. 4. If now we make an allowance of time for the purification, the visit of the Magi, the flight into Egypt, and the remaining there till Herod was dead—for all of which not less than six months can well be required, it follows that the birth of Christ cannot in any case be fixed later than the autumn of A.U. 749.

Another note of time occurs in Luke 3. 1, 2, where John the Baptist is said to have entered upon his ministry in the fifteenth year of Tiberius; and again in Luke 3. 23, where Jesus is said to have been "about thirty years of age" at His baptism. Now, if both John and Jesus, as is quite probable, entered upon their ministry at the age of thirty, in accordance with the Levitical custom (Num. 4. 3, 35, 39, 43, 47), by reckoning back thirty years we may ascertain the year of John's birth, and of course also that of Jesus. Augustus died Aug. 29, A.U. 767; and was succeeded by Tiberius, who had already been associated with him in the government for at least two years, and probably three. If now we reckon from the death of Augustus, the fifteenth year of Tiberius commenced Aug. 29th, A.U. 781; and going back thirty years, we find that John must have been born not earlier than August, A.U. 751, and our Lord of course not earlier than A.U. 752;—a result disagreeing with that obtained from Matthew by three years. If, on the other hand, we reckon from the time when Tiberius was admitted as co-regent of the empire, which is shown to have been certainly as early as A.U. 765, and probably in A.U. 764, then the fifteenth year of Tiberius began in A.U. 778, and it follows that John may have been born in A.U. 748, and our Lord in A.U. 749. In this way the results obtained from Matthew and Luke are more nearly coincident.

A third note of time is derived from John 2. 20, "Forty and six years was this temple in building." Josephus says, in one place, that Herod began to build the temple in the eighteenth year of his reign; while in another he specifies the fifteenth year; *Ant.* 15. 11. 1.; *Wars* 1. 21. 1. He also assigns the length of Herod's reign at thirty-seven or thirty-four years; according as he reckons from his appointment by the Romans, or from the death of Antigonus; *Ant.* 17. 8. 1; *Wars* 1. 33. 8. Herod was first declared king of Judea in A.U. 714; Jos. *Ant.* 14. 14. 4, 5. *Wars* 1. 14. 4. Comp. *Ant.* 14. 16. 4. Hence the eighteenth year of his reign, when Herod began to rebuild the temple, would coincide with A.U. 732; and our Lord's first passover, in the forty-seventh year following, would fall in A.U. 779. If now our Lord at that time was thirty and a half years of age, as is probable, this would carry back the year of His birth to the autumn of A.U. 748.

Further, according to a tradition preserved by the Latin Fathers of the first five centuries, our Lord's death took place during the consulate of the two Gemini, C. Rubellius and C. Fufius, that is, in A.U. 782. So Tertullian, Lactantius, Augustine, etc. See Tertull. *adv. Jud.* ₹ 8. Augustin. *de Civ. Dei,* XVIII. 54. If now the duration of His ministry was three and a half years, then, as before, the year of His birth would be carried back to the autumn of A.U. 748.

Some modern writers, taking into account the abode in Egypt, and also the διετής, "two years," of Matt. 2. 16, have supposed that Jesus must have been from two to three years old at Herod's death; and hence they assume that He was born in A.U. 747. The same year, A.U. 747, is also fixed upon as the date of Christ's birth, by those who, with Keppler, regard the star in the east as having been the conjunction of the planets Jupiter and Saturn, which occurred in that year.

From all these data it would appear that, while our Lord's birth cannot have taken place later than A.U. 749, it *may* nevertheless have occurred one or two years earlier.

The present Christian era, which was fixed by the abbot Dionysius Exiguus in the sixth century, assumes the year of Christ's birth as coincident with A.U. 754. It follows then from the preceding statements, that this our common era begins in any case more than four years too late; that is, from four to five years, at the least, after the actual birth of Christ. This era was first used in historical works by the Venerable Bede, early in the eighth century; and was not long after introduced in public transactions by the Frank kings Pepin and Charlemagne.

In respect to the time of the year when Jesus was born there is still less certainty. John the Baptist would seem to have entered upon his ministry in the spring; perhaps when the multitudes were collected in Jerusalem at the passover. The crowds which followed him imply that it was not winter. The baptism of Jesus in the Jordan, probably six months later, would then have occurred in autumn. It could not well have been in the winter; nor does a winter seem to have intervened. If now we may assume, as is most probable, that John entered on his office when he had completed his thirtieth year; then the time of his birth was also the spring; and that of our Lord, six months later, was the autumn. Archbishop Newcome, quoting from Lardner, has the following remark: "Jesus was born, says Lardner, between the middle of August and the middle of November, A.U. 748 or 749. We will take the mean time, October 1." See Lardner's Works, vol. i. p. 370, 372. Lond. 1835.—There is, on this point, no valid tradition. According to the earliest accounts, the sixth of January, or Epiphany, was celebrated by the oriental church, in the third and fourth centuries, as the festival of the birth and baptism of Jesus. In the Western church, after the middle of the fourth century, the twenty-fifth of December (Christmas) began to be kept as the festival of Christ's nativity; this day having been fixed upon, partly at least, as being the then current winter solstice. Thus, as late as the time of Leo the Great (who died 461), there were many in Rome "by whom this day of solemnity was regarded as honourable, not so much on account of the nativity of Christ, as because of the rising of the new sun, as they call it." The observance of this latter festival (Christmas) spread into the East; while that of the Epiphany, as the baptismal day, was adopted in the West.

See, generally, Lardner's Works, vol. i. Book II. 3. p. 356, sq. Lond. 1835. Gieseler's *Ecclesiastical History*, vol. i. p. 53, Edinburgh, 1846. See also Greswell's *Dissert.* x. vol. i., where it is ably maintained that April 5, A.U. 750, B.C. 4, is the precise date of our Lord's birth.

"This taxing was first made when Cyrenius was Governor of Syria."—Luke 2. 2.

The difficulty in this note of time is that "Cyrenius," or, in the Roman form of his name, Publius Sulpicius Quirinus, is known to have been a "governor," *i.e.*, proprætor (imperial delegate) of Syria in A.D. 6, about ten years *after* Christ's birth, and to have then made a "taxing" or enrolment of the people, on the deposition of Archelaus. This is the taxing referred to, Acts 5. 37. But Luke's statement refers to B.C. 4: how is it to be explained?

Of the many solutions proposed, three may be selected:

1. The phrase *was first made*, might be translated *first took effect*. The emperor Augustus, incensed against Herod, as we know from Roman historians, ordered a census of the kingdom, at the earlier period, as the first step to taking it entirely under the Roman sway. But the imperial purpose was altered before being fully executed, the census was stopped, and only first carried out "when Cyrenius was governor."

2. Or the word *first* may be taken to mean *before*. "The census was made before Cyrenius was governor," as though the evangelist would say, "*This* enrolment must not be confounded with that under Quirinus, ten years later." Greswell, Wieseler, and Robinson strongly maintain this interpretation.

To both the foregoing explanations, however, the most simple and obvious rendering of the passage stands opposed. They are admissible, but hardly natural. St. Luke at least seems to say very clearly that *this* enrolment was made "in the days of Cyrenius;" and, moreover, that it was the first so made, —thus implying, as Paley shrewdly observes, there were two.[a] Admitting two enrolments, however, were there two governorships by Quirinus?

3. The third explanation, first proposed, we believe, by Dr. A. Zumpt in 1855 (see Merivale's *History of Rome under the Empire*, vol. 4, ch. 39), meets the whole difficulty, and preserves the natural sense of the passage. It is, simply, that Quirinus was *twice* governor or proprætor of Syria. The steps in the argument are very ingenious, but could only be given by going into much detail.

The basis of the whole is to be found in the eulogy which, as recorded by Tacitus (*Annals*, 3. 48), was pronounced upon Quirinus after his death, by the emperor Tiberius himself. In this it is stated that Quirinus conquered the Homonadenses, a Cilician tribe; and was afterwards appointed *rector* to Caius Cæsar, the adopted son of Augustus. Now this last appointment, we know from the history, must have been in A.U.C. 753, or B.C. 1, about three years after Christ's birth. The conquest in Cilicia was therefore achieved some time previously, and Cilicia was a part of the province of Syria. But we know again from the Roman annals that three years or thereabouts before Christ's birth Quirinus was pro-consul in Africa. The victory over the

---

[a] *Evidences*, p. 275, Birks' Ed., Religious Tract Society.

omonadenses must therefore be placed between the two dates, and Quirinus accordingly have been in authority in Syria about the time of the Nativity. Further, by a careful examination of the list of Syrian governors[b] as mentioned in History, Dr. Zumpt seems to make it quite clear that this earlier term of office must have fallen in the very year assigned by the evangelist. Thus, instead of being a difficulty, the statement of St. Luke, as Dr. Farrar remarks, has "preserved for us an historical fact" in closest harmony with the known history of the period. For a good sketch of the whole argument, the reader may consult the English edition of Wieseler's *Chron. Synopsis*, pp. 129–135.

List of the Syrian "Governors" (Zumpt).

C. Sentius Saturninus	B.C.	9	A.U.C.	745
P. Quintilius Varus ...	,,	6	,,	748
P. Sulpicius Quirinus	,,	4	,,	750
M. Lollius	,,	1	,,	753
C. Marcius Censorinus	A.D.	3	A.U.C.	756
L. Volusius Saturninus	,,	4	,,	757
P. Sulpicius Quirinus	,,	6	,,	759
Q. Creticus Silanus ...	,,	11	,,	764

Note to § 13.—THE GENEALOGIES.

I. In the genealogy given by Matthew, considered by itself, some difficulties present themselves.

1. There is some diversity among commentators in making out the three divisions, each of fourteen generations, ver. 17. It is, however, obvious that the first division begins with Abraham and ends with David. But does the second begin with David, or with Solomon? Assuredly with the former; because, just as the first begins *from Abraham*, so the second also is said to begin *from David*. The first extends *to David*, and includes him; the second extends *until the carrying away into Babylon*, that is, to an epoch, and not to a person; and therefore the persons who are mentioned as coeval with this epoch, *about the time of the carrying away* (ver. 11), are not reckoned before it. After the epoch the enumeration begins again with Jechoniah, and ends with Jesus. In this way the three divisions are made out thus: Abraham to David, 14; David to Josiah, 14; Jechoniah to Jesus, 14: in all three cases, *inclusive*.

2. Another difficulty arises from the fact, that between Joram and Ozias, in ver. 8, three names of Jewish kings are omitted, namely, *Ahaziah*, *Joash*, and *Amaziah*. See 2 Kings 8. 25 and 2 Chr. 22. 1; 2 Kings 11. 2, 21 and 2 Chr. 22. 11; 2 Kings 12. 21, 14. 1 and 2 Chr. 24. 27. Further, between Josiah and Jechoniah, in ver. 11, the name of

Jehoiakim is also omitted. See 2 Kings 23. 34; 2 Chr. 36. 4. Comp. 1 Chr. 3. 15, 16. If these four names are to be reckoned, then the second division, instead of *fourteen* generations, will contain *eighteen*, in contradiction to ver. 17. To avoid this difficulty, Newcome and some others have regarded ver. 17 as a mere gloss, "a marginal note taken into the text." This indeed is in itself possible; yet all the external testimony of manuscripts and versions is in favour of the genuineness of that verse. It is better therefore to regard these names as having been customarily omitted in the current genealogical tables, from which Matthew copied. Such omissions of particular generations did sometimes actually occur, "because they were wicked and impious," according to the Rabbins. See Lightfoot, *Hor. Heb.* on Matt. 1. 8. A striking example of an omission of this kind, apparently without any such reason, is found in Ezra 7. 1–5, compared with 1 Chr. 6. 3–15. This latter passage contains the lineal descent of the high priests from Aaron to the Captivity; while Ezra, in the place cited, in tracing back his own genealogy through the very same line of descent, omits at least six generations. A similar omission is necessarily implied in the genealogy of David, as given in Ruth 4. 20–22; 1 Chr. 2. 10–12; Matt. 1. 5, 6. Salmon was contemporary with the capture of Jericho by Joshua, and married Rahab. But from that time until David, an interval of at least four hundred and fifty years (Acts 13. 20), there intervened, according to the list, only four generations, averaging of course more than one hundred years to each. But the highest average in point of fact is *three* generations to a century; and if reckoned by the eldest sons they are usually shorter, or three generations for every seventy-five or eighty years. See Sir I. Newton's *Chronol.* p. 53. Lond. 1728.

II. Other questions of some difficulty present themselves, when we compare together the two genealogies.

1. Both tables at first view purport to give the lineage of our Lord through Joseph. But Joseph cannot have been the son by natural descent of both Jacob and Heli (Eli), Matt. 1. 16; Luke 3. 23. Only one of the tables therefore can give His true lineage by generation. This is done apparently in that of Matthew; because, beginning at Abraham, it proceeds by natural descent, as we know from history, until after the exile; and then continues on in the same mode of expression until Joseph. Here the phrase is changed; and it is no longer Joseph who "begat" Jesus, but Joseph "the husband of Mary," of whom was born Jesus who is called Christ."

2. To whom then does the genealogy in Luke chiefly relate? If in any way to Joseph

as the language purports, then it must be because he in some way bore the legal relation of son to Heli, either by adoption or by marriage. If the former simply, it is difficult to comprehend why, along with his true personal lineage as traced by Matthew up through the royal line of Jewish kings to David, there should be given also another subordinate genealogy, not personally his own, and running back through a different and inferior line to the same great ancestor. If, on the other hand, as is most probable, this relation to Heli came by marriage with his daughter, so that Joseph was truly his *son-in-law* (comp. Ruth 1. 8, 11, 12); then it follows that the genealogy in Luke is in fact that of Mary the mother of Jesus. This being so, we can perceive a sufficient reason why this genealogy should be thus given, viz., in order to show definitely that Jesus was *in the most full and perfect sense* a descendant of David; not only by law in the royal line of kings through his reputed father, but also in fact by direct personal descent through his mother.

That Mary, like Joseph, was a descendant of David, is not perhaps expressly said in the New Testament. Yet a very strong presumption to that effect is to be drawn from Luke 1. 27 (see the Note on ¿ 3), and from the address of the angel in Luke 1. 32; as also from the language of Luke 2. 5, where Joseph, as one of the posterity of David, is said to have gone up to Bethlehem, *to enrol himself with Mary his espoused wife*, for this is the meaning of the Greek. The ground and circumstances of Mary's enrolment must obviously have been the same as in the case of Joseph himself.

It is indeed objected that it was not customary among the Jews to trace back descent through the female line, that is, on the mother's side. There are, however, examples to show that this was sometimes done; and in the case of Jesus, as we have seen, there was a sufficient reason for it. See 1 Chr. 2. 22 compared with 1 Chr. 2. 21; 7. 14; and Num. 32. 40, 41. So in Ezra 2. 61, Neh. 7. 63, a certain family is spoken of as "the children of Barzillai;" because their ancestor "took a wife of the daughters of Barzillai the Gileadite, and was called after their name."

¿ 36.—Our Lord's Second Passover.

On the phrase *feast of the Jews* (ἑορτὴ τῶν Ἰουδαίων), John 5. 1, turns mainly the question as to the duration of our Lord's public ministry. John notes distinctly three passovers; John 2. 13; 6. 4; 12. 1. If now this feast be another passover, then our Lord's public labours continued during three and a half years; if not, then the time of His ministry must in all probability be reckoned one year less.

The only reasonable ground of doubt in this case is the absence of the definite article before *feast*. But, even as the text now stands, it *may* assuredly in itself just as well denote the great Jewish festival as any other. The following considerations seem to show that it does most probably thus stand for a passover, viz. the *second* in our Lord's public ministry.

1. The word *feast* (ἑορτή) without the article is put definitely for the passover, in the phrase κατὰ ἑορτήν, Matt. 27. 15; Mark 15. 6; Luke 23. 17. Comp. John 18. 39.

2. In Hebrew a noun before a genitive is made definite by prefixing the article, not to the noun itself, but to the genitive; and this idiom is transferred by the LXX. into Greek. So, too, in the New Testament: Matt. 12. 24, where the article is omitted in the original before *prince*, and nevertheless must be supplied. Hence, in the passage before us, according to the analogous English idiom, we may render the phrase by *the Jews' festival;* which marks it definitely as the passover.

3. It is not probable that John means here to imply that the festival was indefinite or uncertain. Such is not his usual manner. The Jewish festivals were to him the measures of time; and in every other instance they are definitely specified. See chs. 2. 23; 12. 1; 6. 4; 4. 45; 11. 56; 12. 12, 20, etc., all referring to the passover. So, too, the festival of tabernacles, 7. 2; and of the dedication, 10. 22.

4. The plucking the ears of grain by the disciples (¿ 37 and Note), shows that a passover had just been kept; which tallies accurately with this visit of our Lord to Jerusalem.

5. This *feast* could not have been the festival either of Pentecost or of Tabernacles next following our Lord's first passover. He returned from Judea to Galilee not until eight months after that passover, when both these festivals were already past: see Note on ¿ 25.—That it might by possibility have been the Pentecost after a second passover not mentioned, and before that in John 6. 4, cannot perhaps be fully disproved; but such a view has in itself no probability, and is apparently entertained by no one. At any rate, it would also give the same duration of three and a half years to our Lord's ministry.

6. Nor can we well understand here the festival of Purim, which occurred on the fourteenth and fifteenth of the month Adar, or March, one month before the passover: see Esth. 9. 21, 22, 26–28. Against this the following considerations present themselves: (*a*) The Jews did not go up to Jerusalem to celebrate the festival of Purim. The observance of it among that people throughout the world consisted solely in reading the Book of Esther in their synagogues on those days, and making them "days of feasting and joy and of sending portions [dishes] one to another and gifts to the poor," Esth. 9. 22. Jos. *Ant.* 11. 6. 13. Reland, *Antiqq. Heb.* IV.